CULPABLE CAREL

The question of when a person is culpable for taking an unjustified risk of harm has long been controversial in Anglo-American criminal law doctrine and theory. This survey of the approaches adopted in England and Wales, Canada, Australia, the United States, New Zealand and Scotland argues that they are converging, to differing extents, around a 'Standard Account' of culpable unjustified risk-taking. This Standard Account distinguishes between awareness-based culpability (recklessness) and inadvertence-based culpability (negligence) for unjustified risk-taking. With reference to criminal law theory and philosophical literature, the author argues that, when explained appropriately, the Standard Account is defensible and practical. Defending the Standard Account involves analysing in depth a number of controversial matters, including the meaning of advertence/awareness, the role of attitudes such as indifference in culpable risk-taking, and the question of whether negligence should be used in the criminal law.

FINDLAY STARK is a university lecturer in criminal law at the Faculty of Law, University of Cambridge, and also a fellow of Jesus College, Cambridge. His research and teaching centres around various aspects of criminal law, criminal procedure and criminal evidence.

CULPABLE CARELESSNESS

Recklessness and Negligence in the Criminal Law

FINDLAY STARK

Faculty of Law, University of Cambridge

Jesus College, Cambridge

CAMBRIDGE
UNIVERSITY PRESS

CAMBRIDGE
UNIVERSITY PRESS

University Printing House, Cambridge CB2 8BS, United Kingdom

One Liberty Plaza, 20th Floor, New York, NY 10006, USA

477 Williamstown Road, Port Melbourne, VIC 3207, Australia

314-321, 3rd Floor, Plot 3, Splendor Forum, Jasola District Centre, New Delhi - 110025, India

79 Anson Road, #06-04/06, Singapore 079906

Cambridge University Press is part of the University of Cambridge.

It furthers the University's mission by disseminating knowledge in the pursuit of education, learning and research at the highest international levels of excellence.

www.cambridge.org
Information on this title: www.cambridge.org/9781108465120

First published 2016
First paperback edition 2018

A catalogue record for this publication is available from the British Library

Library of Congress Cataloging in Publication data
Names: Stark, Findlay, author.
Title: Culpable carelessness : recklessness and negligence in the criminal law / Findlay Stark.
Description: New York ; Cambridge University Press, 2016.
Identifiers: LCCN 2016017469 | ISBN 9781107038905 (Hardback)
Subjects: LCSH: Negligence, Criminal. | Criminal intent. | Criminal law. | BISAC: LAW / Criminal Law / General.
Classification: LCC K5067 .S73 2016 | DDC 345/.04–dc23 LC record available at https://lccn.loc.gov/2016017469

ISBN 978-1-107-03890-5 Hardback
ISBN 978-1-108-46512-0 Paperback

For Shona, to whom I owe so much more than a book dedication
(but it's a start)

CONTENTS

ACKNOWLEDGEMENTS

This book began life as a PhD thesis written at the University of Edinburgh between 2008 and 2011. I remain grateful to the Arts and Humanities Research Council and the Clark Foundation for Legal Education for funding my doctoral research and to many friends and colleagues (thanked in the thesis itself) who supported me whilst I was carrying it out.

Four people played a particularly crucial role during my PhD studies. James Chalmers and Sharon Cowan supervised the work with great patience. Antony Duff and Victor Tadros examined the thesis and gave me many ideas to feed into this book project. As a result of their encouragement to better the work (and the helpful comments on the proposal and example text from the Press's readers), this book is a very different beast from the PhD thesis. The text has largely been rewritten, and the central argument in the book has expanded, matured and developed. Primarily, the jurisdictional focus has broadened beyond Scotland and England and Wales to include various other Anglo-American systems. Further, more philosophical material has been consulted and referenced, in the hope of moving the theoretical debate on culpable carelessness (my umbrella term for culpable, unjustified risk-taking) beyond the stage it has got to in criminal law theory.

I have been fortunate to have colleagues give their time to comment on various parts of the book as it developed. Thanks are due, on this front, to Matt Dyson, James Edwards, Chloë Kennedy, Fiona Leverick, Arlie Loughlan, Jo Miles, Michael Plaxton and Andrew Simester. Particular thanks must go to James Chalmers, who went (well) beyond the call of duty and read the entire manuscript before submission. I have also had helpful conversations about the ideas in this book with Antje du Bois-Pedain, Mark Dsouza, Peter Glazebrook, Doug Husak, David Ibbetson, Henry Mares, Mark McBride, Jonathan Rogers, John Spencer and Graham Virgo.

Further feedback on parts of the book has been received at various seminars and conferences. Chapter 3 is a more focussed version of a wider-ranging paper that was originally presented to the Centre for Legal Theory, National University of Singapore, August 2013 (and published as 'It's only words: on meaning and *mens rea*' (2013) 72 *Cambridge Law Journal* 155). Chapter 6 (along with ideas from other chapters) was presented at Criminal Law Conversations, Cambridge, June 2015, and Chapter 8 was presented to the Criminal Justice Section of the Society for Legal Scholars conference, York, September 2015. I am thankful to the audience members at these presentations for their comments.

Despite the involvement of so many kind, distinguished and generous people, I remain liable for each and every mistake in this book.

At Cambridge University Press, Finola O'Sullivan has been excellent (and has shown remarkable patience) throughout the process of planning and producing this book. Richard Woodham, Gillian Dadd and Rebecca Jackaman were similarly patient, and helped with preparing the manuscript for submission and planning the cover. I am extremely grateful to Stephanie Sakson for copy-editing the manuscript, to Robert and Cynthia Swanson for preparing the index, and to Anand Shanmugam at SPi for managing the production project.

On the more personal front, I am grateful to my parents for their continued support. I have also had excellent research assistance/emotional support from our cats, and am saddened that Minstrel, who sat on my lap, purring, throughout the writing of my PhD thesis and most of this book, is not here to see the finished product.

Although perhaps a bad thing to admit to at the beginning of a monograph, I cannot quite explain in words how thankful I am to my wife, Shona, for putting up with me whilst I have written this book. She will be very glad that the project is concluded. Shona has had to put up with (too) much, and I look forward to now being able to repay her kindness and patience. The first line of this book is 'We cannot live without risk'. I could not live without her.

FGFS

Jesus College, Cambridge

ABBREVIATIONS

The following abbreviations are used where the context does not make immediately clear which jurisdiction a case or statute originates from.

AK	Alaska, USA
AR	Arkansas, USA
CA	California, USA
Can	Canada
Cwlth	Commonwealth of Australia
DE	Delaware, USA
E&W	England and Wales
FL	Florida, USA
GA	Georgia, USA
HCA	High Court of Australia
IA	Iowa, USA
IL	Illinois, USA
MA	Massachusetts, USA
MD	Maryland, USA
MI	Michigan
MN	Minnesota, USA
MS	Mississippi, USA
NC	North Carolina, USA
ND	North Dakota, USA
NE	Nebraska, USA
NM	New Mexico, USA
NSW	New South Wales, Australia
NY	New York, USA
NZ	New Zealand
OH	Ohio, USA
OK	Oklahoma, USA
PC	Privy Council
Qd	Queensland, Australia
RI	Rhode Island, USA

SA	South Australia
SC	South Carolina, USA
SD	South Dakota
Scot	Scotland
Tas	Tasmania, Australia
UK	The United Kingdom of Great Britain and Northern Ireland
VA	Virginia, USA
Vic	Victoria, Australia
VT	Vermont, USA
WA	Washington, USA
WAus	Western Australia
WV	West Virginia, USA
ZA	South Africa

CASES

Australia

Canada

England and Wales (Including the Judicial Committee of the Privy Council)

European Court of Human Rights

Republic of Ireland

New Zealand

Scotland

South Africa

United States of America

LEGISLATION

Australia

Canada

England and Wales

New Zealand

Scotland

United Kingdom

United States of America (and Related)

Miscellaneous

1

Introduction

We cannot live without risk. The 'chance or probability of a bad outcome'[1] infects every human action. For a legal system to be concerned with *every* instance of risk-taking would thus be unmanageable. When attention turns to the question of which instances of risk-taking the *criminal* law should concern itself with, matters move beyond mere practicalities of enforcement. This is because of what criminal convictions communicate.[2] In Gardner's memorable phrase, the criminal law's declarations intend to 'get personal' in a way that the law's other declarations (awards of civil damages in tort/delict cases, determinations of tax liabilities, etc.) do not.[3] Criminal conviction (and, for some, punishment)[4] carries with it a personalised, and intentionally stigmatic, message of condemnation, aimed not only at censuring wrongdoing, but also at censuring citizens for having engaged in wrongdoing.[5] From this communicative aspect of the criminal conviction, it follows that wrongdoing should reflect adequately on defendants[6] to make such personal

[1] The definition of risk adopted in Stephen Perry, 'Risk, harm, interests and rights', in Tim Lewens (ed.), *Risk: Philosophical Perspectives* (London: Routledge, 2007), p. 190.

[2] The communicative aspects of the criminal law are discussed in more detail below at Chapter 3.

[3] John Gardner, 'On the general part of the criminal law', in R.A. Duff (ed.), *Philosophy and the Criminal Law: Principle and Critique* (Cambridge: Cambridge University Press, 1998), p. 236, at p. 237.

[4] See, generally, R.A. Duff, *Punishment, Communication and Community* (Oxford: Oxford University Press, 2001). See further Joel Feinberg, *Doing and Deserving: Essays in the Theory of Responsibility* (Princeton, NJ: Princeton University Press, 1970), ch. 5; Victor Tadros, *The Ends of Harm: The Moral Foundations of Criminal Law* (Oxford: Oxford University Press, 2011), ch. 5.

[5] Cf. Victor Tadros, *Criminal Responsibility* (Oxford: Oxford University Press, 2005), p. 82. It has been argued that *badness* or *wickedness* is communicated by criminal convictions: Penny Crofts, *Wickedness and Crime: Laws of Homicide and Malice* (London: Routledge, 2013), ch. 1. It is submitted that this view of the message of conviction is too strong.

[6] The term 'defendant' will be used throughout this book unless Canadian, Scottish or South African cases are under consideration (in which case the term 'accused' will be used).

condemnation legitimate. Culpability judgements are the law's means of drawing such meaningful connections between defendants and wrongdoing.[7] Without them, the message of conviction would, it is submitted, be unwarranted and defamatory.[8]

That a defendant took a 'risk' (a concept unpacked in slightly more detail later in this chapter) is not itself a reliable indicator of wrongdoing *or* culpability. First, as will be explained below, taking a risk is not always something that is *prima facie* wrongful, i.e. something requiring justification. Second, even when risk-taking is *prima facie* wrongful, it does not follow that it is *all things considered* wrongful, i.e. that, when all relevant considerations are taken into account, the reasons against taking the relevant risk defeated or excluded the reasons in favour of doing so, rendering the risk-taking unjustified.[9] It is *all things considered* wrongs with which the criminal law ought ultimately to be concerned when it convicts defendants.[10]

It is because of its concern with all things considered wrongdoing that Anglo-American criminal law concentrates on the idea of *unjustified* risk-taking.[11] Importantly, the focus of this book is not on the question of whether risking the interests of others *itself* should be criminalised even where the risked consequence or circumstance does not materialise (in other words, whether simple *endangerment* should be criminalised)[12] or about the idea of justifying risk-taking. Separate books could be

[7] See A.P. Simester, 'A disintegrated theory of culpability', in Dennis J. Baker and Jeremy Horder (eds.), *The Sanctity of Life and the Criminal Law: The Legacy of Glanville Williams* (Cambridge: Cambridge University Press, 2013), p. 178, at p. 180.

[8] There is not space to consider the legitimacy of strict liability in the criminal law. See, however, A.P. Simester (ed.), *Appraising Strict Liability* (Oxford: Oxford University Press, 2005).

[9] Cf. the conception of 'core wrongfulness' in James R. Edwards and A.P. Simester, 'Wrongfulness and prohibitions' (2014) 8 *Criminal Law and Philosophy* 171.

[10] Cf. Antje du Bois-Pedain, 'The wrongfulness constraint in criminalization' (2014) 8 *Criminal Law and Philosophy* 149 (critiqued in Edwards and Simester, 'Wrongfulness and prohibitions').

[11] In this book, 'Anglo-American systems' are characterised by the similarity of their approach to criminal liability. Thus, Scots criminal law is (perhaps controversially) classified as an Anglo-American jurisdiction.

[12] See, however, R.A. Duff, 'Criminalizing endangerment', in R.A. Duff and Stuart Green (eds.), *Defining Crimes: Essays on the Special Part of the Criminal Law* (Oxford: Oxford University Press, 2005), p. 43. Most jurisdictions criminalise some specific instances of endangerment (e.g. around driving). More general offences of reckless endangerment are rarer. Cf. American Law Institute, *Model Penal Code and Commentaries (Official Draft and Revised Comments)*, 3 vols. (Philadelphia: American Law Institute, 1980), vol. 1, s. 211(2).

written about these topics. More will have to be said about them in this book, but the main focus is on the circumstances in which a defendant is *culpable* for taking an unjustified risk with the interests of others.

The term 'culpability' is used loosely in criminal law theory.[13] There nevertheless appears to be an acceptance, in much of the theoretical literature on criminal law, that culpability is demonstrated through the defendant's *insufficient concern* for the interests of others. The idea of insufficient concern for the interests of others links those who hold vastly different perspectives on other issues. For instance, Alexander, Ferzan and Morse and Tadros adopt different approaches to the wider matter of criminal responsibility: Alexander, Ferzan and Morse think choice is the sole basis of responsibility;[14] Tadros explains responsibility in terms of character.[15] They also adopt different accounts of the justification of punishment: Alexander, Ferzan and Morse are retributivists;[16] Tadros supports (in *Criminal Responsibility*, where he develops his thoughts on insufficient concern) a communication view of punishment.[17] They agree, however, that the element of culpability required for a criminal conviction is a demonstration (through choices or 'in-character' behaviour) of *insufficient concern for the interests of others.*[18] Furthermore, focussing on the defendant's lack of sufficient concern for others is one way of understanding accounts of culpable carelessness in terms of 'indifference' towards risk.[19] The basic understanding of culpability as insufficient concern for the interests of others will thus be adopted in this book. It is *the way* in which this lack of concern is demonstrated that is more controversial, and which requires much more explanation.

As will be seen, taking a risk, even an unjustified one, is not in itself a guarantee of culpability.[20] For this reason, Anglo-American criminal law

[13] For an attempt to apply more structure to culpability, see Leo Zaibert, *Five Ways Patricia Can Kill Her Husband: A Theory of Intentionality and Blame* (Peru, IL: Open Court, 2005).

[14] Larry Alexander and Kimberly K. Ferzan with Stephen J. Morse, *Crime and Culpability: A Theory of Criminal Law* (Cambridge: Cambridge University Press, 2009), ch. 2.

[15] See, generally, Tadros, *Criminal Responsibility*.

[16] Alexander and Ferzan with Morse, *Crime and Culpability*, pp. 7–10.

[17] Tadros, *Criminal Responsibility*, ch. 3. Tadros's views on punishment have since changed: see, generally, Tadros, *The Ends of Harm*.

[18] Tadros, *Criminal Responsibility*, pp. 83–90; Alexander and Ferzan with Morse, *Crime and Culpability*, ch. 2.

[19] Some such accounts are discussed in Chapter 7.

[20] See, further, Simester, 'A disintegrated theory of culpability', at pp. 181–183.

has developed (with some notable exceptions discussed in Chapter 2) two culpability concepts designed to link defendants to their unjustified risk-taking: recklessness and negligence. This book is, in large part, an effort to best understand and explain these two culpability concepts and how they secure appropriate findings of blame with regard to unjustified risk-taking (in offences of endangerment) and the materialisation of the risked harm (in completed offences).

The treatment of culpable risk-taking in Anglo-American criminal law has not, to date, been the focus of a monograph. Doctrinal and theoretical discussions of the topic have been the subject of many book chapters and articles – too many to survey meaningfully in this introductory chapter. And yet the proper extent of culpable carelessness, and particularly the place of *inadvertent* unjustified risk-taking (typically identified as *negligence*) within the criminal law's arsenal of fault terms, remains controversial.

As well as continued controversy, there remain important gaps in much of the criminal law literature on culpable carelessness. First, there has been an absence of comparative work analysing the approach towards culpable carelessness in different Anglo-American criminal law jurisdictions. A comparative analysis of the approach towards culpable risk-taking in a range of Anglo-American jurisdictions is carried out in Chapter 2. This comparison demonstrates a trend towards a common model – the 'Standard Account' – which the remainder of the book proceeds to analyse from a theoretical perspective.

Such a general, theoretical explanation of culpable carelessness must engage with concepts that have at times been neglected doctrinally and in the associated literature. The fact that certain aspects of culpable carelessness have been neglected to date is another good reason to dedicate a monograph to the topic. A good example is awareness of risk. Awareness of risk is, as will be seen, crucial to the approach towards culpable carelessness adopted in most Anglo-American systems of criminal law. It usually distinguishes recklessness from negligence: reckless defendants are aware of the relevant risk attendant upon a particular token of behaviour (φ-ing), whereas negligent defendants lack such awareness (but, on some accounts, *ought to possess it*).[21] Incidentally, the line between recklessness and negligence is often the line between criminal and civil

[21] Some accounts of negligence concentrate simply on the defendant's *conduct*, rather than her beliefs about risk. Such accounts are rejected below at Chapter 7, section on 'Conduct: Hart's Insight'.

liability. Negligence is not usually a sufficient form of culpability for serious offences,[22] whilst recklessness typically is.[23]

Given its importance, the concept of awareness of risk ought to be well understood and developed.[24] The concept is, however, 'radically under-theorized'.[25] It is thus worth reflecting in detail on the nature of awareness of risk and on whether it can hold the weight that the Standard Account places upon it. This book provides such reflection on awareness of risk, as well as other important aspects of the debate on culpable carelessness.

The next section of this chapter outlines the book's argument. This overview is followed by a brief discussion of the aspect of wrongdoing involved in unjustified risk-taking.

An Overview of the Argument

As mentioned already, Anglo-American systems of criminal law usually distinguish between two types of culpability for unjustified risk-taking: recklessness and negligence.[26] In everyday language, these concepts have blurred edges:[27] persons are labelled reckless or negligent with little thought to the difference – if any – that exists between these terms.[28] This is a particular problem in relation to recklessness, the extra-legal meaning of which is painfully unclear.[29]

Although unproblematic in the 'everyday' moral context, this variation in definition is inappropriate in relation to the criminal law, with its

[22] The exception is usually involuntary manslaughter, but it will be noted in Chapter 2 that negligence is also used in the law of sexual offences in some jurisdictions.

[23] Some crimes cannot be committed recklessly: e.g. assault requires 'evil intent' in Scotland (*Lord Advocate's Reference (No 2 of 1992)* 1993 JC 43) and murder cannot be committed recklessly in English law (*R* v. *Cunningham* [1982] AC 566).

[24] Glanville Williams, *Textbook of Criminal Law*, 2nd edn. (London: Stephens, 1983), p. 97.

[25] Douglas N. Husak, 'Negligence, belief, blame and criminal liability: the special case of forgetting' (2011) 5 *Criminal Law and Philosophy* 199 at 207. It is explained in Chapter 4 that Husak's point, although valid, is slightly overstated.

[26] As Chapter 2 demonstrates, different terminology is sometimes used. The core distinction between two ways of being culpable for unjustified risk-taking is nevertheless fairly constant.

[27] *Banditt* v. *R* [2005] HCA 80, (2005) 224 CLR 262 (HCA), at [108]. On the matter of whether settled meanings for 'everyday' terms exist, see Gilbert Ryle, 'Ordinary language' (1953) 62 *Philosophical Review* 167.

[28] *R* v. *Taylor* [2004] VSCA 189, (2004) 149 A Crim R 399 (Vic), at [42].

[29] *MacPherson* v. *Brown* (1975) 12 SASR 184 (SA), at 188.

requirement that citizens be warned fairly of potential liability.[30] As Chapter 2 demonstrates, there is a general trend in Anglo-American criminal law towards the Standard Account, with its distinction between awareness-based recklessness and inadvertence-based negligence. Despite this general trend, *absolute* consistency has eluded some Anglo-American systems, even where statutory definitions of recklessness and negligence exist.

There are two main divergences that have occurred in the treatment of terms such as recklessness and negligence. First, some Anglo-American systems have conflated the concept of recklessness (and occasionally negligence) and rules on voluntary intoxication and criminal liability. Motivating such moves is often the thought that becoming acutely voluntarily intoxicated (i.e. intoxicated to the extent that there is a reasonable doubt over whether *mens rea* was formed)[31] is itself careless/'reckless'/'negligent' and that this carelessness supplies the culpability usually satisfied by fault concepts such as recklessness and negligence. This conflation of voluntary intoxication and standard fault elements relating to risk-taking will be objected to in Chapter 2. It has complicated discussions of culpable carelessness unnecessarily in a number of jurisdictions. One of the arguments in this book is thus that discussions of voluntary intoxication should be divorced entirely from accounts of culpable carelessness. If acutely, voluntarily intoxicated defendants are to be held to account for the wrongs they commit in that state, it must be on some basis other than their 'recklessness' or 'negligence' in becoming intoxicated.[32]

Second, even if the core *terms* used in the criminal law are consistent, sometimes Anglo-American systems use different definitions of the words 'reckless' and 'negligent', or different *types* or interpretations of recklessness and negligence (e.g. 'ordinary'[33] and 'gross'),[34] in different contexts. This point threatens to undermine the Standard Account's

[30] The concept of fair warning is discussed below in Chapter 3.

[31] There is general acceptance that lower levels of intoxication are not relevant to criminal culpability – a disinhibited defendant can still be culpable, even if she would not have acted in a prohibited manner had she been sober. See e.g. *R* v. *Sheehan and Moore* [1975] 1 WLR 739 (E&W), at 744.

[32] See, further, Findlay Stark, 'Breaking down *Brennan*' 2009 *Juridical Review* 155 at 167–169.

[33] Courts do not tend to name this type of negligence. They merely differentiate it from 'gross' negligence, or similar concepts.

[34] See e.g. *R* v. *Adomako* [1995] 1 AC 171 (E&W).

generality. In Chapter 3, a defence of such generality will be mounted. It will be argued that *mens rea* terms such as 'recklessness' and 'negligence' *should* be defined and interpreted/applied consistently in the criminal law. This argument is premised mainly on the need for the criminal law to provide clear *ex ante* guidance to citizens, in clear and consistent language. Shifting definitions are not conducive to such clarity and might – it will be contended – lead to a degree of mistrust of the criminal law.

A secondary aspect of the argument for consistency in definition points to how it can limit undue flexibility in *ex post* decisions by courts and juries. Although some flexibility in fault elements is necessary, care must be taken not to surrender too much definitional freedom to judges or, worse, unaccountable jurors. The ultimate conclusion of Chapter 3 is that consistency in the approach to defining and interpreting terms relating to the culpability of unjustified risk-taking is necessary. The rest of the book thus proceeds to analyse the best unitary understanding of the Standard Account of recklessness and negligence in Anglo-American criminal law.

To develop such a model, it is necessary to unpack an idea that is central to the Standard Account: awareness of risk. As mentioned above, most understandings of recklessness are premised on the defendant's awareness of a particular risk attendant upon φ-ing, whilst negligence is typically understood as involving *inadvertent* risk-taking (inadvertence being synonymous, for the purposes of this book, with unawareness of risk). Despite the core role that it plays in delimiting recklessness and separating it from negligence on the Standard Account, awareness of risk merits far more analysis than it has, to date, received. Chapter 4 presents an account of awareness of risk in terms of the defendant's *beliefs* about risk. It is contended that one cannot be aware that there is a certain risk attendant upon φ-ing, unless one believes that that particular risk exists.

What might seem like a mere semantic switch from awareness to belief is actually far more significant, but this becomes clear only once the concept of belief is explored in more detail than it has been in previous discussions. The account of belief presented in Chapter 4 presents beliefs as ascriptions made on the basis of the defendant's dispositions towards thought and conduct. To believe that there is a risk of electrocution attendant upon leaving one's children unattended in the bath near a plugged-in radio, for example, is not simply to have a conscious experience 'My children might be electrocuted'. Such a belief can also properly be ascribed on the basis of fidgeting anxiously when away from the room, regarding a location for the radio to be acceptable only if it is sufficiently far from the water, and so on.

Importantly, on the model defended in Chapter 4, beliefs can *sometimes* be ascribed even when conscious attention is focussed elsewhere. In the bath example, a parent who moves the radio 'without thinking' might be ascribed the belief that there is a risk of electrocution if it is left there, even if his conscious attention is focussed on other household tasks. If beliefs cannot be ascribed in such circumstances, a fair amount of human behaviour becomes much less easier to interpret and understand. If belief is understood in the manner outlined in Chapter 4, such interpretation and understanding becomes easier. It can then be seen how the belief-centred view of awareness of risk maps onto the limited number of available existing criminal law discussions of that concept, and can explain much that has, to date, been avoided by courts in their discussions of recklessness and negligence.

Although some authors have gestured towards a belief-centred account of awareness of risk in the past, some have, however, gone further, and argued that one cannot be aware that there is a risk attendant upon φ-ing unless one *knows* that the relevant risk exists.[35] The accounts of knowledge invoked by criminal theorists are always parasitic on belief,[36] and so to require knowledge is to require *more* than a belief. Chapter 5 demonstrates why conceiving of awareness of risk in terms of knowledge does not fit well with the general structure of criminal liability in Anglo-American systems and is otherwise problematic. It will be concluded that knowledge of risk should not play a role in understanding of the Standard Account of culpable carelessness. The best account of awareness of risk available is the one presented in Chapter 4 – i.e. a defendant is aware that there is a risk attendant upon φ-ing if she *believes* that that specific risk is associated with φ-ing.

Once the concept of awareness of risk has been analysed, it will be necessary to question *why* it is given such a prominent role in Anglo-American accounts of culpable carelessness. This question is answered in Chapter 6, which analyses the relationship between awareness of risk, choice and culpability. The basic premise underlying many accounts of culpable carelessness is that a person can *choose* to take a particular risk

[35] The clearest example is Husak, 'Negligence, belief, blame and criminal liability'.

[36] Some philosophers concentrate on senses of knowledge that are not parasitic on belief. See Keith Hossack, *The Metaphysics of Knowledge* (Oxford: Oxford University Press, 2007), ch. 1.

only if she believes that that risk is associated with φ-ing. For instance, a person can choose to endanger life only if she believes that life will be endangered as a result of her action. That conceptual point about choice will not be doubted in Chapter 6 – it is unimpeachable. Instead, Chapter 6 addresses what will be termed the 'Exclusive Thesis' – the argument that *only* choices can ground culpability.[37]

The Exclusive Thesis, if accepted, has profound implications for the criminal condemnation of inadvertent, unjustified risk-taking, typically understood as the mark of negligence. If choice is *essential* to culpability, culpability cannot exist in the absence of a belief that the relevant risk exists, and inadvertent risk-taking seems beyond the criminal law's grasp.

It will be argued that choices are *important* when it comes to culpability but are not the be-all and end-all of culpability. What is required for culpability is a *suitably* clear demonstration of the defendant's insufficient concern for the interests of others, and the work done so far by theorists to support the Exclusive Thesis does not do enough to show that *only* choices draw a sufficiently clear link between defendants and wrongdoing. The Exclusive Thesis presents an unduly narrow conception of culpability, and what can legitimately be expected of citizens in terms of the formation of beliefs about the risks attendant upon their behaviour.

With the rejection of choice as the *sole* basis of culpability for the taking of unjustified risks, the discussion can move to non-choice-based accounts. Chapter 7 discusses some of the most developed versions of such theories (the insights from others are left to Chapter 8). The contention will not be that these existing accounts are irredeemably flawed. It is rather that the important lessons contained in the accounts discussed in Chapter 7 are clouded by theoretical shortcomings. It will be argued that the lessons gleaned from existing theories can inform an account of negligence that does not share those shortcomings.

Chapter 8 is thus dedicated to constructing a more defensible model of culpability without awareness than exists at present. The best available view is that negligence is an *epistemic* failure – i.e. the failure to form a relevant belief, namely the belief that the relevant risk attendant upon φ-ing exists – rather than a failure simply to *act* as a 'reasonable person' might have. The starting point for negligence as failure of belief (as it will be called) is what the defendant *did* believe and perceive regarding the

[37] For a clear example of this argument, see Alexander and Ferzan with Morse, *Crime and Culpability*, chs. 2 and 3.

situation in which she found herself. If the ingredients of a fresh belief that there is a risk attendant upon φ-ing were there, the question becomes whether the *reason* that the defendant failed to form that relevant belief demonstrates something meaningful about *her* and *her* concern for the interests of others. It will be argued that answering this question requires consideration of whether the defendant's epistemic failure reflects something meaningful enough about the defendant's character to tie her, as an agent, to her wrongdoing.

Chapters 3–8 outline a theoretical model of culpable carelessness that, it will be argued, can explain and justify the Standard Account. It is necessary, however, to be realistic about the limitations of that theory. Chapter 9 thus briefly examines the lessons for doctrine to be gleaned from the theory presented in this book, and the kind of compromises that will be required to make it effective in practice. The aim of Chapter 9 is to demonstrate how the Standard Account's approach to culpable carelessness can be given increased theoretical rigour, whilst remaining practically relevant.

Now that a general overview of the book's argument has been presented, it is helpful to return briefly to the aspect of wrongdoing present in unjustified risk-taking. As explained already, justification is not the focus of this book. It is nevertheless important to say something about it, to answer some queries that would otherwise dog the rest of this book's explanation of culpable carelessness. The next section, however, will necessarily have to be more stipulative than the remainder of the book.

Risks and Wrongdoing

Most Anglo-American definitions of recklessness and negligence expressly require that the defendant's risk-taking is *unjustified*.[38] This is sometimes explained in terms of 'unreasonable' risk-taking,[39] but it is assumed that unreasonable and unjustified amount to the same thing in this context.[40] As noted above, this focus on unjustified risk-taking ensures that the defendant engaged in *all things considered wrongdoing*,

[38] The requirement that the defendant's risk-taking be unjustified is not always spelled out explicitly. See e.g. *R* v. *Cunningham* [1957] 2 QB 396 (E&W) (which remains binding in offences requiring *malice*).

[39] E.g. *R* v. *Stephenson* [1979] QB 695 (E&W) at 704; *A Criminal Code for England and Wales*, 2 vols. (Law Com. No. 177, 1989), vol. 1, cl. 18(c).

[40] See, similarly, R.A. Duff, *Intention, Agency and Criminal Liability: Philosophy of Action and the Criminal Law* (Oxford: Basil Blackwell, 1990), p. 143.

rather than simply justified conduct that has the *initial appearance* of being wrongful, before she is subject to the stigma of conviction.

Despite this crucial role for the concept of unjustified risk-taking, there is scant legislative or judicial guidance on when taking a risk *is* unjustified. The prosecutorial discretion that permeates the Anglo-American criminal law world presumably accounts, in part, for this fact: it is plausible that justified risk-takers, or those whose conduct is not *obviously* unjustified, are not prosecuted. In addition, although there is no room for a detailed analysis here, prosecution appeals from trial decisions tend to be rare in Anglo-American systems. If a defendant is found to be justified, and acquitted, then this conclusion is unlikely to be the subject of appellate proceedings and widespread legal reporting. Furthermore, it will be seen that justification involves questions that are likely to be circumstance specific, and thus stating guidance in advance is likely to be difficult. In more serious cases, jurors will be entrusted to set the limits of justification, and appellate courts will be unwilling to intervene.

In the light of its central role in the Standard Account, the concept of justification is relevant to this book's explanation of culpable carelessness. It is not acceptable, as the courts have, to leave analysis of justification to others. Justification of risk-taking will therefore be examined here briefly, from a theoretical perspective.[41]

Why Is Justification Required?

Justifications exist in a relationship with at least *prima facie* wrongdoing. Absent a token of *prima facie* wrongdoing, there is nothing to be justified.[42] Through its focus on *un*justified risk-taking, the criminal law is thus, implicitly, requiring that the taking of risks with particular interests be justified. This assumption suggests that at least *some* risk-taking with such interests can itself be *prima facie* wrongful. Why might this be thought to be the case?

[41] For a fuller analysis of risk assessment, albeit in the context of regulation rather than the criminal law, see Matthew D. Adler, 'Risk, death and harm: the normative foundations of risk regulation' (2003) 87 *Minnesota Law Review* 1293; Matthew D. Adler, 'Against "individual risk": a sympathetic critique of risk assessment' (2005) 153 *University of Pennsylvania Law Review* 1121.

[42] Cf. R.A. Duff, *Answering for Crime: Responsibility and Liability in the Criminal Law* (Oxford: Hart, 2007), p. 227.

A profitable answer to this question points to *harm*: if taking a particular risk harms the interests of others, then a justification for that harm can legitimately be sought for the defendant's behaviour. There are various competing accounts of the relationship between risks and harms (and, by extension, justification) in the existing literature, and only a brief overview of them can be given here.

One argument for the harmfulness of risk-taking itself would look to the *outcomes* of risk-taking.[43] The most extreme version of this argument would hold that taking a risk, any level of risk, with life is *prima facie* wrongful because that risk might materialise and result in the death of a human being, a grave harm.[44] Any person who wants to take any risk of killing another person must do so only when features of her situation (such as those discussed below) remove the initial perception of wrongfulness.

This account of *prima facie* wrongfulness is implausible, because it suggests that a person has a reason not to behave in a certain way if it carries with it even a microscopic risk of resulting in harm such as death. For instance, when a person crosses the road when signalled to do so by the 'green man' at a pedestrian crossing, there is a risk that a motorist will come speeding past, swerve to avoid the pedestrian, and die in a collision with something on the roadside. It is not *prima facie* wrongful for this microscopic risk to be taken by pedestrians using appropriate crossings. As Gardner points out, 'What calls for justification . . . is that to which there is some rational objection'.[45] No such objection can be raised in relation to the taking of such tiny risks. Given the connection drawn above between conviction and condemnation, the criminal law should

43 There is a lively debate about whether imposing risks on others, even if they do not materialise, is harmful, but there is no space to consider it further here. The debate is nevertheless of core importance, if some conception of the 'harm principle' is adhered to, in discussions of criminalising endangerment. See Claire Finkelstein, 'Is risk a harm?' (2002–2003) 151 *University of Pennsylvania Law Review* 963; Stephen R. Perry, 'Harm, history and counterfactuals' (2003) 40 *San Diego Law Review* 1283; Rahul Kumar, 'Who can be wronged?' (2003) 31 *Philosophy & Public Affairs* 99; John Oberdiek, 'Towards a right against risking' (2009) 28 *Law and Philosophy* 367; John Oberdiek, 'The moral significance of risking' (2012) 18 *Legal Theory* 339.

44 Oberdiek calls this the 'common sense account' in Oberdiek, 'The moral significance of risking', at 343.

45 John Gardner, *Offences and Defences: Selected Essays in the Philosophy of Criminal Law* (Oxford: Oxford University Press, 2007), p. 77. See also Edwards's argument that the criminal law should seek to prohibit only those things that citizens have good reason to avoid doing: James R. Edwards, 'Coming clean about the criminal law' (2011) 5 *Criminal Law and Philosophy* 315 at 319–322.

ask citizens to justify only *significant* instances of wrongdoing, not 'minor' lapses.[46]

A way of rescuing the intuitive plausibility of an outcome-based approach to risks and wrongs is to insist that a risk is *prima facie* wrongful to take, and thus in need of justification, where it is *substantial*.[47] The US Model Penal Code (MPC) grasps this point: its definitions of recklessness and negligence require that the risk the defendant took was unjustified *and* 'substantial'.[48] Even if states have tended to amend the wording of the MPC's provisions on recklessness and negligence, the requirement of substantial risk has generally been retained,[49] pointing towards its importance in many US jurisdictions. Indeed, even in those states that have not followed the MPC's definitions of recklessness and negligence to a very great extent, there are examples of treatments of culpable carelessness where substantial risk-taking is required.[50]

Admittedly, other Anglo-American definitions of culpable carelessness are less clear on whether the substantiality of the relevant risk is important. English law, for instance, has rejected a requirement that the reckless defendant be *aware* of an 'obvious and significant' risk attendant upon her behaviour,[51] but this does not answer the question of whether (irrespective of the defendant's beliefs) the risk *actually* has to be obvious and significant to be the stuff of criminal wrongdoing. Given the implausibility of an account that suggests that *any* risk-taking with interests protected by criminal offences is *prima facie* wrongful, it is submitted that it should be assumed that English law requires the defendant's risk-taking to be substantial. It is submitted that similar

[46] Douglas N. Husak, 'Reasonable risk creation and overinclusive legislation' (1997–1998) 1 *Buffalo Criminal Law Review* 599 at 606; Herbert Wechsler, 'On culpability and crime: the treatment of *mens rea* in the Model Penal Code' (1962) 339 *Annals of the American Academy of Political and Social Science* 24 at 29; Joshua Dressler, 'Does one *mens rea* fit all? Thoughts on Alexander's unified conception of criminal culpability' (2000) 88 *California Law Review* 955 at 957–958. See further the requirement of a 'gross deviation' from standards of risk-taking in American Law Institute, *Model Penal Code*, ss. 2.02(2)(c)–2.02(2)(d).

[47] Cf. the 'High Risk thesis' discussed in David McCarthy, 'Rights, explanation and risks' (1997) 107 *Ethics* 205 at 213–215.

[48] American Law Institute, *Model Penal Code*, ss. 2.02(2)(c)–2.02(2)(d). See, too, H.L.A. Hart, *Punishment and Responsibility: Essays in the Philosophy of Law*, 2nd edn. (Oxford: Oxford University Press, 2008), p. 137.

[49] There are exceptions, where the code refers simply to 'a risk': e.g. 17-A MRSA s. 34(3)–(4); MCA s. 45(43).

[50] E.g. RS ss. 2901(7)–2901(8) (OH).

[51] *R* v. *Brady* [2006] EWCA Crim 2413, at [14]–[16].

assumptions can be made about the other Anglo-American systems surveyed in Chapter 2, even if they – like English law – have not addressed the question of substantiality explicitly.

Room for doubt regarding this assumption might come from the famous English case, *Chief Constable of Avon and Somerset Constabulary* v. *Shimmen*,[52] and so it is worth considering it briefly. In an effort to impress his friends through a show of prowess in the martial arts, and his ability to control his body, Shimmen kicked towards a shop window. Shimmen argued at trial that he had intended to stop short of the window and had taken steps to reduce the risk of breaking the window to what he regarded as an acceptable level. He accepted that he had not excluded the risk altogether. Alas, Shimmen's show of ability failed, the window was smashed, and he was charged with criminal damage, which required recklessness as to the damage or destruction of the window.[53]

One way of understanding Shimmen's claim is that he had removed the substantiality of the risk to the window (in the sense of its statistical probability of being broken) and ought, therefore, to be excluded from criminal liability. He was arguing, in short, that he had not engaged in a token of even *prima facie* wrongdoing. The Court of Appeal disagreed. They asked whether even the reduced risk that the defendant had imposed on the shopkeeper's interest in his property was justified (and concluded that it was not).

The court's call for justification was, on the view presented here, an implicit recognition of the fact that Shimmen had, despite his steps to reduce the risk, still engaged in *prima facie* wrongdoing; the risk remained substantial enough to warrant an answer. Why else would a justification be called for? The court found that even the reduced risk of property damage was unjustified, and the potential basis of recklessness, given the very weak reasons Shimmen presented for endangering the window. This is an appropriate analysis, and the question then becomes whether Shimmen was culpable for breaking the window. The matter of culpability is what the rest of this book is about.

The requirement of substantiality of risk has, despite its apparent solution to the implausibility of bare outcome-based accounts of the

52 (1987) 84 Cr App R 7.

53 Criminal Damage Act 1971, s. 1(1). At the time, awareness of the risk of damage was not strictly required for recklessness in criminal damage cases: *Commissioner of Police for the Metropolis* v. *Caldwell* [1982] AC 341. See now *R* v. *G and Another* [2003] UKHL 50, [2004] 1 AC 1034.

prima facie wrongfulness of risk-taking, been objected to in the past. One objection is premised on the fact that, if a risk must be substantial, then it must be over a certain threshold of probability. Simons has, for instance, suggested a probability of 5 percent (0.05).[54] The difficulty with this approach towards substantiality is that taking even very small risks with important interests (such as another person's life) might still be wrongful, even if the probability of harm eventuating is lower (say, 3 percent (0.03)).[55]

There is, however, no need to assume that the probability of risk relevant to *all* interests in the criminal law will be the same. The level of substantial risk-taking can be sensitive to change in individual offences and the individual interests that they are designed to incorporate.[56] A substantial risk to life, for example, is likely to be much lower, in terms of probability, than a substantial risk to property. Of course, the difficulty is that drawing any line between substantial and insubstantial risks is going to be difficult, even if such lines are sensitive to individual interests.[57] That is a reason to leave the judgement of substantiality to be fact specific (as the MPC definition does), rather than imposing a blanket probability such as that suggested by Simons.

A separate objection to the substantiality criterion is that it collapses into the question of justification for risk-taking. For Alexander, Ferzan and Morse, whether a risk is wrongful to take is a function of the probability of the harm arising, the nature of the harm risked, and the reasons for taking the risk.[58] The substantiality of the risk, rather than being an indicator of *prima facie* wrongdoing, is simply part of the enquiry into whether the risk was *all things considered* unjustified. Alexander, Ferzan and Morse thus question whether the threshold of substantiality has any independent worth, and would like to see it removed from definitions of recklessness such as those found in the MPC[59] (they reject

54 Kenneth W. Simons, 'Should the Model Penal Code's *mens rea* provisions be amended?' (2003) 1 *Ohio State Journal of Criminal Law* 179 at 189.

55 Alexander and Ferzan with Morse, *Crime and Culpability*, pp. 25–27.

56 See also American Law Institute, *Model Penal Code*, p. 236 (n. 13).

57 McCarthy, 'Rights, explanation and risks', at 212. It might be tempting to say any line is going to be arbitrary, but it is not clear that that is true. Consider if 'substantial' was said to mean a 99% probability of harm materialising. On that basis, somebody taking a risk that is 95% likely to result in harm is not taking a 'substantial' risk, which is implausible. If there are clear lines of plausibility, then a charge of *arbitrariness* is misplaced.

58 Alexander and Ferzan with Morse, *Crime and Culpability*, p. 27.

59 See also McCarthy, 'Rights, explanation and risks', at 213–215.

the idea that negligence is an appropriate fault element for the criminal law).[60] If they are right, then it appears that the question of *prima facie* wrongdoing becomes irrelevant. In theory, the taking of a microscopic risk of harm would need to be considered in the light of any possible justifications offered by the defendant.[61] Once again, the main reason for rejecting this thesis is its simple implausibility. The criminal law should not be, even in principle, capable of deployment in relation to trivial instances of risk-taking, even if the threatened outcome is harm to an interest protected by the criminal law.

The risks with which the criminal law is concerned ought, thus, to be substantial *and* unjustified – the MPC definitions of recklessness and negligence have things, to that extent, right. There is, however, a potential stumbling block to using an account of why risk-taking is harmful that is premised on a connection between the risk-taking and the eventual materialisation of harm. Perry explains clearly that the very idea of risk assumes that not all information about a certain situation is known.[62] If all information about a certain set of circumstances were known (all the relevant features of the situation and all the physical forces operating on them), it would be possible to predict with certainty whether the threatened outcome would materialise. To someone possessed of all the facts, probabilistic assessments are stark: outcomes are definitely going to occur (and have a probability of 1), or they are definitely not going to occur (and have a probability of 0).

From the perspective of the criminal law, this fact about risk is both problematic and unproblematic. It is unproblematic in the sense that the criminal law is often assessing circumstances from the *ex post* perspective: a court faced with a defendant charged with a particular offence knows whether or not the relevant risk materialised, and can thus establish whether the probability was 0 or 1. But the criminal law is avowedly concerned with addressing defendants from the *ex ante* perspective. It hopes that defendants can take its commands into account when deciding what to do. No defendant contemplating whether or not to φ is possessed of all the relevant facts about the attached outcomes and circumstances, and this means that she cannot avoid probabilistic assessments of them. This point about the *ex ante* perspective and its

60 Alexander and Ferzan with Morse, *Crime and Culpability*, ch. 3. 61 See ibid., p. 27.
62 See, particularly, Stephen Perry, 'Risk, harm and responsibility', in David G. Owen (ed.), *The Philosophical Foundations of Tort Law* (Oxford: Oxford University Press, 1997), p. 321.

relationship with risk is thus problematic for the criminal law, because it raises the thorny issue of how the extent of a risk (let alone a *substantial* risk) ought to be established.

Answering this question about establishing risk is not easy. As Alexander, Ferzan and Morse explain clearly, the probability of a given outcome from the *ex ante* perspective will depend on the facts that are taken into account, and the reference class that those facts create.[63] To see the impact of reference classes, consider the act of driving. The probability that a given manoeuvre will result in a collision with another vehicle will change depending on the amount of information that is taken into account. For instance, if no facts about the specific vehicle, level of experience of the driver and road conditions are taken into account, the risk of collision will, presumably, be based on national averages. Those averages will create the reference class. But if facts about the specific road are taken into account, then the safety or dangerousness of that particular stretch of road will alter the probability of a collision resulting from the manoeuvre. The reference class will have changed. The same will be true of other facts, such as the experience and ability of the individual driver. The probability of a collision occurring will be higher or lower depending on the various facts taken into account.

The difficulty is knowing, for the purposes of culpable carelessness, how to establish the relevant reference class. Alexander, Ferzan and Morse argue that the only non-arbitrary way to establish the relevant reference class in a criminal case is to allow the defendant to set the reference class, and to rely exclusively on the defendant's beliefs about the risks in her given situation.[64]

From the *ex ante* perspective, Alexander, Ferzan and Morse's focus on the defendant's beliefs might be considered laudable. The defendant's beliefs about the situation she is in will shape her decision-making in the *ex ante* perspective and indicate the extent to which the criminal law's prohibitions can hope to influence the defendant *at that particular moment in time*. Bearing in mind that Alexander, Ferzan and Morse do not think that inadvertent, unjustified risk-taking (commonly called 'negligence') is the stuff of criminal liability,[65] their adoption of a defendant-centred view of the relevant risk's extent at the time of acting makes further sense. Negligent defendants do not believe that there is a particular risk attendant upon φ-ing, and thus the defendant-centred

[63] Alexander and Ferzan with Morse, *Crime and Culpability*, pp. 28–31.
[64] Ibid., pp. 30–31. [65] Ibid., ch. 3.

approach will not work there if it is understood to involve the defendant's extant beliefs about the relevant risk *at the time of acting*.

The defendant-centred view can, however, lead to implausible results. Consider Ross, who believes that φ-ing is 95 percent likely to result in the death of another person (death has a probability of 0.95). If the defendant's beliefs about risk are to be determinative, then the probability of death that is taken into account when asking about the justification of Ross's risk-taking is, presumably, 0.95. That is the case even if Ross is gravely mistaken about the relevant reference class, and the real probability of death based on that reference class is much lower, say 0.05. This line of argument has two important consequences. First, it collapses any meaningful distinction between wrongdoing and culpability. If it is assumed that the reasons that render behaviour wrongful exist independent of the 'subjective' perspective of an actor, then a person can be a wrongdoer even if she does not realise that this is the case.[66] If this is right, then presumably the converse is also true: a person can engage in conduct that is not wrongful, even if she believes that she is acting wrongfully.[67] To put matters another way, wrongdoing is 'objective'.

The second, related, consequence of Alexander, Ferzan and Morse's analysis concerns situations where the defendant's beliefs have absolutely no basis in fact. Consider if Ross's belief about the probability of death is premised on a false belief about a certain feature of the situation (e.g. the conductivity of a certain type of metal).[68] If he had a true belief about the metal, Ross would believe that the risk of death attendant upon φ-ing is 0.05. Assume that this probability of death is high enough to require justification but is overall justifiable to impose, given Ross's reasons for acting in the way he did. For the purposes of criminal culpability, on Alexander, Ferzan and Morse's account, the probability of death that has to be justified appears to be 0.95, which is so divorced from the practical reality of the situation (0.05) as to be implausible. They might well find *culpability*, but in the absence of wrongdoing to which that culpability attaches (i.e. the factual taking of a certain level of risk), that should not be enough for criminal conviction. Criminal convictions, with their

[66] See Edwards and Simester, 'Wrongfulness and prohibitions', at 174–175.

[67] Oberdiek, 'The moral significance of risking', at 344–345. Cf. *R* v. *Taaffe* [1984] AC 539 (E&W).

[68] Cf. the example of the driver with the broken speedometer in Alexander and Ferzan with Morse, *Crime and Culpability*, p. 29.

personalised message about culpable *wrongdoing*, ought not to be imposed in such circumstances. To do so cheapens the communicative enterprise of the criminal law.

If the choice open to the law, in assessing risk, is arbitrariness or implausibility, then the risk-based concepts of recklessness and negligence seem very problematic fault elements. There are, however, alternative approaches which can counter claims of arbitrariness. Johnson, for example, argues that the probability of the relevant outcome should be calculated from those facts that the defendant *believed* to exist, that are in fact *true*.[69] Through this manoeuvre, Johnson manages successfully to construct a non-arbitrary matrix of facts from which to establish the risk attendant upon φ-ing, for the purposes of a criminal trial.

Johnson would thus simply ignore the fact that Ross believes that φ-ing is extremely risky (0.95),[70] as this is not true, because it relies on another belief (about the metal) that is false. This true belief account is also capable of explaining so-called *Caldwell* lacuna cases, which were much discussed in England and Wales in the 1980s.[71] These are cases where the defendant believes (incorrectly) that there is *no* risk at all attendant upon φ-ing. To change the facts of *Shimmen*, imagine if a Tae Kwon Do expert believes that he can stop his kick one inch from a window. He believes that there is absolutely *no* risk of breaking the window. He is wrong, and the window is broken. Bearing in mind the risk must have existed (it materialised), Johnson would ignore the defendant's belief about whether or not the window *could* be broken, and take into account only the defendant's true beliefs (e.g. assuming he had a correct belief about this matter, the distance the defendant believed he was standing from a window when he decided to kick towards it).

69 See Eric A. Johnson, 'Knowledge, risk and wrongdoing: the Model Penal Code's forgotten answer to the riddle of objective probability' (2011) 59 *Buffalo Law Review* 507. Johnson describes such true beliefs as 'knowledge' and finds reference to them in the Model Penal Code's definitions of both recklessness and negligence. See further Eric A. Johnson, 'Is the idea of objective probability incoherent?' (2010) 29 *Law and Philosophy* 419. Cf. the discussion of knowledge below at Chapter 5.

70 See Johnson, 'Knowledge, risk and wrongdoing', at 520.

71 For discussion, see Edward Griew, 'Reckless damage and reckless driving: living with *Caldwell* and *Lawrence*' [1981] *Criminal Law Review* 743; Glanville Williams, 'Divergent interpretations of recklessness III' (1982) 132 *New Law Journal* 313 at 313–314. Despite the academic discussion, a real '*Caldwell* lacuna' case does not appear to have been reported in England and Wales. Cf. *MJJ (A Minor)* v. *Cooper*, unreported, Divisional Court, 2 July 1987 (E&W) (cited in Diane J. Birch, 'The foresight saga: the biggest mistake of all?' [1988] *Criminal Law Review* 4 at 15); *R* v. *Reid* [1992] 1 WLR 793 (E&W), at 812.

From that subset of beliefs, a reference class would be established in a non-arbitrary way, and risk assessed.

Although criminal courts do not tend to expend energy on such assessments, it is submitted that this is because the risk typically is not disputed amongst the parties. If they wish to litigate the issue, they can. In most trials, though, what is focussed upon is the matter of whether the defendant was *aware* of the relevant risk attendant upon φ-ing (and reckless), or whether her unawareness of the relevant risk reflected culpability (in the form of negligence). Those are separate questions to be raised under the heading of culpability.

It is hoped that the account of risks and wrongs presented in the above section has done enough to situate the account of culpability developed in the remainder of this book. The next subsection considers briefly the matter of how *prima facie* wrongful risk-taking might be justified.

Justifying Risk-taking

Risk-taking requires justification where it is *prima facie* wrongful to take the relevant risk, in view of its substantiality. Some such answers to accusations of *prima facie* wrongdoing through the taking of substantial risks will take the form that, all things considered, the defendant was *justified* in φ-ing, that any *prima facie* appearance of wrongdoing was misleading. Hence a distinction between *prima facie* wrongdoing and *all things considered* wrongdoing is required. Justifications defeat findings of *all things considered* wrongfulness, rather than accepting that wrongfulness and denying responsibility or fault.

It is contended here that the question of justification should be resolved, in general terms, by asking what can legitimately be expected of citizens by other citizens in terms of risk-taking.[72] What levels of risk can citizens reasonably ask other citizens to forebear from imposing? This approach towards justification is captured well in Fletcher's conception of unjustified risk-taking as non-reciprocal risk imposition.[73]

[72] See, similarly, Peter Cane, *The Anatomy of Tort Law* (Oxford: Hart, 1997), p. 42.

[73] George P. Fletcher, 'Fairness and utility in tort theory' (1971–1972) 85 *Harvard Law Review* 537 at 548. See, too, Alan Brudner, *Punishment and Freedom: A Liberal Theory of Penal Justice* (Oxford: Oxford University Press, 2009), p. 78. Cf. Rawls's conception of 'reasonable' conduct as honouring fair terms of cooperation and interaction (John Rawls, *Political Liberalism* (New York: Columbia University Press, 1993), pp. 49–50) and Scanlon's 'contractualist' approach to justification (T.M. Scanlon, *What We Owe to Each Other* (Cambridge, MA: Belknap, 1998)).

The basis of Fletcher's view is the point that social interaction necessitates the imposition of some risk on the interests of citizens by other citizens.[74] The state will also often have to impose risks on citizens to facilitate certain activities necessary for the successful flourishing of society. To facilitate movement of persons and goods, for instance, driving is tolerated despite the substantial associated risk to the citizens' lives. Persons are not wrongdoers *simply* for driving.[75]

Risk-taking properly becomes the concern of the law, and particularly the *criminal* law, only when it is *prima facie* wrongful in the light of its substantiality. Further, risk-taking properly becomes the stuff of criminal liability only when it is *all things considered* wrongful, i.e. when it goes beyond what citizens can legitimately be expected to tolerate – for instance, when someone is accused of driving too quickly or in a manner that creates heightened risks of a collision with other road users. It is only after the reciprocal bounds of risk-imposition have been exceeded that the defendant's act of risk-taking becomes unjustified and an instance of *all things considered* wrongdoing.

In employing Fletcher's conception of unjustifiable risk-taking, the 'reasonable person' is a helpful heuristic device. A court can ask whether or not the reasonable person (or, perhaps preferably, reasonable *citizen*)[76] would view the relevant act of risk-taking engaged in by the defendant as socially acceptable, in the light of the defendant's reasons for engaging in it, and the likelihood and severity of the matters risked (factors that provide reasons against engaging in the relevant activity).[77] It is worth noting here that the reasonable person in this context is a *normative*, rather than an empirical, standard.[78] An act of risk-taking might be adjudged unjustifiable even if a majority of people in society perform it regularly.[79]

74 See Hyman Gross, *A Theory of Criminal Justice* (New York: Oxford University Press, 1979), p. 86; Heidi M. Hurd, 'The deontology of negligence' (1996) 76 *Boston University Law Review* 249 at 264; Jenny Steele, *Risks and Legal Theory* (Oxford: Hart, 2004), p. 35.

75 Dan W. Morkel, 'On the distinction between recklessness and conscious negligence' (1982) 30 *American Journal of Comparative Law* 325 at 327.

76 The term 'reasonable citizen' reflects better the fact that the defendant is called to account *as* a citizen before *other* citizens (not merely 'persons'). See Duff, *Answering for Crime*, ch. 2.

77 See Glanville Williams, *Criminal Law: The General Part*, 2nd edn. (London: Stevens, 1961), pp. 59–64. Cf. John C. Coffee, 'Paradigms lost: the blurring of the criminal and civil law models – and what can be done about it' (1991–1992) 101 *Yale Law Journal* 1875 at 1876.

78 See further Cynthia Lee, *Murder and the Reasonable Man: Passion and Fear in the Criminal Courtroom* (New York: New York University Press, 2003), p. 12.

79 Cf. Douglas N. Husak, *Philosophy of Criminal Law: Selected Essays* (Oxford: Oxford University Press, 2010), p. 342.

It is accepted that the model of unjustified risk-taking adopted here is not necessarily concrete.[80] As noted above, an adequate explanation of justification would take up another book. The bounds of socially acceptable risk-taking are in themselves difficult to pin down, and social costs and benefits cannot readily be broken up into determinate, uncontested units.[81] The approach to justification sketched here will thus inevitably allow for difficult moral and political arguments to arise, and those will need to be resolved (typically by the finder of fact).[82] For instance, it will have to be decided whether an instance of risk-taking can be justified by reference to social consequences. Is there a threshold at which social value x can trump the risking of life?[83] The answer is presumably 'Yes', but expanding upon *when* this stage is reached is nigh on impossible. Those types of questions cannot be resolved in this book,[84] but the point that needs to be made here is that strict rules regarding risk-taking's justifiability cannot be set down in advance.[85]

This indeterminate feature of social justification might lead systems of criminal law to seek more precise formulations regarding permissible risk-taking. For instance, a common response in tort law/delict is an analysis that weighs the resource cost of the threatened harm against the resource cost of taking precautions against the risk of its materialisation.[86] Such approaches to justification cannot avoid controversial value judgements, however.[87] How much is a life worth? In what circumstances is there a duty not to pursue certain consequences in the light of their

80 See Larry Alexander and Kimberly K. Ferzan, 'Reply', in Paul H. Robinson, Stephen P. Garvey and Kimberly K. Ferzan (eds.), *Criminal Law Conversations* (Oxford: Oxford University Press, 2009) p. 291, at p. 292.

81 Jules L. Coleman, *The Practice of Principle: In Defence of a Pragmatist Approach to Legal Theory* (Oxford: Oxford University Press, 2001), p. 11.

82 Alan Norrie, *Crime, Reason and History: A Critical Introduction to Criminal Law*, 3rd edn. (Cambridge: Cambridge University Press, 2014), pp. 99–100.

83 There is also the difficult question of whether there are deontological constraints on placing reliance on consequences to risk harm to others. See Larry Alexander, 'Deontology at the threshold' (2000) 37 *San Diego Law Review* 893; Hurd, 'The deontology of negligence'.

84 For a sketch of an account, see Alexander and Ferzan with Morse, *Crime and Culpability*, pp. 93–108.

85 Cf. Paul H. Robinson, 'A functional analysis of the criminal law' (1994) 88 *Northwestern University Law Review* 857 at 882–884.

86 See, classically, *United States* v. *Carroll Towing Co.*, 159 F 2d 169 (2nd Cir. 1947).

87 Claire Finkelstein, 'The inefficiency of *mens rea*' (2000) 88 *California Law Review* 895 at 904. Cf. Carl F. Cranor, 'Towards a non-consequentialist approach to acceptable risks', in Lewens (ed.), *Risk*, p. 45.

infringement of rights? Of course governments (and courts) come to decisions on such matters when deciding, for example, how much resources to spend on keeping a citizen alive, but those judgements are extremely morally and politically contested. All cost–benefit analyses do is cloak those difficult moral and political decisions about what is socially sanctioned risk-taking in the language of economics (and then usually only semi-convincingly). The matter of justification ought to be transparent in its consideration of value and policy judgements concerning the limits of socially acceptable risk-taking, even if these decisions are controversial. Fletcher's approach to risk-taking allows this to happen, even if ultimately it might be a jury that decides such difficult issues, without giving reasons.

It is worth noting that this understanding of justification and wrongdoing demonstrates that the understandings of recklessness and negligence adopted in the Anglo-American world mix up elements that are internal to the defendant (e.g. her awareness of risk, or lack thereof) and those that are external (e.g. whether her risk-taking was wrongful). This is one reason why the division between 'subjective' and 'objective' liability is potentially confusing and ought to be avoided in discussions of culpable carelessness. As long as a focus on justification for risk-taking is maintained, and as long as justification and wrongfulness remain 'objective' matters, no theory of recklessness or negligence will ever be truly 'subjective'.[88] This is one reason why the 'subjective'/'objective' dichotomy will be eschewed, where possible, in this book.

A final, related, concern about Fletcher's social approach to justification is that it is, to a degree, impersonal. This is because there is a possibility of dissonance between what a defendant believed about the clash of values and interests at play in a justificatory decision and the law's assessment of the situation. If the matter of justification does not allow the defendant's view to be determinative, is any condemnation adequately personal to her?[89] Consider Claire, who believes that she is justified in imposing a high risk of death (0.75) upon other citizens in order to get a thrill from firing a shotgun near a crowd. Should this belief about justification be determinative of the matter of whether she lacked

[88] Don Stuart, '*Mens rea*, negligence and attempts' [1968] *Criminal Law Review* 647 at 652; Celia Wells, 'Swatting the subjectivist bug' [1982] *Criminal Law Review* 209 at 210.

[89] See Leo Katz, 'Harm and justification in negligence' (2003) 4 *Theoretical Inquiries in Law* 397 at 408.

justification for her risk-taking and has engaged in all-things-considered wrongdoing? The MPC might be read to suggest that the answer to this question is 'Yes', at least in terms of recklessness: the defendant must consciously disregard *a substantial and unjustified risk*.[90] This suggests that the defendant must actually believe that her action carries with it a risk that is *both* substantial and unjustified, and decide to take the risk anyway.

Such a completely defendant-focussed view would be unsustainable. It would result in the 'absurd'[91] outcome of leaving the criminal law (and citizens' interests) 'subject to the views of heretics and fanatics'.[92] Claire, in the example above, has plausibly overstepped the 'objective' boundaries of socially acceptable risk-taking. A 'personalised' view – where the defendant's views on the justifiability of her action – would miss this point.[93] In order to potentially capture such defendants' wrongdoing, the question of the justifiability of risk-taking should be answered by reference to the court's appraisal of social expectations: to be acting in an *all-things-considered* wrongful manner, the defendant must have taken an 'objectively' unjustified risk. This allows a person to be an all-things-considered wrongdoer, even if she does not believe herself that this is the case at the time of acting. Similarly, it would allow for a person to *not* be an all-things-considered wrongdoer, even if – through heightened risk aversion – she thinks she is.

If too harsh a view was taken of mistakes about justification, then it might be feared that defendants who are *just* beyond the bounds of socially acceptable risk-taking might caught by the criminal law. What if Claire has taken some precautions against the relevant risk, but *just* not enough to render her risk-taking justifiable, and the threatened harm materialises? Imposing criminal liability in such circumstances might be adjudged unfair, on the basis that criminal convictions convey condemnation. The answer to this conundrum is to take a focus on *culpability* seriously. Claire can remain a wrongdoer, but her wrongdoing might be so minor as to not disclose an appropriate level of culpability, in terms of her concern for the interests of others, to

90 American Law Institute, *Model Penal Code*, s. 2.02(2)(d). The MPC commentary is less than clear on this point: ibid., p. 238.

91 Duff, *Intention, Agency and Criminal Liability*, p. 152.

92 Earl Fruchtman, 'Recklessness and the limits of *mens rea*: beyond orthodox subjectivism' (1986–1987) 29 *Criminal Law Quarterly* 315, 421 (published in two parts), at 321.

93 Cf. Brudner, *Punishment and Freedom*, p. 78; Dressler, 'Does one *mens rea* fit all?', at 959.

warrant conviction. The question for the remainder of this book is *when* such culpability exists.

The matter of *why* justification is sought in cases of recklessness and negligence has been addressed, and a sketch of how such justifications could be argued for has been drawn. Such matters have not been subject to detailed doctrinal analysis. Instead, courts and legislatures have focussed more extensively on the question of *culpability* for unjustified risk-taking. It is to those doctrinal treatments that the book now turns.

2

The Doctrinal Trend towards the Standard Account

This chapter argues that a number of major Anglo-American systems of criminal law are converging on an understanding of recklessness in terms of the unjustified taking of a risk of which the defendant was aware, and negligence as a lesser-used fault element concerned with the inadvertent taking of an unjustified risk. This awareness/unawareness-based model will form the basis of the 'Standard Account' of culpable carelessness, the theoretical underpinnings of which will be discussed in the next six chapters.

Two methodological points should be noted at the outset. First, the jurisdictions surveyed in this chapter were chosen principally because of their size,[1] and also because of their historical relationship with English criminal law,[2] and/or their use of shared concepts such as 'recklessness' and 'negligence'. Given that there are historical links between most of these jurisdictions, the chapter first sets out English law's response to culpable carelessness, and argues that it is not entirely consistent. The law on voluntary intoxication will also be considered, because it has become entangled with recklessness in England and Wales, and certain other jurisdictions,[3] leading to a further lack of clarity. The similarly inconsistent approaches taken in Canada, Australia and the United States will then be analysed. After this, the chapter considers the more consistent tack taken in New Zealand before, finally, addressing Scotland's more distinctive response to the issue of culpable carelessness.

[1] In the case of the Republic of Ireland, matters are close in terms of population, but Irish law's approach to recklessness seems similar to English law's following *R* v. *G and Another* [2003] UKHL 50, [2004] 1 AC 1034. See e.g. *DPP* v. *Cagney* [2007] IESC 46, [2008] 2 IR 111.

[2] References to 'English criminal law' should be read so as to include the law of Wales. The historical link is less clear in Scotland, which has always remained an independent criminal jurisdiction. This point is addressed in the section on Scots law.

[3] For instance, Canada and Scotland.

England and Wales[4]

The 2003 decision in *R* v. *G and Another*,[5] although not intended to be of universal application,[6] typifies the approach taken towards recklessness in the vast majority of offences under English criminal law. The House of Lords[7] adopted the following definition of recklessness from the Law Commission's *Draft Criminal Code*:[8]

> A person acts recklessly . . . with respect to (i) a circumstance when he is aware of a risk that it exists or will exist; (ii) a result when he is aware of a risk that it will occur; and it is, in the circumstances known to him, unreasonable to take the risk.

The defendant need not, apparently, be aware that the relevant risk is 'obvious and significant'.[9]

A similar (but distinct) definition of recklessness comes from the case of *R* v. *Cunningham*. There, it was held that the *mens rea* term 'malice', which is used in older offences, incorporated 'recklessness'. 'Recklessness', in this context, covers situations where the defendant has 'foreseen that the particular kind of harm might be done' and nevertheless proceeded with her action.[10]

[4] For historical overviews of the development of recklessness in English criminal law, see Andrew W. Halpin, *Definition in the Criminal Law* (Oxford: Hart, 2004), ch. 3; K.J.M. Smith, *Lawyers, Legislators and Theorists: Developments in English Criminal Jurisprudence* (Oxford: Clarendon, 1998), chs. 5, 9; Findlay Stark, 'Culpable carelessness: recklessness and negligence in Scots and English criminal law', PhD thesis, University of Edinburgh (2011), ch. 3.

[5] [2003] UKHL 50, [2004] 1 AC 1034. To ensure that footnotes are kept to a manageable size, references to the jurisdiction that a case or statute originates from are included (in brackets, after the relevant citation) only where this is unclear from the context.

[6] Lord Bingham, for instance, expressly limited his remarks to the context of criminal damage: *G and Another*, at [28]. This limitation has not been taken particularly seriously in some judgments. See *R* v. *Brady* [2006] EWCA Crim 2413, at [15]; *Attorney-General's Reference (No 3 of 2003)* [2004] EWCA Crim 868, [2005] QB 73, at [12]; *R* v. *C* [2007] EWCA Crim 1068, at [20]; *R* v. *Coley* [2013] EWCA Crim 223, [2014] 1 WLR 1920, at [57].

[7] The Appellate Committee of the House of Lords heard criminal appeals from England and Wales until the UK Supreme Court assumed its jurisdiction on 1 October 2009.

[8] *G and Another*, at [41]. See *A Criminal Code for England and Wales*, 2 vols. (Law Com. No. 177, 1989), vol. 1, cl. 18(c).

[9] *Brady*, discussed above at Chapter 1, section on 'Why Is Justification Required?'.

[10] [1957] 2 QB 396, at 399–400, adopting the definition in C.S. Kenny, *Outlines of Criminal Law*, 16th edn., ed. J.W.C. Turner (Cambridge: Cambridge University Press, 1952), p. 186. The requirement of advertent foresight appears explicitly for the first time in

There is little clarity over exactly what it means for a defendant to be *aware* of, or *foresee*, a risk. For instance, it is not certain whether it is sufficient for the defendant to have a risk at the 'back of his mind' whilst he took it without justification. What if, for instance, the defendant would have responded 'Yes, of course!' if he had been asked about the risks associated with his conduct, but had failed to engage that belief about risk at the time?[11] Although *deliberately* 'closing one's mind' to risk is apparently consistent with the understanding of 'recklessness' in *Cunningham*,[12] and *G and Another*,[13] the Court of Appeal has refused outright to engage with any 'philosophical quibble'[14] over the relevance of the type of 'background' beliefs described in the previous sentence. It will be contended in Chapter 4 that the failure by the English courts (and those in other jurisdictions) to engage with this question is unfortunate. Its resolution impacts on the scope of recklessness on the Standard Account.

Although awareness of risk (whatever that means) is core to the *G and Another* and *Cunningham* definitions of 'recklessness', it would be too quick to conclude that English law adopts an awareness-based model of recklessness in all contexts. Although they are now comparatively rare, other conceptions of recklessness are found in English criminal law. In involuntary manslaughter, for example, it is permissible to direct juries in terms of 'ordinary' recklessness.[15] This is, apparently, synonymous with 'gross' negligence, i.e. negligence which goes 'beyond a mere matter of compensation between subjects and show[s] such disregard for the life and safety of others as to amount to a crime against the State and conduct deserving of punishment'.[16] Despite the use of the (opaque) term 'disregard' in this definition,[17] it does not appear to be necessary that the 'grossly' negligent defendant first foresaw a risk of death and then

Turner's edition of *Outlines* (cf. C.S. Kenny, *Outlines of Criminal Law*, 15th edn., ed. C.G. Phillips (Cambridge University Press, 1947), pp. 171, 189).

11 Cf. the 'conditional subjectivism' discussed in Glanville Williams, 'Recklessness redefined' (1981) 40 *Cambridge Law Journal* 252 at 268–272, and critiqued in R.A. Duff, 'Professor Williams and conditional subjectivism' (1982) 41 *Cambridge Law Journal* 273.

12 *R* v. *Parker* [1977] 1 WLR 600, at 604.

13 *G and Another*, at [58]. See also *R* v. *Booth* [2006] EWHC 192 (Admin), at [22]–[24].

14 *R* v. *Murphy* [1980] QB 434, at 440.

15 *R* v. *Adomako* [1995] 1 AC 171, at 187.

16 *R* v. *Bateman* (1927) 19 Cr App R 8, at 11–12.

17 The question of whether a person can *dis*regard something without first being aware of its existence is returned to below at Chapter 6, section on 'Choice in Doctrine'.

decided to act in spite of it.[18] As 'ordinary' recklessness is synonymous with 'gross' negligence, then it thus appears to be satisfied in cases of inadvertent unjustified risk-taking.

Definitions of recklessness in terms of 'indifference' to risk are similarly uncommon in modern English criminal law, but at least one example of their use can be found.[19] Like the concept of 'disregard', the concept of indifference is equivocal on the question of whether the defendant adverted to the risk of harm at the time of acting.[20] It is thus not clear whether what might be called 'inadvertent indifference' would be sufficient fault to merit conviction.[21]

Negligence

In contrast to recklessness, which is used very often in the drafting and defining of criminal offences requiring *mens rea*, negligence is used sparingly in English criminal law. In fact, the word 'negligence' itself appears extremely rarely in the definition of offences.[22] There are, however, numerous offences, which – although not using the word 'negligence' – require the defendant to exercise reasonable care when performing an activity. In these areas, the standard of carelessness required for conviction is sometimes similar to civil negligence.[23] Other offences of inadvertent carelessness tend towards the above-noted standard of 'gross' negligence, used in involuntary manslaughter.[24] The line between these forms of 'ordinary' and 'gross' negligence seems simply to

[18] *R* v. *Mark and Nationwide Heating Services Ltd* [2004] EWCA Crim 2490. See, further, *R* v. *Stone and Dobinson* [1977] QB 354, at 363–364.

[19] See Uranium Enrichment Technology (Prohibition on Disclosure) Regulations 2004 (SI 2004 No. 1818), reg. 2(2)(a)(ii).

[20] For an argument that 'indifference' does not require awareness of risk, see R.A. Duff, *Intention, Agency and Criminal Liability: Philosophy of Action and the Criminal Law* (Oxford: Basil Blackwell, 1990), ch. 7. Duff's theory of recklessness is discussed below at Chapter 7, section on 'Duff's "Practical Indifference"'.

[21] Failure to advert to an 'obvious' risk is also a recognised fault element under the Uranium Enrichment Technology (Prohibition on Disclosure) Regulations 2004 (SI 2004/1818), reg. 2(2)(b). It is thus not clear if 'indifference' covers any useful ground in that offence.

[22] See David Ormerod and Karl Laird, *Smith and Hogan: Criminal Law*, 14th edn. (Oxford: Oxford University Press, 2015), ch. 6.

[23] See e.g. the standard of 'careless and inconsiderate driving', defined in Road Traffic Act 1988, s. 3ZA.

[24] See e.g. the standard of 'dangerous driving', defined in ibid., s. 2A.

be the extent – in terms of its lack of justification – of the defendant's risk-taking. The focus in such cases is thus on conduct, which will be objected to in Chapter 7.[25] To anticipate the discussion there, it will be contended that conduct-based conceptions of negligence fail to draw an adequately personalised link between defendants and their wrongdoing to merit a criminal conviction.

In other cases, the defendant's faulty carelessness relates to the formation of his beliefs about certain aspects of his behaviour (a theme returned to in Chapter 8), rather than the manner in which that behaviour was performed. This approach is fairly prevalent in sexual offences, with regard to consent or (in limited circumstances) the age of a sexual partner – the prosecution must prove that the defendant did not have a *reasonable* belief about consent or age.[26] An *honest* belief will no longer secure an acquittal, unless it is based on reasonable grounds.[27]

Voluntary Intoxication

The English law of voluntary intoxication merits mention here, because of its relationship with recklessness. If the defendant's state of voluntary intoxication raises a reasonable doubt over whether he formed the relevant *mens rea* at the time of the *actus reus*, he is entitled to be acquitted, but only if the charge is one of 'specific intent'. If the crime is one of 'basic intent', the defendant's voluntary intoxication (however severe) will not secure an acquittal in itself.[28]

There are various theories concerning *why* the defendant's state of voluntary intoxication cannot, by itself, result in an acquittal in crimes of basic intent. The important one, for present purposes, concentrates on the defendant's apparent 'recklessness' in drinking or taking drugs to the extent that he becomes acutely intoxicated. In *DPP* v. *Majewski*,[29] the following thought process was employed: (a) becoming acutely, voluntarily intoxicated is 'reckless'; (b) recklessness tends to be an adequate form of *mens rea* for the *actus reus* elements of 'basic intent' offences; (c) given (a) and (b), the acutely, voluntarily intoxicated defendant has demonstrated sufficient culpability in relation to the *actus reus* of the

25 See Chapter 7, section on 'Conduct: Hart's Insight'.

26 See e.g. Sexual Offences Act 2003, ss. 1(1)(c), 2(1)(d), 3(1)(d), 4(1)(d), 9(c)(i), 10(c)(i).

27 Cf. *DPP* v. *Morgan* [1976] AC 182.

28 See *DPP* v. *Beard* [1920] AC 479; *DPP* v. *Majewski* [1977] AC 443.

29 [1977] AC 443.

'basic intent' offence to merit conviction.[30] In the light of the fact that this thought process has been followed in some of the other jurisdictions surveyed below (e.g. Scotland and Canada), it is worth spending a little time explaining its deficiencies.[31]

First, there is the question of *which* risks the defendant was aware of when becoming acutely, voluntarily intoxicated. In most cases it can be assumed that the defendant's 'recklessness' in becoming voluntarily intoxicated related to a number of risks, such as becoming disorientated or having a hangover the next morning. The defendant's foresight presumably did not relate to the risk of committing a specific crime, unless he had previously acted similarly in an intoxicated state.[32] In accordance with what some English authors have dubbed the 'correspondence principle',[33] recklessness usually requires awareness of the risk of a specific type of conduct occurring, a particular circumstance existing, or a particular consequence materialising. This specificity is laudable, insofar as it ensures a connection between the defendant, as an agent, and her wrongdoing.

The English voluntary intoxication rules do not subscribe to any sense of correspondence. The courts do not ever investigate *what* the defendant believed might emanate from his decision to become acutely intoxicated (assuming people *decide* such things).[34] So the equivalence of acute, voluntary intoxication and recklessness suggested in *Majewski* seems out of place in a system that concerns itself typically with the defendant's awareness of a specific risk.[35]

Secondly, unless becoming acutely intoxicated (the apparent fault element in cases of extreme voluntary intoxication) and the commission

[30] See *Majewski*, at 474–475. The Court of Appeal tried to distance itself from these remarks in *R* v. *Heard* [2007] EWCA Crim 125, [2008] QB 43, at [30]. See Rebecca Williams, 'Voluntary intoxication – a lost cause?' (2013) 129 *Law Quarterly Review* 264 at 267–268.

[31] This section builds on Findlay Stark, 'Breaking down *Brennan*' 2009 *Juridical Review* 155 at 156–160.

[32] A.J.P. Kenny, *Freewill and Responsibility* (London: Routledge, 1978), pp. 65–66; Pillsbury, 'Crimes of indifference', at 186.

[33] See Kenneth Campbell and Andrew Ashworth, 'Recklessness in assault – and in general?' (1991) 107 *Law Quarterly Review* 187 at 192; Jeremy Horder, 'A critique of the correspondence principle in criminal law' [1995] *Criminal Law Review* 759.

[34] Cf. Susan Dimock, 'What are intoxicated offenders responsible for? The "intoxication defense" revisited' (2011) 5 *Criminal Law and Philosophy* 1; Findlay Stark, 'Prior fault' (2014) 73 *Cambridge Law Journal* 8 at 10.

[35] *R* v. *O'Connor* (1980) 146 CLR 64 (HCA), at 85.

of the *actus reus* are viewed as 'one transaction',[36] English law has little way of explaining how there is concurrence of fault and wrongdoing in cases involving acutely, voluntarily intoxicated defendants. Such temporal concurrence is necessitated by general principles of English criminal law.[37] The difficulty in convicting a defendant of a 'basic intent' offence committed at t_2, perpetrated at the height of a 'reckless' drinking spree commenced miles and hours away at t_1, is readily apparent.[38]

Thirdly, difficulties are posed by the confusion over the line between 'basic' and 'specific' intent crimes in English law and those systems that have borrowed this distinction from it. In *R* v. *Heard*,[39] the Court of Appeal suggested (*obiter*) that the line is between fault elements intrinsic to the *actus reus* ('basic intent') and fault elements stretching beyond the bare *actus reus* ('specific intent').[40] This does not divide nicely into recklessness ('basic intent') and knowledge/intention ('specific intent'). Consider aggravated criminal damage:[41] the defendant's *mens rea* must stretch not only to the bare act of criminal damage ('basic intent'), but also to the possibility of endangering the lives of others ('specific intent'). The sober defendant must be at least reckless to both of these elements, and *presumably* the defendant's voluntary intoxication can negate *mens rea* only with regard to endangerment.[42] If the equivalence between recklessness and voluntary intoxication explained English law's approach, why does the defendant's 'reckless' decision to get intoxicated provide one form of recklessness in aggravated criminal damage but not the other?[43]

Given the problems of equating voluntary intoxication with recklessness, a second seam of authority has appeared, which essentially requires

[36] See *Thabo Meli and Others* v. *R* [1954] 1 WLR 228 (PC). That decision, however, was not made in relation to the context of voluntary intoxication.

[37] See A.P. Simester, J.R. Spencer, G.R. Sullivan and G.J. Virgo, *Simester and Sullivan's Criminal Law: Theory and Doctrine*, 5th edn. (Oxford: Hart, 2013), pp. 167–171.

[38] Gerald H. Gordon, *The Criminal Law of Scotland*, 3rd edn., ed. M.G.A. Christie, 2 vols. (Edinburgh: SULI/W. Green, 2000–2001), vol. 1, para. 12.13.

[39] [2007] EWCA Crim 125, [2008] QB 43.

[40] At [31]. See, further, *R* v. *George* [1960] SCR 871 (Can), at 877.

[41] Criminal Damage Act 1971, s. 1(2).

[42] This position was assumed in *Commissioner of Police for the Metropolis* v. *Caldwell* [1982] AC 341, at 359–360. The treatment of voluntary intoxication in that case was not doubted in *G and Another*. See also *Heard*, at [31]; *Coley*, at [57].

[43] The English courts have failed to give a compelling answer, but for a theoretical response, see A.P. Simester, 'Intoxication is never a defence' [2009] *Criminal Law Review* 3 at 10–12.

the court to ignore evidence of the defendant's state of voluntary intoxication.[44] This is problematic, in that it involves the jury having to find *mens rea* (the awareness of a *specific* risk, in most cases of recklessness) where, on the evidence, there might be none. As Simester puts it, this approach is 'highly artificial . . . [i]t rests on a fiction, a deliberately false inference from the facts'.[45] It is perhaps for this reason that this response to the problem of acutely, voluntarily intoxicated wrongdoers has not been taken very seriously by the English courts, but – as will be seen below – it has found favour elsewhere.

The third option is to ask what the defendant *would have been aware of* had he not been intoxicated, and this appears to be the option favoured currently by the English Court of Appeal[46] and, on occasion, the legislature.[47] This approach is unnecessarily complicated for jurors to apply, and still allows for findings of 'recklessness' where, at the time of the *actus reus*, the defendant might have been unaware of the relevant risk(s). He merely *could have* been aware, had he been sober.

What all this means is that, in cases involving voluntary intoxication, English law abuses the concept of recklessness – either by equating it with the defendant's decision to become intoxicated, allowing it to be found through ignoring the facts, or by engaging in a counterfactual enquiry about what might have been. It is submitted that progress can be made only by distinguishing clearly between *mens rea* and the rules on voluntary intoxication. Some of the jurisdictions discussed below have accomplished this feat, and it will be concluded that this is the most sensible way forward.

Summary

It is *almost* universally true that English law defines recklessness in terms of the defendant's awareness of risk, allowing for a clear demarcation between recklessness and negligence, but minor statutory and common law deviations from this model are visible. It appears that English law is on a gradual trajectory towards recognising *only* awareness-based recklessness, but it still has some way to go, and inadvertent negligence is still employed in a limited range of contexts, sometimes in relation to serious offences (manslaughter and some sexual offences).

44 See e.g. *R* v. *Hardie* [1985] 1 WLR 64, at 70.
45 See Simester, 'Intoxication is never a defence', at 5.
46 See the discussion in *Coley*, at [57]. 47 Public Order Act 1986, s. 6(5).

The Law Commission's Draft Criminal Code sought to alleviate definitional strain on the word 'recklessness' by defining it in general terms of awareness of risk.[48] Abuse would still be done to this model in cases involving acute voluntary intoxication. Rather than, for instance, identify voluntary intoxication as an alternative type of fault, the Draft Code would treat the acutely, voluntarily intoxicated defendant as being aware of any risks that he would have foreseen whilst sober[49] (an approach objected to above). The Code has never been implemented. It is unlikely that it ever will be.[50]

Now that the English position has been set out, it is time to investigate how other Anglo-American jurisdictions have fared in explaining culpable carelessness.

Canada

The Criminal Code of Canada (CCC) applies to all Canadian provinces and territories.[51] It does not provide definitions of *mens rea* terms but does use the concepts of recklessness and negligence in some offence definitions.[52]

When defining *recklessness*, the Supreme Court of Canada (SCC) has consistently[53] required that 'the accused persisted in a course of conduct knowing of the risk which it created'.[54] As with English law, the matter of whether this knowledge must be at the forefront of the accused's conscious mind has not been resolved.

48 See the text accompanying note 8, above.

49 Law Commission, *A Criminal Code for England and Wales*, cl. 22(1)(a). Separate provision is made for mistakes made by the defendant, which would only be taken into account if *reasonable*: cl. 22(1)(b), 22(2).

50 See Ian Dennis, 'RIP: the criminal code (1968–2008)' [2009] *Criminal Law Review* 1.

51 Criminal law is reserved to the federal Canadian government by the (UK Parliament's) Constitution Act 1867, s. 91(27).

52 On recklessness, see e.g. (second-degree) murder (Criminal Code, RSC 1985, c. C-46 (hereinafter 'CCC'), s. 229) and aggravated arson (s. 433). The Code's approach to 'criminal negligence' is discussed below.

53 See *R* v. *Sansregret* [1985] 1 SCR 570, at [16]; *R* v. *Hinchey* [1996] 3 SCR 1128, at [117]; *R* v. *Kerr* 2004 SCC 44, [2004] 2 SCR 371, at [88].

54 *R* v. *ADH* 2013 SCC 28, [2013] 2 SCR 269, at [16]. Occasionally, the courts talk in terms that suggest 'assumption' of or 'indifference' towards that foreseen risk is also required: e.g. *R* v. *Leary* [1978] 1 SCR 29, at 34. 'Indifference' does not seem to require more than the decision to take the risk of which the accused was aware. This point is discussed below at Chapter 7, section on 'Attitudinal Accounts'.

Consistency has been undermined slightly by the CCC's definition of 'criminal negligence'. 'Criminal negligence' is sufficient fault for conviction where death[55] or bodily harm[56] results from the accused's act or omission to perform a legal duty. 'Criminal negligence' requires 'wanton or reckless disregard for the lives or safety of other persons'.[57]

This definition is 'notorious in its ambiguity'[58] and – despite using the word 'reckless'[59] – can be viewed as *either* an awareness-based test, involving awareness of a risk of harm or death, *or* a test that would cover some cases of unawareness of risk, based on the accused's departure from the standards of care recognised by a reasonable person. Following initial confusion,[60] the 2008 decision in *R* v. *J(F)* held that 'criminal negligence' requires '*a marked and substantial departure* (as opposed to a *marked departure*) from the conduct of a reasonably prudent [person] in circumstances where the accused either recognized and ran an obvious and serious risk . . . or, alternatively, gave no thought to that risk'.[61] It is thus not quite correct to say that recklessness is *always* understood in an awareness-based manner in Canada.

The difficulty with the decision in *J(F)* is that what might be termed 'ordinary' negligence is also employed in the CCC (although the word 'negligence' itself is found very rarely in the CCC).[62] A question has thus arisen as to how 'ordinary' negligence is to be distinguished from 'criminal negligence'. In *Hundal* v. *R*[63] and *R* v. *Finlay*,[64] the SCC adopted a 'modified objective' test for 'ordinary' negligence in criminal offences: the accused's carelessness must constitute a 'marked departure from the standard of care of a reasonably prudent person', but any incapacity on the part of the accused to foresee the relevant risk(s) must be considered.[65]

55 CCC, s. 220. 56 Ibid., s. 221. 57 Ibid., s. 219.

58 *R* v. *Tutton* [1989] 1 SCR 1392, at 1403.

59 The CCC requires reckless *or* wanton disregard. The courts have not distinguished between these concepts in the context of 'criminal negligence'.

60 The SCC split equally on the definition of 'criminal negligence' in *Tutton*. See, further, *R* v. *Waite* [1989] 1 SCR 1436; *R* v. *Anderson* [1990] 1 SCR 265.

61 *R* v. *J(F)* 2008 SCC 60, [2008] 3 SCR 215, at [9] (emphasis in original).

62 See e.g. CCC, s. 436 ('arson by negligence'). 63 [1993] 1 SCR 867.

64 [1993] 3 SCR 103.

65 See, further, *R* v. *Creighton* [1993] 3 SCR 3; *R* v. *Gosset* [1993] 3 SCR 76; *R* v. *Beatty* 2008 SCC 5, [2008] 1 SCR 49. Cf. H.L.A. Hart, *Punishment and Responsibility: Essays in the Philosophy of Law*, 2nd edn. (Oxford: Oxford University Press, 2008), ch. 6 (discussed below at Chapter 7, section on 'Exploring Hart's Account'.

This 'modified objectivism' is focussed clearly on the accused's *conduct* and does not require awareness of risk on the part of the accused. What distinguishes it from the test for 'criminal negligence' is that, with 'ordinary' negligence, the prosecution need not prove a marked *and* substantial departure from 'objective' standards. In short, the carelessness involved in 'criminal negligence' is *worse* than that found in 'ordinary' negligence. The line between these forms of negligence, which mirrors that between 'ordinary' and 'gross' negligence in English law, is unclear at best.

Voluntary Intoxication

Canada's approach to evidence of the accused's voluntary intoxication is even more complicated than its English equivalent. For cases where the accused is voluntarily intoxicated to the extent that she is in a state akin to insanity or automatism, regard must be had to the SCC's decision in *R* v. *Daviault*[66] and section 33.1 of the CCC.

In *Daviault*, a majority of the SCC decided that the accused could be acquitted if, given her *extreme* state of voluntary intoxication (akin to automatism), there existed reasonable doubt over the formation of *mens rea*. There would be no finding of 'recklessness' in becoming voluntarily intoxicated in these cases.

Despite its very narrow ambit, the majority's judgment proved too much for the Canadian legislature,[67] which soon added section 33.1 to the CCC. This provides that voluntary intoxication cannot negate *mens rea* in 'an offence under [the Code] or any other Act of Parliament that includes as an element an assault or any other interference or threat of interference by a person with the bodily integrity of another person'. Many offences that are commonly committed by voluntarily intoxicated offenders can be brought under section 33.1's remit, rendering it very broad[68] and almost certainly unconstitutional.[69] Where section 33.1 of

[66] [1994] 3 SCR 63.

[67] See Elizabeth Sheehy, 'The intoxication defence in Canada: why women should care' (1996) 23 *Contemporary Drug Problems* 595; Isabel Grant, 'Second chances: bill C-72 and the Charter' (1995) 33 *Osgoode Hall Law Journal* 379.

[68] Don Stuart, *Canadian Criminal Law: A Treatise*, 7th edn. (Toronto: Carswell, 2014), p. 484.

[69] See ibid., 486–487; Heather MacMillan-Brown, 'No longer *Leary* about intoxication: in the aftermath of *R* v. *Daviault*' (1995) 59 *Saskatchewan Law Review* 311 at 332–333; Kent Roach, 'Dialogue or defiance: legislative reversals of Supreme Court decisions in

the CCC does not apply (e.g. property offences), the SCC's decision in *Daviault* will be followed if the accused was voluntarily intoxicated to the extent that she was in a state akin to automatism at the time of the alleged offence.[70]

When the accused is not voluntarily intoxicated to the extent required by *Daviault*, but there remains reasonable doubt over whether *mens rea* was formed, the SCC's decision in *R* v. *Leary*[71] will be followed instead. This implements English law's 'specific/basic' intent dichotomy. Dissentients in the SCC and academic commentators[72] have been refreshingly sceptical about the idea that becoming voluntarily intoxicated is *itself* 'reckless'.[73] There are nevertheless conflations of recklessness and intoxication in some Canadian cases.[74] This equation of intoxication and recklessness is lamentable, given the problems with this approach outlined above.

Summary

Superficially, Canada has remained relatively consistent in its approach to understanding recklessness but has suffered similar problems to English law. The use of recklessness in the definition of criminal negligence has no doubt contributed to the development of a jurisprudence that is as unpredictable as a 'rogue elephant',[75] and – going beyond recklessness – it seems complicated to have different *types* of negligence in different circumstances, with vague lines being drawn between them. Finally, the adoption of the fiction about 'recklessness' in some (though not all) voluntary intoxication cases is problematic. Like England and Wales, then, more thought needs to go into achieving consistency in the approach towards culpable carelessness in Canadian criminal law.

Canada and the United States' (2006) 4 *International Journal of Constitutional Law* 347 at 360–363.

70 *R* v. *Bouchard-Lebrun* 2011 SCC 58, [2011] 3 SCR 575, at [35].

71 [1978] 1 SCR 29.

72 See, particularly, the critique of the 'disjointed, incoherent approach to criminal culpability' underlying this approach, in Tim Quigley, 'Specific and general nonsense?' (1987–1988) 11 *Dalhousie Law Journal* 75 at 102–114.

73 See *Leary*, at 45.

74 E.g. *R* v. *Bernard* [1988] 2 SCR 833, at [76]; *R* v. *Daley* 2007 SCC 53, [2007] 3 SCR 523, at [36]; *Bouchard-Lebrun*, at [31].

75 Stuart, *Canadian Criminal Law*, p. 293. Stuart explains that this is a South African saying, referring to 'a psychotic elephant dangerously running amok' (n. 788).

Australia

It is worth considering each of Australia's nine jurisdictions separately. This is because of variations in their approaches to defining recklessness and separating it from negligence.

Before exploring these differences, it is useful to give a point of explanation for those unfamiliar with Australian criminal law. It is possible to divide the Australian jurisdictions into two clusters. New South Wales (NSW), South Australia (SA) and Victoria are Common Law jurisdictions. Each has a consolidated criminal law statute,[76] but these pieces of legislation do not purport to provide full statements of the criminal law. Judicial decisions can thus still drive the law's development, though it must be noted that more and more of the criminal law of these states is found nowadays in statute.

The second group of jurisdictions is made up of the Australian Capital Territory (ACT),[77] the Northern Territory (NT),[78] Queensland,[79] Tasmania[80] and Western Australia (WAus).[81] These systems have either fully codified their criminal laws or, in the case of the ACT, are on their way to doing so. The federal Australian criminal law, which applies in relation to each state and territory, is also on the way to being fully codified.[82]

The treatment of unjustified risk-taking in these two groups of jurisdictions will be considered separately.

The Common Law Jurisdictions

The various consolidating statutes found in the Australian Common Law jurisdictions do not provide general definitions of *mens rea* terms. The consolidating statutes nevertheless contain reference to recklessness.[83]

[76] Crimes Act 1900 (NSW); Criminal Law Consolidation Act 1935 (SA); Crimes Act 1958 (Vic).

[77] Criminal Code 2002 (ACT), which must be read with the Crimes Act 1900 (ACT).

[78] Criminal Code Act 1983 (NT).

[79] Criminal Code Act 1899 (Qd).

[80] Criminal Code Act 1924 (Tas).

[81] Criminal Code Act Compilation Act 1913 (WAus).

[82] Criminal Code Act 1995 (Cwlth). At present, some offences are still defined in the Crimes Act 1914 (Cwlth).

[83] E.g. Crimes Act 1900 (NSW), s. 35 ('reckless grievous bodily harm or wounding') and Crimes Act 1958 (Vic), s. 27 ('causing serious injury recklessly'). The Criminal Law Consolidation Act 1935 (SA) contains references both to recklessness and 'reckless indifference', without defining these words in relation to *all* offences.

The courts in these jurisdictions have also read recklessness into individual offences.[84]

The relevant courts[85] and legislatures[86] have taken an awareness-centred approach towards defining recklessness in most contexts. For example, at common law, the *mens rea* of murder can be made out where the defendant knows it is *probable* that death or serious injury will result from his conduct.[87] This is clearly an awareness-based conception of *recklessness*, even if it is described often as a type of knowledge (of the relevant risk).[88] Indeed, in NSW, murder has been defined in legislation explicitly by reference to 'reckless indifference' to human life.[89] The HCA has made clear that such indifference requires awareness of the risk of death.[90]

'Reckless indifference' has been defined with similar reference to the defendant's awareness of risk in relation to some other offences.[91] It

[84] *MacPherson* v. *Brown* (1975) 12 SASR 184 (SA), at 188–189 (a case concerning kidnapping under the Criminal Law Consolidation Act 1935 (SA), s. 39).

[85] See e.g. *Ignatova* v. *R* [2010] VSCA 263 (Vic), at [36]–[38] ('causing serious injury recklessly' – Crimes Act 1958 (Vic), s. 17); *R* v. *Abdul-Rasool* [2008] VSCA 13, (2008) 18 VR 586 (Vic), at [67] ('conduct endangering life' – Crimes Act 1958 (Vic), s. 22); *R* v. *Taylor* [2004] VSCA 189, (2004) 149 A Crim R 399 (Vic), at [42] (being 'reckless' as to being a trespasser for the purposes of aggravated burglary – Crimes Act 1958 (Vic), s. 76); *Blackwell* v. *R* [2011] NSWCCA 93, (2011) 208 A Crim R 392 (NSW) ('reckless grievous bodily harm' – Crimes Act 1900 (NSW), s. 35 (although the legislation has subsequently been amended, the awareness-based conception of recklessness still applies: *Chen* v. *R* [2013] NSWCCA 116 (NSW)).

[86] The Criminal Law Consolidation Act 1935 (SA) gives definitions for some specific offences – for instance, s. 21 defines recklessness in terms of awareness of substantial risk of causing harm or serious harm in relation to offences against the person (see also ss. 29A(6), 32AA(6)). Cf. s. 47 (defining 'reckless indifference' in relation to consent – see below). The Crimes Act 1958 (Vic), ss. 318(2)(a)–318(2)(b) defines recklessness with regard to 'culpable driving causing death' as existing where the defendant 'consciously and unjustifiably disregards a substantial risk', and negligence with regard to the 'gross' failure to exercise the care that would be demonstrated by the 'reasonable man'.

[87] *Pemble* v. *R* (1971) 124 CLR 107 (HCA); *La Fontaine* v. *The Queen* (1976) 136 CLR 62 (HCA); *R* v. *Crabbe* (1985) 156 CLR 464 (HCA); *Royall* v. *R* (1991) 172 CLR 378 (HCA). The other Australian jurisdictions are more variable in their definitions of murder. See Simon Bronitt and Bernadette McSherry, *Principles of Criminal Law*, 3rd edn. (Sydney: Thomson Reuters, 2010), p. 506.

[88] See Bronitt and McSherry, *Principles of Criminal Law*, p. 526. The relationship between awareness and knowledge of risk is explored below at Chapter 5.

[89] Crimes Act 1900 (NSW), s. 18. This means that recklessness as to the causing of grievous bodily harm is not sufficient *mens rea* for murder in NSW. See, similarly, Crimes Act 1900 (ACT), s. 12.

[90] See *Royall*.

[91] See e.g. Criminal Law Consolidation Act 1935 (SA), s. 85 ('arson and other property damage'); *Tziavrangos* v. *Hayes* (1991) 55 SASR 416 (SA).

should be noted that the addition of the concept of *indifference* never appears to do much work in these Common Law jurisdictions, in contrast to the Scottish position (at least in common law offences and murder), discussed below. It is not required, for a finding of recklessness in NSW, SA or Victoria, that a separate *attitude* of indifference be proved: the bare choice to take, without adequate justification, a risk of which the defendant is aware is sufficient fault to constitute 'reckless indifference'.[92]

'Reckless indifference' is not *always* defined so as to clearly require awareness of risk, however. For instance, the SA legislature has defined what it means to be 'recklessly indifferent' in relation to rape and other sexual offences so as to include, *inter alia*, cases where the defendant 'does not give any thought as to whether or not the other person is consenting to the act'.[93] This sense of 'reckless indifference' might seem inconsistent with a requirement of awareness of risk of non-consent. To be aware of a risk of non-consent would, presumably, be to 'give thought' to the matter of consent. Then again, if to 'give any thought' to a matter simply means to be thinking *consciously* about that matter (in the 'mind's eye'), then awareness that is at the 'back of the mind', and not being focussed on explicitly might be sufficient for a conviction. As with English and Canadian law, there is no clarification of this matter in the decided cases.

In Victoria, the word 'recklessness' (never mind 'reckless indifference') is not used: the relevant form of *mens rea* is the absence of a reasonable belief in consent in offences such as rape.[94] A similar position exists in NSW, where the absence of a reasonable belief in consent now sits alongside recklessness as a form of *mens rea* in sexual offences.[95] As noted above in relation to English law, the absence of a reasonable belief in consent understanding of fault is arguably a form of negligence, in the sense it entails the failure to form beliefs about the risk of non-consent that would be expected in the circumstances. Both NSW and Victoria thus manage to avoid stretching the concept of

92 See *Banditt* v. *R* [2005] HCA 80, (2005) 224 CLR 262 (HCA). This point is not always clear, particularly in older decisions (e.g. *R* v. *Ashman* [1957] VR 364 (Vic), at 366).

93 Criminal Law Consolidation Act 1935 (SA), s. 47.

94 Crimes Act 1958 (Vic), s. 38(1)(c).

95 Confusingly, both mental states are used as proof of *knowledge*: Crimes Act 1900 (NSW), ss. 61HA(3)(b)–61HA(3)(c). In relation to the previous provisions on consent, recklessness was read to cover a failure to give any thought to the matter of consent: see the summary in *Bochkov* v. *R* [2009] NSWCCA 166 (NSW), at [94].

'reckless indifference' in the context of sexual offences to include *some* inadvertent risk-taking.

Unfortunately, this definitional clarity becomes lost in the context of involuntary manslaughter. There, the concept of 'reckless negligence', and the equivalence of 'recklessness' and 'gross' negligence, complicates matters.[96] These forms of 'recklessness' can be understood to incorporate the taking of grave risks of which the defendant is unaware, i.e. as a more serious form of 'ordinary' negligence, where 'such a great falling short of the standard of care which a reasonable man would have exercised and which involved such a high risk that death or grievous bodily harm would follow that the doing of the act merited criminal punishment'.[97] Thus, awareness of risk is not required for manslaughter, despite the language of 'recklessness' being used on occasion.[98]

Accordingly, *all* of the Australian Common Law jurisdictions know at least two senses of the word 'reckless', premised on awareness and unawareness of risk,[99] even if Victoria and NSW avoid this confusion in the law of sexual offences.

Moving beyond *gross* negligence, what might be termed 'ordinary' negligence is found occasionally in the consolidating statutes of the Common Law jurisdictions. Sometimes, this has been interpreted in terms of 'gross' negligence,[100] but it remains unclear whether other degrees of negligence are available.[101] The standard of care expected of the defendant might thus be variable.

In relation to voluntary intoxication, different rules operate in the Common Law jurisdictions. NSW has enshrined the English intent dichotomy in statute[102] and holds intoxicated defendants to sober standards in offences of negligence.[103] The NSW approach focuses on the

[96] *Mamote-Kulang of Tamagot* v. *R* (1964) 111 CLR 62 (HCA). See, further, *R* v. *Lavender* [2004] NSWCCA 120 (NSW) (overruled by the HCA in *R* v. *Lavender* [2005] HCA 37, (2005) 222 CLR 67 (HCA)).

[97] See *Nydam* v. *R* [1977] VR 430 (Vic), at 445.

[98] See *R* v. *Lavender* [2005] HCA 37, (2005) 222 CLR 67 (HCA).

[99] Cf. *MacPherson* v. *Brown*, at 188–189.

[100] See e.g. Crimes Act 1900 (NSW), s. 54 ('causing grievous bodily harm'); *R* v. *D* (1984) 3 NSWLR 29 (NSW).

[101] Cf. *D*, at 34.

[102] Crimes Act 1900 (NSW), pt. 11A. See also *R* v. *Grant* [2002] NSWCCA 243, (2002) 55 NSWLR 80 (NSW) (all forms of murder, even those premised on 'reckless indifference' to the risk of death, are 'specific intent' offences).

[103] Crimes Act 1900 (NSW), s. 428F.

inadmissibility of evidence of voluntary intoxication in assessing basic intent, rather than the equivalence of voluntary intoxication with recklessness. Victoria and SA have, by contrast, followed the High Court of Australia's rejection of the intent dichotomy in *R* v. *O'Connor*.[104] In those jurisdictions, with certain exceptions,[105] if the defendant can raise a reasonable doubt over whether he had *mens rea*, he is entitled to be acquitted. The 'recklessness' argument used in *Majewski* did not find favour with the High Court of Australia in *O'Connor*.[106] In most cases, no confusion over recklessness and acute voluntary intoxication thus arises in Victoria and South Australia. It is submitted that this is advantageous. If the view is taken that acutely, voluntarily intoxicated offenders are adjudged culpable enough to be held liable for an offence, it should be done through recognising intoxication as an alternative ground of fault.

The Older Codes

For reasons that will become apparent, it is worth considering the treatment of recklessness and negligence in the older codified jurisdictions and the more recent codes separately. The law of voluntary intoxication in the codified jurisdictions can then be analysed.

The older criminal codes (found in Queensland, Tasmania and WA), do not give general definitions of *mens rea* terms, such as recklessness and negligence.[107] The codes of Queensland and WA are, in this respect, identical.[108] Recklessness has, however, been accepted as a synonym for wilfulness in *some* contexts.[109] Furthermore, there is *obiter* support for

[104] (1980) 146 CLR 64.

[105] See Criminal Law Consolidation Act 1935 (SA), ss. 267A–269; Crimes Act 1958 (Vic), s. 37H, 322T.

[106] *O'Connor*, at 85. See also *S* v. *Chretien* 1981 (1) SA 1097 (ZA).

[107] See e.g. Criminal Code Act 1924 (Tas), s. 156(3) (making clear that 'culpable negligence' in culpable homicide will vary with circumstances).

[108] Sir Samuel Griffiths crafted both codes.

[109] See *R* v. *Lockwood, ex p Attorney-General* [1981] Qd R 209 (Qd); Michael J. Shanahan, Paul E. Smith and Soraya Ryan, *Carter's Criminal Law of Queensland*, 16th edn. (Chatswood, NSW: LexisNexis Butterworths, 2006), p. 266. Confusion still arises from some decisions. In *DAB* v. *Capes* [2011] WASC 137 (WAus), for instance, willfulness is defined in terms of the defendant's awareness that a certain result is 'likely' to come about, but proof that the defendant acted 'recklessly' will apparently not do (at [43]).

the view, in WA at least, that recklessness might be sufficient *mens rea* for assault.[110] These understandings of recklessness require awareness of risk on the part of the defendant.[111]

Things become more complicated when attention is paid to negligence. Where negligence is employed by these jurisdictions in the criminal law (which is rarely),[112] it is understood as requiring *more* than civil negligence, but the courts in Queensland and WA have not got much further than that.[113] In involuntary manslaughter, 'gross' negligence can constitute *mens rea*.[114] In *R* v. *Hodgetts and Jackson*,[115] the Queensland Court of Criminal Appeal proposed the following test for 'gross' negligence: 'recklessness involving grave moral guilt'.[116] Recklessness and 'gross' negligence are thus viewed as synonymous in some cases, in common with English law (and, if 'criminal negligence' is synonymous with 'gross' negligence, Canadian law).[117]

Tasmania must be considered separately because its code is materially different from those of Queensland and WA. Section 13 of the Tasmanian code provides that criminal acts must be 'voluntary and intentional'. This has not prevented 'reckless or wanton indifference' from being recognised as a form of *mens rea* for some offences, at least where the basic physical element of the offence is intended by the defendant. Where they are recognised, recklessness and 'reckless indifference' require awareness of risk on the part of the defendant.[118] 'Wilfulness' has also been read in Tasmania so as to include awareness-based recklessness.[119]

[110] *Hall* v. *Foneca* [1983] WAR 309 (WAus), at 313. Cf. *R* v. *Webb, ex pte Attorney-General* [1990] 2 Qd R 275 (Qd), at 286.

[111] Confusion exists over the exact *level* of foresight required. See *R* v. *T* [1997] 1 Qd R 623 (Qd).

[112] See Andreas Schloenhardt, *Queensland Criminal Law*, 4th edn. (Oxford: Oxford University Press, 2015), pp. 92–93.

[113] See *R* v. *Stott and van Embden* [2001] QCA 313, [2002] 2 Qd R 313 (Qd); *Callaghan* v. *R* (1952) 87 CLR 115 (HCA), at 121–124.

[114] See *Callaghan*. [115] [1990] 1 Qd R 456 (Qd). [116] At 463.

[117] Cf. *R* v. *BDD* [2006] QCA 441, [2007] 1 Qd R 478 (Qd), at [16], where the use of the term 'recklessness' was avoided. Phillip McMurdo J suggested judges should avoid confusing recklessness and negligence in jury directions on manslaughter (ibid., at [50]).

[118] See e.g. *R* v. *Valance* (1961) 108 CLR 56 (wounding or causing grievous bodily harm – Criminal Code (Tas), s. 172). See also *Hurst* v. *Tasmania* [2011] TASCCA 12 (Tas).

[119] See, in the context of arson, *R* v. *Hodgson* [1985] Tas R 75 (Tas); *R* v. *Gardenal-Williams* [1989] Tas R 62 (Tas).

The Tasmanian approach to negligence is, by now, familiar. Manslaughter can be committed through the failure to abide by a duty tending towards the preservation of life that demonstrates 'culpable negligence'.[120] What amounts to 'culpable negligence' is a question of fact, for each jury,[121] making it difficult to assess its relationship to other forms of negligence and recklessness.

The Modern Codes

The more recent Australian codes (found in the NT, the Commonwealth and the ACT) contain statutory definitions of recklessness and negligence,[122] and this has created more certainty.[123] Recklessness is defined in terms of awareness of a substantial risk that it is not justified for the defendant to take.[124] Once again, awareness is undefined. Negligence is defined *only* in relation to conduct, and the core question is whether the defendant's behaviour demonstrates 'such a great falling short of the standard of care that a reasonable person would exercise in the circumstances; and . . . such a high risk that the physical element exists or will exist, that the conduct merits criminal punishment for the offence'.[125] The focus is thus on *behaviour*, rather than a failure to be aware of a risk of a certain consequence or circumstance.

Recklessness and negligence are sufficient fault for manslaughter in NT,[126] which allows for a clear bifurcation between these fault elements, avoiding the confusion noted above in relation to other Australian jurisdictions.[127]

120 Criminal Code Act 1924, s. 156(2)(b).

121 Ibid., s. 156(3).

122 Only *some* of the offences contained in the Crimes Act 1900 (ACT) incorporate the Code's definitions. For instance, murder requires 'reckless indifference' (s. 12).

123 Eric Colvin and John McKechnie, *Criminal Law in Queensland and Western Australia: Cases and Commentary*, 5th edn. (Chatswood, NSW: LexisNexis/Butterworths, 2008), para. 1.13.

124 Criminal Code Act 1983 (NT), s. 43AK; Criminal Code Act 1995 (Cwlth), s. 5.4; Criminal Code 2002 (ACT), s. 20.

125 Criminal Code Act 1983 (NT), s. 43AL; Criminal Code Act 1995 (Cwlth), s. 5.5. The same constituent definitional elements appear in a slightly different order in the Criminal Code 2002 (ACT), s. 21.

126 See Criminal Code Act 1983, s. 160(c).

127 The Commonwealth and ACT codes do not have provisions on homicide. The relevant definitions of manslaughter in the ACT do not mention *mens rea* explicitly: Crimes Act 1900, s. 15.

Voluntary Intoxication in the Codified Jurisdictions

With regard to voluntary intoxication, all codified Australian jurisdictions adopt English law's intent dichotomy[128] and typically explain that the standard of care in negligence is not impacted upon by voluntary intoxication.[129] The focus is, as in NSW, on *ignoring* evidence of the defendant's state of intoxication entirely in offences of 'basic intent'. This avoids the conflation of recklessness and intoxication found in English and (to a degree) Canadian law, but still allows for findings of recklessness on the basis of a deliberately fictional account of the evidence. The treatment of voluntary intoxication in these jurisdictions is thus clearer, but far from ideal.

Summary

The Australian jurisdictions appear to be converging on a definition of recklessness in terms of the defendant's taking of an unjustifiable risk of which she is aware – a move that has not proved entirely uncontroversial.[130] There are still minor variations in approach, however, in most Australian jurisdictions (particularly in the context of involuntary manslaughter).

Alive to these difficulties, an Australian Model Criminal Code (MCC) has been in development since the 1990s.[131] The plan was that the remaining Common Law jurisdictions and the older code jurisdictions would harmonise their approach to important matters of criminal law (including *mens rea*) in line with the MCC, to ensure that there were not significant differences in the treatment of identical conduct in different parts of Australia.[132] The project appears to have 'lost momentum'.[133]

[128] Criminal Code Act 1899 (Qd), s. 28; Criminal Code Act Compilation Act 1913 (WAus), s. 28; Criminal Code Act 1924 (Tas), s. 17; Criminal Code Act 1983 (NT), s. 43AS; Criminal Code Act 1995 (Cwlth), s. 8.2; Criminal Code 2002 (ACT), s. 31.

[129] See e.g. Criminal Code Act 1983 (NT), s. 43AT; Criminal Code Act 1995 (Cwlth), s. 8.3; Criminal Code Act 2002 (ACT), s. 32.

[130] See e.g. Andrew Hemming, 'Reasserting the place of objective tests in criminal responsibility: ending the supremacy of subjective tests' (2011) 13 *University of Notre Dame Australia Law Review* 69.

[131] See www.pcc.gov.au/uniform/crime%20(composite-2007)-website.pdf.

[132] Mark Findlay, Stephen Odgers and Stanley Yeo, *Australian Criminal Justice*, 5th edn. (Oxford: Oxford University Press, 2014), pp. 12–13.

[133] See the letter of W. Ross Way to the Laurie Glanfield, Secretary to the Standing Committee of Attorneys-General, 1 November 2007, available at www.lawcouncil.asn.au/

It is useful to note, however, that the MCC adopts the same definitions of recklessness and negligence as used in the modern NT, ACT and Commonwealth codes.[134] The code distinguishes between manslaughter (where one sufficient fault element is recklessness) and 'causing death by criminal negligence',[135] which might clarify the distinction between different types of risk-taking in the context of homicide. It also incorporates the intent dichotomy for cases of voluntary intoxication and the sober reasonable person standard[136] and avoids talk of the 'recklessness' involved in getting into that state. The implementation of these proposals would bring consistency and clarity to the approach towards recklessness and negligence in Australian criminal law, but the wisdom of these reforms would, it is submitted, be best discussed in the light of the theoretical treatment of the Standard Account presented in the next chapters.

The United States

When considering the definitions of recklessness and negligence in US jurisdictions, it is worth looking first to the Model Penal Code (MPC) and then to individual state penal codes.[137] As will become apparent, the MPC's lead has been followed to varying extents.

The MPC's Definitions[138]

The MPC defines recklessness as follows:[139]

> A person acts recklessly with respect to a material element of an offense when he consciously disregards a substantial and unjustifiable risk that the material element exists or will result from his conduct. The risk must

lawcouncil/images/LCA-PDF/a-z-docs/LetterfromLCAPresidenttoSCAGreModelCriminalCodeNovember2007.pdf.

134 Model Criminal Code, ss. 2.2.9–2.2.10. 135 Ibid. ss. 5.1.10–5.1.11.

136 Ibid. ss. 2.3.5–2.3.6. The drafts initially proposed to follow *O'Connor* but failed to gain support: Stephen Gough, 'Surviving without *Majewski*?' [2002] *Criminal Law Review* 719 at 722.

137 For an overview of the pre-MPC situation with regard to recklessness, see David M. Treiman, 'Recklessness and the Model Penal Code' (1981) 9 *American Journal of Criminal Law* 281 at 293–297.

138 See, generally, ibid.

139 American Law Institute, *Model Penal Code and Commentaries (Official Draft and Revised Comments)*, 3 vols. (Philadelphia: American Law Institute, 1980), vol. 1, s. 2.02(2)(c) (hereinafter, MPC).

> be of such a nature and degree that, considering the nature and purpose of the actor's conduct and the circumstances known to him, its disregard involves a gross deviation from the standard of conduct that a law-abiding person would observe in the actor's situation.

The requirement of 'conscious disregard' in the definition of recklessness suggests that the defendant must have been aware of, and perhaps even deliberated over taking, the relevant risk.[140]

The MPC's definition of negligence gives further credence to the view that recklessness requires awareness of risk:[141]

> A person acts negligently with respect to a material element of an offense when he should be aware of a substantial and unjustifiable risk that the material element exists or will result from his conduct. The risk must be of such a nature and degree that the actor's failure to perceive it, considering the nature and purpose of his conduct and the circumstances known to him, involves a gross deviation from the standard of care that a reasonable person would observe in the actor's situation.

The absence of a need for 'conscious disregard' in the definition of negligence, and the idea that the defendant *should have been aware* of the risk, confirms that this is a form of fault premised on the defendant's unjustified *un*awareness of risk.

The MPC is – as its name suggests – a model. Individual states can pick and choose the parts they like. There are, in consequence, variations in the definitions of recklessness and negligence in the US states. No state has reproduced the MPC's definitions *verbatim*, although New Jersey comes very close (merely exchanging the 'law-abiding' person with the 'reasonable' person in its definition of recklessness – it is, indeed, not clear why the standard varies in the MPC's definitions).[142]

Groups of states will be considered together in the next sections, by reference to their position with regard to the MPC. To maintain clarity, there will not be *detailed* consideration of each individual state's approach. Instead, *broad* similarities will be focussed upon.

140 This point is discussed below at Chapter 6, section on 'Choice in Doctrine'.

141 MPC s. 2.02(2)(d).

142 NJSA s. 2C.2–2(b)(3). Pennsylvania makes the same change in its definition of recklessness, and exchanges 'purpose' for 'intent' in its definitions of recklessness and negligence: 18 Pa CSA ss. 302(b)(3)–302(b)(4). For discussion of the MPC's distinction between reasonable and law-abiding persons, see Fletcher, *Rethinking Criminal Law*, p. 262.

Virtually Full Adoption of the MPC's Definitions

First, many states (just under half) have adopted the MPC's definitions (or at least very similar wording to them) when defining recklessness and negligence for the purposes of all offences under their penal codes.[143] These states maintain the MPC's clear divide between awareness-based recklessness and unawareness-based negligence.[144]

The only real difficulty encountered by states that have adopted the MPC definitions to this extent arises when *criminal* negligence must be separated from its civil counterpart – a difficulty that has been encountered in relation to other jurisdictions above. For instance, in Alaska, it appears that 'ordinary' civil negligence will do in at least some contexts, even though the general definition of (criminal) negligence in the Alaskan penal code is very similar to that under the MPC with its requirement of a 'gross deviation' from the standard of care.[145] Other states have been troubled by the relationship between civil and criminal negligence and failed to make much headway with it. New York, for instance, leaves most of this definitional work to the jury.[146]

Virtually Full Adoption of the MPC's Definitions with Different Labels

Second, there are states that have adopted the MPC's general *definitions* but not, at least in all contexts, its labels.[147] Somewhat confusingly,

[143] Included in this category are Alabama (Ala Code 1975 ss. 13A-2-2(3)–13A.2-2(4)); Alaska (AS ss. 11.81.900(a)(3)–11.81.900(a)(4)); Arizona (ARS ss. 13-105.10(c)–13-105.10(d)); Arkansas (ACA ss. 5-2-202(3)–5-2-202(4)); Connecticut (CGSA ss. 53a-3(13)–53a-3(14)); Delaware (11 Del C ss. 231(a), 231(e) (note that s. 231(a) defines 'criminal negligence' – s. 231(d) defines 'negligence' in different terms)); Hawai'i (HRS ss. 702-206(3)–702-206(4)); Maine (17-A MRSA ss. 35(3)–35(4)); Missouri (VAMS s. 562.016(4)–562.016(5)); New Hampshire (NH Rev Stat ss. 626-2(ii)(c)–626-2(ii)(d)); New Jersey (NJSA ss. 2C:2-2(b)(3)–2C:2-2(b)(4)); New York (McKinney's Penal Law s. 15.05(3)–15.05(4)); North Dakota (ND Cent Code ss. 12.1-02-02(1)(c)–12.1-02-02(1)(d)); Oregon (ORS ss. 161.085(9)–161.085(10)); Pennsylvania (18 Pa CSA ss. 302(b)(3)–302(b)(4)); Tennessee (TCA ss. 39-11-302(c)–39-11-302(d)); Texas (VTCA Penal Code ss. 6.03(c)–6.03(d)); Utah (UCA 1953 ss. 76-2-103(3)–76-2-103(4)); Wyoming (WS 1977 ss. 6-1-104(iii), 6-1-104(ix)).

[144] See e.g. *State* v. *Ohnstad*, 359 NW 2d 827 (1984, ND), at 835–836.

[145] See *State* v. *Hazelwood*, 946 P 2d 875 (1997). See, further, the discussion in Wayne R. LaFave, *Criminal Law*, 5th edn. (St. Paul, MN: West, 2010), p. 280.

[146] See e.g. the rather vague discussions of the distinction between civil and criminal negligence in *People* v. *Haney*, 30 NY 2d 328, 284 NE 2d 564 (1972), and *People* v. *Conway*, 6 NY 3d 869, 849 NE 2d 954 (2006).

[147] Included in this category are Kentucky, Illinois and Montana.

when an overall view of US law is being taken, Kentucky's penal code uses the MPC's definition of recklessness to define 'wantonness', and the MPC's definition of negligence to define 'recklessness'.[148] In Kentucky, then, 'recklessness' is defined in terms of risks that the defendant *should have* been aware of. The use of 'wantonness' is found in other penal codes, but not all of these accept the MPC's definition of recklessness, with its focus on conscious choices to disregard risks of which the defendant is aware.[149] In Iowa, for example, 'wantonness' can include the taking of risks of which the defendant was *not* aware.[150]

A further difference in terminology is found in Montana's penal code, where 'negligence' is defined in a way that incorporates the MPC's definitions of *both* recklessness and negligence.[151] This threatens to undermine the usefulness of the awareness/unawareness distinction that the drafters of the MPC were keen to maintain. The question of whether the defendant was aware of the risk or not becomes immaterial to the assessment of liability. For the reasons given later in this book, threatening the Standard Account's distinction between recklessness and negligence is unwise.[152]

Adoption of the MPC's Definitions, with Edits

Third, some state penal codes adopt *parts* of the MPC's definitions of recklessness and negligence but omit others.[153] For example, Colorado adopts the MPC's definition of negligence almost exactly,[154] but the reckless defendant 'consciously disregards a substantial and unjustifiable risk that a result will occur or that a circumstance exists'.[155] The 'gross deviation' part of the MPC's definition – which concerns the question of *justification* – is not, therefore, transposed onto Colorado's definition of recklessness, even if (post-1975)[156] the requirement that the defendant *consciously* disregard a risk is.

[148] KRS s. 501.020(4)–501.020(5).

[149] Cf. Illinois (720 ILCS s. 5-4/6, where the MPC's definition of recklessness is used to define both recklessness and wantonness).

[150] E.g. *State* v. *Conyers*, 506 NW 2d 442 (1993).

[151] MCA s. 45-2-101(43).

[152] See below at Chapter 8, section on 'Tadros's Account of Recklessness (and/or Negligence)'.

[153] Included in this category are Colorado, Nebraska and Washington.

[154] CRSA s. 18-1-501(3).

[155] Ibid. s. 18-1-501(8).

[156] Before 1975, recklessness was defined so as to include 'wanton' risk-taking, and this included the taking of risks that the defendant 'should have known' about.

The advertence/inadvertence dichotomy can even be compromised by seemingly minimal changes in language. In Nebraska, recklessness is defined as:[157]

> acting with respect to a material element of an offense when any person disregards a substantial and unjustifiable risk that the material element exists or will result from his or her conduct. The risk must be of such a nature and degree that, considering the nature and purpose of the actor's conduct and the circumstances known to the actor, its disregard involves a gross deviation from the standard of conduct that a law-abiding person would observe in the actor's situation.

Despite being very close to the MPC's definition of recklessness, the omission of the word 'consciously' before the word 'disregards'[158] has led the Nebraska courts to interpret this as a test that can be satisfied by unjustified unawareness of risk.[159]

Partial Adoption of the MPC's Definitions

Fourth, not all states utilise *both* recklessness and negligence in their general descriptions of culpability, even if they adopt *one* of the MPC's definitions.[160] For example, Louisiana's definition of negligence is *broadly* similar to the MPC's, but the term 'recklessness' is not employed in the code.[161] Indiana, by contrast, is a state where recklessness is defined (somewhat loosely) in MPC terms,[162] but the term 'negligence' is not defined.[163]

157 Neb Rev St s. 28.109.

158 See, similarly, Washington's definition of recklessness: West's RCWA s. 9A.08.010(1)(c) Washington's definition of negligence also omits discussion of the matter of justification: ibid., s. 9A.08.010(1)(d)).

159 *State* v. *Kistenmacher*, 231 Neb 318, 436 NW 2d 168 (1989).

160 Included in this category are Indiana, Kansas, Louisiana and Nevada.

161 LSA-RS ss. 14.10, 14.12 (distinguishing intention from negligence). Admittedly, the definition of negligence is distinct from the MPC's, but the idea of a 'gross deviation' from the standard of care to be expected of a reasonable person flows through both.

162 IC s. 35–41-2-2(c): 'A person engages in conduct "recklessly" if he engages in conduct in plain, conscious and unjustifiable disregard of harm that might result and the disregard involves a substantial deviation from acceptable standards of conduct'.

163 See also Kan Stat Ann s. 21.5202(j) (where the MPC's definition of recklessness is adopted, but negligence is not mentioned).

Non-adoption of the MPC's Definitions

Fifth, there are states that define recklessness and negligence in their penal codes but do not follow the MPC's approach to any real extent.[164] Three examples will be given here, though one has recently changed.

First, until December 2015 Ohio defined recklessness as follows:[165]

> A person acts recklessly when, with heedless indifference to the consequences, he perversely disregards a known risk that his conduct is likely to cause a certain result or is likely to be of a certain nature. A person is reckless with respect to circumstances when, with heedless indifference to the consequences, he perversely disregards a known risk that such circumstances are likely to exist.

The use of 'heedless', 'indifference' and 'perversely' in this definition was contrary to the MPC's desire for sanitised, amoral language.[166] The requirement of *known* risk nevertheless maintained an awareness-based stance.[167] Ohio's definition of negligence is, it should be noted, consistent with inadvertent fault, but again does not resemble the MPC's definition.[168]

Following the 2015 reform, the current definition of recklessness in Ohio is as follows:[169]

> (C) A person acts recklessly when, with heedless indifference to the consequences, the person disregards a substantial and unjustifiable risk that the person's conduct is likely to cause a certain result or is likely to be of a certain nature. A person is reckless with respect to circumstances when, with heedless indifference to the consequences, the person disregards a substantial and unjustifiable risk that such circumstances are likely to exist.

This definition of recklessness remains meaningfully distinct from the MPC's. The removal of the word 'perversely' sanitises slightly the previous definition of recklessness applied in Ohio, but the moralistic

[164] Included in this category are California, Georgia, Idaho, Iowa Nevada, Ohio (though its definition has changed recently – see below) and South Dakota (see SDCL ss. 22-1-2(1)(d)–22-1-2(1)(e)). South Dakota's definition of 'recklessness' (ibid. s. 22-1-2(1)(d)) still requires a 'conscious and unjustifiable disregard of a substantial risk', and so awareness of risk is required. See, further, *State* v. *Olsen*, 462 NW 2d 474 (1990, SD), at 476–477.

[165] RC s. 2901.22(C). Cf. Nevada's definition of 'malice' in terms of 'willful disregard': NRS 193.0175.

[166] MPC, p. 230.

[167] See the discussion of 'full knowledge' of risk being required in *State* v. *Whitaker*, 111 Ohio App 3d 608, 676 NE 2d 1189 (1996).

[168] RC s. 2901.22(D). [169] RC s. 2901.22(C).

language concerning 'heedless indifference' remains. The concept of a 'substantial and unjustifiable' risk is lifted from the MPC, but the requirement that such a risk be *consciously* disregarded (which implies awareness of the relevant risk) is omitted. As noted above, the fact that the risk had to be 'known' suggested a focus on advertence, but that language has been removed, raising afresh the question of whether indifference requires awareness of the relevant risk.

Second, California defines negligence as follows: 'a want of such attention to the nature or probable consequences of the act or omission as a prudent man ordinarily bestows in acting in his own concerns'.[170] Recklessness is not defined but is sometimes used as a synonym for 'criminal negligence' in California.[171] In other contexts, recklessness is equated with 'wilfulness'. In those circumstances, a conscious disregard of risk will be required for culpability.[172]

Finally, there is Georgia's definition of 'criminal negligence' as involving a 'willful, wanton, or reckless disregard for the safety of others'.[173] This does not always appear to require conscious disregard of an acknowledged risk.[174] Similar tests have been interpreted to include inadvertent, unjustified risk-taking elsewhere (e.g. in Virginia).[175]

No General Definitions

Sixth, some state penal codes simply do not define *mens rea* terms for general use in all offences.[176] Often, these states continue to use words

170 Cal Pen Code s. 7(2). Similar definitions of negligence are found in Idaho (IC s. 18-101(2)), Nevada (NRS 193.018) and Oklahoma (21 Olk St Ann s. 93).

171 See *People* v. *Oliver*, 210 Cal App 3d 138, 258 Cal Rptr 138 (1989). Confusingly, the Court of Appeal in *Oliver* talks of criminal negligence giving rise to 'a presumption of conscious indifference to consequences' (at 142).

172 See *People* v. *Lara*, 44 Cal App 4th 102, 51 Cal Rptr 2d 402 (1996).

173 Ga Code Ann s. 16-2-1(b). See, too, the definition of 'recklessness' in terms of 'wilfully or wantonly disregard[ing]' a risk in Iowa (ICA s. 702.16). See, similarly, the definition of 'criminal negligence' in terms of 'reckless disregard' in South Carolina (Code 1976 s. 16-3-60). See also the definition of 'criminal negligence' as, amongst other things 'wanton, reckless or willfull indifference' in Washington, DC: DC St s. 22-934.

174 Most cases are unclear in this regard. See e.g. *Keye* v. *State*, 136 Ga App 707, 222 SE 2d 172 (1975), where the defendant was waving a knife about when he stabbed a friend he (claimed he) did not know was standing near him. His conviction, based on criminal negligence, was upheld.

175 See VA Code Ann s. 18.2-36.1(B); *Banks* v. *Commonwealth*, 41 Va App 539, 586 SE 2d 876 (2003), at 546–547.

176 Included in this category are Florida, Maryland, Massachusetts, Michigan, Minnesota (where the law only defines intention: MSA s. 609.02(9)), Mississippi, New Mexico,

such as 'willful' or 'malicious' in individual offence definitions (language that the drafters of the MPC thought too vague to be useful).[177]

Sometimes, however, recklessness and negligence are employed in the formulation of individual offences. Some such offence definitions will include formulations of recklessness and/or negligence. For instance, in Virginia, it is an offence to recklessly handle a firearm.[178] Recklessness in this context has been discussed in tandem with 'criminal negligence', and – although the courts have been wary of treating the two as synonyms – it is not clear where the line between them is drawn.[179] In these situations, it is hard to compare the state penal code's understanding of recklessness and negligence with that found in the MPC.

A similar problem is encountered when states define negligence in specific contexts. Some states refer to 'ordinary negligence to a high degree'.[180] Where such wording is not used, however, state courts might still interpret *criminal* negligence as requiring only the level of carelessness that satisfies *civil* negligence.[181] Another approach is, as in England and Wales, to define 'gross' negligence in terms of 'reckless disregard' of risk.[182] Even where the word 'reckless' is used in these statutes, it might be interpreted to include inadvertent risk-taking.

An alternative approach is to use the words 'recklessness' and 'negligence' in specific offences but to make no effort to define them in the penal code. It is then left to courts to formulate definitions. In some states the word 'recklessly' has been interpreted in line with the MPC's definition, but not always in relation to *all* uses of the word.[183]

North Carolina, Oklahoma, Rhode Island, South Carolina, Vermont, Virginia and West Virginia. Wisconsin is a difficult jurisdiction to classify. Although criminal recklessness and negligence are defined, the definitions stretch only to certain situations (e.g. where death or serious injury is risked: WSA ss. 939.24(1)–939.25(1)). The definition of recklessness follows the MPC's awareness-based model but not the MPC's wording.

177 MPC, p. 230. 178 VA Code Ann s. 18.2-56.1.

179 There is also a reluctance to define recklessness in general terms: *Darnell* v. *Commonwealth*, 6 Va App 485, 370 SE 2d 717 (1988), at 491 ('The meaning of recklessness … depends on the context').

180 Wis Stat s. 939.25(1).

181 An example is South Carolina. Cf. Code 1976 s. 16-3-60 and *State* v. *Jenkins*, 278 SC 219, 294 SE 2d 44 (1982).

182 See e.g. South Carolina (Code 1976 s. 16-3-60).

183 Minnesota, by contrast, adopts the MPC's definitions of recklessness and negligence in most contexts but not all. For instance, 'reckless driving' can involve a failure to be aware of a risk of which the defendant *should* have been aware. See the useful discussion in *State* v. *Engle*, 743 NW 2d 592 (2008), at 595–596.

The MPC's definition of recklessness has also been rejected on occasion when interpreting individual offence definitions.[184]

It is difficult to establish the definition of recklessness in some states, because the word is used in conjunction with other *mens rea* terms, such as 'willfully'[185] or 'negligently'.[186] Even when there is some clarity, this does not mean that a consistent approach is taken. Massachusetts, for example, seems to want the best of both worlds. There, involuntary manslaughter can be made out through proof of 'wanton or reckless' conduct.[187] This can be understood as acting in unreasonable ignorance of an unjustified risk or disregarding an acknowledged risk.[188]

A similar mess of decisions can be found in jurisdictions where the penal code makes no attempt to define negligence. Some jurisdictions have taken the MPC's line in crimes where inadvertent risk-taking is involved – most usually, involuntary manslaughter. For instance, in Vermont, involuntary manslaughter can be committed recklessly or with criminal negligence.[189] The Vermont courts have adopted the MPC understanding of both these *mens rea* terms.[190]

The courts in other jurisdictions are less clear in their approach to negligence. The Supreme Court of Mississippi has defined 'culpable negligence', in the context of involuntary manslaughter,[191] as:[192]

> that degree of negligence or carelessness which is denominated as gross negligence and which constitutes such a departure from what would be the conduct of an ordinarily careful and prudent man under same circumstances as to furnish evidence of indifference to consequences.

184 See e.g. the approach to Maryland's reckless endangerment statute (now Md Code, Criminal Law, s. 3-204) in *State* v. *Minor*, 326 Md 436, 605 A 2d 138 (1992), at 443.

185 E.g. the offence of 'hazing' found in Rhode Island's penal code (Gen Laws 1956 s. 11-21-1).

186 See e.g. the discussion of the relationship between intention, awareness, recklessness and 'criminal negligence' in *People* v. *Datema*, 448 Mich 585, 533 NW 2d 272 (1995, MI).

187 The various authorities are summarised in *Commonwealth* v. *Pugh*, 462 Mass 482, 969 NE 2d 672 (2012). A similar definition of criminal negligence in terms of 'reckless disregard' exists in some contexts under West Virginia law: W Va Code s. 17C-5-1 ('negligent homicide'); *State* v. *Lawson*, 128 W Va 136, 36 SE 2d 26 (1945) (involuntary manslaughter).

188 See *Commonwealth* v. *Pugh*, 462 Mass 482, 969 NE 2d 672 (2012).

189 *State* v. *Forbes*, 147 Vt 612, 523 A 2d 1232 (1987), at 1235.

190 See e.g. *State* v. *Brooks*, 163 Vt 245, 658 A 2d 22 (1995), at 26–27.

191 Miss Code Ann s. 97-3-47.

192 *Shows* v. *State*, 175 Miss 604, 168 So 862 (1936), at 864. See also *State* v. *Pagotto*, 361 Md 528, 762 A 2d 97 (2000, MD).

This appears to be a species of fault that does not require awareness of risk, as does the approach of other states – even if some of them use terminology such as 'reckless disregard'.[193] The Supreme Court of Mississippi has, however, also defined 'culpable negligence' in the context of involuntary manslaughter as involving the 'conscious and wanton or reckless disregard of the probabilities of fatal consequences to others as the result of the willful creation of an unreasonable risk'.[194] This might be read to require awareness of risk, as can the approach taken by the courts in New Mexico. There, the defendant can be convicted of involuntary manslaughter if he acts in a dangerous manner 'without due caution and circumspection'.[195] This has been interpreted as a requirement for 'criminal negligence', which itself has been interpreted to require awareness on the part of the defendant of the risk of death associated with her conduct.[196]

All in all, then, it is difficult to be certain on the definition of recklessness and negligence in states where the penal code is silent on that matter, and it is possible for inconsistency to reign.[197]

Voluntary Intoxication

The MPC and all US state penal codes have special rules regarding voluntary intoxication and the mental element in crime.[198] The MPC's approach, in cases of recklessness, is to ask what the acutely, voluntarily intoxicated defendant *would have* foreseen had she been sober.[199] This counterfactual approach (familiar to English lawyers) is followed in a

[193] For use of 'reckless disregard' and similar terminology to define negligence, see *Santillanes* v. *State*, 115 NM 215, 849 P 2d 358 (1993, NM), at 365 (cf. *State* v. *Schoonmaker*, 143 NM 373, 176 P 3d 1105 (2008, NM), at 1117); *State* v. *Greene*, 348 So 2d 3 (1977, FL); *State* v. *Davis*, 66 NC App 334, 311 SE 2d 311 (1984, NC), at 336. See also the approach taken towards defining 'gross' negligence under federal law in cases following *US* v. *Pardee*, 368 F 2d 368 (4th Cir. 1966).

[194] *Smith* v. *State*, 197 Miss 802, 20 So 2d 701 (1945) at 706. The court went on to hold that 'gross' negligence in civil law would be insufficient – 'wanton disregard of, or indifference to' life is required for 'culpable negligence' in involuntary manslaughter. See also *Evans* v. *State*, 562 So 2d 91 (1990, MS), at 94–95.

[195] NMSA 1978 s. 30-2-3(B). See, similarly, 14 VIC s. 924(2) (US Virgin Islands).

[196] *State* v. *Henley*, 148 NM 359, 237 P 3d 103 (2010), at 107–108.

[197] See, similarly, Treiman, 'Recklessness and the Model Penal Code', at 284.

[198] See, generally, Mitchell Keiter, 'Just say no excuse: the rise and fall of the intoxication defense' (1997) 87(2) *Journal of Criminal Law & Criminology* 482.

[199] MPC, s. 2.08(2).

number of states, either in their definitions of recklessness (which might lead to confusion between intoxication and *mens rea*),[200] in specific provisions (which is clearer),[201] or both.[202] The relevance of voluntary intoxication to negligence is often left unaddressed.[203]

Other states adopt a less prescriptive approach, by incorporating the 'intent dichotomy' in the code,[204] or through the courts,[205] and conclude that evidence of voluntary intoxication is only *relevant* when it negates a 'specific intent'.[206] This excludes evidence of voluntary intoxication from crimes of recklessness without the apparent need for further enquiry into what *would* have been foreseen by the defendant if sober. This solution has, on occasion, been justified on the basis of implied fault in becoming intoxicated, but this fault tends to be

200 This approach is adopted in Alaska (AS s. 11.81.900(3)), Arizona (ARS s. 13-105.10(c)), Delaware (11 Del C s. 231(e)), Kentucky (Ken Rev Stat Ann s. 501.020(3)), New Hampshire (NH Rev Stat s. 626:2(ii)(c)) and New York (McKinney's Penal Law, s. 15.05(3)).

201 This approach is adopted in Connecticut (CGSA s. 53a-7), Maine (17-A MRSA s. 37(2)), New Jersey (NJSA s. 2C:2-8), Oregon (ORS s. 161.125(2)), Tennessee (TCA s. 39-11-503(b)) and Utah (UCA 1953 s. 76-2-306).

202 See e.g. Alabama (Ala Code 1975 s. 13A-2-2(3), 13A-3-2(b)) and North Dakota (ND Cent Code ss. 12.1-02-02(1)(c), 12.1-04-02(2)).

203 Cf. the Utah Criminal Code, which makes clear that unawareness caused by voluntary intoxication will not negate a finding of negligence (UCA 1953 s. 76-2-306).

204 This approach is adopted in California (CA Penal s. 29.4), Colorado (Col Rev Stat s. 18-1-804), Kansas (Kan Stat Ann s. 21-5205), Louisiana (LSA-RS s. 14.15 (the rule also applies to 'special knowledge')), Minnesota (MSA s. 609.075; *State* v. *Fleck*, 810 NW 2d 303 (2012)), Nevada (NRS s. 193.220), South Dakota (SDCL s. 22-5-5), Washington (West's RCWA s. 9A.16.090), Wisconsin (WSA s. 939.42) and Wyoming (Wyo Stat s. 6-1-202). Even where the rules refer to voluntary intoxication's relevance to 'other states of mind', this is understood to exclude recklessness.

205 Sometimes the code is not clear on the relevance of voluntary intoxication to *mens rea*, as in Illinois (720 ILCS s. 5/6-3; *People* v. *Crosby*, 243 Ill App 3d 1083, 614 NE 2d 199 (1993)) and Oklahoma (21 Okl St Ann s. 153; *Grayson* v. *State*, 687 P 2d 747 (1984)). Other times, the code is simply silent on the matter of voluntary intoxication, but the courts recognise the intent dichotomy. This position is found in Maryland (*Shell* v. *State*, 307 Md 46, 512 A 2d 358 (1986), at 364–367), Massachusetts (*Commonwealth* v. *Henson*, 394 Mass 584, 476 NE 2d 947 (1985), at 953–954), Michigan (*People* v. *Langworthy*, 416 Mich 630, 331 NW 2d 171 (1982), at 172–180), Nebraska (e.g. *Tvrz* v. *State*, 154 Neb 641, 48 NW 2d 761 (1951)), New Mexico (*State* v. *Tapia*, 81 NM 274, 466 P 2d 551 (1970), at 553), North Carolina (e.g. *State* v. *Gerald*, 304 NC 511, 284 SE 2d 312 (1981), at 318–319), Rhode Island (e.g. *State* v. *McGehearty*, 212 RI 55, 394 A 2d 1348 (1978)) and Vermont (e.g. *State* v. *Murphy*, 128 Vt 288, 262 A 2d 456 (1970), at 460).

206 Cf. the position in Iowa (ICA s. 701.5), where evidence of voluntary intoxication may be relevant to proving recklessness.

recognised as *negligence*, rather than recklessness.[207] It is submitted that this view remains unconvincing, because – once again – there is an absence of correspondence. The defendant's foresight of (or even the foreseeability of) the risk relevant to the defendant's wrongdoing is not investigated.

Some states have simply refused to allow voluntary intoxication to constitute a 'defence' at all (including in relation to *mens rea*),[208] and this approach has been found to be constitutional.[209] Some of these jurisdictions contain explicit rules regarding recklessness, whilst others do not.[210] A slightly less drastic tack has been taken in Pennsylvania, where evidence of the defendant's state of voluntary intoxication can 'reduce' first-degree murder to a lower degree of murder but is otherwise deemed inadmissible.[211] There is no confusion, in such circumstances, between *mens rea* and intoxication.

Summary

A majority of US jurisdictions take an awareness-based approach to recklessness, allowing for a clear distinction between it and negligence. Tellingly, given the discussion of other jurisdictions in this chapter, it *tends* to be where recklessness is not defined at all, or where the definition is old, that a different approach can sometimes be detected. The treatment of negligence is, as usual, sometimes variable and opaque. With regard to voluntary intoxication, although few states conflate recklessness and the defendant's intoxication, many rely on a counterfactual recklessness test, which is objectionable for the reasons given above in the section

207 Cf. the discussion in *McDaniel* v. *State*, 356 So 2d 1151 (1978, MS), at 1158–1161.

208 This approach is adopted in Arizona (ARS s. 13-503), Arkansas (*White* v. *State*, 290 Ark 130, 717 SW 2d 784 (1986), at 786–788; ACA s. 5-2-207), Delaware (*Davis* v. *State*, 522 A 2d 342 (1987); 11 Del C s. 421), Florida (West's Fl Stat Ann s. 775.051), Georgia (Ga Code Ann s. 16-3-4(c)), Idaho (Idaho Code Ann s. 18-116), Indiana (IC s. 35-41-3-5), Montana (MCA 45-2-203), Mississippi (*McDaniel* v. *State*, 356 So 2d 1151 (1978)), Missouri (VAMS s. 562.076), South Carolina (*State* v. *Vaughn*, 268 SC 119, 232 SE 2d 328 (1977), at 330–331) and Texas (VTCA Penal Code s. 8.04). An odd approach is taken in Hawai'i: there, the evidence of the defendant's state of voluntary intoxication is admissible but cannot negate *mens rea* (HRS s. 702.230(2)). Ohio allows voluntary intoxication to negate voluntariness, but nothing more: RC s. 2901.21(D).

209 *Montana* v. *Egelhoff*, 518 US 37 (1996).

210 See e.g. Delaware (11 Del C s. 231(e)).

211 18 Pa CSA s. 308. See, similarly, the position in Virginia following *Gills* v. *Commonwealth*, 141 Va 445, 126 SE 51 (1925), and West Virginia following the cases summarised in *State* v. *Bush*, 191 W Va 8, 442 SE 2d 437 (1994).

on English law. Other states avoid confusion between recklessness and voluntary intoxication by adopting a rule rendering evidence of the defendant's intoxication irrelevant to all or certain crimes, but this approach is also objectionable for the reasons given above. Once again, it is submitted that the best approach towards voluntary intoxication cases is to recognise a new form of fault, rather than attempting to deal with it in the context of traditional fault elements such as recklessness.

New Zealand

The Crimes Act 1961 – a partial criminal code that applies throughout New Zealand – does not provide general definitions of *mens rea* terms. This task is left to the courts.[212] Following a brief flirtation with an understanding of recklessness in terms including 'giving no thought at all to the matter' of risk in *R* v. *Howe*,[213] the New Zealand Court of Appeal (NZCA)[214] reasserted the dominance of awareness-based recklessness in *R* v. *Harney*.[215] In common with the MPC, recklessness in New Zealand now requires the 'conscious taking of the risk'.[216]

Although the NZCA conceded in *Harney* that '[t]he statutory context may affect the meaning to be given to "recklessly"',[217] it gave no guidance on when alternative definitions of recklessness might be appropriate.[218] This has not proved problematic. The courts[219] and the legislature[220] have refrained from employing alternative conceptions of recklessness,

212 For an overview, see Simon France, 'The mental element' (1990) 20 *Victoria University of Wellington Law Review Monograph* 43.

213 [1982] 1 NZLR 618, at 624. See Simon France, 'A reckless approach to liability' (1988) 18 *Victoria University of Wellington Law Review* 141.

214 At the time the decisions discussed below were made, the NZCA was the highest New Zealand-based court. On 1 January 2004, the Supreme Court of New Zealand took over the jurisdiction of the (London-based) Judicial Committee of the Privy Council in New Zealand criminal appeals.

215 [1987] 2 NZLR 576.

216 Ibid., at 581.

217 Ibid., at 579. See also *Sutherland* v. *Police* [2006] NZHC 729, at [18].

218 Cf. the discussion of a 'definite policy decision by the legislature' in *R* v. *H* (1989) 4 CRNZ 461, at 464.

219 See e.g. *Smith* v. *Police* (1988) 3 CRNZ 262 (Summary Offences Act 1981, s. 11 ('wilful damage')). Cf. A.P. Simester and Warren J. Brookbanks, *Principles of Criminal Law*, 4th edn. (Wellington: Thomson Reuters, 2012), p. 117.

220 There was, at one time, a proposal to include 'heedlessness' – which would not require awareness of risk – as a *mens rea* term in a New Zealand Criminal Code. See Simon France, 'Reforming criminal law – New Zealand's 1989 code' [1990] *Criminal Law Review* 827 at 833–834.

such as 'indifference'.[221] Thus, although 'objectively' the defendant's risk-taking must be unjustified, it is fair to say that recklessness is *otherwise* 'a purely subjective concept' in New Zealand criminal law.[222] New Zealand criminal law has accomplished a consistency that has eluded many other Anglo-American systems.

The NZCA has long recognised that, in the majority of contexts, criminal negligence requires the same level of 'objective' carelessness as its civil law counterpart.[223] This 'straightforward'[224] approach avoids the confusion other systems have encountered when trying to distinguish civil and criminal negligence. Since 1997, however, 'gross' negligence has been recognised as the relevant *mens rea* to secure conviction in involuntary manslaughter cases. This is understood as 'a major departure from the standard of care expected of a reasonable person',[225] a test comparable to English law's in terms of language and – unless and until the NZCA or New Zealand Supreme Court[226] gives more detailed guidance – opacity.

More clarity has been achieved in the context of voluntary intoxication. A defendant in New Zealand can use evidence of his state of voluntary intoxication to raise a reasonable doubt over *mens rea*, apparently whatever the charge.[227] A defendant cannot, therefore, be adjudged reckless unless the prosecution can prove that, even in spite of his intoxication, he was aware of the relevant risk.[228] No conflation of recklessness and intoxication, and no fiction/counterfactual inquiry is embarked upon.

With regard to negligence, the role of voluntary intoxication is less clear. It has been suggested by Simester and Brookbanks that the

[221] See e.g. *Hohaia* v. *Cairns* (1989) 4 CRNZ 558. Cf. *Waaka* v. *Police* [1987] 1 NZLR 754, at 759 (where 'indifference' is equated with wilful blindness or *knowledge*).

[222] *Taylor* v. *Police* (1990) 6 CRNZ 470, at 471.

[223] *R* v. *Storey* [1931] NZLR 417. *Storey* has been referred to as providing a definition of recklessness (e.g. in *D'Almeida* v. *Auckland City Council* (1984) 1 CRNZ 281, at 281–282), but it is submitted that the court was not attempting to define that term. Reckless is used haphazardly as a synonym for negligence throughout the judgment. See also *R* v. *Myatt* [1991] 1 NZLR 675.

[224] *R* v. *Yogasakaran* [1990] 1 NZLR 399, at 404.

[225] Crimes Act 1961, s. 150A.

[226] The New Zealand Supreme Court was created in 2004.

[227] *R* v. *Kamipeli* [1975] 2 NZLR 610. The option of following *Majewski* in New Zealand has been rejected: *R* v. *Roulston* [1976] 2 NZLR 644, at 654; *R* v. *Meek* [1981] 1 NZLR 499, at 504. The only area of real uncertainty is manslaughter – see *R* v. *Grice* [1975] 1 NZLR 760, at 766; Simester and Brookbanks, *Principles of Criminal Law*, pp. 386–388.

[228] See *R* v. *Tihi* [1990] 1 NZLR 540, at 545.

reasonable person remains sober in offences of negligence, however drunk the defendant was at the time of the *actus reus*.[229]

Summary

New Zealand's approach to differentiating recklessness and negligence is, on the whole, clear (with the possible exception of 'gross' negligence in manslaughter), despite the NZCA's initial reservations about general definitions. The distinction between recklessness and voluntary intoxication drawn by New Zealand law avoids the problems encountered by English law, and thus ensures that the law on *mens rea* is to that extent clearer. New Zealand's criminal law, it is submitted, is one of the clearest examples of the Standard Account of culpable carelessness in Anglo-American law (although, for reasons to be explored in the next chapter, it is regrettable that the possibility of different understandings of recklessness was even countenanced in *Harvey*). It is the Standard Account that will be explored through a theoretical lens in the following chapters.

Before moving to the more theoretical aspects of the debate over culpable carelessness, it is useful to consider the approach of Scots law briefly. This is because Scots law has adopted a distinct approach to defining recklessness and separating it from negligence, which is less dependent on the line between mental awareness and unawareness. It is thus, despite its size, a worthwhile comparator.

Scotland

Some might baulk at the idea that Scotland is an 'Anglo-American' system of criminal law.[230] Despite the Union of the Kingdoms of Scotland and England in 1707, Scots criminal law has always remained independent of English law.[231] Since the 1960s, however, Scots law has been on a gradual Anglo-American trajectory in its understanding of *mens rea* terms.[232] Recklessness is now used as a core *mens rea* term. The more general, undeveloped, concept of 'dole' has been cast off.[233]

[229] Simester and Brookbanks, *Principles of Criminal Law*, p. 385.

[230] This section draws on the more detailed doctrinal survey of Scots law's approach to recklessness contained in Findlay Stark, 'Rethinking recklessness' 2011 *Juridical Review* 163.

[231] Treaty of Union 1706, art. 19.

[232] Due, in no small part, to Sir Gerald H. Gordon's majestic *The Criminal Law of Scotland* (Edinburgh: SULI/W. Green & Sons, 1968).

[233] See the discussion of 'dole' and *mens rea* in Stark, 'Rethinking recklessness', at 165–168.

There are frequent claims in the academic literature that recklessness is 'objective' – i.e. does not require awareness of the relevant risk – in Scots criminal law.[234] This point means that there is little discussion of negligence.[235] The more realistic view is that recklessness is defined in various ways depending on the context. *Some* of these senses of recklessness include inadvertent risk-taking, often coupling it with a focus on the defendant's careless *conduct* or 'indifferent' *attitude*; others focus far more on the defendant's *awareness* of risk, yet still talk in terms of attitudes such as indifference.

It is best to view there as being three distinct forms of recklessness recognised by modern Scots law.[236] First, in most statutory offences, recklessness focuses on the defendant's *conduct* and 'whether the degree [of carelessness] is such as properly to attach . . . the epithet "reckless" . . . [This] requires a judgment to be made quite objectively'.[237] This understanding of recklessness has been employed in various statutory contexts, usually those based on conduct, rather than circumstances or consequences.[238] Its use in common law offences has been criticised by the Scottish courts,[239] leading to the odd idea that the origin of an offence (statute or common law) might determine the understanding of recklessness employed. It is submitted that a conduct-based focus seems more appropriately labelled, from a doctrinal perspective, as *negligence*.[240] As has been seen, this is the terminology employed most usually in Anglo-American systems, even if (as will be explained in Chapter 7),[241] a conduct-based account of negligence is objectionable.

[234] See e.g. Joshua Barton, 'Recklessness in Scots criminal law: subjective or objective?' 2011 *Juridical Review* 143; Eric Clive, Pamela Ferguson, Christopher Gane and Alexander McCall Smith, *A Draft Criminal Code for Scotland with Commentary* (Edinburgh: TSO, 2003), pp. 32–33.

[235] One textbook recommends eschewing talk of negligence, but this is unwise given the lack of clarity over Scots law's approach to recklessness. See P.R. Ferguson and Claire McDiarmid, *Scots Criminal Law: A Critical Analysis*, 2nd edn. (Edinburgh: Edinburgh University Press, 2014), p. 172.

[236] In Stark, 'Rethinking recklessness', it is argued that there are *five* types of recklessness in Scots criminal law. One of these is the sense of 'recklessness' involved in voluntary intoxication cases (see below). The other was relevant to rape at common law, and has now been superseded (see below).

[237] *Allan* v. *Paterson* 1980 JC 57, at 60.

[238] See, further, *Carr* v. *HM Advocate* 1994 JC 203, at 208.

[239] See, most clearly, *Transco plc* v. *HM Advocate (No 1)* 2004 JC 29, at [39].

[240] See, similarly, Sally Cunningham, 'Recklessness: being reckless and acting recklessly' (2010) 21 *King's College Law Journal* 445.

[241] See below at Chapter 7, section on 'Conduct: Hart's Insight'.

Second, in most common law offences, recklessness is defined – following *Quinn* v. *Cunningham*[242] – by reference to the accused's 'utter disregard' of or 'indifference' towards risk.[243] This definition has proved problematic, as it is not entirely clear from the reported cases whether the accused needs to have been aware of a risk before he can be said to have 'disregarded' or shown 'indifference' towards it.[244] The answer to that question appears to vary with context. Little more can be made of the doctrinal position in Scotland here, other than to say that in the most recent detailed treatment of this form of recklessness, the culpable homicide (manslaughter) case *Transco plc* v. *HM Advocate*,[245] a heightened concern with the accused's state of mind and awareness of risk is detectable.[246]

Third, there is 'wicked' recklessness, a form of *mens rea* found in the Scots law of murder. To be 'wickedly' reckless, the accused must intend to cause physical harm to a person[247] and show 'a wicked disregard of fatal consequences'.[248] The accused does not appear to need to be aware of a risk of death attendant upon his actions to be 'wickedly' reckless.[249] Again, this approach to recklessness endorses a view of 'disregard' of risk that does not require that the accused was aware of the relevant risk.

The absence of a requirement that the accused is aware of the risk of death attendant upon his intentional attack can be seen as one of the strengths of 'wicked' recklessness – it can be demonstrated through an unthinking attitude of 'indifference' towards the risk of death.[250] 'Wicked' recklessness is really a judgment about the accused's *attitude* towards the risk of death. It is worth noting that this focus on *the accused's* attitude is surely a 'subjective' matter, even in cases where

242 1956 JC 22. 243 Ibid., at 24–25.

244 Cf. *Harris* v. *HM Advocate* 1993 JC 150, at 165 with *Transco plc* v. *HM Advocate (No 1)* 2004 JC 29, at [33]–[39].

245 2004 JC 29.

246 See, further, Stark, 'Rethinking recklessness', at 177–186. Previously, definitions of culpable homicide included 'gross, or wicked, or criminal negligence': *Paton* v. *HM Advocate* 1936 JC 19 at 22. The preference is now to speak in terms of recklessness and indifference.

247 Presumably, intending to injure A, with indifference to A's life, is sufficient *mens rea* for murder even if B is killed instead. Cf. *Roberts* v. *Hamilton* 1989 JC 91.

248 *HM Advocate* v. *Purcell* [2007] HCJ 13, 2008 JC 131, at [16]. See also *Petto* v. *HM Advocate* [2011] HCJAC 78, 2012 JC 105.

249 Timothy H. Jones, 'The Scottish law of murder' (1989) 105 *Law Quarterly Review* 516, at 518–520; *HM Advocate* v. *Hartley* 1989 SLT 135, at 136; *Broadley* v. *HM Advocate* 1991 JC 108, at 114; *Cawthorne* v. *HM Advocate* 1968 JC 32, at 35–36.

250 See e.g. Duff, *Intention, Agency and Criminal Liability*, pp. 162–163.

it is alleged that his culpability lay in *not* realising there was a risk of death.[251] This once again casts doubt on the efficacy of the 'subjective'/'objective' dichotomy and supports this book's decision not to use it when discussing culpable carelessness.

Now that an intention to cause physical injury is, at base, required for a finding of 'wicked' recklessness, the jury's focus should be more on the accused's *state of mind*. This might make 'wicked' recklessness move further in the advertence-based direction in the future, but it is too early to tell.[252]

Given the confusion over whether awareness of risk is required for recklessness, there is little Scots authority on negligence. Some offences nevertheless endorse negligence-esque fault elements. For instance, in the modern law of sexual offences, the accused has *mens rea* if he fails to form a reasonable belief in consent.[253] This can constitute the unreasonable failure to be aware of an obvious risk of non-consent, which appears to be a form of negligence, broadly similar to the account of negligence defended in Chapter 8.

Voluntary Intoxication

When it comes to the accused's state of voluntary intoxication, Scots law has rejected the English intent dichotomy. If the accused commits an offence requiring *mens rea* whilst acutely, voluntarily intoxicated, he is to be convicted. This position was defended in *Brennan* v. *HM Advocate*[254] on the basis that becoming that intoxicated is 'reckless' and recklessness supplies the fault element for most offences under Scots law (including, in its 'wicked' form, murder). The influence of the House of Lords' thinking about 'recklessness' in *Majewski* (decided just over a year before *Brennan*) is clear. Even in offences that require intention as the relevant form of *mens rea*, evidence of acute voluntary intoxication will not assist the accused. It is assumed that he intended the natural and probable consequences of his (intoxicated) acts.[255]

251 See Victor Tadros, 'The Scots law of murder' in Jeremy Horder (ed.), *Homicide Law in Comparative Perspective* (Oxford: Hart, 2007), p. 187, at p. 196.

252 For criticism of developments post-*Purcell*, see Claire McDiarmid, '"Something wicked this way comes": the *mens rea* of murder in Scots law' 2012 *Juridical Review* 283.

253 This approach is adopted in Sexual Offences (Scotland) Act 2009, ss. 1–9, 11.

254 1977 JC 38, at 51. For criticism of *Brennan*, see Stark, 'Breaking down *Brennan*'.

255 *Ross* v. *HM Advocate* 1991 JC 210, at 214.

The result of this is that Scotland, like England and Wales, has a form of 'recklessness' that exists where the accused was unaware of the relevant risks given his state of voluntary intoxication. The problems noted above, in relation to English law's voluntary intoxication rules, also apply here (if anything, these problems multiply if *intention* is to be assumed). The equation of recklessness with intoxication seems less peculiar in Scotland, however, because recklessness is less regularly (and clearly) defined in terms of awareness of risk.

Summary

Scots criminal law is generally undeveloped in comparison to the other systems discussed in this chapter, and its approach to recklessness and negligence demonstrates this. The question of whether awareness of risk is required has been dodged by the courts through the use of equivocal terms such as 'utter disregard' for or 'indifference' towards risk. Where the position is clearer, Scots law seems far more attitude-based in its approach than the other jurisdictions surveyed above. It is very much an odd one out. If the trend towards concentrating on the defendant's state of mind in homicide cases is representative, however, Scotland might move in a more awareness-based direction in the future. It is simply too early to tell.

The Draft Criminal Code for Scotland defined as reckless the accused who 'is, or ought to be, aware' of a relevant 'obvious and serious' risk.[256] Negligence was not recognised as a form of *mens rea* by the Draft Code's authors. Although the Draft Code is clearer on the absence of a need for the reckless accused person to be aware of the relevant risk attendant upon her conduct, the Draft Code (published in 2003) has not been, and probably never will be, enacted.[257]

Conclusion

It must be accepted that this chapter is a snapshot; the law is stated as it *is*, without tracing its historical development. That history shows, it might be contended, a gradual, often stumbling journey towards the

256 Clive, Ferguson, Gane and McCall Smith, *A Draft Criminal Code for Scotland*, cl. 10.

257 See Eric Clive, 'Codification of the criminal law', in James Chalmers, Fiona Leverick and Lindsay Farmer (eds.), *Essays in Criminal Law in Honour of Sir Gerald Gordon* (Edinburgh: Edinburgh University Press, 2010), p. 54.

distinction between recklessness and negligence in terms of the defendant's awareness of risk[258] and recognition that voluntary intoxication is a separate issue (perhaps a distinct way of being culpable) from recklessness and negligence. Some systems of criminal law simply have farther to go than others. Certainly, the Standard Account of culpable carelessness is that recklessness involves awareness of a particular risk, whilst negligence concerns a failure to be aware of that risk (or, potentially, a failure to meet a certain standard of conduct). This allows, it is submitted, the theoretical conclusions reached in the following chapters to inform development (where necessary) of the main Anglo-American jurisdictions surveyed here. There is not a need, in other words, for an *English* theory of culpable carelessness, a *New Zealand* theory, and so on.

The Standard Account raises a number of questions, which are explored in the following chapters. First, is the Standard Account correct to centre on *one* understanding of recklessness and negligence, or is it defensible in theory to have more than one definition of these terms? As seen in this chapter, many jurisdictions that have not codified *mens rea* terms have this divergence in definition in at least *some* contexts (and some codified definitions are susceptible to variable interpretation). It will be argued in Chapter 3 that such variable definitions (and interpretations) are indefensible: if different senses of culpable risk-taking are thought to exist, then different words should be used to mark them out consistently through the criminal law.

Second, there is the question of what is meant by *awareness* of risk. This question, which has seldom been approached by courts or legislatures, and relatively infrequently by theorists, is answered in Chapters 4 and 5. It will be contended in Chapter 4 that awareness of risk entails *belief*, and belief should be understood in terms of the defendant's dispositions. An alternative account of awareness of risk, in terms of *knowledge* of risk, will be rejected in Chapter 5.

Third, it must be asked why awareness of risk has the role it does in the Standard Account. Chapter 6 explains awareness of risk's importance in terms of its connection with choice, and how a defendant's choices – in the light of her awareness of the associated risks – can make culpability judgments particularly stable. It will nevertheless be doubted that choice is the *sole* mark of culpability, which opens the door to considering when defendants who are *unaware* of the risks attendant upon their conduct

258 Cf. Jeremy Horder, 'Two histories and four hidden principles of *mens rea*' (1997) 113 *Law Quarterly Review* 95.

can be culpable. Chapter 7 contends that many existing accounts of culpability without awareness, some of which employ notions such as 'indifference', are flawed. In Chapter 8, an alternative understanding of culpable inadvertence in terms of a failure of *belief* regarding risk (rather than a bare failure to reach a standard of *conduct*) is developed. The chapter will consider limitations that should be placed on the *extent* of criminal negligence, that is, the range of offences in which negligence should operate as an acceptable fault element.

Once the above questions have been addressed, Chapter 9 considers some practical implications of this book's theoretical defence of the Standard Account.

3

Consistency in Definition

The 'Standard Account' of culpable, unjustified risk-taking in the Anglo-American systems surveyed in Chapter 2 distinguishes between two fault elements: recklessness and negligence. It defines these words (or their equivalents) consistently, as do very many jurisdictions that have codified *mens rea* terms. It was noted in Chapter 2 that, in a few of the Anglo-American systems that have not codified their *mens rea* terms, *multiple* definitions of recklessness (usually provided by the courts) exist, even if the *main* one is presented in terms of awareness of risk. Decisions on recklessness (and negligence)[1] might be limited to specific contexts, opening the door to alternative understandings in other circumstances.[2] There might also be multiple forms of negligence (some co-extensive with recklessness) existing in a system of criminal law. For instance, many systems have struggled (or simply not tried) to distinguish 'gross' or 'criminal' negligence and its civil counterpart.[3] The risk of variation is real even in systems which have codified the *definition* of recklessness – it is not inconceivable that courts could *apply* that definition differently in different contexts (though the experience of those codified jurisdictions that have defined recklessness and negligence, particularly Australia and the United States, is that this has not happened regularly).

This chapter presents an argument for the consistent definition of recklessness and negligence in the criminal law. The argument could be applied more widely to core criminal law concepts, but making that claim

[1] See e.g. 'criminal negligence' under Canadian criminal law (Criminal Code, RSC 1985, c. C-46, s. 219), discussed above at Chapter 2, section on 'Canada'.

[2] See e.g. *R* v. *G and Another* [2003] UKHL 50, [2004] 1 AC 1034 (E&W), at [28]; *R* v. *Abdul-Rasool* [2008] VSCA 13, (2008) 18 VR 586 (Vic), at [67]; *Darnell* v. *Commonwealth*, 6 Va App 485, 370 SE 2d 717 (1988, VA), at 491; *R* v. *Harney* [1987] 2 NZLR 576 (NZ), at 579.

[3] See e.g. the vague guidance given to jurors on this distinction in English involuntary manslaughter cases following *R* v. *Adomako* [1995] AC 171. See also *People* v. *Conway*, 6 NY 3d 869, 849 NE 2d 954 (2006, NY).

here is unnecessary.[4] Presenting this argument will justify the remainder of the book's search for the most defensible, consistent understandings of recklessness and negligence, and the references to generic tokens of behaviour (which will be shortened, for convenience, to φ), rather than specific tokens of distinct wrongs such as killing or having non-consensual sex.[5]

Defending Multiple Definitions

There are, in the criminal law theory literature, defences of the practice of defining *mens rea* terms differently in relation to different contexts or offences. Tadros presents such a defence in the context of a wider discussion of the 'general' part of the criminal law – i.e. those rules and principles that apply across all, or at least two categories, of offences.[6] *Mens rea* terms are aspects of the 'general' part[7] because they are, at least usually,[8] used across different categories of offences. This is the case with both recklessness and negligence (even though negligence tends to be used in fewer contexts than recklessness in Anglo-American systems of criminal law).

Tadros does not, however, think that this avowed generality means that *mens rea* terms such as recklessness and negligence must be overly 'general', i.e. defined uniformly throughout the criminal law. This is because, Tadros explains, different categories of offence, and even different offences within each category, are sensitive to what might be called 'localised concerns'. The principles, policies and other types of moral and political argument that bear upon a polity's understanding of culpable wrongdoing will vary from context to context.[9]

4 The claim is expanded to cover intention in Stark, 'It's only words'.

5 See, however, the discussion of negligence and criminalisation below at Chapter 8, section on 'Virtue Ethics and a Liberal Criminal Law'.

6 Victor Tadros, 'The system of the criminal law' (2002) 22 *Legal Studies* 448.

7 It is possible to be more specific. For instance, Gardner suggests *mens rea* terms are part of the 'definitional general part': John Gardner, 'On the general part of the criminal law' in R.A. Duff (ed.), *Philosophy and the Criminal Law: Principle and Critique* (Cambridge: Cambridge University Press, 1998), p. 205, at p. 205.

8 In some Anglo-American systems, particular *mens rea* terms are found only in relation to certain offences. For example, in English law, 'dishonesty' is used principally in property offences (see e.g. Theft Act 1968, s. 1; Fraud Act 2006, ss. 2–4).

9 See also John Gardner, 'Wrongs and faults', in A.P. Simester (ed.), *Appraising Strict Liability* (Oxford: Oxford University Press, 2005), p. 51, at p. 72. There is not space here to enter the debate over what principles and policies are, and what role they ought to play

For instance, Tadros thinks that an understanding of intention in terms of foresight of a virtual certainty, as is found in the English law of murder,[10] works well in some offences (his examples include murder, theft and causing grievous bodily harm with intent)[11] but is less appropriate where the harm threatened is usually less serious (his examples include incitement, criminal damage and attempts at less serious offences such as common assault).[12] In those latter contexts, Tadros thinks that finding intention in foresight of a virtual certainty is illegitimate, because it is likely to miss the core culpable wrongdoing that the criminal law is aiming to combat. In consequence it would be 'crude' to define such a crucial *mens rea* term as intention, which is used throughout the criminal law, uniformly.[13]

Although Tadros does not consider recklessness and negligence in detail,[14] there is no reason to think that his argument could not be applied in relation to those *mens rea* terms. Consider whether there could be different understandings of recklessness, premised on the defendant's awareness or unawareness of risk or her attitude towards risk (Chapter 2 showed that there are, to different extents, in various Anglo-American jurisdictions). The localised concerns which impact on how culpable wrongs should be conceived of in the law of property offences mean, the argument would go, that an awareness-based understanding of recklessness should be applied there. Where these concerns change, perhaps because the defendant was at fault for not recognising the relevant risk, recklessness might be understood in a wider sense.[15]

in the criminal law. They are used simply as shorthand for the various types of arguments that can affect the decision over what constitutes culpable wrongdoing. See, however, John Gardner, 'Ashworth on principles', in Lucia Zedner and Julian V. Roberts (eds.), *Principles and Values in Criminal Law and Criminal Justice: Essays in Honour of Andrew Ashworth* (Oxford: Oxford University Press, 2012), p. 3.

10 In the English law of murder, a jury *may* find intention when the defendant foresees that it is *in fact* virtually certain that a certain result will occur: *R* v. *Woollin* [1999] 1 AC 82. The decision in *Woollin* was limited to the context of murder (at 90).

11 Tadros, 'The system of the criminal law', at 453. 12 Ibid., at 454. 13 Ibid., at 455.

14 This is slightly odd – Tadros was writing at a time when English law's definition of recklessness in criminal damage cases relied on the reasonable person's foresight (*Commissioner of Police for the Metropolis* v. *Caldwell* [1982] AC 341), rather than the defendant's, whereas in offences against the person the defendant's awareness of a risk of some physical harm was crucial to understanding recklessness (*R* v. *Savage and Parmenter* [1992] 1 AC 699). For the contemporary English position, see Chapter 2, section on 'England and Wales'.

15 This is one way of understanding the case of *R* v. *Parker* [1977] 1 WLR 600 (E&W), where the defendant was unreasonably angry and failed to note the risk of property

In the context of manslaughter, where the law is concerned with the taking of risks with people's lives, it might be appropriate to have an even wider conception of recklessness, premised on the failure to recognise obvious risks of death.[16] Given these points, the adoption of *one* understanding of the word 'reckless' would, on this view, be over-simplistic and potentially damaging to the criminal law's enterprise of defining culpable wrongdoing accurately. An argument for understanding negligence differently in separate contexts could be raised on similar grounds.

Before challenging Tadros's defence of multiple definitions of the same *mens rea* term in the following sections, it is important to be clear about what aspects of his account are not disputed here. There is no problem with Tadros's endorsement of a conservative approach to defining culpable wrongdoing, which is opposed to attempts to create 'grand theories' which explain in general terms large swathes of the criminal law and are likely, as a result, to miss important distinctions.[17] Tadros's fear, for instance, is that if the understanding of recklessness in terms of awareness of risk were applied across the criminal law (and negligence were to continue to be limited to specific contexts), some offences would not be defined in a way that reflects fairly the relevant moral and political concerns relating to the defendant's culpability or the nature of his wrongdoing. Grand theories will tend to do this, and there is an obvious evil to be avoided here. The criminal law might well fail to maintain its necessary moral legitimacy if its rules are clumsy and indifferent to what are no doubt important concerns in the eyes of the citizens bound to live according to the criminal law's declarations, lest they be punished.

Furthermore, Tadros is correct that, to avoid this evil, different offences need different fault elements. What is taken issue with here is the idea that this makes it proper for courts and legislatures to use the *same term/concept*, such as recklessness, or indeed negligence, to mean different things in different contexts. Tadros and the courts in some of the Anglo-American jurisdictions discussed in Chapter 2 appear to think (most usually in the context of recklessness) that the argument from

damage attendant upon slamming a plastic phone receiver down on its plastic cradle. See the discussion of *Parker* below at Chapter 8, section on 'No Beliefs about Risk'.

16 See the discussion of the English law of manslaughter above at Chapter 2, section on 'England and Wales'. See also the discussion of 'criminal negligence' in Canadian criminal law above at Chapter 2, section on 'Canada'.

17 For doubts about 'grand theory', see R.A. Duff, 'Theorizing criminal law: a 25th anniversary essay' (2005) 25 *Oxford Journal of Legal Studies* 353; R.A. Duff, *Answering for Crime: Responsibility and Liability in the Criminal Law* (Oxford: Hart, 2007), pp. 7–8.

competing localised concerns of principle, policy, etc. validates this approach. At times, they have been willing to view important *mens rea* concepts such as recklessness as mere words – empty vessels to be filled with whatever meaning courts think the context calls for – rather than key tools in a communicative enterprise.

It is the increased popularity of the view that criminal law and criminal justice ought to be communicative exercises that first gives rise to the suspicion that this apathy towards the uniform definition of core *mens rea* terms, such as recklessness and negligence, is misguided. The next section explains how a focus on communication and discretion can be used to build a case for the clear and uniform definition of general *mens rea* terms including recklessness and negligence, whilst meeting Tadros's worry about localised concerns.

An Alternative Approach

The principle of fair warning – that citizens should not, in principle,[18] be utterly surprised to find out that they have committed a criminal offence – is of core importance to any defensible system of criminal law.[19] It helps to secure the rule of law, insofar as it ensures that the criminal law is capable of guiding conduct.[20]

A crucial aspect of fair warning is that citizens should have adequate access to clear and stable guidance on what is proscribed as culpable wrongdoing, so that they can reasonably easily avoid criminal punishment.[21] A key aspect of the *communicative* enterprise of criminal law is

[18] Anglo-American criminal law does not typically allow ignorance of the law to excuse criminal wrongdoing. This approach to ignorance of law is, despite initial impressions, compatible with the principle of fair warning – see below at Chapter 6, section on 'Choice and Fair Warning'.

[19] For discussion, see Glanville Williams, *Criminal Law: The General Part*, 2nd edn. (London: Stevens, 1985), pp. 578–588; Winnie Chan and A.P. Simester, 'Four functions of *mens rea*' (2011) 70 *Cambridge Law Journal* 381 at 388–393; Andrew Ashworth and Jeremy Horder, *Principles of Criminal Law*, 7th edn. (Oxford: Oxford University Press, 2013), pp. 62–65; A.P. Simester, J.R. Spencer, G.R. Sullivan and G.J. Virgo, *Simester and Sullivan's Criminal Law: Theory and Doctrine*, 5th edn. (Oxford: Hart, 2013), pp. 26–31.

[20] On the necessity of law to guide conduct, see John Rawls, *A Theory of Justice: Revised Edition* (Cambridge, MA: Harvard University Press, 1999), pp. 210–212; Joseph Raz, *The Authority of Law: Essays on Law and Morality*, 2nd edn. (Oxford: Oxford University Press, 2009), ch. 11; John Finnis, *Natural Law and Natural Rights*, 2nd edn. (Oxford: Oxford University Press, 2011), p. 283.

[21] Raz, *The Authority of Law*, pp. 214–216; Edward Griew, 'Consistency, communication and codification – reflections on two *mens rea* words', in P.R. Glazebrook (ed.), *Reshaping*

to provide such guidance. Effective communication, it will be contended here, requires a language that is comprehended by all potential and existing parties in a criminal case. It is not fostered by malleable definitions of fault elements that vary with context. In the next sub-sections, this argument will be developed from Duff's discussion of punishment, language and communication.[22]

Duff on Communication

Duff's core point is that, if trials are communicative endeavours leading to convictions (and, on Duff's view, punishments) that communicate authoritative censure, it is important that those involved in the criminal justice process can communicate with each other throughout, and this requires a shared language. It is not simply lawyers and judges who must be able to communicate effectively with the language of the law and be able to understand its nuances and inconsistencies. The language of the criminal law should be accessible to those lay actors who must argue about it to avoid the pain of punishment. It must also be accessible to those laypersons called to give judgment on their peers, be they jurors or lay judges (depending on the system of trial). And it must be accessible to those lay members of the public who hear of the case, for instance through the media. Absent such accessibility, the wider message of criminal liability could be lost in translation.[23]

A crucial aspect of this accessible language, for Duff, is that it allows citizens to argue about and (if they disagree with the courts' view) ultimately to understand the nature of their alleged/proven culpable

the Criminal Law Essays in Honour of Glanville Williams (London: Stevens, 1978), p. 57, at p. 68. On the nature of such guidance, see Andrew Ashworth, *Positive Obligations in Criminal Law* (Oxford: Hart, 2013), ch. 3.

22 R.A. Duff, *Punishment, Communication and Community* (Oxford: Oxford University Press, 2001), pp. 188–193. That section of Duff's book develops points first made in R.A. Duff, 'Law, language and community: some preconditions of criminal liability' (1998) 18 *Oxford Journal of Legal Studies* 189 at 197–201.

23 This point brings up considerations relating to the 'fair labelling' of offenders. See Ashworth and Horder, *Principles of Criminal Law*, pp. 77–79; James Chalmers and Fiona Leverick, 'Fair labelling in criminal law' (2008) 71 *Modern Law Review* 217. Fair labelling might itself be able to play a role in guiding conduct: Victor Tadros, 'Fair labelling and social solidarity', in Lucia Zedner and Julian V. Roberts (eds.), *Principles and Values in Criminal Law and Criminal Justice: Essays in Honour of Andrew Ashworth* (Oxford: Oxford University Press, 2012), p. 67, at p. 72.

wrongdoing. Duff is concerned primarily that those being tried are able to understand arguments and declarations regarding the normative nature of their acts (why they are *wrongful*) and their mental states and attitudes (why they are *culpable*), but it will be contended here that this kind of argument goes beyond Duff's *ex post* perspective and applies also in the area of *ex ante* guidance. It is from the anticipatory perspective that the need for clear and uniform definitions of *mens rea* terms, including recklessness and negligence, begins to become clear.

In planning their lives, citizens must be able to understand properly the nature of what the law declares to be a criminal offence, and it is obvious that this will usually be conducted without the benefit of legal advice. Duff's points about the ability to *translate* the law for laypersons (developed in a discussion on the *trial*) are thus less crucial here.[24] In the trial, such translation is readily available; in fact in many systems the state provides it through arrangements such as legal aid. But by the trial stage, a vital avenue for communication has already been missed. It is surely vital that citizens can *avoid* being put on trial in the first place by understanding clearly the law's normative notions of wrongdoing and culpability and acknowledging the steps needed to avoid committing offences.[25] The law should thus be clear in its message, and applied consistently, so that non-specialists can utilise it effectively at the stage of planning their conduct, as well as in later stages of the criminal process. This need for clarity is particularly vital in the criminal law context, as misunderstandings can have severe consequences.

It is necessary to clarify exactly what effective communication is thought to involve.

The Boundaries of Definition

The paragraphs above might be read to constitute an argument in favour of adopting 'ordinary' understandings of core criminal law concepts,[26] which could be grasped easily by laypersons by (moral) intuition. For those familiar with the history of *mens rea* terms in England and Wales,

[24] Duff, *Punishment, Communication and Community*, p. 189.

[25] See, similarly, *McBoyle* v. *US*, 283 US 25 (1931), at 27.

[26] It is doubtful that such 'ordinary' understandings of words exist. A useful introduction is Gilbert Ryle, 'Ordinary language' (1953) 62 *Philosophical Review* 167.

this pursuit of 'ordinariness' will bring up (bad) memories of the search for the 'ordinary' or 'popular' meaning of recklessness in *Commissioner of Police for the Metropolis* v. *Caldwell*.[27]

Caldwell had a grudge against his former employer, an hotelier. In order to settle the score, a drunken Caldwell started a small fire at the hotel. The fire was extinguished quickly, but ten guests were staying in the hotel at the time, and their lives could have been put in danger by Caldwell's actions. He was thus charged with aggravated criminal damage, which requires intention or recklessness as to the damage or destruction of property, *and* intention or recklessness as to the endangerment of life.[28]

For the majority of the House of Lords, Lord Diplock decided that an awareness-based conception of recklessness was just *one* possible understanding of that term:[29]

> [Recklessness] presupposes that if thought were given to the matter by the doer before the act was done, it would have been apparent to him that there was a real risk of its having the relevant harmful consequence; but, granted this, recklessness covers a whole range of states of mind from failing to give any thought at all to whether or not there is any risk of those harmful consequences, to recognising the existence of the risk and nevertheless deciding to ignore it.

Lord Diplock thought these various ways of taking an unjustified risk were *equally blameworthy*[30] and clearly felt the law was being unduly constrained from recognising *moral* culpability in practice by its 'obsession'[31] with a choice between two exclusive accounts of recklessness (one premised on awareness of risk, the other not).[32]

The decision in *Caldwell* resulted in uncertainty over the definition of recklessness in English law,[33] uncertainty that existed both for courts applying the law *ex post* and from the *ex ante* perspectives of citizens hoping to avoid criminal liability. The House of Lords eventually

[27] [1982] AC 341, at 351. On this history of recklessness before and after *Caldwell*, see Findlay Stark, 'Culpable carelessness: recklessness and negligence in Scots and English criminal law', PhD thesis, University of Edinburgh (2011), ch. 3.

[28] Criminal Damage Act 1971, s. 1(2). Note that no *actual* endangerment of life needs to be proved – the defendant must simply be reckless as to the possibility of endangerment.

[29] *Caldwell*, at 351. [30] Ibid., at 352. [31] Ibid.

[32] See, further, Alan W. Norrie, *Law and the Beautiful Soul* (London: Glasshouse, 2005), p. 85; Alan W. Norrie, *Law, Ideology and Punishment: Retrieval and Critique of the Liberal Idea of Criminal Justice* (Dordrecht: Kluwer, 1991), p. 176.

[33] See e.g. *R* v. *Morrison* (1989) 89 Cr App R 17, at 19.

vanquished *Caldwell* in *R* v. *G and Another*,[34] but as Chapter 2 demonstrated, other understandings of recklessness continue to exist on the fringes.[35] A consistent definition of recklessness would remove the uncertainty altogether.

This is not to say that the majority's search for an 'ordinary' understanding of recklessness in *Caldwell* was folly. It is important that, if laypersons are to understand the language in which it expresses itself, the criminal law is related sufficiently to terms that non-lawyers employ in their everyday lives.[36] So, although Lord Edmund-Davies (who dissented in *Caldwell*) was correct to express the aspiration that '[t]he law ... compiles its own dictionary ... what was originally the common coinage of speech acquires a different value in the pocket of the lawyer ...',[37] the law's understanding of core terms, like *mens rea* words, must not become too esoteric.

To see why, consider if recklessness were to be defined as aiming to bring about a certain result. This would surely be an understanding of recklessness that had strayed too far from 'ordinary' understandings, as it seems more akin to everyday understandings of (so-called *direct*) intention.[38] The language of the law, if it bore absolutely no relation to the language of laypersons, would be beyond citizens not because it was applied inconsistently (perhaps it would be applied consistently by faithful judges and juries), but rather because it had drifted too far from the normal language of blame utilised by citizens.[39] The law must be anxious to avoid this result. This is because a convincing account of the criminal law's legitimacy, on communication grounds, is that citizens should be able to identify with the criminal law and view it as *theirs*, rather than some 'alien' imposition.[40] Inaccessible language is likely to appear 'alien'.

34 [2003] UKHL 50, [2001] 1 AC 1034.

35 See Chapter 2, section on 'England and Wales'.

36 See, similarly, Neil MacCormick, *Rhetoric and the Rule of Law* (Oxford: Oxford University Press, 2005), pp. 126–127.

37 *Caldwell*, at 357.

38 In English law, for instance, there are strictly two forms of intention (at least in murder and certain other contexts). These are direct intention (a useful synonym is *purpose*) and indirect intention (acting in the face of an actual and acknowledged virtual certainty that a particular result will come about). For a critique of English law's approach, see M. Cathleen Kaveny, 'Inferring intention from foresight' (2004) 120 *Law Quarterly Review* 81.

39 Duff, *Punishment, Communication and Community*, pp. 190–191.

40 Ibid., pp. 192–193. See also John Gardner, *Offences and Defences: Selected Essays in the Philosophy of Criminal Law* (Oxford: Oxford University Press, 2007), pp. 45–53.

This is, however, as far as the argument for 'ordinary' understandings of criminal law concepts like recklessness and negligence goes. It sets boundaries within which the law should operate when defining its concepts in *semantic* terms.[41] The mistake in *Caldwell* was to think that, once those boundaries were identified, the law's definitional work was largely done.

Recklessness can thus sensibly be defined, as it is somewhat consistently in *most* Anglo-American systems, as the taking of a substantial and unjustified risk, whilst being *aware* of that risk. This is close enough to the 'everyday' language and normative understanding of recklessness to be comprehended by a layperson, and this ensures that – although the law has adopted a definition of recklessness which might not quite match perfectly a layperson's intuitive understanding[42] – communication is possible because it is *close enough* and semantically graspable. Citizens could understand easily that they ought not to take certain risks that they believe to be attendant on φ-ing, or else they might be punished.

The difficulty complained of here arises where that definition of recklessness is not applied consistently (or a jury is 'left to its own devices')[43] and begins to overlap in some contexts with other *mens rea* terms, such as negligence. As the citizen grasps recklessness in one context, he is surprised or embarrassed to learn that it might mean something else in another. Although both of these definitions might end up being close to an intuitive understanding of recklessness, matters are complicated by the difference in semantic understanding propagated by the courts (and sometimes the legislature). This is not conducive to citizens feeling confident in their ability to plan and communicate via the language of *their* law, a law that respects them as planning agents.[44] This has implications for the certainty with which citizens can view their prospective conduct or argue about their alleged misdeeds. Given the special context of the criminal law, such uncertainty can have particularly severe consequences, which ought to be avoided.

If the language of the law and the language of extra-legal discourse are to be bridged successfully, so that a communication about culpable

[41] And the law ought to define terms within these boundaries, rather than asking juries to do it themselves, if only for reasons of accountability. See, further, Adrian Briggs, 'Judges, juries and the meaning of words' (1985) 5 *Legal Studies* 314.

[42] See *Caldwell*, at 357.

[43] *R* v. *Taylor* [2004] VSCA 189, 149 A Crim R 399 (Vic), at [42].

[44] See, further, Raz, *The Authority of Law*, pp. 221–222.

wrongdoing can be engaged in at the planning stage of conduct, it is crucial that citizens can be on firm ground in their understanding of the normative *and* semantic contours of *mens rea* concepts, rather than on shifting sands. They should not feel, when trying to engage with the criminal law's content on such a core matter, that they are engaged in a discussion with Humpty Dumpty, where the meanings and content of certain terms can change unexpectedly, frustrating real dialogue.[45] If a statute or common law offence can be committed recklessly or negligently, that should mean *one* thing, rather than various things. It is submitted that the best understanding of the Standard Account must strive for this consistency in definition of recklessness and negligence (and, it will be suggested below, avoid distinguishing between extremely similar concepts such as 'ordinary' and 'gross' negligence).

This account of consistency in definition raises immediate objections, which will be dealt with in the following sections.

Robinson on Conduct and Adjudication

The first challenge to the communicative account sketched above arises from the work of Paul Robinson, who has done most to divide criminal prohibitions and defences into 'rules of conduct' and 'principles of adjudication'.[46] As Robinson explains, rules of conduct are addressed to citizens and ought to be clear and concise in order to give meaningful *ex ante* guidance and communicate to the public the criminal law's prohibitions.[47] Principles of adjudication, by contrast, do not guide the behaviour of citizens. They are useful instead from an *ex post*

[45] See Lewis Carroll, *Through the Looking Glass and What Alice Found There* (London: Dent, 1929), p. 123 ('"When *I* use a word," Humpty Dumpty said, in rather a scornful tone, "it means just what I choose it to mean – neither more nor less."')

[46] His most important works in this area are Paul H. Robinson, 'Rules of conduct and principles of adjudication' (1990) 57 *University of Chicago Law Review* 729, and *Structure and Function in Criminal Law* (Oxford: Oxford University Press, 1997). Robinson credits the rediscovery of the conduct/adjudication distinction to George Fletcher and Meir Dan-Cohen. See George P. Fletcher, *Rethinking Criminal Law* (Boston: Little, Brown, 1978), pp. 456–459; Meir Dan-Cohen, 'Decision rules and conduct rules: on acoustic separation in criminal law' (1983–1984) 97 *Harvard Law Review* 625. See also Richard Singer, 'On classicism and dissonance in the criminal law: a reply to Professor Meir Dan-Cohen' (1986) 77 *Journal of Criminal Law and Criminology* 69.

[47] Paul H. Robinson, 'Structuring criminal codes to fulfill their function' (2000–2001) 4 *Buffalo Criminal Law Review* 1 at 7. The question of whether the criminal law prohibits, or merely declares pre-existing wrongs, is skipped over here, but see Duff, *Answering for Crime*, pp. 85–87.

perspective, when a court is assessing the blameworthiness of the defendant's alleged wrongdoing.

Given that courts are accorded time for thought and reflection about the defendant's behaviour (time which the defendant might often be denied), Robinson contends that principles of adjudication can be drafted more imprecisely than rule of conduct, lest their ability to assess blameworthiness accurately be compromised.[48] A simple explanation for the variation found in the definition of recklessness and negligence in some Anglo-American systems, then, is that *mens rea* terms such as recklessness (and *perhaps* negligence) are *always* principles of adjudication: they play no part in giving *ex ante* guidance to citizens, and thus it does not matter if they are confusing or not.[49] If lawyers *can* understand these terms, and judges and juries *can* – with suitable direction – apply them, then that is sufficient. The argument for clear and uniform definitions of *mens rea* terms presented above thus fails. A more nuanced approach, such as that defended by Tadros, will presumably be better able to capture the distinct forms of culpable, unjustified wrongdoing that are the concern of the criminal law.

There are three responses to this argument. First, Robinson provides uniform definitions of *mens rea* terms (based on the MPC's) in his draft 'Code of Adjudication' appended to the most worked-through model of his theory.[50] This suggests that Robinson does not, in fact, think different understandings of these terms will be needed for different adjudicative contexts, unless of course courts warp those statutory definitions extensively.

Second, Robinson himself notes that *mens rea* terms are not *always* principles of adjudication, because sometimes they will play a part in defining a wrong.[51] His work has concentrated on inchoate

48 Robinson, 'Rules of conduct and principles of adjudication', at 770; Paul H. Robinson, 'Fair notice and fair adjudication: two kinds of legality' (2005–2006) 154 *University of Pennsylvania Law Review* 335 at 378.

49 Robinson, 'Rules of conduct and principles of adjudication', at 769. Peter Alldridge once supported this line of thinking: Peter Alldridge, 'Rules for courts and rules for citizens' (1990) 10 *Oxford Journal of Legal Studies* 487 at 489, 494–495. Cf. Peter Alldridge, 'Making criminal law known', in Stephen Shute and A.P. Simester (eds.), *Criminal Law Theory: Doctrines of the General Part* (Oxford: Oxford University Press, 2002), p. 103, at pp. 113–115.

50 Robinson, *Structure and Function in Criminal Law*, p. 237.

51 Robinson, 'Rules of conduct and principles of adjudication', at 737–739. See, further, Fletcher, *Rethinking Criminal Law*, pp. 566–569; Chan and Simester, 'Four functions of *mens rea*', at 385–388.

offences[52] – where *mens rea* is an essential part of establishing when a person has 'crossed the line' into criminal liability – but Chan and Simester also give the example of theft.[53] It is not wrong, in itself, to pick up an item of property such as a bag. It *is* wrong, however, to pick up a bag knowing that it belongs to someone else and intending to deprive the true owner permanently of her property in dishonest circumstances.[54] It is submitted that recklessness can play a similar, wrong-defining role in certain circumstances: it is wrong to pick up a bag knowing it belongs to someone else, aware of a risk (which is, in the circumstances, unjustifiable to take) that it cannot be returned, in dishonest circumstances. If this is the case, then surely those *mens rea* terms which make conduct wrongful need to be defined clearly to ensure that citizens are capable of planning their affairs so as to avoid potential criminal liability. Those *mens rea* terms are, after all, elements of conduct rules. They ought, then, to be expressed in clear and consistent language upon which confident plans regarding liability can be made.[55]

Admittedly, it is not immediately obvious how negligence can contribute to the wrongfulness of an 'objectively' neutral piece of conduct. It might be thought that the answer is simple: negligence is about careless conduct (in certain circumstances, a wrong) itself. But that is not the best understanding of negligence available, because – as explained in Chapter 7[56] – a conduct-based view of negligence draws an insufficient link between defendants and wrongdoing to warrant the condemnation of conviction. As will be explained in far greater detail in Chapter 8, the fault of negligence is best understood as consisting in the culpable failure to possess a belief about the risks attendant upon φ-ing. It is the absence of the kind of mental state that can be spoken to by the law's commands immediately at the time of engaging in behaviour. As will be explained below, this does not mean that negligence is necessarily anathema to a system of law premised on fair warning.[57] It is submitted that conceiving

[52] See e.g. Robinson, *Structure and Function in Criminal Law*, pp. 133–134, 157–164. Despite noting the importance of *mens rea* in inchoate offences, Robinson's 'Code of Conduct' states simply, 'You may not attempt to commit a crime' (p. 218). This is unclear with regard to whether *mens rea* matters – suggesting that Robinson's codes of conduct and principles of adjudication distinction is drawn too sharply.

[53] Chan and Simester, 'Four functions of *mens rea*', at 385–386.

[54] See Theft Act 1968 (E&W), s. 1.

[55] See, similarly, Gardner, 'Wrongs and faults', at p. 70.

[56] See section on 'Conduct: Hart's Insight'.

[57] See below at Chapter 8, section on 'Virtue Ethics and a Liberal Criminal Law'.

of negligence as a failure of belief also does not necessarily mean that negligence can be susceptible to variation in definition.

Even if this answer regarding negligence is not accepted, the contention here is that the need for consistency in definition anyway stretches beyond those *mens rea* terms that constitute partly the wrong that the defendant is alleged to have perpetrated. If the criminal law prohibits the intentional causing or risking of a certain result, then a person who takes the time to think about whether or not he *is* intending a result (or simply taking the risk of its occurrence) is entitled, surely, to guidance on the possible penal consequences. If this is the case, then surely it *does* make sense to direct citizens not to do certain actions when they are doing them with certain mental states or in the absence of a specific mental state, such as a belief that there is a risk attendant upon φ-ing.[58] Indeed, negligence (which it is difficult to conceive of as a (positive) 'mental state')[59] could play a role here: the defendant should be given guidance on when *lacking* the relevant mental state (belief that a particular risk exists) might result in liability for the taking of an unjustified risk. Some writers seem to note that this is *the* role of *mens rea* terms: to ensure that fair warning and *ex ante* guidance were available to the defendant prior to the alleged offence.[60] This suggests that Robinson is too restrictive in his concession that *mens rea* terms are not *always* aspects of principles of adjudication.

As argued above, since the criminal law is a communicative enterprise, such *ex ante* guidance as can be provided through the law's definitions of its *mens rea* terms should be presented clearly. Malleable definitions of *mens rea* terms including recklessness and negligence hinder this process unnecessarily and reduce the polity's confidence that the criminal law belongs to *it*. Uniform definitions would help to avoid this difficulty, and this policy should be applied to all *mens rea* states, including recklessness and negligence.

[58] See, in a similar vein, Dan-Cohen, 'Decision rules and conduct rules', at 652; R.A. Duff, 'Rule-violations and wrongdoing', in Stephen Shute and A.P. Simester (eds.), *Criminal Law Theory: Doctrines of the General Part* (Oxford: Oxford University Press, 2002), p. 47, at pp. 69–70. There are more convincing reasons for excluding defences from offence definitions, but they are beyond the scope of this book. See, however, Fletcher, *Rethinking Criminal Law*, p. 457.

[59] Indeed, this is often presented as a (poor) reason why negligence is not the stuff of criminal liability. This view is rejected below at Chapter 6, section on 'Choice and *Mens Rea*'.

[60] Dan-Cohen, 'Decision Rules and Conduct Rules', at 662; H.L.A. Hart, *Punishment and Responsibility: Essays in the Philosophy of Law*, 2nd edn. (Oxford: Oxford University Press, 2008), pp. 181–182.

Third, even if a system of law were reformed in order to implement Robinson's dichotomy between conduct and adjudication, it would presumably still use the same *mens rea* words to give both *ex ante* and *ex post* guidance about wrongdoing and culpability. It would seem then that the definition of terms such as intention and recklessness would have to be consistent and clear in some contexts (where they form part of a rule of conduct for citizens) but not in others (where they become part of a principle of adjudication for courts). This would produce a perplexing account of the criminal law, and it must be remembered that not all of those who Robinson would give principles of adjudication to will be trained legal specialists. Jurors would, it is assumed, soon get confused if they understood recklessness in one context, but not in another. Those planning their conduct might plausibly be puzzled when they hear of court judgments that can be explained only by reference to the defendant's *mens rea* (or lack thereof) and that fail to accord with their 'conduct rule' understandings. Again, this would shake their confidence in the criminal law's declarations of culpable wrongdoing. It is therefore submitted that uniform definitions and a wide range of distinct fault terms used across the criminal law would remain necessary from a communicative perspective, even if Robinson's conduct/adjudication distinction were applied faithfully.

Even if it is doubted that negligence is in the same position as intention and recklessness, in the light of the fact that it cannot make a morally neutral piece of conduct (picking up property belonging to another) wrongful, it is submitted that it should be defined consistently, as requiring the same level of departure from expected standards regarding the formation of beliefs about risk.[61] This is the reason that this book will not defend different *types* of negligence ('gross', 'criminal', etc.). It would be unnecessarily complicated to define *some mens rea* terms consistently (in virtue of their wrong-making potential) and others inconsistently. In short, if some *mens rea* words *must* be defined consistently, then *all mens rea* words *should* be defined consistently. This is the approach that will be taken in the remainder of this book.

Robinson's conduct/adjudication dichotomy does not, then, render redundant the communicative argument outlined above. It is now necessary to consider a second objection.

[61] See below at Chapter 8.

'Thin Ice' and Discretion

The second attack on the communicative account offered above concerns its transition from *normative* to *semantic* clarity. It might be wondered whether such a move is necessary or whether it would defeat the purpose of the criminal law in punishing culpable wrongdoing.

This objection arises from a qualification to the requirement of fair warning of potential criminal liability: the 'thin ice principle'.[62] The idea behind this principle is that, as long as citizens can appreciate that their conduct is of *dubious* legality, they are sufficiently warned about the prospect of punishment.[63] In continuing to behave in this state of uncertainty, the citizen takes the risk of criminal liability and must take the consequences.

This point could be taken to mean that, in the context of *mens rea* words such as recklessness and negligence, variation in definition would be permissible so long as all definitions remained sufficiently close to the morally intuitive understanding mentioned above that citizens could be on 'thin ice'. In such cases, citizens presumably could sense their conduct sailed close to the wind and would not be surprised unfairly if they were held liable for an offence. If so, the argument for uniformity in definition falls away: all that can be argued for is that *mens rea* words should be defined within the broad parameters of everyday (moral) understanding.[64] Multiple definitions of terms such as recklessness and negligence would, on this view, be permissible. Lord Diplock was right in *Caldwell* after all.

There are two responses available to this claim. The first is that the 'thin ice principle' is itself not conducive to a clear criminal law that citizens can feel confident in utilising when planning their conduct. In short, the endorsement of 'thin ice' undermines the requirement of fair warning to a large extent. It is hence a troubling principle, more troubling than has perhaps been recognised in the criminal law literature to

[62] See Williams, *Criminal Law*, pp. 589–590; Douglas N. Husak, *Philosophy of Criminal Law* (Totowa, NJ: Rowman & Littlefield, 1987), pp. 69–72; Andrew Ashworth, 'Interpreting criminal statutes: a crisis of legality?' (1991) 107 *Law Quarterly Review* 419 at 443–444; *Knuller (Publishing, Printing and Promotions) Ltd* v. *DPP* [1973] AC 435 (E&W), at 463, 488.

[63] On some accounts, mere negligence as to being on 'thin ice' might be sufficient to secure fair warning. See Douglas N. Husak, 'Strict liability, justice and proportionality', in A.P. Simester (ed.), *Appraising Strict Liability* (Oxford: Oxford University Press, 2005), p. 81, at p. 99.

[64] See Gardner, *Offences and Defences*, pp. 43–45.

date. This point about 'thin ice' will no doubt strike some people as being unproblematic because of the very function of the principle – to catch those who, although not caught by a *core* understanding of fault, are still, given their awareness of the dubiety of their conduct, *bad enough* to warrant conviction.[65]

But acceptance of that viewpoint would lead to something of a Pyrrhic victory, because of a second, more troubling, concern over discretion.[66] The 'thin ice principle' might allow a wide margin of appreciation for criminal justice actors, including those in the courts, in their definition or application of *mens rea* concepts. The risk is that this allows arbitrary distinctions (just *when* is this definition of recklessness to be applied?) and bias to creep into the criminal justice system, as well as usurping the legislature's role in criminalisation decisions.[67] An additional benefit of adopting clear and consistent definitions of *mens rea* terms is that it would ensure that the discretion accorded to bodies such as the police and courts to 'do justice' in individual cases would be reduced to a degree that these dangers could be minimised.[68]

There is still the question, however, of what to do if there are perceived gaps in the definition of fault elements, through which those who *should* be convicted of an offence are escaping. Furthermore, there remains a need to respond to the localised principles that Tadros identified as being so important. These points are discussed in the next section.

Practical Concerns

It has been argued that, if the criminal law is to live up to its communicative ideal, citizens must be able to understand (normatively and semantically) and use the language of wrongdoing and culpability adopted by the courts and the legislature in planning their conduct. Similarly, if the discretion accorded to criminal justice actors is to be

65 Ashworth, 'Interpreting criminal statutes', at 443.

66 See also Larry Alexander and Kimberly K. Ferzan with Stephen J. Morse, *Crime and Culpability: A Theory of Criminal Law* (Cambridge: Cambridge University Press, 2009), p. 300.

67 Raz, *The Authority of Law*, p. 218; Ashworth and Horder, *Principles of Criminal Law*, p. 65.

68 Even those who support discretion in the definition of concepts such as *mens rea* accept that this power must be controlled to avoid damaging respect for the criminal justice system: Paul H. Robinson, 'Legality and discretion in the distribution of criminal sanctions' (1988) 25 *Harvard Journal on Legislation* 393 at 398.

controlled adequately, the criminal law's *mens rea* terms should be defined clearly and consistently. This argument means that recklessness and negligence should be defined in *one* way throughout the criminal law, which coheres with the approach of the Standard Account of culpable carelessness, which Chapter 2 argued a number of major Anglo-American systems of criminal law are now, to varying extents, converging around.

But what are the courts and the legislature to do if they accept the argument from communication made in this chapter, yet want to ensure that the law can react appropriately to the competing principles and policies which affect different areas of the criminal law? As noted above, Tadros suggests that the courts may, in interpreting *mens rea* terms such as recklessness, be conservative (defining recklessness in relation to a particular context, such as a single type of offence) and not seek to make generalisations which might prejudge the treatment of recklessness in distinct parts of the law. This approach results, however, in the courts using a small number of *mens rea* terms in different ways and leads to the potential confusion pointed to above. A better solution, it is submitted, would be to expand the range of *mens rea* terms presently utilised in the criminal law and ensure that, when they were used, these words are defined consistently across offences.[69]

The benefit of using different *terms*, rather than different *definitions*, is obvious. It would avoid the need for the courts to *decide* (in systems where they have the freedom to decide) when recklessness is to be defined with reference to awareness of risk and when it ought not to be. The decision on the definition of a *mens rea* word would be left to the legislature in drafting an offence (which would, as a happy side effect, ensure the legislature made clear what form(s) of *mens rea* it intended to be relevant to a particular component of the *actus reus*). This would allow recklessness and negligence to have *one* meaning, and leave any 'gaps' in culpability to be filled in, by the legislature, using other words (themselves defined consistently). That said, the terms and concepts used should be meaningfully distinct, so the invocation of standards such as 'gross' negligence, as opposed to 'ordinary' negligence, ought to be avoided.

Consider the definition of recklessness developed in the context of the English law of rape in the 1980s. By the late 1970s, rape required an

[69] See, similarly, Griew, 'Consistency, Communication and Codification', at p. 68.

intention to have sexual intercourse and either knowledge that the woman[70] was not consenting or recklessness as to her consent.[71] If recklessness was understood to mean that the defendant was aware of the risk of non-consent in this context, then that would mean that a man who failed to become aware of blatantly obvious signs of non-consent from his partner would have (in theory) to be acquitted of rape. At least some such defendants are going to be more morally reprehensible than some actors who are aware of a risk of non-consent (i.e. the defendant who notes a minuscule risk of non-consent but hopes it will not materialise).[72] The wholesale exclusion of those defendants who were simply *indifferent* to the matter of consent (and thus unaware of the risk of non-consent) from conviction and punishment was unacceptable; again, localised concerns pointed towards the expansion of the law's understanding of recklessness in this context to capture some defendants who were not aware of the risk of non-consent at the relevant time.[73] It is therefore not incredibly surprising that the English courts moved to consider an 'indifferent', inadvertent defendant as being 'reckless' and thus culpable.[74]

This move by the English courts no doubt did violence to the idea of awareness-based recklessness (which was already in tatters following *Caldwell*, a case discussed earlier in this chapter), but it is quite clear that the judges might have felt that they had no other choice. They could not simply declare that indifference was a new form of *mens rea*, distinct from recklessness (as, following the argument presented in this chapter, would have been preferable).[75] So the integrity of recklessness in terms of awareness of risk was further surrendered (beyond the extent to which the majority's decision in *Caldwell* had already done so) in order to

70 A man could not be raped under English law until 1994.

71 *DPP* v. *Morgan* [1976] AC 182, a decision which had influence elsewhere: e.g. *Jamieson* v. *HM Advocate* 1994 JC 88 (Scot) and *Pappajohn* v. *R* [1980] 2 SCR 120 (Can).

72 Finbarr McAuley and J. Paul McCutcheon, *Criminal Liability: A Grammar* (Dublin: Round Hall Sweet & Maxwell, 2000), p. 288.

73 On the question of whether 'indifference' to risk can be demonstrated where there is no awareness of risk, see below at Chapter 7, section on 'Some General Criticisms'.

74 'Indifference' played a large part in the law of sexual offences during the *Caldwell* era: see e.g. *R* v. *Kimber* [1983] 1 WLR 1118 (E&W).

75 Although this solution would have been *preferable*, it is not necessarily ideal. The fault element of rape, and related sexual offences, should be the failure to form a belief in non-consent when this could legitimately be expected of the defendant, rather than 'indifference'. See below at Chapter 7, section on 'Distinguishing Recklessness and Negligence' (on Duff's treatment of 'practical indifference' in rape) and at Chapter 8, section on 'Virtue Ethics and a Liberal Criminal Law' (on negligence as failure of belief in sexual offences).

ensure that those who surely deserved punishment for their culpable wrongdoing got it.

Decisions such as these on the definition of recklessness no doubt 'did justice', but only at a price: the clarity of the law for laypersons. Furthermore, the English courts exercised discretion in the definition of recklessness in areas such as rape that was not subject to clear boundaries. It is submitted that it would have been preferable for the courts to maintain a uniform definition of *mens rea* terms such as recklessness and require parliamentary intervention. For instance, the legislature has, through the Sexual Offences Act 2003, amended the definition of the *mens rea* of rape in English law to more clearly locate culpable wrongdoing, without endangering the clarity of the definition of recklessness in other contexts.[76] If the defendant does not have a reasonable belief in consent, he is to be convicted if his partner was, in fact, not consenting.[77] As noted in Chapter 2, this is an approach that other Anglo-American systems have adopted. The type of case mentioned above – where the defendant failed to form the belief that his partner was not consenting, despite obvious the signs – is thus captured well, and recklessness in English criminal law can go back to meaning (usually) the unjustified taking of risk of which the defendant is aware. This makes it easier to argue about the application of the law of rape to particular circumstances, and makes it clear to citizens (in normative and semantic terms) what the polity takes to constitute rape, and what positive steps defendants must take to avoid liability.

Judges would do well to spur on such legislative clarifications in those systems where they are needed. If a statute defines a crime in terms of recklessness, but the defendant clearly was not aware of the relevant risk, he might still *appear* culpable (and perhaps, though not always, he was on 'thin ice'). The trial judge might reach the conclusion that, had the legislature thought about it, they would have included inadvertent unjustified risk-taking within the ambit of the offence. The judge may feel inclined, in light of this conclusion, to fudge the issue of awareness for the jury, as English judges did in relation to rape in the 1980s.

[76] This claim regarding clarity might be objected to. It is not clear *to whom* the defendant's belief in consent must appear reasonable: Sharon Cowan, '"Freedom and the capacity to make a choice": a feminist analysis of consent in the criminal law of rape', in Vanessa E. Munro and Carl Stychin (eds.), *Sexuality and the Law: Feminist Engagements* (Abingdon: Routledge-Cavendish, 2007), p. 51, at pp. 60–61.

[77] Sexual Offences Act 2003, s. 1.

Appellate courts might well accept this, claiming that this is one instance where – because of the types of concerns local to that offence – recklessness includes those unjustified risk-takers who unreasonably fail to become aware of the relevant risk(s) associated with their conduct. But the point is that this move would be based on supposition and no real democratic discussion of the localised concerns that the criminal law is meant to reflect. It is submitted that it would be preferable to permit the occasional 'injustice' to occur, in order to allow a proper discussion about the various arguments concerning wrongdoing and culpability to take place in the legislature.

A Criminalisation Concern

The obvious danger with the argument for unitary definition put forward in this chapter is that legislatures might, hoping to avoid unmerited acquittals, make every offence overbroad, with the lowest form of fault element possible. They could, for example, make all offences capable of commission through negligence or (if they can justify it) offences of strict liability, to ensure that no 'culpable' wrongdoers go free. This is no doubt a concern, but it would make it very clear to the public what the legislature was doing. However tough on crime 'the public' is thought to be in certain Anglo-American jurisdictions,[78] if every offence had a flimsy fault element (or no fault element at all) attached to it, convictions would be avoided through 'jury equity', and citizens would soon become attuned to the fact that the criminal law no longer reflected anything like *their* ideas about wrongdoing and culpability. As contended above, this would compromise the moral legitimacy of the criminal law and jeopardise the sense of obligation that citizens have towards it. It must be asked whether the legislature would take this sort of risk. The experience of those modern criminal codes that *do* define *mens rea* terms suggests that recklessness will typically be the baseline of fault for serious offences, not negligence.[79] It is submitted, then, that the concern about

[78] It is difficult not to have sympathy with Horder's view that '[l]ay people are not the wild-eyed retributivists that it suits many liberal-progressive scholars or would-be law reformers to regard them as being': Jeremy Horder, *Homicide and the Politics of Law Reform* (Oxford: Oxford University Press, 2012), p. 42.

[79] See American Law Institute, *Model Penal Code and Commentaries (Official Draft and Revised Comments)*, 3 vols. (Philadelphia: American Law Institute, 1980), vol. 1, s. 2.02(4).

overcriminalisation expressed above is not unreal – and would have to be guarded against – but it is less significant than it might otherwise be.[80]

What *is* required is keen attention to the role of different *mens rea* terms in criminalisation decisions.[81] The decision on which *mens rea* term to deem sufficient for culpability in relation to a specific token of wrongdoing will take into account different 'localised concerns'. But this does not mean that the definition of terms such as recklessness and negligence need themselves be susceptible to variation. The best understanding of the Standard Account would not admit of such variation, and so this book will refuse to do so.

An Over-inclusiveness Concern

A final worry about the argument for unitary definition presented here is that it might lead to the development of a very rich *mens rea* vocabulary. There might be 'indifferent risk-taking', 'acutely, voluntarily intoxicated risk-taking' (if the mistake of conflating intoxication and recklessness/negligence is made)[82] and so on, and this would result in a clunky and confusing approach to *mens rea*. This is not necessarily the case. Again, if attention is paid to those jurisdictions that have codified their *mens rea* terms, they seldom have that many, and it is possible to be able to cater to special cases such as intoxication in distinct provisions. Although there have been calls for a greater diversity of *mens rea* terms in some such jurisdictions,[83] there have also been calls for less,[84] and – ultimately – the question is whether a real gap in culpability is demonstrated to exist. This book is concerned with culpable, unjustified risk-taking, and the best understanding of the Standard Account. It will thus argue about the best definitions of recklessness and negligence.[85] Once these terms are

[80] For a useful introduction to the problem of overcriminalisation, and potential checks on legislative power in the criminal context, see Douglas N. Husak, *Overcriminalization: The Limits of the Criminal Law* (Oxford: Oxford University Press, 2007).

[81] Cf. Chan and Simester, 'Four functions of *mens rea*', at 393–395.

[82] The conflation of voluntary intoxication and recklessness is objected to above in Chapter 2.

[83] See Kenneth W. Simons, 'Rethinking mental states' (1992) 72 *Boston University Law Review* 463; Alan C. Michaels, 'Acceptance: the missing mental state' (1997–1998) 71 *Southern California Law Review* 953.

[84] See e.g. Alexander and Ferzan with Morse, *Crime and Culpability*, ch. 2.

[85] It was argued in Chapter 2 that rules on voluntary intoxication should be dealt with entirely separately from recklessness and negligence.

understood in the terms described in the remaining chapters, no significant gap in culpability for risk-taking is visible.

Conclusion

For concerns of fair warning and the control of courts' discretion, consistent definitions of the terms 'recklessness' and 'negligence' should be employed. The Standard Account, with its single definitions of recklessness and negligence, is thus superior to more multifaceted models, found principally in un-codified jurisdictions or those jurisdictions with elderly criminal codes that do not define *mens rea* concepts comprehensively. In the light of this conclusion, the following chapters proceed on the basis that the search is for the best *unitary* understanding of recklessness and negligence.

For the same reasons, it will be assumed in the next two chapters that the concept of awareness of risk ought to be defined consistently (in terms of the defendant's beliefs about the risks attendant upon her conduct), rather than being susceptible to variation. The next two chapters consider the best unitary understanding of awareness of risk.

4

From Awareness to Belief

Chapter 2 argued that Anglo-American systems of criminal law have sometimes failed to adopt consistent understandings of recklessness and negligence, and Chapter 3 explained why this is problematic. The following chapters thus move towards achieving the best understanding of the 'Standard Account' of culpable risk-taking, which utilises *unitary* definitions of recklessness and negligence.[1] Before the best understandings of recklessness and negligence can be approached, it is useful to clarify the concept that is meant to do the work of separating them: awareness of risk.

Awareness of risk lies at the heart of the Standard Account of culpable carelessness in Anglo-American criminal law. Reckless defendants are *aware* of the risks attendant upon their behaviour, risks that, in the circumstances, it is not justifiable to take.[2] (For convenience, the defendant's behaviour will be referred to, when being considered in the abstract, as 'φ-ing'.) Negligent defendants are unjustifiably *not* aware of those risks at the time that they take them.[3] If the concept of awareness of risk is so important, then it is sensible to establish exactly what it consists of. That is the purpose of the next two chapters. Once this purpose has been achieved, it can then be asked (in Chapter 6) whether – and, if so, why – awareness of risk deserves its pivotal role in the Standard Account.

Despite its centrality to the Standard Account, it was noted in Chapter 2 that the main Anglo-American systems of criminal law have failed to explain the concept of awareness of risk in any depth. Indeed, the Court of Appeal of England and Wales once suggested that questions

[1] It was argued in Chapter 2 that voluntary intoxication rules should be separated entirely from recklessness and negligence.

[2] On justifying risk-taking, see above at Chapter 1, section on 'Justifying Risk-taking'.

[3] As seen in Chapter 2, some systems conceive of negligence as being about *conduct*, whilst others address it in terms of lacking awareness of a particular risk. The lack of awareness view will be preferred below in Chapter 8.

about different aspects of awareness constituted a 'philosophical quibble', not worth engaging with unless absolutely necessary.[4] Husak alleges that the position is hardly better in criminal law theory. He remarks that it is 'scandalous' that[5]

> Virtually all of the commentary written by both friends and foes of liability for negligence seemingly presupposes that we agree about what awareness is and whether or not a given defendant possesses it. Of course, most cases are clear. In my judgment, however, this pivotal topic is radically under-theorized.

This criticism of the current theoretical literature is expressed too strongly. As will be seen, *some* theoretical work on the concept of awareness of risk has been done,[6] although an alternative way of reading it will be suggested. Husak nevertheless has a point: the literature on this 'pivotal topic' is not incredibly expansive, and *certain* aspects of awareness of risk are undeveloped. The next two chapters aim to advance the discussion of various aspects of awareness of risk that, it is contended, are crucial to gaining the best understanding of that concept for use in the Standard Account.

The argument in this chapter is split into three sections. First, it will be contended that to be aware of a particular risk associated with φ-ing requires a *belief* that the relevant risk exists. This contention raises the question of what it means to say that a defendant *believes* a certain proposition (shortened, hereafter, to *p*), such as that there is a risk attendant upon φ-ing. In the second part of the chapter, a dispositional account of belief – i.e. one that views beliefs as being things that are *ascribed* to a person, in the light of her dispositions towards thought and behaviour – will be defended. Third and finally, the chapter explains how

4 *R v. Murphy* [1980] QB 434, at 440. The Court of Appeal distinguished between 'knowledge which is stored in the brain and available if called upon' and 'knowledge which is actually present because it has been called upon'. The view was taken that, as the offence (reckless driving) was based on *conduct*, it was not worth engaging with the 'quibble'. See, further, Glanville Williams, *Criminal Law: The General Part*, 2nd edn. (London: Stevens, 1961), p. 170; *R* v. *Bello* (1978) 67 Cr App R 288 (E&W), at 290–291; Gerald H. Gordon, *The Criminal Law of Scotland*, 3rd edn., ed. M.G.A. Christie, 2 vols. (Edinburgh: SULI/W. Green, 2000), vol. 1, para. 7.27.

5 Douglas N. Husak, 'Negligence, belief, blame and criminal liability: the special case of forgetting' (2011) 5 *Criminal Law and Philosophy* 199 at 207.

6 A point noted in Michael S. Moore and Heidi M. Hurd, 'The culpability of negligence', in Rowan Cruft, Matthew H. Kramer and Mark R. Reiff (eds.), *Crime, Punishment and Responsibility: The Jurisprudence of Antony Duff* (Oxford: Oxford University Press, 2011), p. 311, at p. 316 (n. 23).

this dispositional, belief-based understanding of awareness of risk maps onto, and allows for a reconceptualisation of, the existing literature on the topic of awareness of risk. It will be argued that this literature can and should be understood in terms of the defendant's dispositions towards thought and behaviour, and the beliefs that can properly be ascribed in the light of them. So understood, the concept of awareness of risk becomes less mysterious, and, it will be contended, easily adoptable in the context of the criminal law.

The Necessity of Belief

'Being aware that there is a particular risk attendant upon φ-ing' is, it will be contended in this book, co-extensive with 'believing that there is a particular risk attendant upon φ-ing'. The more modest claim to be made at this stage is that awareness of p necessarily entails a belief that p. Consider the following example. Jo is in her back garden, which backs onto some woods that are popular with dog walkers.[7] She has recently purchased (legally) a second-hand rifle and wants to check its accuracy. Just as Jo takes aim at a target propped against the wall at the back of her garden, her neighbour shouts, 'Are you aware you might kill someone walking in the woods?'

Jo reacts with visible surprise and responds verbally (and, for the sake of argument, honestly) that she was not aware of that particular risk when she took aim. She explains that she thought that the wall would stop any stray bullets. On further reflection (prompted by the neighbour's interruption), Jo now recognises that a bullet might well go over or through the wall, or ricochet, and kill a dog walker.

The contention here is that Jo's claim that she lacked awareness of the risk of death is really a claim that, before the neighbour's intervention, she lacked a *belief* that such a risk existed. Awareness of p requires a belief that p. It is further suggested that Jo's surprised responses to the neighbour's question demonstrate that she lacked the dispositions that would be expected of somebody who believed that there was a risk of killing another person attendant upon her conduct before the neighbour's question.[8] This is why it would be inaccurate to say of Jo that, before

[7] This example is based, loosely, on the facts of *Cameron* v. *Maguire* 1999 JC 63 (Scot) (discussed below at Chapter 8, section on '*Cameron* v. *Maguire*').

[8] See H.H. Price, *Belief* (London: George Allen & Unwin, 1969), p. 276.

the neighbour's intervention, she *believed* that firing the rifle might kill someone. The suggestion here is that it would be natural, in these circumstances, to say that the absence of a belief that a risk of death existed is fatal to the proper ascription of *awareness* of that risk to Jo, as well. If awareness of risk is necessary for recklessness, then the absence of belief is similarly fatal to a finding of that form of fault in Jo's circumstances.

The thought is, then, that a person cannot be said to be 'aware' of a specific risk attendant upon a particular token of φ-ing without believing that that specific risk exists. Linkage to the *specific* risk relevant to the defendant's wrongdoing is required because it is to *that wrongdoing* that the defendant, as an agent, must be tied, before the personalised condemnation of a criminal conviction is deployed legitimately. This is the element of truth in what is referred to as the 'correspondence principle', i.e. the idea that a defendant's fault ought to track the discrete elements of the *actus reus*.[9]

To be clear, Jo is unaware of the relevant risk even if she had relevant background beliefs about risks in general that *could* (in appropriate circumstances) lead to the manifestation of further dispositions, which *themselves* would merit the ascription of a belief about the relevant risk to her.[10] Although in such circumstances, it appears that Jo has at least some of the ingredients for the formation of a belief about the specific risks associated with her conduct (much more will be said about this topic in Chapter 8), she does not actually form that specific belief before the neighbour's intervention. Upon being asked about the risks attendant upon her conduct, Jo *then* exhibited the relevant dispositions towards thought and behaviour that merit the ascription to her of the belief that firing the rifle at the wall carries with it a specific risk of killing a person. Only *then* could Jo be said to be aware of that particular risk and

[9] See Kenneth Campbell and Andrew Ashworth, 'Recklessness in assault – and in general?' (1991) 107 *Law Quarterly Review* 187 at 192; Jeremy Horder, 'A critique of the correspondence principle in criminal law' [1995] *Criminal Law Review* 759; Victor Tadros, *Criminal Responsibility* (Oxford: Oxford University Press, 2005), pp. 94–95.

[10] See the distinction between dispositional beliefs and dispositions *to* believe defended in Robert Audi, 'Dispositional beliefs and dispositions to believe' (1994) 28 *Noûs* 419. It is submitted that it would be implausible to say that Jo had the relevant belief about risk all along and that the neighbour merely reminded her of it. What evidence of the dispositions consistent with the proper ascription of that belief is available before the neighbour's intervention? See Philip Pettit, *The Common Mind* (Oxford: Oxford University Press, 1993), p. 47.

potentially reckless with regard to it[11] (if, as will be contended in Chapter 6, there is good reason to believe that recklessness requires awareness of risk).

The position to be defended in Chapter 8 is that Jo's fault before the stage at which the neighbour intervened might, at best, be one of *negligence*. More will be said about the nature of negligence, its place in the criminal law and its relationship with recklessness in due course. For now, it is necessary to consider further the dispositional account of belief that has been sketched in the preceding paragraphs and explore its implications for the criminal law's understanding of awareness of risk.

Believing That *p*

If awareness of/that *p* requires a belief that *p*, then an obvious question arises: what does it mean to believe that *p*? There is, in Anglo-American criminal law doctrine and theory, little clarity over what it means for a defendant to believe that *p*. To an extent, this vagueness is understandable. Belief is very rarely a *mens rea* term in its own right in the Anglo-American systems surveyed in Chapter 2.[12]

Another possible explanation for the scarcity of legal material on this topic is that it is thought to be self-evident what it means to have a belief,[13] that believing is, as the Court of Appeal of England and Wales once put it, 'something which everybody is concerned with almost every day of their lives'.[14] The Court of Appeal appears to think that, if a concept is encountered often enough, it will be understood readily, and so further reflection and elaboration upon its nature is unnecessary. As well as being questionable both empirically and philosophically, this approach is in stark contrast to the extensive efforts of courts and

[11] The question of whether she *is* reckless depends on whether she chose to take the relevant risk, despite her awareness, and whether that choice reflects on her in the appropriate way. See below at Chapter 6.

[12] See, however, Serious Crime Act 2007 (E&W), ss. 45(b), 46(1)(b); Theft Act 1968 (E&W), s. 22(1). See also the list of (principally English and US) examples in Stephen Shute, 'Knowledge and belief in the criminal law', in Stephen Shute and A.P. Simester (eds.), *Criminal Law Theory: Doctrines of the General Part* (Oxford: Oxford University Press, 2001), p. 171, at pp. 172–182.

[13] Cf. *R* v. *Harris* (1987) 84 Cr App R 75 (E&W), at 78 ('"knowledge or belief" are words of ordinary usage in English').

[14] *R* v. *Reader* (1978) 66 Cr App R 33, at 36.

legislatures in the Anglo-American world to explain other core *mens rea* terms such as intention and, indeed, recklessness.[15] Admittedly, if belief is encountered less frequently in the courts, fewer opportunities for such elaboration and clarification will arise. This scarcity of opportunity nevertheless suggests that the courts should be *more* anxious to explain belief clearly, and in detail, when they have the chance. That citizens possess beliefs and encounter the beliefs of others on a daily basis will thus not serve as a *justification* for the failure of Anglo-American courts and legislatures to explain clearly their views on the concept of belief. The fact that beliefs are encountered often in ordinary life is merely an *explanation* for the absence of a clear understanding of belief in law, and a poor one at that.

Some criminal law writers have endeavoured to analyse belief in slightly more detail than Anglo-American courts and legislatures. Many existing accounts tend, however, to be short and negative. Belief is not accorded the same length of treatment as other *mens rea* terms such as intention and recklessness (perhaps because of the scarcity of doctrinal material on the topic). Those discussions that do exist explain what belief *is* by pointing to when belief ascriptions are unwarranted. For example Ashworth and Horder posit that to hold a belief is to 'act without any significant doubt on the [relevant] matter'.[16] This description hints at two important aspects of belief.

First, there is the degree of confidence that the believer is disposed to place in the relevant proposition being true.[17] It is important to bear in mind here the distinction between entertaining a proposition and believing that same proposition to be true. A person can accept *p* for the sake of argument, without believing that *p*. In such circumstances, that person does not have the requisite level of confidence (the appropriate attitude) with regard to the truth of *p* to be said to *believe* it.[18] Similarly, a person

[15] For detailed surveys of these definitional efforts in the context of English law, see Andrew Halpin, *Definition in the Criminal Law* (Oxford: Hart, 2004).

[16] Andrew Ashworth and Jeremy Horder, *Principles of Criminal Law*, 7th edn. (Oxford: Oxford University Press, 2013), p. 480. Cf. *R* v. *Hall* (1985) 81 Cr App R 260 (E&W), at 264.

[17] See Shute, 'Knowledge and belief in the criminal law', pp. 183–184; Stephen P. Garvey, 'What's wrong with involuntary manslaughter?' (2006–2007) 85 *Texas Law Review* 333 at 343.

[18] For further exploration of the distinction between belief and acceptance, see L. Jonathan Cohen, *An Essay on Belief and Acceptance* (Oxford: Oxford University Press, 1992), ch. 1; Raimo Tuomela, 'Belief versus acceptance' (2000) 2 *Philosophical Explorations* 122.

can *suspect* that *p*, but not *believe* that *p*.[19] The difference between these terms is surely the degree of confidence placed in the truth of *p*.[20]

Second, Ashworth and Horder's brief discussion of belief captures the point, to be returned to below, that the defendant's behaviour is an important matter when considering the proper ascription of a belief to a person. That a person is disposed to act as though *p* is true is a good indication (though, as will be seen, not an irrefutable one) that the ascription to her of a belief that *p* is warranted. Despite the fact that it captures this point, it would nevertheless be preferable if Ashworth and Horder's description of the concept of belief was positive, i.e. if it identified the necessary and/or sufficient conditions for saying that a defendant believes that *p*, rather than providing an indication of one instance (where the defendant harbours significant doubts about the truth of *p*) when those necessary and/or sufficient conditions are not satisfied.[21] The difficulty with the negative approach towards defining belief is that it is not clear how many other conditions that would defeat the ascription of a particular belief to a particular defendant exist (if any). A positive account of belief should be able to avoid this ambiguity by stating envisaged necessary conditions of having a belief, and is thus more desirable in principle.

A negative definition of the 'fuzzy'[22] concept of belief need not be a sign of unhelpfulness or defeatism if, as some philosophers have suggested, no positive alternative is readily available.[23] Some criminal law writers have, however, attempted to advance a more positive account of

[19] Garvey, 'What's wrong with involuntary manslaughter?', at 343; *Hall*, at 264.

[20] See, further, Sophie Matthiesson, 'Should the law deal with reckless HIV infection as a criminal offence or as a matter of public health?' (2010) 21 *King's Law Journal* 123 at 127. Of course, utter confidence in the truth of *p* is typically conceived of not in terms of belief but in terms of knowledge (the subject of the next chapter). The point, for the purposes of the present discussion, is that the degree of confidence that a person is disposed to place in *p* being true is important to the proper ascription of a belief that *p*. Ashworth and Horder note this point.

[21] On the desirability of positive definitions, see Glanville Williams, *The Mental Element in Crime* (Jerusalem: Magnes Press, 1965), p. 16.

[22] Eric Schwitzgebel, 'A phenomenal, dispositional account of belief' (2002) 36 *Noûs* 249 at 250.

[23] See e.g. Aaron Z. Zimmerman, 'The nature of belief' (2007) 14(11) *Journal of Consciousness Studies* 61 at 61 ('barring trivial examples, the concept of belief is not equivalent to the content of any definite description'); David Hume, *A Treatise of Human Nature*, 2 vols., ed. David F. Norton and Mary J. Norton (Oxford: Oxford University Press, 2007), vol. 1, 1.3.7(7).

the circumstances in which it is appropriate to ascribe a belief that *p* to a defendant, and their endeavours are worth considering further. Their earlier efforts will, ultimately, form the foundation of the dispositional account of belief (and thus awareness of risk) defended in this book.

It is necessary to begin by dispensing with an account of belief that might seem intuitively plausible.

A Straw Man?

As remarked above, precious few detailed accounts of belief exist in the criminal law literature. Most writers who discuss belief do not make any effort to define it or to explain when belief-ascriptions are warranted. It is thus difficult to know what their account of belief is, and accordingly impossible to establish whether they have fallen into error. In the light of the vagueness of the concept of belief in most of the criminal law literature, it is useful to dismiss an intuitively appealing, but ultimately implausible, positive definition of belief. The following understanding of belief is not found explicitly in the criminal law literature. It is presented here briefly, so that it can be cleared from consideration, with the caveat that it may well be a straw man argument.

The envisaged view would hold that belief is simply a phenomenal matter: a person believes that *p* is the case if she has a conscious, mental experience of *p* – a thought such as 'This is risky, because . . .'[24] Presumably, in the light of the important distinction between entertaining a proposition and believing that same proposition, an appropriate degree of confidence in the truth of *p* would also be required before the defendant can be said properly to believe that *p*. Otherwise, a person can 'believe' that Berlin is the capital of Spain simply by entertaining that conscious thought. That would be an implausible result.

Even if an attitudinal component regarding the truth of *p* were added to the bare phenomenal account of belief sketched above, that account would remain woefully inadequate. A person can properly be said to believe that *p* even when *p* is not being focussed on consciously.[25]

[24] Simons refers to belief as a 'cognitive' matter in Kenneth W. Simons, 'Rethinking mental states' (1992) 72 *Boston University Law Review* 463 at 539. He makes clear that such cognitive states do not necessarily result in a fully conscious experience: at 529–530.

[25] See Michael S. Moore, *Placing Blame: A Theory of the Criminal Law* (Oxford: Oxford University Press, 1997), p. 629.

Consider if Guy believes that George Washington was the first President of the United States.[26] If all that this sentence means is that Guy is focussing consciously on that proposition about George Washington, and has some appropriate attitude towards its truth, then when his conscious attention is focussed elsewhere, Guy's belief presumably ceases to exist. But it can be assumed that (absent some form of mental disorder), if asked a few minutes later about the first President of the United States, Guy would again think of George Washington. Or he would be disposed to correct someone who said that the first President was Thomas Jefferson. Even when his mind wanders onto other topics, Guy presumably retains the dispositions towards thought and conduct that one would expect someone who believes that George Washington was the first President of the United States to have. In those circumstances, it does not appear to be an abuse of language to ascribe the relevant belief about George Washington to Guy, even when he is focussing his conscious attention on a tennis match, or preparing dinner, or anything other than the relevant fact about George Washington. Indeed, even when Guy is asleep, it would still be valid to ascribe the belief about George Washington to him. This is because, once awake, Guy will still be disposed to think, act and react in the way that someone who had the relevant belief would.[27]

The alternative to accepting that a belief that *p* can be ascribed appropriately even when *p* is not being thought about consciously is to hold that, somewhat implausibly, beliefs are formed and evaporate conterminously with the believer's phenomenal experience. On this view, Guy would believe (and thus be 'aware') that George Washington was the first President of the United States only intermittently, when that proposition was being entertained in his 'mind's eye'. Again, this account is not defended explicitly in the context of recklessness and negligence, presumably because of its implausibility.

Of those theorists who have paid real attention to the matter of what it means to believe that *p*, the tendency has been to concentrate not *simply* on conscious experience (though such experiences are important, for reasons that will be explained), but also on the believer's wider

[26] This example is taken from John R. Searle, *Mind: A Brief Introduction* (Oxford: Oxford University Press, 2004), p. 166. See, further, Robert Audi, *Epistemology: A Contemporary Introduction to the Theory of Knowledge* (New York: Routledge, 2011), p. 86.

[27] See Searle, *Mind*, p. 169. D.M. Armstrong, 'Perception and belief', in Jonathan Dancy (ed.), *Perceptual Knowledge* (Oxford: Oxford University Press, 1988), p. 127, at p. 131.

dispositions, particularly towards behaviour. It will be contended that these (often short) accounts offer a more promising grounding for the best understanding of awareness of risk for use in the Standard Account.

Dispositional Accounts of Belief

Griew,[28] White[29] and Husak[30] have followed philosophers such as Ryle by defining belief positively in terms of the defendant's dispositions.[31] On the most defensible reading of these views, beliefs are *ascribed* to an agent on the basis of her existing dispositions, rather than simply what she is focussing her attention on consciously – in her 'mind's eye' – at any given moment. For the purposes of discussion, it is useful to adopt Schwitzgebel's definition of a disposition:[32]

> *Dispositions* can be characterized by means of conditional statements of the form: If condition C holds, then object O will (or is likely to) enter (or remain in) state S. O's entering state S we may call the *manifestation* of the disposition, C we may call the *condition of manifestation* of the disposition, and the event of C's obtaining we may call the *trigger*.

The criminal law's concern, in trials, will be with viewing *ex post* the manifestation of the defendant' dispositions towards thought and behaviour *at the time of the unjustified risk-taking*, in response to appropriate triggers, such as perception of features of the situation regarding the relevant risk.[33]

Different dispositional accounts of belief exist, and it is useful to begin by explaining the one that is often termed 'behaviourism'.

[28] Edward Griew, 'Consistency, communication and codification – reflections on two *mens rea* words', in P.R. Glazebrook (ed.), *Reshaping the Criminal Law: Essays in Honour of Glanville Williams* (London: Stevens, 1978), p. 57, at p. 70.

[29] Alan R. White, *Misleading Cases* (Oxford: Clarendon, 1991), p. 133.

[30] See Husak, 'Negligence, belief, blame and criminal liability', at 210.

[31] See, classically, Gilbert Ryle, *The Concept of Mind* (London: Penguin Books, 1999), pp. 32–33. See also R.B. Braithwaite, 'The nature of believing' (1932–1933) 33 *Proceedings of the Aristotelian Society* 129.

[32] Schwitzgebel, 'A phenomenal, dispositional account of belief', at 250. There is not space here to consider all of the features of dispositions in philosophy. For an overview of the current field, see Troy Cross, 'Recent work on dispositions' (2012) 72 *Analysis* 115.

[33] On the role of perception in belief formation, see below at Chapter 8, section on 'A Preliminary Sketch of Belief Formation'.

Behaviourism

On a simple, 'logical' behaviourist, view (with which Ryle is, perhaps unjustifiably, often associated),[34] the ascription of a belief that *p* to a person is warranted where that person is disposed to *behave* as if he had the relevant degree of confidence in *p* being the case.[35] Again, nobody in the culpable carelessness literature has defended a bare behaviourist conception of belief,[36] but such accounts were at one point popular in the philosophical literature. They are thus worth exploring briefly here.

Consider the following example. Duncan is walking home and approaches a street corner where a large hedge obstructs the view of what is coming the other way. He slows down as he approaches the corner. The behaviourist claim is that the ascription to Duncan of a belief in the risk of collision with a cyclist or pedestrian coming around the corner, which can be mitigated by slowing down, can be made simply on the basis of his conduct and the predictions that can be made from it regarding his future conduct. The relevant question is whether Duncan's conduct is the kind of behaviour that would be exhibited by someone acting as though such a risk existed. Beliefs are important, on this view, only insofar as they explain and predict behaviour.

The behaviourist's contention is that this type of behavioural question, and particularly the prediction of *future* behaviour, is all that matters. There is no need to ask Duncan what *he* took himself consciously to believe – what he experienced mentally, or 'said to himself'[37] – before a certain belief can be attributed to him. The claim is that Duncan's actions and reactions warrant the ascription of certain beliefs, and (on some accounts) his verbal reporting of a conscious experience that he thought he had the relevant belief at the time of acting would be simply another piece of behaviour to take into account.[38] Such self-reporting is not, however, necessary for the proper ascription of a belief – other behaviour might warrant the same conclusion.

[34] Ryle's account is far more nuanced: see Schwitzgebel, 'A phenomenal, dispositional account of belief', at 259–260.

[35] See Ryle, *The Concept of Mind*, pp. 117–118. The main other form of behaviourism is 'methodological' behaviourism, which denies that beliefs are useful in explaining human behaviour. See Moore, *Placing Blame*, p. 630.

[36] There are, however, hints of such an account in Richard Posner, 'The jurisprudence of skepticism' (1987–1988) 86 *Michigan Law Review* 827 at 868–871.

[37] Cf. *Hall*, at 264.

[38] Cf. Price, *Belief*, pp. 256–259; B.F. Skinner, *Science and Human Behavior* (New York: Macmillan, 1953), p. 280.

It is worth repeating that this ascription of a belief that there was a risk attendant upon not slowing down does not even depend on an inference *back to* what was going on in Duncan's mind. The behaviourist claim is not that conduct is 'external' evidence of an 'internal' mental state of believing that *p*.[39] That process of inference from 'external' action to 'internal' conscious mental experience is the mark of dualism, i.e. the idea that a person consists in a physical body (which can be observed by other people) and a non-physical mind (which cannot). For present purposes, it is sufficient to note that behaviourists aim to avoid the involvement of dualistic mental states in their explanations and predictions of human behaviour, principally because they find them unhelpfully mysterious or irrelevant, for reasons that need not be considered further here.[40] Dualism is, however, a topic to be returned to below, in the context of Duff's theory of 'practical indifference'.[41] Although not a behaviourist in the sense described above, Duff is sceptical about dualism, and this attitude informs his account of recklessness.

The difference between the behaviourist and the dualist claims is, nevertheless, important for understanding the account of belief presented here. It is the difference between thinking (i) that to behave in a certain way *is itself* what merits the ascription of a belief that *p* and (ii) that to behave in a certain way is simply *evidence* of an inner mental state (to which the believer has privileged access), the existence of which merits the ascription of (or is co-extensive with) a belief that *p*.[42] Those who would subscribe to the latter view are perhaps in danger of identifying a phenomenal mental state (e.g. consciousness of risk) with the belief that *p*.[43] This brings with it the risk of embracing the implausible account of belief sketched above. A wider 'mental state' – based account of belief would avoid this difficulty, but none has been forthcoming, at least explicitly, in the literature on culpable risk-taking.

A bare, behaviourist description of belief nevertheless has its limitations, which is perhaps why it too has not been defended explicitly in the criminal law literature in this area. The main difficulty with behaviourism in the context of ascribing culpability is that it is not always improper to

39 See, further, Moore, *Placing Blame*, pp. 630–633.

40 See R.A. Duff, *Intention, Agency and Criminal Liability* (Oxford: Blackwell, 1990), ch. 6.

41 Duff's account of recklessness is explored below in Chapter 7.

42 Cf. J.F.M. Hunter, 'Believing' (1980) 5 *Midwest Studies in Philosophy* 239 at 247.

43 Even if they do not, they owe an explanation of *what* the relevant mental state *is* that is being evidenced in behaviour: Eric Schwitzgebel, 'In-between believing' (2001) 51 *The Philosophical Quarterly* 76 at 82.

ascribe a belief that *p* to two people who behave in vastly different ways, in the light of their *other* properly ascribed beliefs and desires, etc.[44] A range of behavioural responses is consistent with the ascription of a belief that *p*. Katri walks out of the door wearing a jacket, whilst Jill does not. A behaviourist observer might conclude that Katri should be ascribed the belief that it is cold outside, whilst Jill should not. Appropriate predictions about future behaviour could then follow.

The difficulty with this analysis is that it might instead be the case that Katri *desires* to avoid getting cold, whilst Jill does not. Consider if Jill would respond, if prompted, that it is cold, would encourage others to dress warmly, would dress her child warmly, etc. If she has these *other* dispositions towards behaviour that are consistent with the ascription of a belief that it is cold outside, and they are simply not visible in her conduct in the circumstances (because other people and her children are absent), then the conclusion that Jill does not hold the belief that it is cold might be considered counter-intuitive. *Particular* acts seem neither necessary nor sufficient to lead to the proper ascription of a belief that *p*.

One way of overcoming this difficulty is to read in further conditions that must be satisfied before Jill will behave in line with the behaviour to be expected of a holder of the relevant belief, e.g. the presence of another person or her children. On this view, Jill would rightly be said to believe that it is cold outside, because of the range of hypothesised behavioural dispositions she *would* display in those altered circumstances. This means, however, that behaviourist accounts of the dispositions required for the proper ascription of a belief that *p* would become extremely specific, as they seek to capture all of the preconditions for the performance of the relevant behaviour that would be expected of someone who held the relevant belief.[45] Furthermore, the validity of these ascriptions becomes particularly vulnerable epistemically, because of their heavy reliance on counterfactual propositions about what an agent *would* do in different circumstances. If the evidence available is the person's behaviour alone, then the ascription of beliefs seems an extremely difficult

[44] See Eric Schwitzgebel, 'Knowing your own beliefs' (2009) 39(1) *Canadian Journal of Philosophy* 41 at 44; John R. Searle, *The Mystery of Consciousness* (New York: New York Review of Books, 1997), p. 138.

[45] For discussion, see Cohen, *Belief and Acceptance*, p. 9. Cf. the argument for a more contextualised understanding of moral responsibility, less dependant on *generic* traits, in John Doris, *Lack of Character: Personality and Moral Behaviour* (Cambridge: Cambridge University Press, 2002).

enterprise. If beliefs about risk are to do useful work in the criminal law, it ought to be easier to ascribe them, so that the finder of fact can reach a decision in an individual case.

As a result of these shortcomings of behaviourism, more nuanced dispositional accounts of belief have been presented in the philosophical literature. These seek to *build on* behaviourism's dispositions towards action and reaction, by also consulting a wider pool of evidence when considering the ascription of beliefs to an agent. It is submitted that, when it comes to gaining the best understanding of awareness of risk on the Standard Account, these more nuanced accounts of belief are more promising than behaviourism. It will be further argued that, ultimately, a more nuanced dispositional account of belief comes close to the existing legal position in some Anglo-American systems. It thus fits well with a theoretical explanation of that position.

Schwitzgebel's Account of Belief

A useful, wider dispositional account of belief is presented by Schwitzgebel, who conceives of the proper ascription of beliefs in terms of the coherence of an agent's dispositions with a 'dispositional stereotype'.[46] A 'dispositional stereotype' is a set of dispositions that ordinary people would expect agents who hold the particular belief to conform to, at least ordinarily. For Schwitzgebel, there are three types of disposition that are crucial to belief ascription,[47] all of which are relevant to the context of awareness of risk.

First, as the behaviourists note, there are dispositions to behave in certain ways. Walking to work, I can ascribe to the person walking ahead of me the belief that continuing along this road will lead her to reach her intended destination. Again, the appropriateness of this ascription does not appear to rest on a claim about what she is experiencing mentally (though it does presume some level of rationality on her part).[48] She certainly need not be repeating, 'This road leads to where I want to go' to

[46] See Schwitzgebel, 'A phenomenal, dispositional account of belief'. [47] Ibid., at 252.

[48] For a philosophical defence of this presumption of rationality, and the importance of viewing ourselves and others as 'planning agents', see Michael E. Bratman, *Intention, Plans and Practical Reason* (Cambridge, MA: Harvard University Press, 1987). See, further, Peter Cane, 'Fleeting mental states' (2002) 59 *Cambridge Law Journal* 273 at 280–283; Zimmerman, 'The nature of belief', at 64–65; Daniel C. Dennett, *The Intentional Stance* (Cambridge, MA: MIT Press, 1987).

herself, silently, for my belief ascription to be valid. This is not to say that my belief ascription is bound to be correct – perhaps she is hopelessly lost, mentally disordered, or absent-mindedly wandering, with no particular intended destination. It is nevertheless possible for the ascription to take place properly, without appealing to the idea that the walker's behaviour allows me to infer the existence of a silent inner monologue about where she was going, on the basis of which a belief can be ascribed properly.[49]

Accepting this point is not, however, to endorse bare behaviourism and to attempt to eliminate phenomenal experiences from what it means to believe that *p* is the case. The second types of disposition identified by Schwitzgebel are phenomenal, which means that they give rise to certain mental experiences. Upon seeing the corner, Duncan remembers consciously the time he was nearly knocked over by an over-eager cyclist and feels anxious. Such a mental image, and conscious experience of foreboding, might be said to merit the ascription of a *belief* to Duncan that this risk exists. Similarly, if Jill has the mental experience of thinking that it is cold outside, then she might (within limits, to be discussed below) be ascribed properly the belief that it is cold outside, even if her behaviour suggests the opposite conclusion. The woman walking ahead of me in the street might harbour grave conscious doubts about whether this road does in fact lead to her intended destination, perhaps rendering insecure my initial ascription of belief to her, which was based on her observed behaviour alone.[50]

Schwitzgebel views the agent's phenomenal experiences, the manifestations of dispositions towards conscious experiences, as important. He does not, however, prize them over all other evidence in his quest to analyse the proper conditions for the ascription of belief. Having a particular phenomenal disposition is, for him, *part* of what it means to be properly ascribed the belief that *p* is true, but it is not *necessary* for the appropriate ascription of a belief that *p* is true.[51] A person *can* be

[49] Duff, *Intention, Agency and Criminal Liability*, p. 160.

[50] Of course, a behaviourist might reply that the only *evidence* of such phenomenal experiences available to a third party, such as a criminal court, will be self-reporting by the agent. And such self-reporting is merely an instance of behaviour, from which an ascription of belief can be made. It is submitted that not much turns on this knotty point for the purposes of explaining the concept of awareness on the Standard Account.

[51] Cf. David J. Chalmers, *The Conscious Mind: In Search of a Fundamental Theory* (Oxford: Oxford University Press, 1996), p. 20.

described appropriately as believing that *p* is the case, even if she does not manifest a relevant phenomenal disposition on a particular occasion. The person walking ahead of me on my way to work might be thinking about cats or an ill relative, etc. Similarly, a person can have a particular phenomenal experience (a thought such as 'This is risky . . .') whilst behaving in a way that seems inconsistent with a belief that a danger exists. These phenomenal and behavioural dispositions are parts of a pool of evidence that might mean belief that *p* is the case can be ascribed to an agent. The propriety of that ascription does not, however, rely on a perfect union of behaviour and phenomenal experience. This is a point that will be returned to later in this chapter.

Schwitzgebel's third type of disposition is cognitive, concerning matters such as how to solve a mathematical problem. This type of disposition might be relevant to calculations about risk and mistakes made in assessing whether a certain risk exists or not. Cognitive dispositions are less visible in the existing literature on culpable carelessness but will make occasional reappearances in the remainder of this book.

Schwitzgebel's nuanced, dispositional account of when an agent can be said properly to believe that *p* is eminently suited to the criminal law context. Indeed, something like it has been defended by White in a previous, short (two-page) discussion of belief in the criminal law: 'Believing that *p* is normally a disposition to behave as if *p* or appropriately to *p*, where "behaving" covers both acting and reacting, both in word and deed, with both external and internal responses, both cognitively and emotionally.'[52] White's description of when it is 'normally' proper to ascribe a belief that *p* to a defendant speaks to the behavioural, phenomenal and cognitive dispositions identified by Schwitzgebel. It is not obvious from White's work why the caveat 'normally' is included, however. This hesitation about the proper nature of belief does not appear necessary, and will thus not be defended here.

It is worth noting, at this stage, an obvious counter-argument to Schwitzgebel and White's position. This is that they endorse an account of belief that is far too vague for the purposes of the criminal law, and thus inappropriate for offering even part of the explanation of when taking a certain risk with the interests of others is the mark of culpability. The next section analyses this criticism and ultimately rejects it.

[52] White, *Misleading Cases*, p. 133.

Complicating Beliefs

Why might the dispositional account of belief sketched in the previous section prove problematic for use as part of the Standard Account? Consider Duncan again. Sometimes when he approaches the hedge, Duncan has the phenomenal experience of foreseeing – in his 'mind's eye' – the cycling collision, but fails routinely to behave in accordance with it by slowing down. He fails to warn others who are visiting his home about the danger. He does not experience a thought about the risk mentally every time he walks home. In short, Duncan fails to respond in the various ways that someone might be expected to respond, if he were to be appropriately ascribed the belief that there was a risk of being hit by a cyclist if caution is not exercised at the relevant corner. Duncan simply has, on occasion, the relevant phenomenal experience that would be expected of someone credited appropriately with that belief.

There is a range of explanations for the lack of consistency in Duncan's responses. Most obviously, perhaps he *does* believe that he might collide with a cyclist but is simply unmoved by this belief. He does not care if he collides with another pedestrian/cyclist. This explanation seems to prize phenomenal dispositions above all else (the relevant phenomenal disposition appears to be the only one demonstrated in this case). It has already been asserted that a bare phenomenal account of belief is problematic.

Another explanation is that Duncan does *not* merit the ascription of the relevant belief, because he lacks the full set of dispositions that would be expected of a believer.[53] This conclusion does not necessarily follow. Failing to have *all* of the relevant dispositions that one would expect a person with certain beliefs to display is not in itself unusual. Consider the case of a person who is afraid to stand close to the edge of the observation level at the top of the Empire State Building. Such a disposition is presumably consistent with the dispositional stereotype of a person who believes that the building is not structurally sound. What if, however, that person is, despite this fear, disposed to avow in speech that the building is structurally sound, to encourage others to visit the building, to

[53] See, similarly, Price, *Belief*, p. 256; Roger A. Shiner, 'Intoxication and responsibility' (1990) 13 *International Journal of Law and Psychiatry* 9 at 21. Cf. Ruth B. Marcus, 'Some revisionary proposals about belief and believing' (1990) 50 *Philosophy and Phenomenological Research* 133 at 143.

climb the stairs without trepidation, etc.? He is simply terrified when presented with the view at the top.

Tamar Szabó Gendler labels such outlying dispositions towards thought and behaviour as 'aliefs' (more specifically, 'norm-discordant aliefs').[54] She explains, 'An alief is, to a reasonable approximation, an innate or habitual propensity to respond to an apparent stimulus in a particular way.'[55] Aliefs are, Gendler contends, beliefs' irrational cousins. An alief will not change with new evidence,[56] she suggests, whilst a belief will. In consequence, the person in the Empire State Building might be described as having an *alief* regarding the structural soundness of the building (he is disposed to act inconsistently with his other dispositions), rather than a *belief* that it is not structurally sound.

If aliefs are defined so as to be non-responsive to new evidence, they appear to form quite a narrow category. A person who alieves that the building is not structurally sound can take steps to address this. She can expose herself to the building often, in an attempt to avoid the undesired reaction (she might engage, in other words, in immersion therapy).[57] Duncan can attempt to change his habit of not slowing down to make it consistent with his reflective judgments about the risk of collision and the desirability of avoiding such mishaps. Of course, such a strategy might not *always* work, but it might at least *sometimes* work.[58] Some things that might seem, initially, to be aliefs are thus sensitive to correction through habituation.[59] Aliefs appear to be the remainder, which is presumably relatively small.

Given the potentially very small area that they cover, it might be wondered whether adding aliefs to beliefs is worth the effort. A simpler, alternative explanation for a person who, despite acting in a way incompatible with a belief that *p*, yet has phenomenal experiences that might be expected of a believer, is that he holds conflicting

[54] See Tamar S. Gendler, 'Alief and belief' (2008) 105 *Journal of Philosophy* 634; Tamar S. Gendler, 'Alief in action (and reaction)' (2008) 23 *Mind and Language* 552, both reproduced in Tamar S. Gendler, *Intuition, Imagination and Philosophical Methodology* (Oxford: Oxford University Press, 2010).

[55] Gendler, 'Alief in action (and reaction)', at 553.

[56] On the connection between belief and evidence, see below at Chapter 8, section on 'A Preliminary Sketch of Belief Formation'.

[57] Eric Schwitzgebel, 'Acting contrary to our professed beliefs or the gulf between occurrent judgment and dispositional belief' (2010) 91 *Pacific Philosophical Quarterly* 531 at 539.

[58] See, further, the discussion of negligence as failure of belief below at Chapter 8.

[59] See Gendler, 'Alief in action (and reaction)', at 566.

dispositions.[60] Perhaps this is the situation that Duncan is in, in which case it is difficult to tell what beliefs he should really be ascribed (if any). Accepting that it is not crystal clear *what* Duncan believes, and suspending judgment, seems a simpler and preferable solution to this type of case than the endorsement of concepts such as aliefs. In the context of culpable carelessness, such conflicting dispositional evidence would mean entertaining reasonable doubt over whether the defendant believed that a relevant risk existed (and thus was 'aware' of that risk) and acquitting her of an offence requiring recklessness.

None of the points in the previous paragraph should be particularly surprising: few people have completely integrated and coherent systems of dispositions, even if they strive for them,[61] and sometimes establishing what another person believes is difficult.[62] Furthermore, there is scope for argument with a person about what they believed. If a person's dispositions towards thought and behaviour are at odds with one another, external observers might sometimes be able to ascribe beliefs correctly in circumstances where the believer herself cannot.[63] The believer might well be self-deceived as to the significance of her dispositions towards action and reaction.[64] A brief point of clarification should be made here: the believer of course has privileged access to her phenomenal experiences and need not *infer* them ('What am I thinking?').[65] But if beliefs are not identified with phenomenal experience alone, then a person can be mistaken about the beliefs she holds.

Inconsistencies in disposition will, in some cases, remove the appropriateness of a belief attribution. If *all* that Duncan does is sometimes report a mental experience of risk, and yet otherwise fails to act in the

[60] See, generally, E. Schwitzgebel, 'Acting contrary to our professed beliefs'. Cf. the discussion of 'cognitive dissonance' in Moore and Hurd, 'The culpability of negligence', at p. 319.

[61] Cf. the classic discussion of 'consonance' between what an agent takes herself to believe and her behaviour in Leon Festinger, *A Theory of Cognitive Dissonance* (Stanford, CA: Stanford University Press, 1957), ch. 1.

[62] Cohen, *Belief and Acceptance*, p. 33.

[63] Marcus, 'Some revisionary proposals about belief and believing', at 141–142. The ascription of beliefs that a believer would not identify herself as holding must not be taken too far: Price, *Belief*, p. 105.

[64] Self-deception has not been discussed at great length in the literature on culpable carelessness. See Garvey, 'What's wrong with involuntary manslaughter?', at 374–378; Moore and Hurd, 'Punishing the awkward, the stupid, the weak and the selfish', at 155–156.

[65] See T.W. Smyth, 'Unconscious desires and the meaning of desire' (1972) 56 *Monist* 413 at 418.

way that might be expected, a claim that he *believes* in the content of that experience might be insecure on a nuanced dispositional account such as Schwitzgebel's. The ascription might still be warranted – perhaps, as noted above, the defendant's failure to act in accordance with the relevant behavioural dispositions belies his lack of concern about the particular risk(s) believed to exist, rather than the absence of belief(s) altogether. Duncan's failure to behave as might be expected of a person whose dispositions warrant the ascription of a belief that *p* is also consistent, however, with his not *really* believing that *p* is the case at all. In the criminal law context, a finder of fact is going to have to make the best of the evidence available, having received instruction in the task. The finder of fact will have to decide whether they are sure, beyond reasonable doubt, that the defendant's manifested dispositions towards thought (if reported to the finder of fact) and behaviour warrant the ascription of a belief that there is a particular risk attendant upon φ-ing.[66]

Schwitzgebel accepts that there is no non-arbitrary way of establishing the point at which a person possesses sufficient dispositions (and of which type) to merit the ascription of a particular belief.[67] If a defendant has three of the ten various dispositions that we might expect him to have if he believes that *p*, then does he believe that *p*? What if he has seven? What kind of explanations for failures to respond in appropriate ways will be consistent with a belief that *p*? What these questions (which cannot be answered in advance of a particular factual scenario) demonstrate is that it is not clear that belief is a binary matter, once a dispositional account of that concept has been embarked upon.[68] A person might, in light of her conflicting dispositions, be 'in-between' believing that *p* and not believing that *p*.[69] Juries can be given guidance on these dispositional aspects of belief sketched above and (as they are at present) on the importance of consulting a wide pool of evidence, but ultimately the law cannot be too prescriptive.[70]

[66] The dispositions will have been manifested because the finder of fact will be asking this question after the alleged wrongdoing has been performed.

[67] Schwitzgebel, 'A phenomenal, dispositional account of belief', at 252–253; Pettit, *The Common Mind*, p. 32.

[68] Cf. Leo Katz, *Bad Acts and Guilty Minds: Conundrums of the Criminal Law* (Chicago, IL: University of Chicago Press, 1987), pp. 208–209.

[69] See Schwitzgebel, 'In-between believing'.

[70] This pool of evidence should include the reactions of the defendant to the materialisation of the risk. See, similarly, *McDowall* v. *HM Advocate* 1998 JC 194 (Scot), at 198.

If it is to make use of the concept of belief and avoid straying too far from the everyday ascriptions of belief that are entered into by citizens, the criminal law will need to pay attention to the nuance and fluidity that has been detected above in relation to the attribution of belief. It might appear unsatisfactory – from the point of legal certainty and consistency – to allow the finder of fact to draw an arbitrary line, which leaving belief or awareness undefined would encourage them to do.[71] There is, however, not necessarily a knockdown Rule of Law argument that means a dispositional analysis of belief must be abandoned. In cases involving recklessness, the judge or jury could be asked to consider whether *they* consider that the defendant acted, and/or had a phenomenal experience, and/or employed a cognitive process, in a manner consistent with the dispositions that point towards the propriety of the ascription of a belief that there was a specific risk involved in φ-ing. This approach would, in essence, involve the jury in setting the dispositional stereotype that they take to be relevant to the ascription of a belief in risk and seeing – from all of the evidence available (within the confines of the existing rules of evidence) – whether the defendant measured up to it adequately. As long as this approach was adopted consistently, it is submitted that the Rule of Law is respected adequately. A difficulty would emerge if belief was understood in very different ways in different contexts, for the reasons explained in Chapter 3. But that is not what is proposed here.

The explanation of belief above is similar to what juries around much of the Anglo-American world are directed to do in cases involving recklessness: from all the evidence the jury is asked whether the defendant was aware of the relevant risk. That is consistent with taking not only the defendant's testimony of his mental experience, but also his actions and behavioural responses, and perhaps his cognitive processes (if evident), into account when deciding whether he had the dispositions that are consistent with believing that *p*. But this is not to endorse dualism – to say that *all* the jury has is 'external' evidence that might point towards an elusive 'internal' mental state of belief or awareness of risk. True, Anglo-American courts make that connection between action and mental state often.[72] The contention here is that this inference from the 'external' to the 'internal' is not, however, a *necessary* step. Sometimes the ascription of a belief that there is a risk is merited even where the defendant's conscious mind is focussed on other matters. To deny this is

[71] Cf. White, *Misleading Cases,* p. 134.

[72] See Duff, *Intention, Agency and Criminal Liability*, pp. 28–29.

tantamount to doubting that the person walking in front of me believes that doing so will lead her to her destination, if her conscious attention is focussed elsewhere.

Now that a dispositional, belief-centred account of awareness of risk has been outlined, it is useful to map it onto the existing literature on that topic. This process will demonstrate how a dispositional account of belief can offer simpler explanations than accounts describing different types of conscious experience or 'levels' of belief. It will be contended that gaining real clarity on awareness of risk is aided by seeing things dispositionally.

Revisiting the Existing Literature

In his earlier work, Duff distinguished between three levels of knowledge, which are relevant to the discussion of awareness of risk: *explicit*, *tacit* and *latent* knowledge.[73] Although presented in terms of knowledge, rather than belief,[74] Duff's model provides a useful structure for the analysis of the views of those criminal law theorists who have debated the relationship between phenomenal experience, cognition and behaviour. It will be contended that each of Duff's forms of knowledge is comparable to a type of *disposition* encountered above. Rather than describing three *sorts* of knowledge or belief, Duff is better understood to be explaining three types of dispositional situation relevant to the ascription of beliefs about risk and the formation of beliefs about risk.

Explicit Knowledge

'Explicit knowledge' refers to propositions contemplated consciously by the defendant – for instance the express, conscious thought 'Performing this action is risky . . . I might kill someone.'[75] Such knowledge has also been referred to as 'reflective'[76] or 'occurrent'[77] to indicate the need for conscious entertainment of the relevant proposition.

[73] R.A. Duff, '*Caldwell* and *Lawrence*: the retreat from subjectivism' (1983) 3 *Oxford Journal of Legal Studies* 77 at 80.

[74] The role of knowledge in descriptions of awareness of risk is discussed below at Chapter 5.

[75] See Duff, '*Caldwell* and *Lawrence*', at 80.

[76] Garvey, 'What's wrong with involuntary manslaughter?', at 343.

[77] Galen Strawson, *Freedom and Belief* (rev. edn.) (Oxford: Oxford University Press, 2010), p. 117.

Another writer describes explicit knowledge as 'consciousness of risk'.[78] This label marks out the importance of conscious attention being paid to the relevant proposition but comes potentially unstuck when consideration is given to the fact that the boundaries of the term 'conscious' are controversial. The concept of consciousness will be returned to later in this book.[79] A short detour to consider the meaning of consciousness is necessary here, however, to clarify the boundaries of the term.

Criminal law theorists and philosophers use the word 'consciousness' to mean different things. For instance, following Freud,[80] Moore identifies the relevant sense of consciousness at work in explicit knowledge by referring to the believer's phenomenal, mental experience – to what she is paying attention to at a particular moment in time.[81] There must be 'some datable mental process [that] is occurring that we experience, and . . . our attention is directed upon that mental experience'.[82] On this view, the reader is (hopefully) *consciously* aware of the words on this page because they are the focus of attention, and thus are experienced mentally.[83] For Moore, the conscious should be compared with the 'preconscious'. The preconscious consists of those mental states that guide conduct, without being focussed on consciously. What marks out something as *pre*conscious, as opposed to another type of state, is that it *can* be focussed on consciously through a (minor) act of will.[84] Examples of this process will be given below, in the discussion of *tacit* knowledge. For now, it is sufficient to note that Moore contends that, as the preconscious is still part of the agent's mental states, it can still play a role in her practical

[78] Eric Colvin, 'Recklessness and criminal negligence' (1982) 32 *University of Toronto Law Journal* 345 at 361.

[79] See the discussion of Ferzan's 'opaque' recklessness, below at Chapter 6, section on 'Ferzan's "Opaque" Recklessness'.

[80] See Sigmund Freud, *The Standard Edition of the Complete Psychological Works of Sigmund Freud*, ed. J. Strachey, 24 vols. (London: Vintage, 2001), vol. 19, pp. 14–15. For criticisms of a focus on a Freudian model, see Neil Levy, *Consciousness and Moral Responsibility* (Oxford: Oxford University Press, 2014), pp. 5–6.

[81] See Michael S. Moore, *Law and Psychiatry: Rethinking the Relationship* (Cambridge: Cambridge University Press, 1984), p. 127; Michael S. Moore, *Act and Crime: The Philosophy of Action and Its Implications for Criminal Law* (Oxford: Oxford University Press, 1993), p. 151. See also Chalmers, *The Conscious Mind*, p. 4.

[82] Moore, *Law and Psychiatry*, p. 127.

[83] The relationship between attention and consciousness is somewhat controversial amongst experts in consciousness – see Christopher Mole, 'Attention and consciousness' (2008) 15 *Journal of Consciousness Studies* 86.

[84] Moore, *Act and Crime*, pp. 151–152.

reasoning, and thus conduct guided by preconscious mental states can still be the subject of responsibility.[85] Preconsciousness is, in other words, important for Moore; he simply wishes to distinguish it from consciousness.

The description of explicit knowledge as 'consciousness of risk' is, accordingly, supported by Moore's usage of the term 'consciousness'. Other writers, however, would caution against Moore's using the term 'consciousness' to describe *only* phenomenal experiences. For instance, Dennett distinguishes between $aware_1$ (which is synonymous with Moore's 'consciousness') and $aware_2$ (which is, arguably, synonymous with Moore's 'preconsciousness').[86] Dennett thinks that both $aware_1$ and $aware_2$ are states of consciousness: to be conscious of something is to be *either* $aware_1$ *or* $aware_2$ of that thing. This is why the label 'consciousness of risk' is unclear.

Regardless of whoever is right about the proper extent of the term 'consciousness', Duff's explicit knowledge is – for the purposes of the discussion in this chapter – what Moore identifies as consciousness, and Dennett refers to as $awareness_1$.

With this clarification made, it is necessary to make another one. A difficulty with the term 'consciousness' is that it can be used in two senses: intransitive (i.e. Hana is conscious when awake, unconscious when asleep) and transitive (i.e. Hana is conscious *of/that p*).[87] It is important to be clear on which sense of the word is intended here. In this discussion, consciousness is being used in the transitive sense.

Now that it is clear what explicit knowledge is taken to be, it can be seen that it can be described in dispositional terms. Explicit knowledge is, it is submitted, the manifestation of a disposition to have a certain phenomenal experience in certain circumstances. The presence of such

85 Michael S. Moore, 'Responsibility and the unconscious' (1979–1980) 53 *Southern California Law Review* 1563 at 1624–1626; Moore, *Law and Psychiatry*, p. 326.

86 See Daniel C. Dennett, *Content and Consciousness* (Routledge & Kegan Paul, 1969), ch. 6. Moore seems to accept this equation: Moore and Hurd, 'The culpability of negligence', at 318 (n. 30). It is not entirely clear that Moore's 'preconscious' awareness must *always* be guiding action, but many of his examples of such a mental state are of habitual action. It is thus unclear whether the simple ability to report back mentally a proposition in appropriate circumstances would count as 'preconscious' awareness. Cf. Daniel I.A. Cohen, 'The jurisprudence of unconscious intent' (1996) 24 *Journal of Psychiatry and Law* 511 at 555.

87 See Stanislas Dehaene et al., 'Conscious, preconscious, and subliminal processing: a testable taxonomy' (2006) 10 *Trends in Cognitive Sciences* 204 at 204.

a disposition might provide a basis for the ascription of a belief to a defendant. If Rajiv has the 'explicit' phenomenal experience of thinking 'I might kill someone if I proceed with my plan . . .', triggered by his perception of those features of the situation which give rise to that risk, then this might provide grounds for ascribing to him a belief that his action might kill someone. Whether that ascription is merited would depend, ultimately, on the coherence of his *other* dispositions (towards behaviour and cognition) with the relevant dispositional stereotype that someone who holds the relevant belief would be expected to live up to. Again, the judge or jury would have to consult as wide a pool of evidence as possible in order to establish whether it is correct to ascribe the relevant belief to a defendant.

As will be seen in the next section, Duff's 'tacit knowledge' is similarly explicable in terms of dispositions and belief ascriptions.

Tacit Knowledge

As Duff explains, tacit knowledge is '*shown* in my actions and reactions: in the way my actions are patterned towards my goals; in what I say if asked about what I am doing; in my lack of surprise when [for example] fire behaves as fire usually does, or my surprise if it does not'.[88] Other writers refer to this form of knowledge as 'dispositional',[89] which is telling (although, given the account of belief developed above, potentially confusing).

It is submitted that what Duff identifies as tacit knowledge, when put into the language employed above, is the coherence of the agent's behaviour – her actions and reactions[90] – with manifestations of a relevant dispositional stereotype. His discussion of the structure of actions also points towards the manifestation of cognitive dispositions. The defendant who is *tacitly* aware of a risk attendant upon φ-ing will have *manifested* a sufficient number of the relevant behavioural and/or cognitive dispositions in her actions (e.g. her hesitance in acting, the way in which she plans her behaviour) and reactions (e.g. her lack of surprise at the

[88] Duff, '*Caldwell* and *Lawrence*', at 88 (emphasis in original). On the connection between belief ascriptions and surprise, see Price, *Belief*, pp. 275–277; Dennett, *The Intentional Stance*, p. 81.

[89] Garvey, 'What's wrong with involuntary manslaughter?', at 344.

[90] See, further, Cohen, *Belief and Acceptance*, p. 9.

result) to merit the ascription of the belief that the relevant risk existed at the time she took it.[91]

The finding that a defendant had tacit knowledge of risk is not, for Duff, rendered null and void by the absence of an explicit, conscious thought such as 'This is risky . . .' at the time the risk was taken. Were tacit knowledge co-extensive with conscious thought in this manner, then it would be indistinguishable from explicit knowledge. As Duff indicates, a person's actions can be guided towards the agent's ends, in the light of her beliefs, even when those actions and beliefs are not being focussed on consciously.[92] This idea might be difficult to grasp at first but should become clearer through the consideration of examples.

First, consider Ellie, who works at King's College, Cambridge. On her way to work, and lost in thoughts of legal theory, Ellie is stopped by a tourist, who asks for directions to the college. Ellie contemplates the tourist's question mentally and responds with appropriate directions, demonstrating the dispositions towards thought and action that merit the ascription of a belief to her that the college is, say, two streets away, on the right. Assuming such a process means focussing mental attention on the proposition that the college is two streets away, on the right, then Ellie now has explicit knowledge (in Duff's terminology) of its location. Before the tourist's intervention, however, the knowledge of the college's location existed but was tacit. It was guiding Ellie's conduct (otherwise, she would not be successful in finding her way to work), even without the associated inner, mental monologue ('King's College is this way . . . right turn ahead . . .'). The tacit nature of this knowledge freed up conscious space for other worthy tasks, such as thinking about legal theory.[93]

As Moore notes, the content of what Duff calls tacit knowledge can usually become explicit through a minor act of will.[94] Through attending

[91] Cf. Husak, 'Negligence, belief, blame and criminal liability'. Husak contends that beliefs should be discovered through *both* evidence of manifested dispositions and (non-leading) questioning about other dispositions that were present but not manifested (at 216). It is submitted that this approach will fail to distinguish meaningfully between what the defendant believed at the time of φ-ing and what the defendant is now, following questioning at trial, capable of believing. On the account presented in this book, the distinction between extant and potential beliefs is the line between recklessness and negligence, and it will be argued at the close of Chapter 8 that this line should be clear.

[92] See, further, D.M. Armstrong, *Belief, Truth and Knowledge* (Cambridge: Cambridge University Press, 1973), p. 21.

[93] See Moore, *Act and Crime*, p. 152.

[94] See, similarly, the discussion of 'explicit beliefs' in Galen Strawson, *Freedom and Belief*, pp. 117–118.

consciously to the matter, Ellie can render explicit that which was guiding her conduct. The relevant information was preconscious but is now conscious, in Moore's terminology; Ellie had awareness$_2$ but now has awareness$_1$ in Dennett's terminology. What is important about tacit knowledge, on Moore's account, is that there is some form of mechanism within the defendant that allows for this conscious experience of the relevant proposition.[95] Without such a mechanism, the mental state that guides and explains the defendant's behaviour would be beyond her conscious grasp, and thus – as Moore pointed out – beyond the scope of her practical reasoning.[96] But, to be clear, to be 'tacitly' or 'preconsciously' aware of a risk does not require that such a conscious grasping takes place: it is a matter of the possession of the relevant *capacity* to take a matter into account in conscious deliberation over what to do, at the time of acting, that determines the extent of the agent's responsibility. It is not the *exercise* of that capacity that counts.[97]

It is submitted that this point about capacity can be linked back to the dispositional theory of belief defended earlier in this chapter. If a person is not disposed to *ever* have the relevant phenomenal experience consistent with the ascription of a belief that *p*, then any such ascription is probably unwarranted. This explains why the law should, even on the dispositional account presented in this book, still care about the *capacity* to have the relevant phenomenal experience consistent with a belief that a particular risk attends φ-ing.

One other point of clarification should be given before another example of tacit knowledge is presented. It would be peculiar to think of the 'move' from preconscious to conscious knowledge as a process of inference – i.e. to think that Ellie focussed consciously on what her actions disclosed ('What am I doing?'). Rather, through attending to the tourist's question, Ellie had a phenomenal experience that was in line with the dispositional stereotype with which her conduct also cohered. She was disposed to have a particular phenomenal experience in certain circumstances, just as she was disposed to act and react in terms of her behaviour in certain circumstances (e.g. by changing direction at the appropriate point in the journey). Ellie is not in the position of an external observer, charged with establishing what ascriptions of belief are appropriate in the light of her own behaviour, reported phenomenal

95 Searle, *Mind*, pp. 166–167. 96 See above note 85.

97 See the discussion of Ferzan's 'opaque' recklessness below at Chapter 6, section on 'Ferzan's "Opaque" Recklessness'.

experiences and employed cognitive processes. Her explicit knowledge that *p* simply *is* her phenomenal experience of the fact that *p*. She has 'privileged access' to this experience.[98]

(This does not mean, for the reasons explained above, that Ellie's conscious experience is the definitive source of authority on what she believes.[99] It might be appropriate, all things considered, to say that Ellie does not *really* believe that *p*, if – for example – the relevant phenomenal experience is divorced entirely from her other dispositions towards thought, action and reaction, but she is unable to see this, perhaps because she is self-deceived.[100] It would not be appropriate to deem Ellie mistaken about her phenomenal experiences in the same way. This is why it is vitally important to distinguish between those experiences and her beliefs.)

It is worth considering a second, popular example of the explicit/tacit distinction: driving. Although learning to drive requires a lot of (explicit) conscious concentration, the movements involved soon become habitual, so the thought 'Time to change gear . . .' need not occupy the driver's conscious mind.[101] These manoeuvres will ultimately be completed smoothly and without the need to think them through consciously.[102]

Similarly, the risks associated with certain manoeuvres, which must be contemplated consciously by a learner ('It's risky if I don't check the blind spot . . .'), can soon guide behaviour without focussed mental attention.[103] Experienced drivers look 'automatically' in the blind spot. The driver's conscious attention can remain focussed on the conversation with a passenger, listening to the radio, and so on, and she will typically drive successfully, i.e. without taking unjustified risks of colliding with other road users. If the driver wishes to, however, she can focus consciously on the individual aspects of the risks attendant upon driving and make conscious decisions about them.[104] Consider driving in snow,

[98] Moore, *Law and Psychiatry*, p. 256.

[99] Ibid. The same point can be made about desires: Thomas W. Smyth, 'Unconscious desires and the meaning of desire' (1972) 56 *The Monist* 413 at 422.

[100] See Ilman Dilman, *Freud and the Mind* (Oxford: Basil Blackwell, 1984), p. 53.

[101] John McCrone, *Going Inside: A Tour Round a Single Moment of Consciousness* (London: Faber, 1999), p. 135; Duff, *Intention, Agency and Criminal Liability*, p. 159.

[102] Cf. John R. Searle, *Intentionality: An Essay in the Philosophy of Mind* (Cambridge: Cambridge University Press, 1983), pp. 150–151.

[103] Moore, *Act and Crime*, pp. 129–130; Peter Carruthers, *Consciousness: Essays from a Higher-Order Perspective* (Oxford: Oxford University Press, 2005), pp. 71–72.

[104] Moore, *Act and Crime*, p. 152.

where such increased, 'explicit' concentration is required, or teaching a learner driver how and when to change gear safely.[105] The actor need not make such information about driving in the snow or changing gear explicit in order to drive in normal conditions successfully. Life would be lived at a much slower pace if people did have to focus their conscious attention on elements of ordinary actions and the attendant risks in this way.[106]

Thus far, then, it has been seen that Duff's explicit and tacit knowledge find their analogues in the dispositional account of belief advanced above. The next section demonstrates that latent knowledge can be similarly described in dispositional terms.

Latent Knowledge

Latent knowledge is, on Duff's account, the defendant's knowledge about risk in general, which can be employed in order to determine whether a specific risk exists in a particular scenario.[107] It is also referred to as 'passive' knowledge,[108] 'experiential' knowledge[109] and – perhaps most usefully – 'background' knowledge[110] in the criminal law theory literature.

As will be explained in much greater detail in Chapter 8, latent knowledge of risks in general is obviously useful in the formation of beliefs about the riskiness of *a specific instance* of

105 Daniel C. Dennett, *Consciousness Explained* (Boston: Little, Brown, 1991), p. 277.

106 Christopher Hookway, 'Epistemic norms and theoretical deliberation' (1999) 12 *Ratio* 380 at 384–386; McCrone, *Going Inside*, p. 135; Martha C. Nussbaum, *Upheavals of Thought: The Intelligence of Emotions* (Cambridge: Cambridge University Press, 2001), p. 72; Nomy Arpaly, *Unprincipled Virtue: An Inquiry into Moral Agency* (Oxford: Oxford University Press, 2002), p. 21.

107 Duff, '*Caldwell* and *Lawrence*', at 80. See, similarly, Kenneth W. Simons, 'Dimensions of negligence in criminal and tort law' (2002) 3 *Theoretical Inquiries in Law* 283 at 302. Potentially confusingly, because of the above discussion of Moore's use of Freudian theory, Freud described the preconscious as a form of 'latent' awareness: Freud, *The Standard Edition of the Complete Psychological Works of Sigmund Freud*, vol. 19, pp. 14–15.

108 Victor Tadros, *Criminal Responsibility* (Oxford: Oxford University Press, 2005), p. 257; Kenneth W. Simons, 'Does punishment for "culpable indifference" simply punish for "bad character"? Examining the requisite connection between *mens rea* and *actus reus*' (2002–2003) *Buffalo Criminal Law Review* 219 at 251; M. Wasik and M.P. Thompson, '"Turning a blind eye" as constituting *mens rea*' (1981) 32 *Northern Ireland Legal Quarterly* 328 at 331.

109 Colvin 'Recklessness and criminal negligence', at 361.

110 Tadros, *Criminal Responsibility*, p. 250; Garvey, 'What's wrong with involuntary manslaughter?', at 342.

φ-ing.[111] Catriona's belief that her friend's expensive vase is at risk of being smashed if it is knocked is a vital ingredient for the formation of the belief that it would be risky for her – at this moment – to allow her young children to play near it. There are, however, other ingredients required for the formation of the *specific* belief that allowing her children to play here, now, is risky. She must believe, for instance, that the vase is in the room, that the children might knock the vase, and so on. In short, as will be explained in greater detail in Chapter 8, the formation of the dispositions consistent with a belief that there is a risk attendant upon φ-ing relies on the presence of various 'background' beliefs (themselves to be understood in terms of the defendant's dispositions), and the drawing of the relevant inferences from them and the defendant's perceptions.

Much latent knowledge is – like tacit knowledge – capable of being made explicit (i.e. experienced mentally) through an act of will, though this might sometimes be time-consuming (e.g. trying to remember a fact about the conductivity of certain metals that was learnt a long time ago).[112] The process of turning conscious attention to a piece of latent knowledge can, however, be easy. If prompted, most people can explain confidently and without significant effort the risks attendant upon reversing a car without turning around, and other risky aspects of driving.[113] Again, such latent knowledge does not, on Duff's account, spring into existence simply upon conscious reflection – the agent had the relevant latent knowledge before the question was posed.

As with explicit and tacit knowledge, latent knowledge can be conceived of in terms of the agent's dispositions. To possess latent knowledge of a risk attendant upon φ-ing is, it is submitted, a disposition to, in appropriate circumstances, behave in a certain way, have a certain phenomenal experience or employ a certain cognitive process.[114] Explicit and tacit knowledge are examples of the *manifestation* of the defendant's dispositions that point to the appropriateness of the ascription of a belief that a particular risk is associated with φ-ing. Latent beliefs are dispositional, too, but point rather to beliefs about other matters

[111] Tadros, *Criminal Responsibility*, pp. 250–251.

[112] Colvin, 'Recklessness and criminal negligence', at 362.

[113] See also Kimberly K. Ferzan, 'Opaque recklessness' (2000–2001) 91 *Journal of Criminal Law & Criminology* 597 at 631; Jeremy Horder, 'Gross negligence and criminal culpability' (1997) 47 *University of Toronto Law Journal* 495 at 510–511; *Murphy*, at 440.

[114] Michael S. Pardo and Dennis Patterson, *Minds, Brains and Law: The Conceptual Foundations of Law and Neuroscience* (Oxford: Oxford University Press, 2013), pp. 138–140.

(e.g. information from which a belief that a particular risk is associated with φ-ing could have been formed).[115]

It has thus been seen that each of Duff's types of knowledge finds its analogue in the earlier discussion of the dispositions relevant to the proper ascription of beliefs to a person, on the basis of their behaviour, cognitive processes and reported phenomenal experiences. The next section will discuss a variation on Duff's tripartite scheme, and how it compares to the dispositional account of awareness presented in this chapter.

An Alternative Model

Duff later abandoned the tripartite categorisation of types of knowledge. He collapsed explicit and tacit knowledge together into 'actual' knowledge and contrasted 'actual' knowledge with 'latent' knowledge.[116] The advantage of this move is that it makes clear that explicit and tacit knowledge are relevant to criminal liability only when guiding conduct[117] – when they are 'online' in Levy's terminology.[118] I can have explicit (but not 'actual') knowledge of the risks attendant upon φ-ing whilst sitting at my desk thinking about risks, simply by focussing conscious attention on those risks.[119] ('Is it risky to leave the gas on in the oven overnight?') Without a connection between this knowledge and an action, it is nevertheless difficult to see its relevance to my criminal liability. What is given by the Standard Account is an explanation of the circumstances in which a defendant can be culpable *regarding* a wrong – in this context, the taking of an unjustified risk with another person's protected interest in an offence of endangerment, or the materialisation of risk in complete offences. Such an explanation must draw an explanatory link between the defendant as an agent and the instance of wrongdoing for which she is responsible.[120] If my explicit knowledge of the risks attendant upon φ-ing is engaged when I am not actually doing the wrong thing by φ-ing, then it cannot explain why my φ-ing was culpable. In the absence of a token of wrongdoing, the question about my culpability never arises.

[115] See the discussion of such background beliefs below at Chapter 8, section on 'A Preliminary Sketch of Belief Formation'.
[116] Duff, *Intention, Agency and Criminal Liability*, pp. 159–160.
[117] Shute, 'Knowledge and belief in the criminal law', at 187 (n. 71).
[118] Levy, *Consciousness and Moral Responsibility*, p. 32. [119] See ibid., p. 33.
[120] Cf. A.P. Simester, 'Responsibility for inadvertent acts' (2005) 2 *Ohio State Journal of Criminal Law* 601 at 606.

It is useful, in order to clarify this point further, to make a point that will be returned to in the next chapter.[121] It does not appear to be incredibly important that a person can have what appears to be fault (*mens rea*) if there is never a question of a wrong (*actus reus*) being perpetrated. Although it is an obvious point, it is worth stating explicitly: the reason I am not criminally liable, when sitting at my desk thinking about risks, is that I am *doing nothing wrong*. What Duff's discussion of 'actual' knowledge might be used to indicate is the need for a union of wrongdoing and culpability, of (broadly) *actus reus* and *mens rea*.

Might the language of 'actual' knowledge be salvageable, if understood as requiring a union between φ-ing being wrongful and a defendant's culpability for φ-ing? It is submitted that the answer is 'No'. The language of 'actual' knowledge collapses the important explanatory distinctions between explicit and tacit knowledge.[122] Duff's decision to combine explicit and tacit knowledge speaks to his general anti-dualist project in *Intention, Agency and Criminal Liability*.[123] Duff's general approach, analysed in more detail in Chapter 6, is to move from attempting to interpret *mental events* to attempting to interpret *actions*, in their social context. Although he is not a behaviourist,[124] it is submitted that Duff, like them, comes close to under-emphasising the importance of phenomenal experience, in order to avoid what he regards as the pitfalls of dualism (which, it will be remembered, is the idea that human beings consist of a body which is observable and a mind that is not). No such project regarding dualism is being pursued here, and thus the distinction between explicit and tacit knowledge – between phenomenal experience and action-guiding information, capable of being focussed on consciously – shall be maintained.

When understood in this manner, and translated into the terminology of beliefs ascribed on the basis of manifested dispositions towards thought and behaviour, Duff's account is instructive. This is because of its useful identification of *tacit* knowledge, the form of knowledge that guides actions and reactions, even without conscious attention being paid to it. The argument to be developed in the coming chapters is that, on the

121 See section on 'The Absence of Justification'.

122 It has also been pointed out that the actual/latent distinction suggests that latent knowledge is not *actual* knowledge, when surely it is: Horder, 'Gross negligence and criminal culpability', at 510 (n. 52).

123 See Duff, *Intention, Agency and Criminal Liability*, ch. 6. See also Shiner, 'Intoxication and responsibility'.

124 See Duff, *Intention, Agency and Criminal Liability*, pp. 124–126.

best understanding of the Standard Account, tacit knowledge – when conceived of in terms of dispositions towards behaviour and cognition consistent with the ascription of a belief about a particular risk – marks the borderline between recklessness and negligence. The reckless defendant manifests a sufficient number of *dispositions* to merit the ascription to him of a belief that there is a specific, substantial risk attendant upon φ-ing and is unmoved by that belief in circumstances that show him to be insufficiently motivated by the interests of others. Again, it is worth noting again explicitly that the manifestation of a phenomenal disposition is not a *necessary* condition for awareness of risk. The negligent defendant's manifested dispositions towards thought and behaviour, by contrast, does not merit the ascription of a belief that such a risk exists but demonstrates her insufficient concern with the interests of others in failing to *form* that belief, in the light of her *other* beliefs and perceptions regarding the situation. It is in this way that, it will be contended, the reckless defendant more clearly demonstrates her lack of concern for the interests of others. This is why, it will be concluded, the line between recklessness and negligence should always be clearly maintained. If the Standard Account is understood in this way, it is submitted that it is defensible in theory.

Conclusion

This chapter has presented an account of awareness of risk in terms of beliefs in risk and has explained belief in terms of the coherence of the believer's behaviour, phenomenal experience and cognitive processes with a dispositional stereotype. It has then mapped this account onto the existing literature, using Duff's types of knowledge as a useful guide. It has been demonstrated that Duff's original types of knowledge (and their equivalents in the work of other theorists) can be explained in dispositional terms, and that dispositional approach will be maintained for the remainder of this book.

This move from knowledge to belief and disposition is advantageous. The language of knowledge, when used in relation to culpable carelessness, can raise problems, with which this book will have to deal. Some doctrinal and theoretical sources refer to awareness of risk in terms of *knowledge* of risk, which – as will be demonstrated in the next chapter – means they require *more* than a belief that the relevant risk exists. It will be shown there that this move from belief to knowledge is problematic and should be resisted.

5

Beyond Belief: Knowledge and Awareness of Risk

It has been argued that, on the 'Standard Account' of culpable carelessness in the Anglo-American systems surveyed in Chapter 2, awareness of risk should be understood in terms of *believing* that a particular risk exists. Belief should, in turn, be understood in terms of the coherence of the defendant's dispositions towards thought and behaviour with a relevant 'dispositional stereotype'.[1] Some of the existing literature on awareness, and its relationship with consciousness, has been re-explained in these terms.[2] This chapter addresses a different aspect of the criminal law theory literature on recklessness and negligence, which conceives of awareness that a certain proposition is the case (shortened, for ease of reading, to *p*) in terms of *knowledge* that *p*. The understandings of knowledge employed in this literature are always parasitic on belief, and thus these arguments are to the effect that *more* than belief should be required for awareness of risk on the Standard Account. This argument will be rejected in this chapter.

The chapter begins by outlining a knowledge-based argument about awareness of risk presented by Douglas Husak. It then analyses the understanding of knowledge in terms of foresight of a virtual certainty, which is adopted in many Anglo-American systems of criminal law in relation to *consequences*. This understanding of knowledge encounters difficulties. This leads to consideration of an alternative account, which conceives of knowledge in terms of justified true belief. The various problems with this account will be explained, before it is concluded that understanding awareness of risk in terms of knowledge is deeply problematic in the context of the criminal law. The better account of awareness of risk, for use in relation to the Standard Account, is in terms of the defendant's beliefs about risk alone, i.e. the view defended in Chapter 4.

[1] A term borrowed from Eric Schwitzgebel, 'A phenomenal, dispositional account of belief' (2002) 36 *Noûs* 249.

[2] See above at Chapter 4, section on 'Revisiting the Existing Literature'.

Husak on Knowledge

In his recent, helpful discussions of awareness of risk, Husak presents the 'speculative and tentative' view that awareness of risk is co-extensive with *knowledge* of risk.[3] To be aware of the risks attendant upon a piece of conduct (φ-ing), the defendant must *know* about those risks. On this view, knowledge of risk is the 'essence' of recklessness.[4] If negligence is to unjustifiably lack awareness of a risk, then it follows that, on Husak's proposal, to be negligent is to unjustifiably *lack* knowledge of the risks associated with φ-ing.

Husak's claim that knowledge that there is a risk is co-extensive with awareness that there is a risk attracts support from various sources. First, Anglo-American courts have on occasion suggested that a reckless defendant *knows* the relevant risk exists,[5] and have, in other contexts, equated awareness that *p* with knowledge that *p*.[6] It should be noted, however, that these equations of knowledge and awareness were not the product of detailed argument or apparent reflection. The courts of the main Anglo-American systems have failed to engage fully with the concept of awareness, particularly in the context of recklessness and negligence.

It is worth noting that Husak also reads the American Law Institute's Model Penal Code (MPC) to require knowledge of risk in its definition of recklessness[7] (a definition that, as seen in Chapter 2, has virtually been

[3] Douglas N. Husak, 'Negligence, belief, blame and criminal liability: the special case of forgetting' (2011) 5 *Criminal Law and Philosophy* 199 at 208; Douglas N. Husak, 'Distraction and negligence', in Lucia Zedner and Julian V. Roberts (eds.), *Principles and Values in Criminal Law and Criminal Justice* (Oxford: Oxford University Press, 2012), p. 81, at p. 83. See, further, Daniel M. Treiman, 'Recklessness and the Model Penal Code' (1981) 9 *American Journal of Criminal Law* 281 at 351–352, 354.

[4] John E. Stannard, 'Subjectivism, objectivism and the Draft Criminal Code' (1985) 101 *Law Quarterly Review* 540 at 541. See, similarly, Larry Alexander and Kimberly K. Ferzan with Stephen J. Morse, *Crime and Culpability: A Theory of Criminal Law* (Cambridge: Cambridge University Press, 2009), p. 33. Cf. G.R. Sullivan, 'Knowledge, belief and culpability', in Stephen Shute and A.P. Simester (eds.), *Criminal Law Theory: Doctrines of the General Part* (Oxford: Oxford University Press, 2002), p. 207, at p. 207.

[5] E.g. *R* v. *ADH* 2013 SCC 28, [2013] 2 SCR 269 (Can), at [16]; *R* v. *Stephenson* [1979] QB 695 (E&W), at 703; *Royall* v. *R* (1991) 172 CLR 378 (HCA), at 395.

[6] See e.g. *Atwal* v. *Massey* [1971] 3 All ER 881 (E&W), at 882. See also Criminal Code Act 1995 (Cwlth), s. 5.3.

[7] See American Law Institute, *Model Penal Code and Commentaries (Official Draft and Revised Comments)*, 3 vols. (Philadelphia: American Law Institute, 1980), vol. 1, s. 2.02(2)(c).

adopted by many, though certainly not all, US states).[8] This is because the MPC's definition of knowledge requires the defendant to be *aware* of certain matters (awareness is undefined), and Husak 'supposes' that this same understanding of awareness must apply in cases of recklessness.[9] One difficulty with this analysis is that the MPC does not require the reckless defendant to be 'aware' of a risk explicitly.[10] It requires the 'conscious disregard' of a ('substantial and unjustifiable') risk. Presumably, Husak would contend, such disregard can be demonstrated only where the defendant *is* aware of the risk.[11] Furthermore, the MPC's definition of negligence mentions the defendant's failure to be 'aware' (again undefined) of the relevant risk attendant upon φ-ing.

Second, the Oxford English Dictionary defines awareness in terms of knowledge.[12] Chapter 3 explained that, because it must be lived by, and in serious cases applied by, laypersons, it is important that Anglo-American criminal law's concepts cohere with 'everyday', 'ordinary' understandings to an extent, as long as they are defined consistently within those boundaries. Thus an ordinary language understanding of awareness of risk, in terms of knowledge of risk, should not be discarded lightly by the criminal law, in its efforts to communicate judgments of wrongdoing and culpability.

Given the above points, Husak's view that awareness that there is a risk attendant upon φ-ing should mean *knowledge* that there is a risk attendant upon φ-ing, and not merely a *belief* that such a risk exists, needs to be explored further. One difficulty with proceeding with such an inquiry is that criminal law doctrine and theory have defined knowledge in different ways. The form of knowledge relied on by doctrine and theory is, however, always parasitic on belief. In the light of the criminal law's refusal to utilise them, this chapter will accordingly not consider *other* types of knowledge (such as knowledge from perception), which

[8] Notably, in the Washington penal code, the MPC wording has been amended to deem reckless a person who '*knows of* and disregards a substantial risk': Wash Rev Stat ss. 9A.08.010(1)(c) (emphasis added).

[9] Husak, 'Negligence, belief, blame and criminal liability', at 208.

[10] Admittedly, knowledge *is* mentioned in the MPC's definition of recklessness (and also its treatment of negligence), but this was intended by the drafters to pertain only to the substantiality of the risk and the justification of the defendant's taking it. See Eric A. Johnson, 'Knowledge, risk and wrongdoing: the Model Penal Code's forgotten answer to the riddle of objective probability' (2011) 59 *Buffalo Criminal Law Review* 507 at 516.

[11] This point is returned to in the next chapter's consideration of the concept of *choice* and its relationship with recklessness.

[12] See www.oxforddictionaries.com/definition/english/awareness?q=awareness.

epistemologists have discussed at length.[13] It will be remembered that the purpose of this book is to offer the best theoretical yet practical account of the Standard Account. It is not an exercise in what knowledge might mean in an 'ideal' system of criminal law.

Believing That It Is Virtually Certain That There Is a Risk

One common understanding of the *mens rea* term 'knowledge',[14] which finds some support in relation to *consequences* in Anglo-American doctrine and theory, defines knowing that *p* in terms of a belief that *p* is true to a certain degree of probability.[15] Typically,[16] the line is drawn at the stage of virtual certainty: Gerry knows a certain proposition (*p*) when he believes that it is virtually certain that *p*.[17] In the light of the discussion of belief-ascriptions in Chapter 4, this belief should be ascribed where Gerry is disposed to think and behave in a sufficiently similar manner to someone who should be said to believe that it is virtually certain that *p*. He should assent to the proposition that it is virtually certain that *p*, act as though it is virtually certain that *p*, have relevant conscious experiences regarding the virtual certainty of *p*, and so on.

The definition of knowledge in terms of virtual certainty should be more controversial than it has been to date in criminal theory, because it allows defendants to *know* things that are not true. Suppose that Gerry can be ascribed the belief that it is virtually certain that, if he flicks a light switch, the building will explode, killing everybody inside. He is cautious around the light switch, would report verbally that the relevant risk exists to the requisite degree of certainty, would assent to others saying the risk is real, will see in 'his mind's eye' the

[13] See H.H. Price, *Belief* (London: George Allen & Unwin, 1969), pp. 86–91; D.M. Armstrong, *Belief, Truth and Knowledge* (Cambridge: Cambridge University Press, 1973), ch. 10; Keith Hossack, *The Metaphysics of Knowledge* (Oxford: Oxford University Press, 2007), ch. 1; Blake Mayers-Shulz and Eric Schwitzgebel, 'Knowing that *p* without believing that *p*' (2013) 47 *Noûs* 371.

[14] And sometimes the general concept of knowledge: H.A. Pritchard, 'Knowing and believing', in A.P. Griffiths (ed.), *Knowledge and Belief* (Oxford: Oxford University Press, 1967), p. 60, at pp. 62–63.

[15] American Law Institute, *Model Penal Code*, s. 2.02(2)(b) can be read in this way – see Alexander and Ferzan with Morse, *Crime and Culpability*, p. 32.

[16] Though not always – see, e.g. Criminal Code Act 1995 (Cwlth), s. 5.3, which defines knowledge in terms of awareness that *p* 'exists or will exist in the normal course of events'.

[17] See, e.g. American Law Institute, *Model Penal Code*, s. 2.02(2)(b)(ii).

consequences of flicking the switch and would warn others of the risk. In fact, no such risk of explosion or death exists. It is submitted that, as a simple matter of what words mean, Gerry does not *know* the building will explode if he flicks the switch, because the building will not, in fact, explode in those circumstances. In short, a person can *know* something only if it is, as a matter of fact, true.[18] Although it makes sense to speak of false beliefs (even in virtual certainties),[19] 'false knowledge' is more difficult to make sense of.[20]

Additionally, if awareness of risk were synonymous with knowledge of risk, and knowledge meant a belief in virtual certainty, this would lead to counter-intuitive conclusions. It would mean, for instance, that Henry is aware of a risk attendant upon φ-ing only if he is *virtually certain* that there is a risk attendant upon φ-ing. If Henry thinks it is merely very likely there was a risk attendant upon φ-ing, he would not be aware of that risk, and thus could not even begin to be reckless as to that risk on the Standard Account. Consider, however, if Henry contemplates the risks attendant upon φ-ing and concludes that it is merely probable that, if he proceeds with φ-ing, there is a risk that another person will be injured as a direct result. He acts, reacts and has phenomenal experiences consistent with the ascription of this belief. The conception of knowledge as a belief in the virtual certainty of an outcome seems to lead to the conclusion that Henry is unaware of the risk of injury associated with φ-ing. But it is submitted that he *is* aware of that risk – he can (presumably) investigate the risk further, explain it to others, warn them of it, take steps in his practical reasoning and conduct designed to avoid the risk, and so on. The account of awareness that is parasitic on beliefs in virtual certainties leads to implausible conclusions about what agents are aware of, and that is why it should be dispensed with in relation to the Standard Account's understanding of awareness of risk.

Husak does not adopt the first understanding of knowledge, and thus avoids this air of unreality.

[18] This perhaps explains the House of Lords' insistence, in the English case of *Woollin*, that a belief that it is virtually certain that death or serious bodily harm will occur is insufficient for so-called oblique intention (arguably a form of knowledge). The virtual certainty must *also* exist in fact: *R* v. *Woollin* [1999] 1 AC 82, at 96.

[19] See Stephen Shute, 'Knowledge and belief in the criminal law', in Stephen Shute and A.P. Simester (eds.), *Criminal Law: Doctrines of the General Part* (Oxford: Oxford University Press, 2002), p. 171, at pp. 184–185.

[20] See Armstrong, *Belief, Truth and Knowledge*, pp. 137–138.

Justified, True Belief

Husak instead adopts the famous, though by no means universal, philosophical understanding of knowledge as justified true belief (what might be termed the 'tripartite account').[21] Husak contends that a belief that there is a risk associated with φ-ing is necessary but not sufficient for awareness that there is such a risk. To constitute awareness of risk, the defendant's belief that there is a risk must also be *justified* and *true*.

This account of knowledge is superior to the virtual certainty model, in terms of its relationship with an ordinary language understanding of knowledge. This is because the tripartite account links knowledge with truth. A person cannot, on Husak's understanding of knowledge, *know* something that is in fact false. In the example above, Gerry does not know (because it is not true) that there is a risk the building might explode, resulting in the deaths of those inside it, if he flicks the light switch. The tripartite account gets to the appropriate conclusion in this case: Gerry merely believes (falsely, and presumably without adequate justification) that this risk exists, on the assumption that he has a sufficient number of dispositions consistent with the proper ascription of that belief.

Oliver Johnson suggests another advantage of the tripartite model of knowledge. He claims that the tripartite model coheres with what most laypeople mean when they use the noun 'knowledge', or the verb 'to know', in the sense of knowledge/knowing *that p*.[22] Johnson thinks that, upon reflection, a layperson might well conclude that, for Andrew to know that leaving the Christmas tree lights on overnight carries with it a risk of fire, the following must happen: (a) Andrew must believe that this conduct involves a risk of fire (which will involve him possessing various dispositions, as explained in the previous chapter); (b) Andrew must be able to offer adequate justification for having the dispositions relevant to the ascription of that belief (perhaps Andrew has been informed by a reliable government advertising campaign about the dangers of leaving the Christmas tree lights on overnight, and this has shaped his

[21] Husak, 'Distraction and negligence', p. 83. The tripartite account of knowledge also underpins Johnson, 'Knowledge, risk and wrongdoing'.

[22] Oliver A. Johnson, 'The standard definition' (1980) 5 *Midwest Studies in Philosophy* 113 at 114. Another sense of knowing is 'knowing how' (e.g. knowing how to play the piano). This sense of knowledge is not relevant here, but see, however, Jason Stanley and Timothy Williamson, 'Knowing how' (2001) 98 *Journal of Philosophy* 411.

dispositions);[23] and (c) leaving the Christmas tree lights on for too long must *in fact* carry with it the risk of fire. This posited coherence with lay understanding suggests that the tripartite account of knowledge could potentially be employed in the criminal law.

Despite these points about ordinary language and understanding, it is submitted that two points weigh against employing the tripartite account of knowledge in order to better understand the Standard Account's concept of awareness of risk. The first reason is that an enquiry into whether the defendant's extant beliefs about risk are *justified* is, in the context of the criminal law, often unnecessary and problematic. What is more important, in this context, is the defendant's motivation with regard to the beliefs she has. Second, when used as an account of *knowledge*, the tripartite account suffers from serious philosophical deficiencies, which the criminal law should not ignore. These points will be considered in turn, before it is concluded that simple *belief* that a particular risk exists (as explained in the previous chapter) ought to be sufficient for a finding of awareness of risk on the Standard Account.

The Absence of Justification

When employing the *mens rea* concept of knowledge, Anglo-American criminal law seems unconcerned about the defendant's justification for having the dispositions consistent with the proper ascription of certain beliefs. It will be contended that this is entirely appropriate where the defendant's belief is that there is a risk attendant upon φ-ing (even though a different approach will be adopted in Chapter 8 in cases where the defendant positively believes there is *no* such risk).[24]

The law's ambivalence to the matter of justification in cases where the defendant holds the belief relevant to culpability can be seen in the MPC's definition of knowledge, which distinguishes between conduct, circumstances and consequences. On the reading of the MPC that is most compatible with the tripartite account, the knowing defendant must – in relation to conduct and circumstances – be aware (believe)[25] that he is performing certain conduct/that a circumstance exists (i.e. the

[23] Such adverts used to be prevalent in the United Kingdom.

[24] At Chapter 8, section on 'Incorrect Beliefs about Risk'.

[25] It is assumed that the matter of justification cannot be smuggled back in simply through understanding 'awareness' here to meaning justified true belief.

truth condition).[26] (As mentioned above, to know that a *consequence* will come about is, on the MPC's model, to be practically certain that the result will materialise.)[27]

The MPC's definition of knowledge in relation to conduct and circumstances includes no requirement that the defendant have adequate justification for forming the dispositions consistent with the ascription of the relevant belief.[28] There is no need – on the face of the MPC – for an enquiry into the reasons for which the defendant was disposed appropriately towards *p*, and such reasons are essential to the matter of justification of belief.[29]

Consider Kyle, who has the relevant dispositions consistent with a belief that he is carrying prohibited drugs in a sealed package because (and only because) Terry, a pathological liar, has told him that is the case. In the event, the package really *does* contain prohibited drugs (a circumstance element). It would appear that Kyle *knows* (in law) that what he is possessing is prohibited drugs (the relevant circumstance), on the reading of the MPC mentioned above: he is aware (he believes) that he is in fact possessing prohibited drugs (the truth condition). Assuming beliefs based *solely* on the testimony of persons thought by the believer to be pathological liars are unjustified, Kyle nevertheless fails to form knowledge on the tripartite account. He lacks a justification for holding that dispositions that warrant the ascription to him of his true belief. On the tripartite account of knowledge, Kyle *believes* (unjustifiably) that he possesses drugs, and this belief is incidentally true. He does not *know* that he possesses drugs.

This lack of concern about the defendant's justification for having dispositions that merit the ascription of a belief[30] is fortunate. Presumably – absent reliable testimony from the defendant, who has good reason to lie – the prosecution would be unable in most cases to prove beyond reasonable doubt that the defendant possessed adequate justification for

26 American Law Institute, *Model Penal Code*, s. 2.02(2)(b). The truth condition is not strictly necessary, on the MPC's definition of knowledge, as seen below.

27 Ibid., s. 2.02(2)(b)(ii).

28 It also mixes together a *mens rea* element (belief that *p*) and part of the *actus reus* (the fact that *p*). This point is returned to later in this chapter.

29 This view relies on the adoption of what Kvanvig refers to as a 'subjective' account of justification for belief. See Jonathan L. Kvanvig, 'Subjective justification' (1984) 93 *Mind* 71.

30 At least in cases where the defendant is not suffering from mental disorder (a matter beyond the scope of this book).

having the dispositions consistent with the ascription of the relevant belief. It might also be wondered why such proof matters. The defendant who persists in her conduct, despite her properly ascribed belief that it involves risks, seems to demonstrate just as much culpability where her beliefs are unjustified as when they have adequate justification. She fails to be moved by her beliefs, and in doing so demonstrates insufficient concern for the interests of others – the gist of culpability.

Absent a concern with justification, and assuming that in these circumstances Kyle could be convicted of an offence involving *known* possession of drugs, the MPC might be read to conceive of knowledge regarding conduct and circumstances in terms of beliefs that turn out to be true.[31] If so, it is not clear what this definition of knowledge adds to the account of awareness sketched in the previous chapter: there is a belief that *p* (a matter of *mens rea*), and, to result in a conviction, it must coincide with the fact that *p* (a matter of *actus reus*).[32] If that is all that is, in fact, required for knowledge in cases like Kyle's, then it would be far simpler, semantically, to refer to the 'subjective'[33] *mens rea* element of *belief*, not knowledge, and leave the matter of whether the matter is true as an 'objective' element of the *actus reus*.[34] It is submitted that this is exactly what the criminal law should do. If the layperson would think that knowledge requires justified true belief (as Johnson suggests), then to ensure *ex ante* clarity and limit the discretion of *ex post* application, the law should avoid using the word 'knowledge' when it does not mean to appeal to the idea of justification and wishes to bifurcate between the matters of belief (*mens rea*) and truth (*actus reus*).[35]

It is worth noting that the rejection of the requirement of justification does not render the criminal law unduly harsh, as might be feared. Defendants who, without adequate justification, form the dispositions consistent with the ascription of a belief that there is a risk attendant

[31] See, similarly, *R* v. *Saik* [2006] UKHL 18, [2007] 1 AC 18 (E&W), at [26].

[32] See, further, Kenneth W. Simons, 'Rethinking mental states' (1992) 72 *Boston University Law Review* 463 at 541.

[33] 'Subjective' is used, reluctantly, in preference to 'internal', in order to avoid the connotation that *mens rea* is simply about an 'internal' mental state to which only the defendant has direct access. Cf. the discussion of dualism above at Chapter 4, section on 'Behaviourism'.

[34] Note here that the belief must be that there is a particular risk attendant upon φ-ing (a risk that, in the circumstances, it is unjustified for the defendant to take), and it is assumed that *mens rea* elements will not exist independently of *actus reus* elements.

[35] See above at Chapter 3.

upon φ-ing are not in jeopardy of automatic conviction. First, although awareness of risk is *necessary* for recklessness on the Standard Account, it is not *sufficient*. As explained in the next chapter, the defendant must also, through her failure to be moved by that belief, demonstrate insufficient concern for the interests of others. That is not envisaged as being a trivial standard.

Second, without an *actus reus* of factual unjustified risk-taking in a general endangerment offence (if such offences are included in the relevant jurisdiction), or the materialisation of the relevant risk in complete offences, there can be no conviction, even if there is awareness of risk and a failure to be moved adequately by it.[36] The justification criterion appealed to by Husak is not, in short, saving defendants from unmerited convictions. It can thus be discarded without rendering those with beliefs that there is a risk attendant upon φ-ing automatically in peril of conviction. It is still up to them whether to choose to take the risk, and that risk-taking must have a basis in fact.

Despite these points about justification, Husak might contend that important work is nevertheless being done by all elements of the tripartite account, i.e. that the criminal law *ought to* adopt the tripartite account of knowledge in the context of awareness of risk, even if it does not do so at present. It would even be coherent to contend that the argument above has pointed only to the inappropriate use of the word 'knowledge' when that is not what the criminal law *means*, rather than a problem with the tripartite account itself. It is thus necessary to probe the idea of justified true belief further, which means considering the 'infamous but slightly irritating'[37] problems raised by 'Gettier cases'.[38] It will be argued in the next section that Gettier cases cannot be avoided by the criminal law, and this will lead to the conclusion that the tripartite account of knowledge should not be used in relation to awareness of risk.

Gettier Cases

Gettier cases demonstrate that a person can hold a justified true belief that *p* without it seeming appropriate to say that she knows that *p*.

[36] This book does not deal with offences of strict liability and assumes that some form of fault must be proved in relation to each aspect of the *actus reus*.

[37] Jonathan Dancy, *Introduction to Contemporary Epistemology* (Oxford: Blackwell, 1985), p. 26.

[38] See Edmund L. Gettier, 'Is justified true belief knowledge?' (1963) 23 *Analysis* 181.

A clear example of a Gettier case, for those readers unfamiliar with them, is as follows. Chloë is clearing out the attic of her recently purchased house when she sees what she takes to be a pistol.[39] What she sees is, in fact, a realistic-looking toy left by the previous owner. Unbeknownst to Chloë, the previous owner has *also* left a real pistol in a box in another part of the attic, which Chloë has never looked in. Chloë lives in a jurisdiction where it is an offence to knowingly possess a firearm without a licence. Assuming that she has no licence, and that 'possession' is read widely enough to cover her leaving the toy in her attic, does Chloë *know* there is a firearm in the attic?

Gettier's point is that, if the tripartite test applied by Husak is used, then it appears the answer is, 'Yes, she does know'. On that basis, Chloë is aware that there is a firearm in the attic. First, Chloë believes that there is a (real) pistol, a firearm, in her attic. Second, assuming that her perceptions are typically accurate, she has adequate justification for being disposed to thought and behaviour in a manner that warrants the ascription of the relevant belief to her. Epistemically responsible agents can surely trust in perceptions that are typically accurate.[40] Third, it is true that there is a firearm in the attic.

The difficulty raised by Gettier is that it would be peculiar to describe Chloë as *knowing* that there is a firearm in her attic, because of the apparent logical disconnect between the (coincidentally true and justified) belief she is ascribed properly and the true, factual position. The thought is that, if Chloë is to be counted as knowing that *p*, her justification for holding the dispositions consistent with believing that *p* had better explain logically the relationship between her ascribed beliefs about *p* and the facts about *p*.[41] Chloë is not in such a position. Her ascribed belief is merely coincidentally true, and it seems ludicrous to credit her with knowledge regarding the firearm.[42] It is possible (if not likely) that ordinary speakers would not consider her as having knowledge, and so the criminal law

[39] See the similar example in Roderick Chisholm, *Theory of Knowledge*, 3rd edn. (Englewood Cliffs, NJ: Prentice-Hall International, 1989), p. 93.

[40] I have encountered resistance to the idea that a false belief can be justified. See, however, Price, *Belief*, pp. 80–81; Victor Tadros, *Criminal Responsibility* (Oxford: Oxford University Press, 2005), pp. 244–245.

[41] Philip Kitcher, 'The naturalists return' (1992) 101 *Philosophical Review* 53 at 60.

[42] Linda Zagzebski, 'The inescapability of Gettier problems' (1994) 44 *Philosophical Quarterly* 65 at 66; Anthony M. Dillof, 'Transferred intent: an inquiry into the nature of criminal culpability' (1997–1998) 1 *Buffalo Criminal Law Review* 501 at 529–530.

should be loath to do so, lest it risk consistent *ex ante* guidance and *ex post* application.[43]

If the criminal law *were* to credit Chloë with knowledge of the firearm in her attic, then her liability would also turn on luck in a crucial way. She would have *mens rea* if there was a firearm (which she has not seen or heard about) but not have *mens rea* if the firearm (which she has not seen or heard about) is absent. Any defender of a tripartite knowledge requirement in the Standard Account would need to justify that practice, which stretches well beyond existing examples of moral luck and responsibility for outcomes in the criminal law.[44]

Indeed, any version of the Standard Account of recklessness and negligence that relies on the tripartite conception of knowledge should address Gettier cases, but the fact that many criminal law theorists have skimmed over the issue of what it means to be aware of a risk means that no real defence has been mounted.[45] Husak, for instance, does not address Gettier cases in his recent work on recklessness and negligence. In one paper, he mentions Gettier cases briefly in a footnote, and explains that he hopes they are irrelevant for the purposes of understanding awareness of risk.[46] He then moves from a requirement of knowledge to, in effect, a requirement of bare belief. First, he notes that harm will have come about (or, in a general endangerment offence, an unjustified risk must have been taken) for the question of culpability to arise. It must, in other words, be *true* that the defendant took the risk of harm that would be the subject of the relevant belief.[47] Second, Husak assumes that, if the reasonable person would have been aware of the relevant risk, the defendant must have

43 See above at Chapter 3.

44 Crediting Chloë with knowledge would also raise difficulties of epistemic luck more generally. This topic cannot be dealt with meaningfully here. See, however, Duncan Pritchard, *Epistemic Luck* (Oxford: Oxford University Press, 2005).

45 This position can be contrasted with the field of evidence law. For recent engagements with Gettier cases, see Michael S. Pardo, 'The Gettier problem and legal proof' (2010) 16 *Legal Theory* 37; Mark McBride, 'Reply to Pardo: unsafe legal knowledge?' (2011) 17 *Legal Theory* 67; Michael S. Pardo, 'More on the Gettier problem and legal proof: unsafe nonknowledge does not mean knowledge must be safe' (2011) 17 *Legal Theory* 75.

46 Husak, 'Negligence, belief, blame and criminal liability', at 208 (n. 35). Johnson notes but does not discuss Gettier's paper – see 'Knowledge, risk and wrongdoing', at 513 (n. 26), 574.

47 Husak, 'Negligence, belief, blame and criminal liability', at 208. Cf. Douglas N. Husak and Craig A. Callender, 'Willful ignorance, knowledge and the "equal culpability" thesis: a study of the deeper significance of the principle of legality' [1994] *Wisconsin Law Review* 29 at 44–51.

possessed adequate justification for believing that there was a risk attendant upon his conduct.[48] This might be to assume too much, as the defendant's *reasons* for which the dispositions consistent with a belief might be formed may be different from the reasonable person's. Furthermore, if the defendant forms an unreasonable (but coincidentally true) belief that there is a risk upon φ-ing, it is not clear why culpability cannot be manifested in his failure to be moved sufficiently by it (as the example of Kyle, above, demonstrates). It is not clear, from his recent work, whether Husak thinks these points matter in the context of recklessness and negligence.

However doubtful Husak's assumptions might be, his side-lining of the issues of truth and justification entails that his focus is largely on the concept of *belief*. His discussion of awareness is thus not far removed from that adopted in Chapter 4 (indeed, he cites, but does not develop, Schwitzgebel's insights).[49] It is that belief-based account, rather than one based on knowledge, which should be preferred when trying to best understand awareness of risk on the Standard Account.

The argument here is that it is problematic to pay even lip service to knowledge in the definition of awareness of risk. This is because it is not apparent that Gettier's work *is* irrelevant to the context of awareness of risk. Consider Matt, who wants to watch the big football game. Just before the game starts, Matt sees a rash on Nicky, his infant daughter's, arm. Matt experiences consciously the thought that this is a possible sign of meningitis, and fidgets, nervously, unable to give full concentration to the game when it starts. Assume that Matt has adequate justification for being disposed to think and behave in this way, based on what he has heard about meningitis from a government advertising campaign (as used to be prevalent in the UK). The thought that Nicky might have contracted meningitis leads Matt to form a further thought, and experience further anxiety, that her life might be in danger (because the government advertising campaign drew this link). In such circumstances, it is submitted that Matt should be ascribed a belief that continuing to watch the game means taking a risk with Nicky's life.[50]

[48] Husak, 'Negligence, belief, blame and criminal liability', at 208.

[49] Ibid., at 209 (n. 41), citing Eric Schwitzgebel, 'In-between believing' (2001) 51 *Philosophical Quarterly* 76.

[50] Frank does not *need* to believe that he is taking an *unjustified* risk in order to be culpable, for the reasons explained above at Chapter 1, section on 'Justifying Risk-taking'. Nevertheless, if he *does* have such a belief, the case for potential culpability is even clearer.

Unbeknownst to Matt, the rash has been caused by a mild allergic reaction to the detergent used to wash Nicky's clothing. It is not a sign of meningitis. Nicky nevertheless has contracted meningitis, and has simply not yet developed the tell-tale rash or been able (as a result of her age) to communicate effectively the other symptoms she is experiencing. Nicky's life is, in fact, in danger if she does not receive medical attention, and it is not, in fact, justified for Matt to continue watching the game, rather than seek help. On the tripartite model, Matt *knows* that he is taking an unjustified risk with Nicky's life if he sits down to watch the game: he has a justified, true belief to that effect.

This conclusion is, however, just as odd as Chloë *knowing* that there is a firearm in her attic. Matt's justified belief is, like Chloë's, only coincidentally true, and the ascription of knowledge to him seems unmerited. Matt is 'aware' of the risk only in the sense that he is appropriately said to (justifiably) *believe* that that risk exists. The question then becomes whether he is moved sufficiently by Nicky's interests, in the light of his beliefs about her plight.

What this example demonstrates is that, if a tripartite knowledge requirement is to be defended in relation to the Standard Account's understanding of awareness, Gettier cases will raise difficulties. Given that it is not the task of this chapter to defend a knowledge requirement (quite the opposite), only brief possible defences of a tripartite model of knowledge will be offered. The consequences of mounting these defences indicate why a simple belief requirement will nevertheless be preferable for the *criminal law's* understanding of awareness of risk.

Grasping the Nettle

One response to Gettier problems is simply to contend that Chloë *does* (*in law*) know that there is a firearm in her attic, and Matt *does* (*in law*) know that there is an unjustified risk being taken with his Nicky's life. Knowledge would then mean, in law, (justified) beliefs that turn out, even coincidentally, to be true.[51]

Such an account of knowledge is immune from Gettier counterexamples, because it dispenses with the link between reasons for having the dispositions consistent with believing that p and the fact that p. It

[51] Cf. Crispin Sartwell, 'Knowledge is merely true belief' (1991) 28 *American Philosophical Quarterly* 157; Robin Charlow, 'Wilful ignorance and criminal culpability' (1991–1992) 70 *Texas Law Review* 1351 at 1375.

must again be asked, however, whether it is even worth using the language of knowledge to describe this form of awareness. An approach more in keeping with Anglo-American criminal law's distinction between *actus reus* and *mens rea* is to require simply that the defendant *believes* that, for instance, there is a risk attendant upon φ-ing. It is only where there actually *is* such a (unjustified) risk, or it materialises (the truth condition), that an *actus reus* will have occurred. Only then is culpability needed to explain why the defendant's unjustified risk-taking, and/or its results, reflects on the defendant in a way that makes the personalised censure of a criminal conviction appropriate.

In Matt's case, for example, if Nicky does not have meningitis, she will not be seriously ill or die, or even be in danger of these harms. Matt's awareness (belief) that there is an unjustified risk being taken with Nicky's life plays an important part in explaining why he *could* be *culpable*, but there is no wrong *for which* he is culpable. The culpability inquiry does not even get off the ground.[52]

Conceptually, this bifurcation between *actus reus* and *mens rea* is desirable; it possesses a better 'fit' between a theoretical account of awareness and the existing practices of the main Anglo-American systems of criminal law.[53] In terms of clarifying the language of the criminal law, the language of belief, rather than knowledge, is also commendable. It is doubtful that an ordinary person would say that Chloë *knew* there was a firearm in her attic or that Matt *knew* that he was taking an unjustified risk with Nicky's life. The law should thus not employ this understanding of knowledge, despite its initial plausibility.

Grasping the nettle, and accepting that knowledge simply means 'beliefs which turn out to be true' is an undesirable solution to Gettier cases.

Accommodating Gettier

An alternative way of preserving a knowledge requirement in the Standard Account would be to insist on the tripartite model of knowledge and adapt it to counter Gettier cases. This could be done by reading different matters (such as a causal link between the belief that *p* and the fact that *p*)

[52] See, similarly, Don Stuart, *Canadian Criminal Law: A Treatise*, 6th edn. (Toronto: Carswell, 2011), p. 233.

[53] On such 'fit', see Ronald M. Dworkin, *Taking Rights Seriously* (Cambridge, MA: Harvard University Press, 1977), ch. 4.

into the concept of justification or by searching for another form of 'warrant' for knowledge.[54] The philosophical literature contains many attempts to accommodate Gettier cases, some more convincing than others.[55] Again, the point of this section is not to suggest which one *should* be adopted but to bring out the fact that anybody who wishes to defend a tripartite knowledge requirement in the Standard Account's understanding of awareness of risk should adopt a response to the Gettier counter-examples, and deal with its consequences. No existing response is utterly consequence-free.

Consider the famous, and initially promising, 'truth-tracking' account of knowledge presented by Nozick.[56] Nozick presents the following conditions for knowledge: (1) p must be true; (2) the agent (α) must have a justified belief that p; (3) if p were untrue, then α would not believe that p; and (4) if, in changed circumstances, p were still true, then α would still believe that p.

Nozick's truth-tracking theory of knowledge explains why Chloë does not *know* that there is a firearm in her attic, and Matt does not *know* that an unjustified risk is being taken with Nicky's life. Even if there were no firearm in the attic, Chloë would still believe that there was (on the basis of her misperception) and thus condition (3) of Nozick's test is not satisfied. Matt would be in a similar position: even if Nicky had not contracted meningitis (so no unjustified risk were, in fact, being taken with her life), he would still believe that he was taking an unjustified risk with her life by not seeking medical attention for her. Additionally, if the toy were removed from the attic, Chloë would not believe that there was a firearm in the attic, even though there was in fact one. If the rash were not there, Matt would not form the belief that Nicky's life was

54 On warrant, see Alvin Plantinga, *Warrant: The Current Debate* (Oxford: Oxford University Press, 1993).

55 For summaries, see Dancy, *Introduction to Contemporary Epistemology*, pp. 27–34; Zagzebski, 'The inescapability of Gettier problems'; John Turri, 'Is knowledge justified true belief?' (2012) 184 *Synthese* 247; Stephen Hetherington, 'The Gettier problem', in Sven Bernecker and Duncan Pritchard (eds.), *The Routledge Companion to Epistemology* (London: Routledge, 2011), p. 119; Jonathan J. Ichikawa and Matthias Steup, 'The analysis of knowledge', in Edward N. Zalta (ed.), *The Stanford Encyclopaedia of Philosophy* (Fall 2013 edition), available at http://plato.stanford.edu/entries/knowledge-analysis/.

56 See Robert Nozick, *Philosophical Explanations* (Cambridge, MA: Belknap, 1981), pp. 172–196. Nozick's version of this argument is just one 'sensitivity'-type account of knowledge. For discussion of others, see David Enoch, Levi Spectre and Talia Fisher, 'Statistical evidence, sensitivity and legal knowledge' (2012) 40 *Philosophy & Public Affairs* 197.

in danger, even though it would be. Thus condition (4) would not be met in either case.

Nozick's account of knowledge therefore gets to what seems to be the right conclusion: Chloë *justifiably believes* that there is a firearm in her attic, but does not *know* there is, and Matt *justifiably believes* that he is taking an unjustified risk with Nicky's life, but does not *know* he is. If a jury used Nozick's account of knowledge, there would be no need for 'jury equity' – they would be able to acquit the defendants of offences requiring knowledge because of their failure to satisfy conditions (3) and (4).

Nozick's response to Gettier nevertheless opens up problems with which supporters of a tripartite knowledge requirement in the Standard Account would have to deal. First, Nozick still enquires after the *justification* of the believer's belief, and it was explained earlier in this chapter that asking after such justifications is best avoided in the criminal law, at least where the defendant has the belief relevant to culpability for an instance of wrongdoing (e.g. that there is a risk attendant upon φ-ing).

Second, Nozick's model turns the *truth* of the defendant's belief that there is a risk from an aspect of *actus reus* into an aspect of *mens rea*, and – again, as noted above – it is not clear why this would be necessary or desirable when considered in the context of Anglo-American criminal law, which typically adheres to the *actus reus*/*mens rea* distinction.

Third, there is the question of *how* the finder of fact is to work out what the defendant might have believed in different circumstances. Such hypothetical questions are crucial when addressing stages (3) and (4) of Nozick's test, but they raise profound epistemic difficulties. How is a jury meant to establish what Chloë or Matt *would have* or even *probably would have*[57] believed had the circumstances been different? It will be argued in Chapter 7 that there are further reasons to doubt the efficacy of using hypotheticals too liberally to assess culpability in criminal law theory and practice.[58] These concerns would need to be countered by defenders of a Nozickian knowledge requirement in the Standard Account's understanding of awareness of risk.

Defenders of Nozick's view of knowledge as a model for *criminal law* would also have to explain how the counterfactuals could be *proved* in a

[57] See Enoch, Spectre and Fisher, 'Statistical evidence, sensitivity and legal knowledge', at 204.

[58] See the discussion of Jeremy Horder and Kenneth Simons' accounts of counterfactual culpability, below at Chapter 7, section on 'Criticisms of Counterfactual Choice'.

criminal trial. How is the prosecution to establish beyond reasonable doubt what the defendant *would* (or *most probably would*) have believed in an alternative universe? Such practical concerns should not be ignored by a criminal theorist searching for the 'best' understanding of awareness for use in the Standard Account of recklessness and negligence. The 'best' interpretation of the criminal law's concepts must not only explain and justify those concepts in theory, but also take into account the practical context of the criminal trial. If the Nozickian theory is unduly vulnerable epistemically, then it might lead to unjustifiably high prospects of both unmerited acquittals and wrongful convictions, which is undesirable in terms of the criminal justice system's legitimacy.

Ultimately, then, responses to Gettier problems such as Nozick's are unacceptable for the criminal law context. A requirement of mere *belief* that a risk exists, such as the one defended in Chapter 4, does not suffer from these difficulties. It is thus submitted that Husak's requirement of *knowledge* (which, as noted above, he comes close to surrendering) is unnecessary and problematic. A defendant is aware of a risk attendant upon φ-ing when she *believes* such a risk exists.

Conclusion

It should be reiterated that Husak's account of awareness of risk in terms of *knowledge* is 'speculative and tentative'.[59] Indeed, he appears to not be too wedded to the knowledge requirement – much of what he argues in his more recent work on recklessness and negligence concerns *beliefs* that risks exist (and he understands beliefs in a dispositional sense, though develops his position much less than the previous chapter did).[60] The main lesson from this chapter has been that even talk of knowledge in this context (talk found from time to time in doctrinal discussions) complicates matters unnecessarily and should be avoided. On the best interpretation of the Standard Account of recklessness, a defendant is *aware* of a risk when she *believes* that it exists. For the reasons outlined above, the defendant need *not* believe that it is *virtually certain* that a certain risk exists in order to be aware of that risk.

This book's analysis of awareness of risk is now complete. The focus now shifts to considering why awareness of risk has been given such a pivotal role in Anglo-American accounts of culpable carelessness.

[59] See above at note 3.

[60] See Husak, 'Negligence, belief, blame and criminal liability', at 209–210.

6

The Significance of Awareness of Risk

The previous two chapters have analysed the concept of awareness of risk and concluded that it would be best to conceive of it in terms of the defendant's *beliefs* about risk, rather than her *knowledge* of risk. It was contended that a proper analysis of belief, for the purposes of the criminal law, is dispositional: a person believes that there is a risk attendant upon her behaviour (φ-ing) if her dispositions towards thought and behaviour cohere with what would, stereotypically, be expected of somebody who holds the relevant belief about risk.

It is now time to address a question of vital importance to the 'Standard Account' of culpable carelessness around which the Anglo-American jurisdictions surveyed in Chapter 2 are, to varying extents, converging. *Why* is awareness of risk – the presence of a belief regarding the relevant risk associated with φ-ing – significant? Why does it play the role of separating two culpable mental states (usually called recklessness and negligence) and typically delineating the contours of criminal liability for 'serious' offences (on the basis that negligence is a comparatively exceptional fault element)?

A useful answer to these questions (though, as will be seen, not one that is often discussed doctrinally) points to the connection between beliefs and *choices*. Choices are limited by beliefs: a person cannot be said to have chosen to take a particular risk if she did not believe that it existed.[1] Although she might have chosen to do something else – for example, pull her car out of the driveway – she will be choosing to take the risk of hitting another person, injuring them, only if she believes that this particular risk is associated with her manoeuvre.[2] Without a belief about the relevant risk, no relevant choice to take it is made.

[1] R.A. Duff, *Intention, Agency and Criminal Liability: Philosophy of Action and the Criminal Law* (Oxford: Blackwell, 1990), p. 154; Galen Strawson, *Freedom and Belief* (rev. edn.) (Oxford: Oxford University Press, 2010), p. 121.

[2] See, further, A.P. Simester, 'A disintegrated theory of culpability', in Dennis J. Baker and Jeremy Horder (eds.), *The Sanctity of Life and the Criminal Law: The Legacy of Glanville*

Culpability is a means of drawing a personalised connection between a defendant and her wrongdoing. In the context of culpable carelessness this requires that the defendant's wrongdoing reflect on *her*, as a reasoning agent, in the appropriate way. If choice is a *necessary* (even if not a sufficient)[3] condition for such a meaningful reflection of agency, then only the taking of risks that the defendant believed to exist should be concentrated on by the criminal law when assessing culpable carelessness.[4] If *un*awareness of risk is the mark of negligence (as it tends to be in Anglo-American criminal jurisdictions), then negligence typically[5] involves no choice to take a risk, because the defendant does not believe the relevant risk exists at the time of acting. If choice is a *necessary* component of culpability – a view that will be termed the 'Exclusive Thesis' – then negligence involves no culpability of the sort that ought to be required for a criminal conviction.[6] The Exclusive Thesis has obvious doctrinal implications: if it is right, then most Anglo-American systems of criminal law are making a 'mistake'[7] in including negligence in their arsenal of fault terms.

Not all theorists who think that choice is important to culpability accept that it is a *necessary* condition of culpability. Many writers think that choice is but *one* basis of culpability and are agnostic on the question of whether (or positively accept that) alternative acceptable bases of criminal fault are available. On such accounts, it is at least possible that

Williams (Cambridge: Cambridge University Press, 2013), p. 178; Michael S. Moore, *Placing Blame: A Theory of the Criminal Law* (Oxford: Oxford University Press, 1997), p. 413. There is not space here to examine the issue of so-called act descriptions, but see Kimberly K. Ferzan, 'Opaque recklessness' (2000–2001) 91 *Journal of Criminal Law & Criminology* 597 at 604–605.

3 One analysis of the defence of coercion/duress, for example, would not deny that the defendant made a *choice* to engage in wrongdoing, but would deny that she is culpable/blameworthy for doing so.

4 A particularly clear example of such an argument is Larry Alexander and Kimberly K. Ferzan with Stephen J. Morse, *Crime and Culpability: A Theory of Criminal Law* (Cambridge: Cambridge University Press, 2009), chs. 2–3.

5 It is theoretically possible to *choose* to risk being unaware of a particular risk at a future time. This point is discussed below at Chapter 7, section on 'An Earlier Disregarding of the Relevant Risk'.

6 Theorists who reject *criminal liability* for negligence need not deny that *in other contexts* negligence is blameworthy.

7 Alan Brudner, *Punishment and Freedom: A Liberal Theory of Penal Justice* (Oxford: Oxford University Press, 2009), p. 79. Brudner's explanation of why choice is required for criminal culpability is explored below, section on 'Choice and Punishment'.

culpability can be, as Simester terms it, 'disintegrated',[8] and theorists can 'switch horses'[9] from choice-based culpability in order to accommodate (at least some cases of) negligence. For example, negligence might be explicable not on the basis of choice but on the basis of the defendant's unexercised capacity to take more care when deciding what to do[10] or her demonstration of some defect of motivation or character in relation to the relevant risk.[11]

This chapter has two purposes. The first is to craft an account of the significance of choice to criminal culpability. Creating such an account is crucial to understanding *why* choice is important to culpability, and *how* important it is. The second purpose of this chapter is to test, and ultimately reject, arguments in favour of the Exclusive Thesis. Although certainly *important* to criminal culpability, choice is not the be-all and end-all of criminal culpability.[12] This conclusion opens the door to consideration in the next two chapters of explanations of culpable carelessness that do not require the defendant to make a choice to take a particular risk at the time of the risk-taking.[13]

It is useful to begin by explaining that, as a matter of doctrine, the significance of choice is unclear, a point that necessitates the more theoretical approach adopted in the remainder of this chapter.

Choice in Doctrine

Doctrinally, discussions of the gist of criminal culpability are quite rare and often undeveloped. Although, as Chapter 2 demonstrated, many Anglo-American systems of criminal law agree (to varying extents) about

[8] See Simester, 'A disintegrated theory of culpability'.

[9] Kimberly K. Ferzan, 'Don't abandon the Model Penal Code yet! Thinking through Simons's rethinking' (2002–2003) 6 *Buffalo Criminal Law Review* 185 at 193.

[10] See, famously, H.L.A. Hart, *Punishment and Responsibility: Essays in the Philosophy of Law* (Oxford: Oxford University Press, 1968), ch. 6 (discussed below at Chapter 7, section on 'Exploring Hart's Account'). See also Andrew Ashworth and Jeremy Horder, *Principles of Criminal Law*, 7th edn. (Oxford: Oxford University Press, 2013), p. 184; cf. Andrew Ashworth, 'Belief, intent and criminal liability', in John Eekelaar and John Bell (eds.), *Oxford Essays in Jurisprudence: Third Series* (Oxford: Oxford University Press, 1989), p. 30.

[11] See Victor Tadros, *Criminal Responsibility* (Oxford: Oxford University Press, 2005), ch. 9 (discussed below at Chapter 8, section on 'Tadros's Account of Recklessness (and/or Negligence)'); Simester, 'A disintegrated theory of culpability'; below at Chapter 8.

[12] See, similarly, Jeremy Horder, 'Cognition, emotion and criminal culpability' (1990) 106 *Law Quarterly Review* 469 at 474.

[13] Some of the accounts discussed in Chapter 7 require the defendant to have made a choice regarding risk at an earlier time.

the importance of awareness of risk in their discussions of culpable risk-taking, there is little discussion of *how* awareness of risk draws a connection between a defendant and his unjustified risk-taking. Typically, in their definitions of terms such as recklessness and negligence, courts and legislatures invoke an idea such as the 'disregard' of a (often substantial and unjustifiable) risk, but it is not clear that these formulations necessarily involve ideas of *choice*. To disregard something is to 'pay no attention to ... [or] ignore' it.[14] Recall that choices are limited by beliefs. If 'disregard' is understood so as to involve paying *no* attention to something, it is possible that a person can disregard that of which she is not aware.[15] This is why the Scottish conception of recklessness in terms of 'utter disregard'[16] of risk does not resolve the question of whether an accused must be aware of the relevant risk in order to be reckless.[17] The same is arguably true of the concept of 'indifference' towards risk, though deeper consideration of that matter will be delayed until the discussion of Duff's theory of 'practical indifference' in the next chapter.

Admittedly, many US jurisdictions have adopted the Model Penal Code's requirement that a defendant '*consciously disregard*' a substantial and unjustifiable risk.[18] The use of the term 'conscious' might suggest that the defendant must have a mental experience of *deciding* to take the relevant risk.[19] Whether such a mental experience should be required for recklessness is a matter that will be returned to below in the discussion of Ferzan's work on recklessness.[20] Setting those US jurisdictions that have adopted the requirement of 'conscious disregard' aside, though, the linkage between awareness and wrongdoing is unclear in most doctrinal accounts of recklessness. In the light of this doctrinal lack of clarity, recourse must be taken to criminal law theory.

It is useful to begin by establishing a working definition of choice.

[14] www.oxforddictionaries.com/definition/english/disregard.

[15] For discussion of this point, see Williams 'A reply to Mr Duff' (1982) 41 *Cambridge Law Journal* 286 at 287; *State* v. *Olsen*, 462 NW 2d 474 (1990, SD), at 476–477; James Chalmers, '*Lieser* and misconceptions' 2008 *Scottish Criminal Law* 1115 at 1118.

[16] *Quinn* v. *Cunningham* 1956 JC 22.

[17] See the discussion of Scots law above at Chapter 2, section on 'Scotland'.

[18] American Law Institute, *Model Penal Code and Commentaries (Official Draft and Revised Comments)*, 3 vols. (Philadelphia: American Law Institute, 1980), vol. 1, s. 2.02(2)(c).

[19] This point is clear in Connecticut's definition of recklessness, which requires that the defendant is 'aware of and consciously disregards' the relevant risk: CGSA s. 53a-3(13).

[20] Below at section on 'Ferzan's "Opaque" Recklessness'.

Choice: A Working Definition

Although choice is a concept employed frequently in debates over criminal culpability, it is rarely defined.[21] This leads to the suspicion, as Pillsbury puts it, that in much writing 'the definition of choice may depend on [the author's] view of responsibility and not the other way around'.[22] Even where a definition of choice is given, difficulties are not avoided. Definitions might avowedly pick out only certain of choice's facets,[23] meaning that attacks on choice are attacks on distinct *features* of choice. Another definitional problem can be caused by defining choice negatively, by picking out situations where a choice is not made (e.g. when a person is in a state of automatism) or is somehow not a sure basis upon which to blame a defendant (e.g. duress).[24] The argument is that whatever is left over once all such exceptional cases are identified is 'choice', but that leaves 'choice' as a broad category, with little room for important distinctions in *kinds* of culpability.[25]

Given these pitfalls, it is worth developing a working, positive definition of choice. A suitable definition would be in terms of *the act of expressing a person's preference for one set of reasons that she believes to exist, over another set of reasons that she believes to exist.*[26] It is submitted that this definition coheres sufficiently with a popular dictionary definition of choice – 'the act of choosing between two or more possibilities'[27] – to satisfy the communicative aspirations of the criminal law.[28]

As will be seen in greater detail later on in this chapter, it is the link between a defendant's expression of preferences and her choices that explains why the defendant can usually[29] be blamed for φ-ing when she has chosen to φ or to risk engaging in φ-ing. To anticipate the later

21 A point made in Horder, 'Cognition, emotion and criminal culpability', at 474.

22 Samuel H. Pillsbury, 'The meaning of deserved punishment: an essay on choice, character and responsibility' (1991–1992) 67 *Indiana Law Journal* 719 at 738.

23 See, e.g. R.A. Duff, *Criminal Attempts* (Oxford: Oxford University Press, 1996), p. 148 (offering a 'minimal notion of choice . . . in terms of intention and belief').

24 Anon, 'Negligence and the general problem of criminal responsibility' (1971–1972) 81 *Yale Law Journal* 949 at 966–971.

25 Cf. Simester, 'A disintegrated theory of culpability', at pp. 187–188.

26 It is possible to conceive of this as a choice between conflicting desires: Kimberly K. Ferzan, 'Don't abandon the Model Penal Code yet! Thinking through Simons's rethinking' (2002–2003) 6 *Buffalo Criminal Law Review* 185 at 209.

27 www.oxforddictionaries.com/definition/english/choice.

28 See above at Chapter 3.

29 Absent circumstances that render the choice unreflective of the defendant's agency.

discussion, the argument is that if risk-taking is chosen, then it is typically traceable in a meaningful way to the defendant's wider motivational set-up.[30] On this view, usually choices make risks (and their materialisations) *belong* to the actor in a particular way.[31] This is why choices have 'obvious and immediate moral significance'.[32]

Thus far a brief sketch (which will be fleshed out in due course) has been given of *why* choices are significant to culpability. It is not clear, however, how to get from choices being *significant* to their being the *sole* mark of culpability. That is what is required for the Exclusive Thesis to be supported.

It might be thought that progress towards defending the Exclusive Thesis could be made by focussing on the idea of culpability as *insufficient concern for the interests of others.*[33] There is, however, nothing in the definition of culpability as 'insufficient concern for others' that ties a theorist to the view that *only* choices can ground culpability. Other authors who conceive of culpability as insufficient concern have refused to endorse the Exclusive Thesis.[34] In fact, the notion of insufficient concern for others might suggest that culpability should be understood (at least partially) by reference to the relationships between the defendant and others,[35] and the expectations regarding thought and reflection that flow from them, a theme returned to below.

What is needed to support the Exclusive Thesis is an alternative, positive argument. Such arguments are admittedly hard to find in the existing literature. A more popular strategy is to argue *negatively*, by pointing to various problems with non-choice-based conceptions of

30 See, similarly, John Deigh, 'Responsibility', in John Deigh and David Dolinko (eds.), *The Oxford Handbook of Philosophy of Criminal Law* (Oxford: Oxford University Press, 2011), p. 194, at p. 197.

31 George Sher, *Desert* (Princeton, NJ: Princeton University Press, 1987), p. 161; Sher, *Who Knew? Responsibility without Awareness* (Oxford: Oxford University Press, 2009), p. 74; C.T. Sistare, 'Models of responsibility in criminal theory: comment on Baker' (1988–1989) 7 *Law and Philosophy* 295 at 301–302; Duff, *Intention, Agency and Criminal Liability*, p. 154.

32 T.M. Scanlon, 'The significance of choice', in Sterling M. McMurrin (ed.), *The Tanner Lectures on Human Values, VIII* (Cambridge: Cambridge University Press, 1988), p. 149, at p. 151.

33 See Larry Alexander and Kimberly K. Ferzan, 'Culpable acts of risk creation' (2007–2008) 5 *Ohio State Journal of Criminal Law* 375 at 378.

34 E.g. Tadros, *Criminal Responsibility*, pp. 61–66.

35 See, further, V.F. Nourse, 'Hearts and minds: understanding the new culpability' (2002–2003) 6 *Buffalo Criminal Law Review* 361.

culpability (and, in particular, character-based theories of culpability).[36] The approach taken in the remainder of this chapter is thus to look to some features of choice that might be thought to support the Exclusive Thesis and to consider some objections to non-choice-based accounts of culpability. Other criticisms of non-choice-based accounts of culpability will be held over until later chapters if they are relevant to the arguments discussed there.

The first significant feature of choice concerns the presence of alternative options.

Choice and Alternatives

One reason why choices might be thought especially important to culpability is that a choice presupposes the expression of the defendant's preference for one option over another and ensures that the defendant had alternative options open to her.[37] This is not the place for a discussion of the debate over free will and determinism,[38] and it should be sufficient to probe briefly the connection between alternative possibilities and responsibility.[39] Before this topic can be addressed, though, it is necessary to take a brief detour into explaining responsibility and its connection with culpability. Responsibility 'means different things to different people'.[40] Some general points can, nevertheless, be made. Theories of responsibility seek to demonstrate when an actor can be held accountable (to another person or institution) for various things, including her behaviour. At its most basic, the type of responsibility that is meant here entails *answerability*.[41]

36 For a critique of the dichotomy between choice and character that such accounts suggest, see R.A. Duff, 'Choice, Character and Criminal Liability' (1993) 12 *Law and Philosophy* 345.

37 Duff, *Intention, Agency and Criminal Liability*, pp. 44–47.

38 A useful overview of the main positions relevant to criminal responsibility is Alexander and Ferzan with Morse, *Crime and Culpability*, pp. 13–15. Other helpful introductions are A.J.P. Kenny, *Freewill and Responsibility* (London: Routledge, 1978); Galen Strawson, 'The Impossibility of Moral Responsibility' (1994) 75 *Philosophical Studies* 5.

39 Some writers doubt that Frankfurt's refutation of the so-called Principle of Alternative Possibilities (PAP) is in fact relevant to determinism. See John M. Fischer, 'The importance of Frankfurt-style argument' (2007) 57 *The Philosophical Quarterly* 464 at 465.

40 Pamela Hieronymi, 'Responsibility for believing' (2008) 161 *Synthese* 357 at 359.

41 See ibid.; Duff, *Answering for Crime*, p. 15.

The answer that an agent gives, when called to account, will depend on her reasons for behaving in a particular way.[42] This aspect of responsibility brings in consideration of 'reason-responsiveness', i.e. the agent's ability to notice and respond to the reasons that bear upon her in a given situation.[43] Theorists rarely say more than that criminal responsibility requires responsiveness to reasons. It is not clear, for example, *which* reasons must be capable of being responded to for an agent to be responsible.[44] As responsibility is not the focus of the investigation here, this question can be left to one side.[45] It is sufficient to note that responsibility deals with calling a reason-responsive person to account and that criminal responsibility is a special kind of this practice – i.e. the public calling to account of a citizen, by the state, for her alleged wrongdoing.

Defendants thus must first be reason-responsive agents who can be subject to the attribution of moral appraisals before any question of calling them to account arises. This must certainly be the case before any question of whether a reactive attitude, and particularly a personalised finding of condemnation for wrongdoing, is warranted.[46] Responsibility for wrongdoing is, on the view outlined here, a necessary condition for criminal culpability for wrongdoing.[47]

If a person is responsible only if she had alternative options available to her, then she cannot be culpable in the absence of such alternatives. It is thus necessary to consider whether responsibility for φ-ing requires that alternative options were, in fact, available to the defendant.[48] If it does, then the Exclusive Thesis seems to be defensible.

[42] For an introduction, see Joseph Raz, *Practical Reason and Norms* (rev. edn.) (Oxford: Oxford University Press, 1999), ch. 1.

[43] For descriptions of this capacity, see John M. Fischer and Mark Ravizza, *Responsibility and Control: A Theory of Moral Responsibility* (Cambridge: Cambridge University Press, 1998), ch. 3; Stephen J. Morse, 'Rationality and responsibility' (2000–2001) 74 *Southern California Law Review* 251 at 253–255; Gary Watson, 'Reasons and responsibility' (2001) 111 *Ethics* 374; Tadros, *Criminal Responsibility*, pp. 55–57; Duff, *Answering for Crime*, pp. 39–40.

[44] Douglas N. Husak, 'Answering Duff: R.A. Duff's *Answering for Crime*' (2010) 29 *Law and Philosophy* 101 at 105–109.

[45] See, however, the references in Duff, *Answering for Crime*, p. 39 (n. 2).

[46] See Massimo Renzo, 'Responsibility and answerability in the criminal law', in R.A. Duff et al. (eds.), *The Constitution of Criminal Law* (Oxford: Oxford University Press, 2013), p. 209, at pp. 209–210.

[47] Cf. Michael S. Moore, 'Intention as a marker of moral culpability and legal punishability', in R.A. Duff and Stuart Green (eds.), *Philosophical Foundations of Criminal Law* (Oxford: Oxford University Press, 2011), p. 179, at pp. 182–184.

[48] This is sometimes termed the 'liberty of indifference': Kenny, *Freewill and Responsibility*, p. 25.

The Principle of Alternative Possibilities (PAP) encapsulates the view that alternative options are necessary for responsibility: 'S is morally responsible for something S has done only if S could have done otherwise'.[49] The unconvincing nature of PAP can be demonstrated by consideration of Frankfurt's famous thought experiments.[50] Consider Tom, who decides to vote for candidate A in an election. Unbeknownst to Tom, he has been hypnotised by Gemma so that, if Tom forms the intention to vote for Candidate B, he will immediately form an intention to vote for Candidate A. In the end, Tom does not waver from his plan to vote for Candidate A, and Gemma's intervention does not impact upon Tom's reasoning.

Intuitively Tom is responsible for voting for Candidate A because he did so on the basis of his own reasons, rather than as a result of Gemma's intervention. Nothing 'external' to Tom, as a choosing agent, intervened to break the connection between his agency and the state of affairs chosen.[51] The choice he made is a reflection of *his* intentions, desires and beliefs, rather than anybody else's.[52] It would be insulting to his agency to deny that he is responsible for voting for Candidate A, despite the absence of alternative options.[53]

This argument suggests that alternative possibilities are *not* required for responsibility. If choice requires the *actual* existence of alternative options, then choice is not required for responsibility for φ-ing, either – a conclusion defended by Tadros.[54] It is not clear, however, that choice *does* require the actual existence of such options – Tom *chose* to vote for Candidate A, even if he could not do otherwise because of Gemma's intervention.

It might be argued that choice is important then not because it presupposes that *actual* alternatives were available to the chooser, but merely because it presupposes that the chooser *thought* that alternatives were available and demonstrated through her decision which alternative she prefers.[55] Tom had the *experience* of being able to choose between

[49] Fischer, 'The importance of Frankfurt-style argument', at 464.

[50] See Harry G. Frankfurt, *The Importance of What We Care About: Philosophical Essays* (Cambridge: Cambridge University Press, 1988), ch. 1. See also John Locke, *An Essay Concerning Human Understanding* (Oxford: Oxford University Press, 1975 [original: 1690]), ch. 21, para. 10.

[51] For sustained discussion of this idea, see Fischer and Ravizza, *Responsibility and Control.*

[52] Duff, *Criminal Attempts*, p. 148; Fischer and Ravizza, *Responsibility and Control*, p. 37.

[53] Tadros, *Criminal Responsibility*, p. 62. [54] Ibid.

[55] It might be suggested that true autonomy requires the experienced options have to be suitably important to the defendant, but that suggestion need not be considered further

Candidate A and Candidate B, even if Gemma's intervention would have made it impossible for him to vote for Candidate B. A way of arguing for the Exclusive Thesis thus would be to contend that responsibility for φ-ing requires the *experience* of having alternatives to φ-ing.

It is important to note that the experience of choice would impose an even weaker constraint on responsibility than PAP. Even in the most egregious circumstances (such as where a defendant is threatened with death or serious violence if she does not cooperate), the defendant will still *experience* having alternative options (even if those alternatives are unpalatable).[56] The point is not that duress and similar circumstances remove an experience of alternatives, and choice, but rather that the defendant's options are constrained to the extent that it would be unwarranted to hold that her decisions reflect something meaningful about her general motivational structure.[57] The value of such reflections will be returned to briefly at the end of this chapter.

The experience of choice is thus a weak requirement, but should it be retained? Tadros has rejected the argument that even the experience of choice is required for responsibility for φ-ing by using the following example:[58]

> Suppose that there is a criminal offence of knowingly having proscribed drugs on one's property. Del is asked by Xavier if, in return for £100, he will stash some drugs for him. Del needs the money and agrees. Surely that is all we need to know to say that he is responsible for completing the offence of having proscribed drugs on his property. Now suppose that we discover that he has heard that, if he will not stash the drugs voluntarily, Xavier will break into his house whilst he is away and stash the drugs there anyway. Suppose that there is no acceptable way of preventing Xavier from doing this. Consequently, Del has no choice but to have the drugs knowingly stashed in the house. Surely this new fact will make no difference as to whether he is responsible for stashing the drugs ... Consequently the experience of choice cannot be relevant to determining responsibility. We are interested only in the actual process of Del's reasoning in *v*ing, not in the possibilities that were available to him.

here. See, however, Joseph Raz, 'Autonomy, freedom and the harm principle', in Ruth Gavison (ed.), *Issues in Contemporary Legal Philosophy: The Influence of HLA Hart* (Oxford: Clarendon, 1987), p. 313, at pp. 316–318; Joseph Raz, *The Morality of Freedom* (Oxford: Clarendon, 1988), p. 373.

56 Tadros, *Criminal Responsibility*, p. 65.

57 See, further, Frankfurt, *The Importance of What We Care About*, ch. 3.

58 Tadros, *Criminal Responsibility*, pp. 65–66.

It is submitted that Tadros has not, in fact, exhausted the experience of choice in his example. The two states of affairs faced by the person described are distinct: in one case, the drugs are placed in the house with the defendant's assent (expressing a preference of hers); in another they are planted there without assent (thereby not expressing a preference). The defendant does experience the choice over *how* the drugs come to be in the house (this is why she can act for her own reasons), and this seems significant enough to maintain the importance of the experience of choice. Tadros has not done enough, in short, to support the claim that choice – if understood as requiring only the *experience* of choice – is 'irrelevant' to responsibility, including criminal responsibility.[59] All he has done is demonstrate, once again, that the *actual* existence of alternative options is not necessary for responsibility for a given state of affairs.

That said, it is still not yet clear that salvaging the *experience* of choice provides a firm grounding for the Exclusive Thesis. Although a person who experiences a choice might be *particularly close* to the results of that choice, it is not clear why *less secure* reflections of agency could not be possible. What is required for the Exclusive Thesis to succeed is an argument that *only* choices reflect meaningfully *enough* on defendants to secure criminal culpability. It is submitted that the experience of choice cannot, in itself, do that work.

The next section addresses an alternative argument for the Exclusive Thesis, premised on deliberation and the defendant's control over states of affairs.

Choice and Control

It might be thought that there is a close relationship between expressing a preference for one option over another and deliberation. Choices, on this view, would be marked out not only by the experience of having alternatives, but also by the presence of deliberation.[60]

It is not clear that deliberation is an *essential* element of the concept of choice.[61] It is important to remember that, however loosely the term is

[59] The claim of irrelevance is made in the heading on ibid., p. 61.

[60] Claire Finkelstein, 'Responsibility for unintended consequences' (2005) 2 *Ohio State Journal of Criminal Law* 579 at 593; Horder, 'Criminal culpability', at 201. See also Duff, *Intention, Agency and Criminal Liability*, p. 141.

[61] Tadros, *Criminal Responsibility*, p. 64.

used nowadays, the verb 'to deliberate' is defined so as to involve 'long and careful' or 'slow and careful' consideration of options.[62] This suggests that the idea of deliberation brings in ideas of explicit, *conscious* consideration (i.e. a mental experience)[63] of the options that a defendant believes to be open to her. It is difficult to see how 'long and careful' or 'slow and careful' consideration of options can be an activity not involving explicit, extensive conscious reflection and deliberation.

The concept of *choice*, in general, does not seem *necessarily* to involve deliberation, thus understood.[64] If it did, then very little of what a person does would seem to be chosen by her, which is counter-intuitive. It is relatively unusual for acts to be deliberated upon at any length before being carried out,[65] and the spheres of responsibility and choice do not seem – at least in everyday moral practices – to be so limited.[66] In everyday moral practices, persons can make choices on impulse – the very absence of deliberation – and be responsible for those choices. Indeed, the fact that a decision was made on impulse, without deliberation, is very often a ground for criticising someone's choices (e.g. the new TV bought by someone without due consideration for her bank balance). Impulsivity is not, it seems, a ground for saying that no choice at all was made; it does not seem incorrect to speak of 'impulsive choices'.[67] If that is the case, then deliberation is not necessarily an aspect of choice after all. The Exclusive Thesis would not, then, necessarily bring in a requirement of explicit, conscious consideration of options. It would require merely an experience that there is not simply one option available to the defendant and the expression of a preference for an option that is suitably reflective of the defendant's wider agency.

It has so far been argued that it is possible to conceive of *choices* being made without the engagement of long deliberation and conscious awareness.[68] It might nevertheless be denied that choices that do not

[62] www.oxforddictionaries.com/definition/english/deliberate.

[63] See the discussion of consciousness above at Chapter 4, section on 'Explicit Knowledge'.

[64] Duff, 'Choice, character and culpability', at 348; Pillsbury, 'Crimes of indifference', at 125.

[65] James B. Brady, 'Punishment for negligence: a reply to Professor Hall' (1972–1973) 22 *Buffalo Law Review* 107 at 110.

[66] Some writers believe that responsibility *should* be more limited, but accept that this is contrary to some people's intuitions. See, e.g. Neil Levy, 'Restoring control: comments on George Sher' (2008) 36 *Philosophia* 213 at 217.

[67] Cf. Horder, 'Criminal culpability', at 201.

[68] See, further, Michael S. Moore and Heidi M. Hurd, 'The culpability of negligence', in Rowan Cruft, Matthew H. Kramer and Mark R. Reiff (eds.), *Crime, Punishment and Responsibility: The Jurisprudence of Antony Duff* (Oxford: Oxford University Press, 2011), p. 311, at p. 319.

involve conscious contemplation at all are the ones relevant to *criminal* responsibility. On this view, the Exclusive Thesis requires not only a *choice*, but also a particular *type* of choice. Ferzan presents the most developed version of this argument, in her discussion of 'opaque' recklessness.[69] The next section expresses doubts about the feasibility of defending this particular conception of the Exclusive Thesis with Ferzan's argument.

Ferzan's 'Opaque' Recklessness

Ferzan begins by distinguishing between 'conscious' and 'preconscious' aspects of decision-making. The conscious/preconscious divide will be remembered from Chapter 4.[70] To summarise, on Ferzan's view, *conscious* propositions are focussed on and experienced mentally, whereas *preconscious* propositions exist at a level that *can be* focussed on mentally but need not be to successfully guide behaviour.[71]

Ferzan is concerned about defendants who have a mixture of preconscious and conscious mental states at the time of taking an unjustified risk with the interests of others. Consider the driver who accelerates, even though the upcoming traffic light is turning from green to amber. At this moment, the driver might not experience mentally a thought such as 'This is dangerous because . . .' – particularly if she is used to speeding through red lights.[72] Instead, a more abstract sense of risk or danger might be all that she experienced mentally, even if – had she stopped to think about that risk or danger – the defendant would 'immediately prattle off the reasons why running the light is dangerous'.[73] In other words, the exact nature of the risk (of which the defendant is dimly consciously aware) is preconscious. Such actors are not reckless in the *purest* sense, Ferzan thinks, because they are not *consciously* disregarding a concrete belief about the risks attendant upon φ-ing. Ferzan still thinks such defendants to be intuitively culpable,[74] and therefore proposes

[69] See Ferzan, 'Opaque recklessness'. Ferzan's account is adopted in Alexander and Ferzan with Morse, *Crime and Culpability*, pp. 55–56. Cf. Stephen J. Morse, 'Reasons, results and criminal responsibility' [2004] *University of Illinois Law Review* 363. At points, Morse accepts that negligent defendants have adequate control to be responsible for their unjustified risk-taking: see e.g. at 393, 404.

[70] Section on 'Explicit Knowledge'.

[71] Ferzan, 'Opaque recklessness', at 629–630.

[72] Cf. Tadros, *Criminal Responsibility*, p. 257.

[73] Ferzan, 'Opaque recklessness', at 630.

[74] Ibid., at 600.

to extend the law's understanding of recklessness to accommodate conscious decisions to take a risk, the nature of which the defendant is preconsciously aware.[75] In other words, to be 'opaquely' reckless, the defendant must have some nagging, explicit, psychological experience of abstract risk or danger, have the information regarding that risk available to her in her preconscious and proceed without thinking consciously about that preconscious information. This mixture of conscious and preconscious aspects of the defendant's mental state regarding risk is the boundary of recklessness, and culpability, for Ferzan.[76]

Ferzan thinks that although a *choice* to disregard a risk can be made at the preconscious level, those choices that are *fully* preconscious (i.e. made with no conscious experience at all) are not something with which the criminal law should be concerned. This is because, she explains, a person has an adequate sense of control over her behaviour only when she *consciously* decides to disregard a risk or danger (even if the exact nature of that risk or danger is held only on a preconscious level). If a person is held responsible for her preconscious decision-making about risk, she is apparently held responsible in violation of the principle that 'ought' implies 'can'.[77]

Two points about Ferzan's account are, with respect, mysterious.

First, it is not clear how distinct what might be called 'pure preconscious decision-making' and 'opaque' recklessness are. As Moore has noted, many persons who are preconsciously aware of a proposition or piece of behaviour will also be 'dimly' consciously aware of that proposition or behaviour.[78] Ferzan does not explain in detail how much conscious awareness of 'riskiness' is required, and thus 'opaque' recklessness might well fold into preconscious decision-making in many cases.[79] It should be noted that other theorists have doubted that stark lines can be drawn in this area and maintain that consciousness exists on a

[75] Ibid., at 629. [76] Ibid., at 638.

[77] Ibid., at 637–638. The 'ought' implies 'can' principle will be used as though it was an uncontroversial premise. It is not – see James W. Smith, 'Impossibility and morals' (1961) 70 *Mind* 362; Sharon Ryan, 'Doxastic compatibilism and the ethics of belief' (2003) 114 *Philosophical Studies* 47.

[78] Michael S. Moore, *Act and Crime: The Philosophy of Action and Its Implications for the Criminal Law* (Oxford: Oxford University Press, 1993), p. 154.

[79] See also Moore and Hurd, 'Punishing the awkward, the stupid, the weak and the selfish', at 153.

continuum, rather than in categorically distinct states.[80] Ferzan does not engage with these points in great detail.[81]

Third, Ferzan's point about the amount of control required by the criminal law needs to probed. She begins by suggesting that 'for us to believe that the actor is responsible, she must be *able* to reason through her actions and choose to do wrong' (emphasis added).[82] It is important to note that what is required by Ferzan at this stage is an *ability* to reason through actions consciously, not the *exercise* of that ability.

To explain the relevant ability in more detail, Ferzan relies on Moore's statement that responsibility requires 'the *power* or *ability* to give effect to one's choices',[83] 'the *power* or *ability* to appraise the moral worth of one's proposed actions' (emphasis added).[84] Again, it is important to note these statements point to a *capacity* to engage in conscious reflection about the moral quality of one's actions. A person who is utterly unconscious (e.g. someone who is asleep) lacks the relevant power or ability, and to hold her responsible for her (dreamed) thoughts would be unfair. This is because such an actor has insufficient control over her (dreamed) thoughts to conform them to the law's commands.[85] A finding of responsibility here would, Moore concludes, violate the principle that 'ought' implies 'can'.

Ferzan notes correctly that there is a significant difference between a person who is unconscious and dreaming and someone who is awake but not consciously reasoning through each of her actions and the associated risks.[86] She nevertheless concludes that a person who makes a 'preconscious decision' (as Ferzan would explain matters) is nevertheless *also* not capable of being held responsible for her risk-taking without violating the 'ought' implies 'can' principle.[87] *Some* level of conscious awareness of risk is required.

[80] Useful introductions are Deborah W. Denno, 'Crime and consciousness: science and involuntary acts' (2002–2003) 97 *Minnesota Law Review* 269, and Deborah W. Denno, 'Criminal law in a post-Freudian world' [2005] *University of Illinois Law Review* 601.

[81] See the short treatment of this point in Ferzan, 'Opaque recklessness', at 641.

[82] Ibid., at 636.

[83] Michael S. Moore, 'Responsibility and the unconscious' (1979–1980) 53 *Southern California Law Review* 1563 at 1624.

[84] Ibid. [85] Ibid., at 1622.

[86] Alexander and Ferzan with Morse, *Crime and Culpability*, p. 55.

[87] Ferzan, 'Opaque Recklessness', at 638.

The move from a *capacity* to consciously reason through actions to a requirement that that capacity be *exercised* is quite swift in Ferzan's paper. She adopts Dennett's distinction between 'behavioural' awareness ('*p* is the content of an internal event in A at time *t* that is effective in directing current behaviour') and 'introspective' awareness ('*p* is the content of the input state of A's speech center at time *t*').[88] Ferzan concludes that 'introspective' awareness is required for responsibility, because '[w]ithout triggering our speech centers, we are not reasoning through our actions and are not appraising their moral worth'.[89] There is not, in purely preconscious cases, a sufficiently clear expression of the defendant's 'psychological feeling about the harm she is imposing' to ground a finding of criminal culpability.[90]

It is not clear, however, what, other than intuition[91] leads Ferzan to the conclusion that a person is responsible for a state of affairs *only* if the 'speech centres' have been 'triggered'.[92] It should be noted that Moore, upon whom Ferzan places reliance, manages to avoid the conclusion that consciousness of the wrong-making features of φ-ing is *necessary* for responsibility for wrongful φ-ing. The power or ability relevant to responsibility is present, Moore explains, when knowledge of the wrong-making components of φ-ing is 'recaptured by one's extended memory',[93] i.e. *preconscious.* This type of awareness is all that Moore requires for responsibility, and thus he avoids Ferzan's narrow conclusion that a *conscious* decision not to investigate the *preconscious* information about the risks attendant upon conduct is required. What is required for Moore is simply a disposition to, in certain circumstances, have the relevant phenomenal experience consistent with the ascription of a belief that there is a risk attendant upon φ-ing (the relevant wrong-making feature of the defendant's behaviour).[94]

If matters were left there, then the Exclusive Thesis would still be supportable: the defendant would still have to have a disposition that

[88] Ibid., at 637–638; Daniel C. Dennett, *Content and Consciousness* (Abingdon: Routledge, 1969), p. 133.

[89] Ferzan, 'Opaque Recklessness', at 638.

[90] Kimberly K. Ferzan, 'Holistic culpability' (2006–2007) 28 *Cardozo Law Review* 2523 at 2534.

[91] On the point of intuition, see Moore, 'Responsibility and the unconscious', at 1623–1624.

[92] A similar complaint can be made regarding Alexander and Ferzan with Morse, *Crime and Culpability*, p. 79.

[93] Moore, 'Responsibility and the unconscious', at 1625.

[94] See, similarly, William Wilson, *Central Issues in Criminal Law Theory* (Oxford: Hart, 2002), pp. 120–121.

seems relevant to the ascription of a belief that there is a risk attendant upon φ-ing. Moore nevertheless refuses explicitly to reach this conclusion in the relevant paper. He explains that a person who does not have a conscious or preconscious sense of the wrong-making features of her behaviour *could have done otherwise* (satisfying the 'ought' implies 'can' principle), where she *could* have got into a position where she was aware of the wrong-making features of her situation:[95]

> This is the problematic sense in which ... one guilty of a negligent omission *could have* done other than he did. This does not mean that he had the same power to avoid doing evil as one who consciously knows what he is doing. Rather, it means he could have placed himself in a position to have had that power if he had paid more attention to himself and the world around him. In this sense, responsibility for negligence may sometimes attach to unconsciously intentional actions or attempts *but this is not the degree of responsibility that is the concern of this [a]rticle.* [Emphasis added]

In other words, Moore does not think that all of those who are not consciously or preconsciously reasoning through their actions are necessarily *incapable* of being held responsible for their behaviour without violating the principle of 'ought' implies 'can'. Instead, he thinks that the basis of responsibility in such cases is simply less secure, which would be a ground for according less indignation towards the defendant for her risk-taking and its results.[96] For Moore, choice demonstrates that the defendant's course of conduct was the product of her will,[97] providing a *vital* link between the defendant's agency, her behaviour, the risks it involves and the options that she discounted in deciding what to do.[98] But it need not *necessarily* be the *only* link.

Ferzan could maintain that the wider sense of control spoken to above is simply insufficient for criminal responsibility and culpability. This point about criminal law, inadvertence and control has long been

[95] Moore, 'Responsibility and the unconscious', at 1625–1626.

[96] See, similarly, Carl Ginet, 'The epistemic requirements for moral responsibility' (2000) 34 *Noûs* 267 at 271. Moore has at times accepted that negligence can in principle be criminally culpable but simply must be explained on some basis other than choice: *Placing Blame*, pp. 413–414. For his most recent thoughts, see Michael S. Moore and Heidi Hurd, 'Punishing the awkward, the stupid, the weak, and the selfish: the culpability of negligence' (2011) 5 *Criminal Law and Philosophy* 147.

[97] See, similarly, Brenda M. Baker, '*Mens rea*, negligence and criminal law reform' (1987–1988) 6 *Law and Philosophy* 53 at 69. See also the discussion of wilfulness and recklessness in *R* v. *Lockwood, ex pte Attorney-General* [1981] Qd R 209 (Qd).

[98] Thomas Baldwin, 'Foresight and responsibility' (1979) 54 *Philosophy* 347 at 354.

debated,[99] largely because it is so difficult to establish what level of control should be required for criminal responsibility.

Citizens ought to be able to exercise at least *some* control over the matter of whether they open themselves up to the 'authoritative disavowal'[100] of criminal liability,[101] and the harm of punishment.[102] Beyond that, though, waters are murkier. Control (like the similar concept of *voluntariness*) is a 'vague and imprecise'[103] concept, and most theorists who have considered it have expressed reservations about whether they can give a full account of it.[104] It is plain, however, that the amount of control required for criminal responsibility is typically considered as being wider than the conscious choices envisaged by Ferzan.[105] As Duff points out, the idea that *only* choices (let alone *conscious* choices) are subject to the requisite level of control is 'straightforwardly false'.[106]

Reflection on the idea of control and criminal responsibility suggests that the central concern should be whether a defendant could reasonably[107] have avoided φ-ing through making alternative choices in the past.[108] Control is a matter of whether 'it is up to [a person] whether or not X is the case: insofar as it is within [her] power both to bring it about that X is the case and to bring it about that X is not the case . . . Control is

[99] See e.g. Hart, *Punishment and Responsibility*, pp. 149–151.

[100] Joel Feinberg, *Doing and Deserving: Essays in the Theory of Responsibility* (Princeton, NJ: Princeton University Press, 1970), p. 101.

[101] Duff, *Answering for Crime*, p. 59. Cf. Andrew Botterell, 'Understanding the voluntary act principle', in Francois Tanguay-Renaud and James Stribopoulos (eds.), *Rethinking Criminal Law Theory: New Canadian Perspectives in the Philosophy of Domestic, Transnational and International Criminal Law* (Oxford: Hart, 2012), p. 117.

[102] Nicola Lacey, *State Punishment: Political Principles and Community Values* (London: Routledge, 1994), p. 62.

[103] Douglas N. Husak, 'The alleged act requirement in criminal law', in John Deigh and David Dolinko (eds.), *The Oxford Handbook of Philosophy of Criminal Law* (Oxford: Oxford University Press, 2011), p. 119.

[104] Duff, *Answering for Crime*, p. 58; Douglas N. Husak, 'Does criminal liability require an act?', in R.A. Duff (ed.), *Philosophy and the Criminal Law: Principle and Critique* (Cambridge: Cambridge University Press, 1998), p. 60, at p. 77.

[105] Cf. Levy, *Consciousness and Moral Responsibility*, p. 111.

[106] R.A. Duff, 'Subjectivism, objectivism and criminal attempts', in A.P. Simester and A.T.H. Smith (eds.), *Harm and Culpability* (Oxford: Clarendon, 1996), p. 19, at p. 35.

[107] For a sketch of such a reasonableness-based account, see Husak, 'Does criminal liability require an act?', p. 78. See also the discussion of prospective responsibilities in Duff, *Answering for Crime*, pp. 72–75.

[108] Duff, *Intention, Agency and Criminal Liability*, p. 108. See also Douglas N. Husak, '"Broad" culpability and the retributive dream' (2011–2012) 9 *Ohio State Journal of Criminal Law* 449 at 472.

[about] how far the world is responsive to . . . agency'.[109] This account of control goes well beyond the boundaries of the Exclusive Thesis.[110] That a person *could have* made a particular choice in the past, and thereby averted wrongdoing, would be enough to satisfy this account of control,[111] and 'a hypothetical choice is no choice at all'.[112]

In fact, reflection on the idea of control shows it to be a fairly limited constraint on criminal liability, which could easily accommodate inadvertent risk-taking.[113] Consider Aristotle's account of culpable ignorance. Aristotle contends that negligent actors are responsible where 'it was in their power not to be ignorant, because it was up to them whether they took care'.[114] He believes that a person, in shaping her character, can foster careless habits or, alternatively, endeavour to perform the actions of a careful person (habituating herself to perform further careful actions and, ultimately, become a careful person). Aristotle is thus interested in whether a person's voluntarily formed character explains her ignorance. If a person develops her character in such a way that she fails to foresee risks that she ought to (if she were properly motivated), in the absence of compulsion (or other voluntariness-defeating conditions), then Aristotle would hold her responsible for her ignorance and her wrongdoing.[115] She could have avoided the ignorance and the wrongdoing through making alternative choices. She had a sense of control that it is not immediately clear is inappropriate for criminal responsibility.[116]

Similarly, in Chapter 8, it will be argued that defendants can be culpable for their unjustified risk-taking if, despite their not believing a risk exists, they *could* (and should) have exercised more care in the formation of their beliefs.[117] The issue of control will be returned to in

109 Duff, *Answering for Crime*, p. 57. See also Robert Kane, 'Responsibility, luck and chance: reflections on free will and indeterminism', in Gary Watson (ed.), *Free Will*, 2nd edn. (Oxford: Oxford University Press, 2003), p. 299, at p. 318.

110 Husak, 'Does criminal liability require an act?', p. 76.

111 See Robert M. Adams, 'Involuntary sins' (1985) 94 *Philosophical Review* 3 at 8.

112 Peter Cane, *Responsibility in Law and Morality* (Oxford: Hart, 2002), p. 97 (n. 110).

113 Duff, *Answering for Crime*, pp. 60–61.

114 Aristotle, *Nicomachean Ethics*, trans. Roger Crisp (Cambridge: Cambridge University Press, 2000), III.5.1114a.

115 See e.g. Joseph Raz, 'Responsibility and the negligence standard' (2010) 30 *Oxford Journal of Legal Studies* 1 at 15–18. See also Joseph Raz, *From Normativity to Responsibility* (Oxford: Oxford University Press, 2011), ch. 13.

116 Cf. Jerome Hall, 'Negligent behavior should be excluded from criminal liability' (1963) 63 *Columbia Law Review* 632 at 634–641.

117 See also Wilson, *Central Issues in Criminal Law Theory*, p. 105.

Chapter 8, but it is submitted that enough has been done here to raise significant doubts about Ferzan's argument. It is an insecure foundation for the Exclusive Thesis.

The next subsection considers an alternative control-based argument that might be used to ground some version of the Exclusive Thesis.

Control and the Conscious Centre of Will

An alternative control-based defence of the Exclusive Thesis, which – like Ferzan's – would concentrate on conscious choices, would allege that anything outside a person's conscious centre of the will (her conscious practical reasoning) is beyond the defendant's control. Such an account might be alleged to be 'Kantian', but this is perhaps misguided in the context of the Exclusive Thesis. Kant said relatively little about choice[118] and – on one reading, at least – allowed the *maxims* that guide a person (and are the base of responsibility) to be beyond her conscious grasp.[119]

Leaving Kant aside, Sher has demonstrated persuasively that there are shortcomings to accounts of responsibility that conceive of agents simply as conscious centres of will. Principally, this view is suspicious because it does not cohere with how most persons view themselves and the extent of their responsibilities to others.[120] Crucial to responsible agency and an adequate conception of the self is not simply the ability to be moved by desires at will, but also the ability to reflect on those desires and make decisions about the kind of persons we want to be (attentive, caring, etc.).[121] As long as this general reflective capacity is intact, then it is submitted that responsibility is still a possibility.[122]

[118] See Jennifer K. Uleman, *An Introduction to Kant's Moral Philosophy* (Cambridge: Cambridge University Press, 2010), pp. 27–31.

[119] See ibid., pp. 34–35. [120] See, particularly, Sher, *Who Knew?*, pp. 126–128.

[121] Gerald Dworkin, *The Theory and Practice of Autonomy* (Cambridge: Cambridge University Press, 1988), p. 15; Laura W. Ekstrom, 'Alienation, autonomy and the self' (2005) 29 *Midwest Studies in Philosophy* 45 at 48; Hilary Bok, 'Freedom and practical reasoning' in Gary Watson (ed.), *Free Will*, 2nd edn. (Oxford: Oxford University Press, 2003), p. 162; Christine M. Korsgaard, *The Sources of Normativity* (Cambridge: Cambridge University Press, 1996), p. 189; Frankfurt, *The Importance of What We Care About*, p. 12.

[122] See Deigh, 'Responsibility', at 199. Dworkin would also require that reflections have not themselves been manipulated in a particular way – Dworkin, *The Theory and Practice of Autonomy*, pp. 16–20. Cf. the discussion of 'alienation' below at Chapter 8, section on 'A Wider View: Reflecting Character'.

Furthermore, in important respects, responsibility practices are interpersonal.[123] It is an impoverished account of responsibility that views agents as isolated islands of conscious will, rather than persons capable of further thought about how their behaviour might impact on the interests of others.[124]

On the wider view of responsibility outlined here, it is of course possible to disown[125] some non-conscious behaviour (such as accidental behaviour or conduct carried out whilst sleepwalking)[126] as not being expressive at all of agency. It is not clear, however, that *negligent* behaviour must always be disowned as involuntary or *insufficiently* voluntary for the purposes of the criminal law.[127] To argue otherwise would, to appropriate an argument made in another context by Brudner, 'treat human beings as unreflective, nose-to-the-ground seekers of satisfaction incapable of meeting expectations of foresight premised on a capacity for thought'.[128] This is not to say that a conscious centre of will model of criminal responsibility treats people (perversely) as automatons, but merely to argue that it lets agents off the hook too readily for their failures of reflection on their behaviour and the risks that attach to it.[129] It is not a compelling basis for the Exclusive Thesis.

Individual Autonomy

It might be wondered if exchanging a focus on control or the defendant's centre of consciousness for one on *individual autonomy* would justify the Exclusive Thesis. Although individual autonomy is sometimes linked with choice (although rarely only *conscious* choice) in a manner that suggests the Exclusive Thesis holds,[130] individual autonomy is – like

[123] Sher, *Who Knew?*, p. 124. [124] See Adams, 'Involuntary sins', at 11.

[125] On the idea of ownership and motivation, see Fischer and Ravizza, *Responsibility and Control*, ch. 7.

[126] See A.P. Simester, 'On the so-called requirement for voluntary action' (1997–1998) 2 *Buffalo Criminal Law Review* 403 at 415–416; Douglas N. Husak and Brian P. McLaughlin, 'Time-frames, voluntary acts, and strict liability' (1993) 12 *Law and Philosophy* 95 at 110.

[127] Simon Bronnit and Bernadette McSherry, *Principles of Criminal Law*, 3rd edn. (Sydney: Lawbook, 2010), p. 187.

[128] Brudner, *Punishment and Freedom*, p. 63.

[129] See, further, Angela M. Smith, 'Control, responsibility and moral assessment' (2008) 138 *Philosophical Studies* 367 at 382.

[130] See e.g. Ashworth and Horder, *Principles of Criminal Law*, pp. 24–25.

many other concepts – overworked to the extent that its meaning is often unclear.[131] It can be understood in wider senses[132] which encompass aspects of a person's capacity for thought and her wider character, and her relationships with others, etc.[133] Such a wider view of autonomy, like the account of responsible agency outlined above, recognises again that defendants are not simply islands of conscious awareness, with no control over anything beyond that.[134] Individual autonomy could involve taking responsibility for the kind of individual one is, and the aspects of a situation that one *could have* (but did not) advert to.[135] For instance, Ashworth and Horder understand that, although individual autonomy is respected through concentrating on a defendant's choices, it is also given due weight when an inadvertent actor is punished for failing to reach a standard of care she *could* have reached.[136]

Summary

The problem with the (broadly) control-based accounts of the Exclusive Thesis discussed in this section, then, is that they explain too little,[137] ignoring 'deeply held'[138] or 'rooted'[139] intuitions about blame for inadvertence.[140] People *are* blamed for their inadvertent carelessness far more than even Ferzan admits,[141] and this gives the Exclusive Thesis an

131 Arpaly, *Unprincipled Virtue*, p. 118.

132 See, further, Peter Allmark, 'An Aristotelian account of autonomy' (2008) 42 *Journal of Value Enquiry* 41.

133 Ashworth and Horder, *Principles of Criminal Law*, p. 25.

134 Cane, *Responsibility in Law and Morality*, p. 99.

135 See Baker, '*Mens rea*, negligence and criminal law reform', at 60, Lacey, *State Punishment*, p. 77.

136 Ashworth and Horder, *Principles of Criminal Law*, pp. 181–185.

137 Simester, 'A disintegrated theory of culpability', p. 187.

138 Heidi M. Hurd, 'Introduction: symposium on *Crime and Culpability*' (2010) 29 *Law and Philosophy* 371 at 371.

139 Andrew D. Leipold, 'A case for criminal negligence' (2010) 29 *Law and Philosophy* 455 at 456.

140 Sistare, 'Models of responsibility in criminal theory', at 313; Brenda M. Baker, 'Theorizing about responsibility and criminal liability' (1992) 11 *Law and Philosophy* 403 at 428.

141 See Leo Zaibert, 'For negligence liability', in Paul H. Robinson, Stephen P. Garvey and Kimberly K. Ferzan (eds.), *Criminal Law Conversations* (Oxford: Oxford University Press, 2009), p. 281, at p. 282.

intuitive implausibility.[142] Although they are not co-extensive,[143] it seems sensible that moral and criminal culpability should not be worlds apart.[144] There should at least be a good reason to put distance between the two, and the arguments from deliberation, control and autonomy considered in this section have not offered one.

The arguments in this section should not be read to suggest that negligence could *always* necessarily be utilised as a fault element in the criminal law. As will be explained in Chapter 8, there might be reasons why citizens should *not* be required to think further about certain risks.[145] The contention is rather that the reasons discussed thus far for viewing negligence as *never* being a suitable ground of culpability for the purposes of the criminal law are unconvincing.

The next section considers an alternative argument in favour of the Exclusive Thesis, which is based on the requirement of fair warning.

Choice and Fair Warning

It was accepted in Chapter 3 that the criminal law's principle of fair warning is an integral part of the Rule of Law. Citizens should not be surprised to find that they are criminals. This point about surprise might be linked to a concern with awareness: a person is fairly warned of impending criminal liability, on this view, only if she is *aware* (believes) that she is performing the conduct, and risking the circumstances or consequences, prohibited by law.[146]

This would be a tremendously generous interpretation of the requirement of fair warning. To see this, compare the rule that ignorance of the criminal law is no excuse, a commonplace of Anglo-American jurisdictions.[147] What this rule amounts to is recognition that there is no

142 George P. Fletcher, 'Remembrance of Essays Past', in Russell L. Christopher (ed.), *Fletcher's Essays on Criminal Law* (Oxford: Oxford University Press, 2013), p. 269, at p. 277.

143 John Gardner, 'Criminal law and the uses of theory: a reply to Laing' (1994) 14 *Oxford Journal of Legal Studies* 217 at 219; Hall, 'Negligent behaviour', at 641.

144 See, similarly, Claire Finkelstein, 'Responsibility for unintended consequences' (2004–2005) 2 *Ohio State Journal of Criminal Law* 579 at 599.

145 At Chapter 8, section on 'Virtue Ethics and a Liberal Criminal Law'.

146 There is a hint of this view in Andrew Ashworth, *Positive Obligations in Criminal Law* (Oxford: Hart, 2013), p. 113.

147 This rule is, of course, rarely recognised wholeheartedly. See, e.g. A.T.H. Smith, 'Error and mistake of law in Anglo-American criminal law' (1985) 14 *Anglo-American Law Review* 3.

requirement, in order to convict the defendant of an offence, that she was aware that her conduct was *criminal.* It is sufficient that the defendant *could* reasonably have acquainted herself with the law.[148] One reason that ignorance of law is not a defence is because – at least in theory – it was reasonably *possible*, through alternative choices, for the defendant to acquaint herself with the law and avoid inadvertently breaching it.[149] If the law is not published, for example, then ignorance of the law ought to excuse, because there was no realistic prospect of being able to avoid that ignorance through choosing differently.[150] But if there was a reasonable opportunity to consult the law, then the defendant's claim of ignorance is less obviously a sound ground for complaint.[151] That ignorance was reasonably avoidable.

Fair warning, in general, could be understood to function like ignorance of law. It is instructive, in this regard, to consider T.M. Scanlon's argument about responsibility and objections to being harmed.[152] In essence, on Scanlon's model, an agent's objections to being harmed can be weakened substantially if she was placed in a sufficiently good position to avoid a certain state of affairs through the exercise of her choices. To make this discussion less abstract, and see the connection between choice, belief and avoidability for Scanlon, consider the following example.[153] A local authority decides to move some hazardous waste away from a water supply, but doing so will release some of the hazardous chemicals into the air. Despite a number of precautions, the local authority knows that at least *some* hazardous chemicals (enough to cause physical damage to anybody exposed to them) will escape into the air. The further step of warning residents to stay indoors during the move is thus taken. Scanlon introduces three people who walk into the area of the contaminated waste (call them Antje, Graham and Claudio).[154]

148 For a theoretical defence of this view, see Ashworth, *Positive Obligations in Criminal Law*, ch. 3.

149 For other arguments, see James Chalmers and Fiona Leverick, *Criminal Defences and Pleas in Bar of Trial* (Edinburgh: SULI/W. Green, 2006), pp. 262–265.

150 See, e.g. *R* v. *Lim Chin Aik* [1963] AC 160 (PC).

151 See the discussion of *negligence* with regard to learning the law in Douglas N. Husak, 'Ignorance of law and the duties of citizenship' (1994) 14 *Legal Studies* 105 at 114–115.

152 Scanlon, *What We Owe to Each Other*, ch. 7; Victor Tadros, *The Ends of Harm: The Moral Foundations of Criminal Law* (Oxford: Oxford University Press, 2011), ch. 8.

153 Scanlon, *What We Owe to Each Other*, pp. 256–264.

154 Scanlon distinguishes between four people, but the distinction between two of them is irrelevant for current purposes.

Antje hears the local authority's warnings and believes that the waste is being disposed of, and thus – on the account being sketched here – chooses to *walk into an area contaminated with waste and be exposed to the hazardous chemicals*. Her complaint about being harmed is weak because she was put in a position where she could, through appropriate choices, have avoided that state of affairs. Given what she could easily have chosen (staying indoors, going on holiday, etc.), avoidance was particularly easy in Antje's case, making her complaint about exposure *particularly* weak.

Graham is also reached by the warnings but has forgotten about them by the time of the move (so does not believe, at the relevant time, that he is entering an area with contaminated waste). Graham chooses, for example, *to walk near the lake* but does not (as Antje does) choose to *walk into an area contaminated with waste and be exposed to the hazardous chemicals*. The absence of the relevant beliefs about the waste and the hazard (because the relevant information about has been forgotten) removes the appropriateness of the ascription of such a choice to Graham. Scanlon thinks, however, that Graham *is*, like Antje, without a strong complaint about being exposed to the waste. Because he received the warning, Graham was put in a position where his choices *could have* prevented exposure (for instance, he could have left himself a note to remind him of the move). Although choice is crucial to responsibility in Antje and Graham's cases, it is *not* the choice to bring about the relevant risk; it is whatever choice or choices were made that led to the situation where the risk was not avoided, despite an *adequate* opportunity to do so being presented.

Scanlon's choice-based account thus does not support the Exclusive Thesis unless the argument is that it is *only* where awareness of risk is required that a citizen has an adequate opportunity to avoid wrongdoing and is fairly warned of impending liability and the potential harm of punishment. For the reasons given above in the section on control, it is submitted that this would be an unacceptably narrow view to take of people's ability to reflect on their behaviour and its potential consequences.

Simplistically, things get better for the Exclusive Thesis as Scanlon's discussion continues. Claudio never hears the warnings and has a legitimate complaint, Scanlon argues, on the basis that he was not put in a sufficient position where he could adequately have avoided exposure through his choices. If Claudio did not believe at any stage that there was a risk of being exposed to the waste, he cannot have altered his choices in the light of such information.

It might be argued that a negligent defendant can never be held responsible for her wrongdoing because, being unaware of the risks she is taking, she is not able to change her conduct in response to them. She is like Claudio. But that would be to misunderstand Scanlon's point. Scanlon argues that the state will have a more *difficult* time justifying the use of negligence as a marker of responsibility, because it is harder for citizens to avoid liability and punishment through their choices than where advertence to at least a risk of wrongdoing is required.[155] What would be required for responsibility for inadvertent wrongdoing to be legitimate on a Scanlonian model would thus be that the state puts defendants in a *sufficient* position that they are able through reasonable steps to avoid being negligent. It could, for instance, limit the contexts in which negligence will secure criminal culpability, warn them of penal liability for negligence, engage in educational measures to alert citizens to particular risks and impose liability only where the defendant had the background beliefs about risk that were necessary to form the *specific* belief that φ-ing was risky[156] and the general intellectual capacities required to form that belief.[157] Such limits on the ambit of negligence in the criminal law, which will be discussed at greater length in Chapter 8, ensure that the requirement of fair warning is satisfied adequately. The requirement of fair warning does not support the Exclusive Thesis.[158]

The next section discusses an alternative strategy for defending the Exclusive Thesis, which centres on the link between awareness and punishment.

Choice and Punishment

There is no room here to survey every conceivable theory of punishment, so only a small sample will be analysed. Consequentialist conceptions of punishment, particularly those concerned with harm reduction, can be

155 See, similarly, Moore, *Placing Blame*, p. 414.

156 It is submitted that this would be enough to satisfy the so-called correspondence principle, insofar as the defendant is held responsible only for risks she *could* reasonably have been expected to form beliefs about. 'Correspondence' is not, necessarily, an awareness-based idea. See, further, Tadros, *Criminal Responsibility*, pp. 94–95.

157 Ashworth and Horder, *Principles of Criminal Law*, p. 74.

158 For a different argument for the same conclusion, see Moore, *Placing Blame*, pp. 414–415.

dismissed quickly.[159] An argument for the Exclusive Thesis would run as follows. (1) The end of punishment (which legitimates it) is the reduction of unjustified risk-taking; (2) the only people who will avoid risk-taking are those who are aware that their conduct involves it; (3) therefore (1 and 2), the end of punishment is not capable of being pursued where the defendant is unaware that she is taking a risk (which is, in the circumstances, unjustified); (4) therefore (1, 2 and 3), punishment should be available only where the defendant was aware of the risks attendant upon φ-ing (risks which it is, in the circumstances, unjustified for her to take).[160]

This argument assumes that warning citizens that they will be held liable (and holding them liable) for their negligent risk-taking would not encourage them (and others)[161] to alter their choices to ensure that they take more care regarding risks in the future.[162] This assumption requires empirical backing, which is never presented.[163] If it is accepted that punishment for negligence *could* (in principle) lead to a reduction in inadvertent, unjustified risk-taking, then the consequentialist argument sketched above is weakened substantially. It is worth noting that accepting this argument means accepting that recklessness and negligence seek to inform citizens' practical reasoning at different stages: recklessness speaks to citizens at the time of acting, whereas negligence hopes to influence choices at an earlier stage.[164] This point is unproblematic.[165]

[159] The literature on culpable carelessness has not developed this argument in relation to other consequentialist conceptions of punishment (perhaps because such theories have declined in popularity as modern awareness-based conceptions of *mens rea* have come more into favour).

[160] See e.g. Jerome Hall, *General Principles of Criminal Law*, 2nd edn. (Indianapolis, IN: Bobbs-Merrill, 1960), pp. 137–139; Gross, *A Theory of Criminal Justice*, p. 351.

[161] A distinction may be drawn between *specific* and *general* deterrence: Andrew Ashworth, *Sentencing and Criminal Justice*, 6th edn. (Cambridge: Cambridge University Press, 2015), pp. 83–84.

[162] See E.M. Curley, 'Excusing rape' (1976) 5 *Philosophy and Public Affairs* 325 at 345; Daniel C. Dennett, *Elbow Room: The Varieties of Free Will Worth Wanting* (Cambridge, MA: MIT Press, 1984), pp. 142–143; Hart, *Punishment and Responsibility*, pp. 156–157; Stephen J. Schulhoffer, 'Harm and punishment: a critique of emphasis on the results of conduct in the criminal law' (1973–1974) 122 *University of Pennsylvania Law Review* 1497 at 1541; A.D. Woozley, 'Negligence and ignorance' (1978) 53 *Philosophy* 293–306, at 301; J.M. Morris, 'The structure of criminal law and deterrence' [1986] *Criminal Law Review* 524, at 531; American Law Institute, *Model Penal Code*, p. 243.

[163] '[C]onjectures about deterrence abound' in debates over negligence liability: Douglas N. Husak, *Philosophy of Criminal Law* (Totowa, NJ: Rowman and Littlefield, 1985), p. 132.

[164] Kenny, *Freewill and Responsibility*, pp. 88–89.

[165] Cf. Alexander and Ferzan with Morse, *Crime and Culpability*, p. 80.

An alternative argument in the existing literature on culpable carelessness links awareness of risk together with the retributive duty to undergo suffering.[166] The contention is that only those who were aware of the risk of causing harm can deserve punishment for unleashing that risk upon the world and/or causing the eventual harm. One of the problems[167] of retributivist theories of punishment is that it is debatable what constitutes negative desert.[168] It is not immediately clear why desert must *necessarily* be determined only on the basis of advertent wrongdoing. It is at least possible to argue that inadvertent wrongdoing *deserves* to be punished,[169] even if punishment is regarded as a severe sanction in such situations (and should thus be used relatively sparingly).[170] If the argument is that desert requires control, and inadvertent wrongdoers lack that control, then the arguments outlined earlier in this chapter can be re-deployed.

Brudner presents a different and less easy to counter retributivist argument.[171] For him, a choice to infringe the rights of others is central to culpability because of what it represents. His starting point is Hegel's view concerning social interaction,[172] which holds that the limits of a person's autonomy (and her rights) are determined by the limits on the autonomy (and rights) of others. Under such a system, one person's freedom ends where another's begins:[173] for instance, a person's right to walk where she pleases is circumscribed by the property and privacy rights of others. It is, for Brudner, a fundamental duty of citizenship to respect the boundaries of autonomy and rights, and to cross them only with the consent of those whose autonomy and rights will thereby be infringed.[174]

Given this view of society, Brudner can explain the centrality of awareness to criminal responsibility and culpability. Advertently[175]

166 See ibid., pp. 16–17; Moore, *Placing Blame*, p. 416.
167 For others, see David Boonin, *The Problem of Punishment: A Critical Introduction* (Cambridge: Cambridge University Press, 2008), ch. 3.
168 Moore, *Placing Blame*, p. 206; Paul H. Robinson, *Distributive Principles of Criminal Law: Who Should Be Punished, How Much?* (Oxford: Oxford University Press, 2008), ch. 7.
169 Kenneth W. Simons, 'Culpability and retributive theory: the problem of criminal negligence' (1994) 5 *Journal of Contemporary Legal Issues* 365 at 365.
170 Peter W. Low, 'The Model Penal Code, the common law and mistakes of fact: recklessness, negligence or strict liability?' (1987–1988) 19 *Rutgers Law Journal* 539 at 554.
171 Brudner, *Punishment and Freedom*, ch. 2.
172 See Georg W.F. Hegel, *Philosophy of Right*, trans. S.W. Dyde (Mineola, NY: Dover, 2005 [original: 1896]).
173 Brudner, *Punishment and Freedom*, p. 59.
174 See also Robert Nozick, *Anarchy, State and Utopia* (Oxford: Basil Blackwell, 1974), p. 58.
175 If the defendant is mistaken concerning the bounds of autonomy, defiance of the social order is presumably cannot be shown: Stephen P. Garvey, 'Passion's puzzle' (2004–2005)

(perhaps with an explicit, mental experience of risk)[176] going beyond the reciprocal confines of autonomy, without consent, and impacting upon the freedom of others is a symbolic disavowal of the impeded party's status as an end, the duties of citizenship and the bonds of society.[177] Punishment is a necessary evil, which reasserts the social boundaries of autonomy that the offender has threatened. It does so by limiting the *offender's* autonomy.[178] Through this process, one failure to respect the socially protected thresholds of individual autonomy breeds another,[179] reinforcing the social structure that the offender's advertent wrongdoing threatens to undermine.

This account of punishment means that the state is involved, necessarily, in the infringement of offenders' rights.[180] In imprisoning an offender, for instance, the state ensures that she is no longer free to exercise her individual autonomy as she could before offending.[181] Without the offender's consent, this would – for Brudner – be just as wrong as the offender's wrongful conduct against her fellow citizen(s).[182] It would no longer be an infringement, and would become a violation. This explains why choice is the cornerstone of Brudner's theory: it is only when an offender has *chosen* to do wrong that she can be said to have implicitly consented to (or *willed*) punishment.[183] In such cases, the offender is 'treated in accordance with his dignity and honour' rather than 'as a dog'.[184] Absent this choice and willing, punishment is an

90 *Iowa Law Review* 1677 at 1728. Despite this, Brudner admits of exculpatory mistakes only where the 'Thinking Agent' would have made the same error: Brudner, *Punishment and Freedom*, p. 82.

176 Brudner does not expend much time on consciousness, but see ibid., pp. 92–93.

177 See, further, Jean Hampton, '*Mens rea*', in Ellen F. Paul, Fred D. Miller and Jeffrey Paul (eds.), *Crime, Culpability and Remedy* (Oxford: Basil Blackwell, 1990), 1; William E. Conklin, *Hegel's Laws: The Legitimacy of a Modern Legal Order* (Stanford, CA: Stanford University Press, 2008), pp. 142–143.

178 Brudner, *Punishment and Freedom*, p. 77.

179 Importantly, Brudner thinks that the unforeseen, but foreseeable, consequences of a choice to do wrong may impact on the level of punishment: Brudner, *Punishment and Freedom*, p. 62.

180 Cf. Douglas N. Husak, *Overcriminalization: The Limits of the Criminal Law* (Oxford: Oxford University Press, 2008), p. 96.

181 Punishment thus contains an element of 'dominance' over the offender. See, further, George P. Fletcher, 'What is punishment imposed for?' (1994) 5 *Journal of Contemporary Legal Issues* 101 at 110–111.

182 See also Nozick, *Anarchy, State and Utopia*, pp. 51–52; C.S. Nino, 'A consensual theory of punishment' (1983) 12 *Philosophy and Public Affairs* 289.

183 Brudner, *Punishment and Freedom*, p. 78.

184 Hegel, *Philosophy of Right*, s. 99.

unjustifiable raising of 'a cane against a dog'.[185] The offender's rights are violated, rather than permissibly infringed.

It will be remembered that a belief that φ-ing is a possible outcome of the defendant's choice is a requirement of a choice to φ. Brudner thus requires advertence to the feature of the defendant's behaviour that makes her conduct a wrongful interference with the rights of others. Advertent wrongdoing and risk-taking is thus viewed as the core of culpability in (Brudner's envisaged) liberal society.[186] Brudner therefore supports only the use of (awareness-based) recklessness in the criminal law and decries inadvertent negligence liability in the *criminal* law as a 'mistake' made by Anglo-American systems.[187]

Brudner's defence of the Exclusive Thesis is intimidating. This is because it is linked so thoroughly to a view of the proper boundaries of autonomy, the place of punishment and the relationship between citizens in a liberal democracy. The first difficulty is, however, that the liberal democracy Brudner writes about is not reflected in the criminal law of his native Canada or elsewhere in the Anglo-American world. His theory can thus be accused of creating a 'map of imaginary terrain',[188] a criminal law that is so removed from doctrinal situations like those described in Chapter 2 that it seems alien.[189] In fact, it might be wondered whether Brudner's theory is *too* grand and whether implicit theoretical allegiances cloud his treatment of specific issues such as recklessness and negligence.[190] He might have *assumed* (wrongly) that a person cannot inadvertently threaten others' autonomy, in the sense that demonstrates implicit consent to

185 Ibid.

186 Importantly, like most writers who support the Exclusive Thesis, Brudner views negligence as *morally blameworthy*; it simply does not fit his view of criminal fault: see Alan Brudner, 'Is negligence blameless?', in Paul H. Robinson, Stephen P. Garvey and Kimberly K. Ferzan (eds.), *Criminal Law Conversations* (Oxford: Oxford University Press, 2009), p. 285.

187 Ibid., p. 79.

188 Nicola Lacey, 'Contingency, coherence and conceptualism: reflections on the encounter between "critique" and "the philosophy of the criminal law"', in R.A. Duff (ed.), *Philosophy and the Criminal Law: Principle and Critique* (Cambridge: Cambridge University Press, 1998), p. 9, at p. 16.

189 See also Ronald Dworkin, *Law's Empire* (London: Fontana, 1986), p. 65; Douglas N. Husak, 'Retribution in criminal law theory' (2000) 37 *San Diego Law Review* 959 at 969.

190 George P. Fletcher, *The Grammar of Criminal Law: American, Comparative and International* (Oxford: Oxford University Press, 2007), pp. 57–58.

be punished, by failing to acknowledge a risk that any properly motivated citizen would have foreseen.[191]

It must also be doubted whether the link between choices to do wrong and choices to undergo punishment is as valid or strong as Brudner suggests.[192] His claim is, of course, not empirical. Even those defendants who *intend* to bring about harm are very unlikely to consent to the *legal consequences* of punishment (or the risk of punishment).[193] The empirical connection between a reckless defendant and consent to punishment is presumably weaker still. Brudner is alive to this difficulty and requires only that a 'Thinking Agent' in the defendant's position *would* realise the connection between her wrongdoing and the state's punishment.[194] This reply still leaves a space between the defendant's willing of her own punishment and the thinking Agent's reckoning that such an interference with autonomy is justified on the basis of the defendant's wrongdoing. It is submitted that Brudner does not explain in a secure manner how punishment is justified *to the defendant*, when he has neither empirically consented to such treatment nor actually engaged in the thought process of the thinking Agent.

These points mean that Brudner's thesis is not a compelling account of why *only* choices to take particular risks of harm matter when assessing responsibility and culpability, which is required for the Exclusive Thesis to succeed. It is thus not a threat to the wider notions of culpable carelessness discussed in later chapters.

The focus can thus now move to a final argument for the Exclusive Thesis, which is based on the connection between awareness and *mens rea*.

Choice and *Mens Rea*

A final objection to culpability for inadvertence, which might be used to justify the Exclusive Thesis, is premised on the maxim *actus non facit*

191 Ibid., p. 313. See also Alan Norrie, 'Alan Brudner and the dialectics of criminal law' (2011) 14 *New Criminal Law Review* 449 at 459–461. Brudner thinks that such suggestions make a 'soup' of liability, rather than a clearly defined meal with separate ingredients: Alan Brudner, 'A reply to critics of *Punishment and Freedom*' (2011) 14 *New Criminal Law Review* 495 at 505.

192 See Alice Ristroph, 'When freedom isn't free' (2011) 14 *New Criminal Law Review* 468 at 473–480.

193 See, similarly, T.M. Scanlon, *The Difficulty of Tolerance* (Cambridge: Cambridge University Press, 2003), pp. 226–230.

194 Brudner, *Punishment and Freedom*, pp. 3–5. See, further, Alan Brudner, 'A reply to critics of *Punishment and Freedom*' (2011) 14 New Criminal Law Review 495 at 512.

reum nisi mens sit rea, that '[a]n act does not make a man guilty of a crime, unless his mind be also guilty'.[195] If the defendant does not believe that a risk exists, she cannot, the argument goes, have a culpable mental state – *mens rea* – at the time of taking the risk. She cannot, therefore, be held criminally liable for the inadvertent taking of an unjustified risk.

The popularity of this argument has waned,[196] perhaps because it rests on extremely unstable foundations. First, however laudable a statement of principle, no Anglo-American legal system adopts the *actus non facit reum* principle wholeheartedly – unless the word 'crime' is read particularly restrictively, so as to exclude all strict liability offences. If the *actus non facit reum* principle is read to exclude negligent wrongdoing, then it is even less descriptively apt.

Second, inadvertence *can* perhaps be described as a 'mental state' – it is the state of *not* having a particular belief (more specifically, the belief that there is a relevant risk attendant upon φ-ing).[197] This argument is weakened, however, by the fact that the mental state so described is *negative*, and so will be left to one side for now. The explanation of negligence as failure of belief in Chapter 8 will nevertheless explain when such 'negative' mental states can be useful in understanding culpable carelessness.

Third, as Fletcher points out, although that *actus non facit reum* principle 'is widely quoted, no one seems entirely sure of its relevance'.[198] It first appeared in the work of Coke[199] and is used in relation to two examples: where a person has committed what would now be embezzlement[200] (which was not a crime whilst Coke was writing) and where a person has killed himself whilst *non compos*

195 *Haughton* v. *Smith* [1975] AC 476 (E&W), at 491 (emphasis removed).

196 For early examples of this argument, see J.C. Smith, 'The guilty mind in the criminal law' (1960) 76 *Law Quarterly Review* 78 at 90; Robert P. Fine and Gary M. Cohen, 'Is negligence a defensible basis for penal liability?' (1966–1967) 16 *Buffalo Law Review* 749 at 750; Rupert Cross, 'The mental element in crime' (1967) 83 *Law Quarterly Review* 215 at 219.

199 Cf. Hart, *Punishment and Responsibility*, p. 148; Glanville Williams, 'Recklessness redefined' (1981) 40 *Cambridge Law Journal* 252 at 256.

198 George P. Fletcher, 'The theory of criminal negligence: a comparative analysis' (1970–1971) 119 *University of Pennsylvania Law Review* 401 at 411. See, further, M.J. Zimmerman, 'Negligence and moral responsibility' (1986) 20 *Noûs* 199 at 213.

199 Edward Coke, *Third Part of the Institutes of the Laws of England* (London: E&R Brook, 1648).

200 Ibid., p. 107.

mentis.[201] In both examples, the defendant would not be guilty of an offence, but the reason why seems to be different in each case. As Fletcher explains:[202]

> The first actor did not have the requisite intent to be guilty of larceny; the second was not accountable for his act of suicide. It is tempting to focus solely on the larceny hypothetical and argue that in invoking the concept of *mens rea*, Coke meant merely to say that the actor must have the intent proscribed by law in order to be guilty of the offence ... Yet this interpretation of Coke is hardly compatible with his analysis of suicide by a nonresponsible actor. In the latter case, the absence of *mens rea* is the absence of responsibility, not the absence of a particular intention or mental state proscribed by law.

Mens rea can therefore be understood in a more general sense meaning 'responsibility', rather than just 'advertent mental state'. If that move is made, then the discussion is back largely where it started: why would responsibility in the criminal law be determined entirely by advertent mental states?[203] Admittedly, this understanding of *mens rea* depletes the descriptive significance of that term in modern criminal law scholarship,[204] but it is clearly still at work in parts of Anglo-American criminal law (e.g. in the law of involuntary manslaughter in many jurisdictions).

If negligence is demonstrated (as it will be in Chapter 8) to be a sound basis for criminal culpability – in the sense that it shows meaningfully the defendant's insufficient concern for the interests of others – then the wider understanding of *mens rea* could be marshalled in its support.[205] If the allegation is that '*mens rea*' is now understood exclusively in an awareness-based sense, this is an example of selective definition; preconceptions about responsibility and fault are dictating the realm of *mens rea*, not the other way around. There is nothing in the history of *mens rea* that suggests that it *must* be understood as 'culpable mental state'[206]

201 Ibid., p. 54. 202 Fletcher, 'The theory of criminal negligence', at 411–412.

203 See, similarly, Hart, *Punishment and Responsibility*, pp. 139–140; Husak, *Philosophy of Criminal Law*, p. 135; Baker, '*Mens rea*, negligence and criminal law reform', at 78; Kyron Huigens, 'Virtue and criminal negligence' (1997–1998) 1 *Buffalo Criminal Law Review* 431 at 439.

204 J.W.C. Turner, 'The mental element in crimes at common law' (1938) 6 *Cambridge Law Journal* 31 at 32; Glanville Williams, *Textbook of Criminal Law*, 2nd edn. (London: Stevens, 1983), p. 91 (n. 5).

205 Cf. George P. Fletcher, *Rethinking Criminal Law* (Boston: Little, Brown, 1978), p. 262.

206 Cf. Kimberly K. Ferzan, 'Holistic culpability' (2006–2007) 28 *Cardozo Law Review* 2523 at 2527.

or require awareness of risk. The *actus non facit reum* principle cannot be the basis of the Exclusive Thesis.

Thus far, a range of arguments for the Exclusive Thesis – i.e. that choice is a necessary condition of responsibility and culpability – have been found to be unconvincing. Other arguments for the Exclusive Thesis will be left for the next two chapters, where they crop up more naturally. It has not been denied, however, that choice is *important* to responsibility. The next section explains why choices are *important*, to see if this importance suggests an alternative argument for the Exclusive Thesis.

The Significance of Choice

One way of explaining the importance of choice to culpability can be built on Harry Frankfurt's famous thesis concerning identification and wholeheartedness.[207] Frankfurt contends that a person acts freely when she acts on the basis of desires that she identifies with, i.e. desires she desires to have. This account can be adapted to explain the prominence of choice as an aspect of culpability. Michael is faced with a choice between A-ing and B-ing. He desires both options, and deliberates over them. Here, Michael might reflect on which of the desires he desires to motivate him – does he desire his desire to A or his desire to B? If Michael desires to desire to A, identification has taken place with the desire to A, and A-ing reflects on Michael in a meaningful way.[208] If A-ing is wrongful, and the choice to A demonstrates insufficient concern for the interests of others, then Michael is culpable in the sense that the criminal law ought to require. If Michael desires to B, and simply cannot stop himself from A-ing, such a meaningful reflection of agency is in jeopardy, or so Frankfurt's theory suggests.[209]

Thus described, Frankfurt's analysis seems unrealistic. Just as many chosen acts are not deliberated on (at least consciously, in the chooser's 'mind's eye'), not many people do think reflectively about the desires they

[207] Frankfurt, *The Importance of What We Care About*, ch. 12.

[208] The discussion here glosses over whether there can be higher order desires, and whether that fact leads to problems of infinite regress. See, however, Frankfurt, *The Importance of What We Care About*, p. 164; Tadros, *Criminal Responsibility*, pp. 31–40.

[209] See Frankfurt, *The Importance of What We Care About*, ch. 2.

wish to desire. If identification truly required such conscious deliberation over desires, then very little human action would be reflective of agency. Frankfurt's model would then be implausibly narrow.

This particular difficulty can be solved by arguing that, in choosing to A, a person *has* identified more strongly with his desire to A than with his desire to B.[210] Choosing to risk a certain consequence (or take the risk that a certain circumstance exists) could similarly be said to align the actor with that consequence or circumstance in a special way.[211] This implicit identification with the desire to act, despite the risks of which the defendant is aware, would provide a potential basis upon which to reflect that person's agency in A-ing and open him up to appropriate reactive attitudes with regard to A-ing (and the consequences of the attached risks), such as the condemnation attendant upon a criminal conviction. What will matter, ultimately, is whether the defendant's failure, in choosing to φ, to be moved by her belief about the risks attendant upon φ-ing, demonstrated that she had insufficient concern for the interests of others.

Sometimes, as Frankfurt emphasises, there will be such pressures on a person that her choices do not reflect adequately her general motivational framework. A person will act on motivations that are 'alien' to her, a concept discussed in much more detail in Chapter 8, in relation to negligence.[212] It is envisaged that 'alienation' is much more likely to be a concern in cases of negligence, given the absence of a *choice* to take the relevant risk. The criminal law already caters to cases where choices are not meaningfully reflective of agency through defences such as 'necessity' (to the extent that various Anglo-American systems accept such a defence)[213] and duress. Absent exceptional factors such as duress, there is a strong argument that choices to behave in a certain way despite believing that doing so risks harm to others reflect something very important about individuals and provide a sure basis upon which to make moral assessments of them with regard to their chosen

[210] See ibid., p. 170; Andrew Eshleman, 'Responsibility for Character' (2004) 32 *Philosophical Topics* 65.

[211] See Duff, *Intention, Agency and Criminal Liability*, p. 154; A.P. Simester, 'Responsibility for inadvertent acts' (2004–2005) 2 *Ohio State Journal of Criminal Law* 601 at 603. Cf. Moore, *Placing Blame*, p. 551.

[212] At Chapter 8, section on 'A Wider View: Reflecting Character'.

[213] English law, for instance, is opaque on the question of when 'necessity' is a defence. See Findlay Stark, 'Necessity and *Nicklinson*' [2013] *Criminal Law Review* 949.

wrongdoing. Choices might be thought particularly important because the necessary limits of belief tie the concept of choice very neatly into the chooser's epistemic perspective, meaning any message about responsibility is likely to be *highly* personal.[214]

Understood in the manner sketched above, the inquiry into culpability is, in cases of choice, relatively sanitised,[215] with difficult moral and political questions sidestepped[216] (except, perhaps, in cases of perceived 'alienation', which it is assumed – again – will be rare in cases of choice, absent duress- and necessity-type scenarios). Choice, in short, can typically provide a particularly *clear* and *solid* basis for culpability. All that is disputed here is that choice is the be-all and end-all of criminal responsibility.[217]

Conclusion

Choices are important to responsibility and culpability. They draw particularly clear links between a defendant's agency and her wrongdoing, such as to usually (absent exceptional situations, of the type to be discussed in more detail in Chapter 8) make the personalised condemnation of conviction appropriate. Such clarity means that findings of culpability for chosen wrongdoing can be particularly secure and that the amount of blame that can be assigned to an agent can accordingly be large.

What has been doubted in this chapter is that there is simply no *other* way of establishing a link between defendants and wrongdoing sufficient to condemn and punish. The Exclusive Thesis – which holds that choice is a *necessary* condition for responsibility and culpability – is unconvincing and should not be endorsed. The Exclusive Thesis will necessarily have to be returned to again, in later chapters, when choice-based objections to the account of negligence defended in this book are

214 Baker, '*Mens rea*, negligence and criminal law reform', at 69.

215 Kenneth W. Simons, 'Rethinking mental states' (1992) 72 *Boston University Law Review* 463 at 482–483. Cf. Jeremy Horder, 'Questioning the correspondence principle: a reply' [1999] *Criminal Law Review* 206 at 208.

216 John Gardner and Heike Jung, 'Making sense of *mens rea*: Antony Duff's account' (1991) 11 *Oxford Journal of Legal Studies* 559 at 575; Alan W. Norrie, 'Subjectivism, objectivism and the limits of criminal recklessness' (1992) 12 *Oxford Journal of Legal Studies* 45 at 58.

217 Cf. K.W. Simons, 'Culpability and retributive theory', at 389.

considered. This mix of positive and negative arguments explains why the Exclusive Thesis is difficult to pin down, and no doubt accounts for its pervasiveness in much discussion of criminal culpability. This chapter has argued that its prevalence is, however, unwarranted. The next chapter critiques a number of existing theories of culpability without awareness, which further challenge the Exclusive Thesis.

7

Culpability beyond Awareness of Risk

Some Existing Accounts

The previous chapter gave the positive case for the importance of the concept of awareness of risk to the 'Standard Account' of culpable carelessness in Anglo-American criminal law. Awareness brings in consideration of belief, which in turn brings in considerations of choice. Choices typically[1] link defendants particularly clearly to their unjustified risk-taking, thus making plain the matter of culpability – the linkage of a defendant to her wrongdoing in an adequately personalised manner.

It was nevertheless contended that this positive case for viewing awareness as important to culpability was not sufficient to ground (some version of) the Exclusive Thesis, i.e. the argument that awareness of risk is a *necessary* (if not sufficient) condition of criminal culpability. An alternative, negative argumentational strategy, adopted by some Exclusive Theorists, is to contend that non-awareness-based conceptions of culpability are flawed. Typically, the boon of the choice theorist is character theories,[2] but other theories have also been objected to.[3] This is a less effective manner of defending the Exclusive Thesis, because it demands that *all* conceivable alternative accounts be dismissed, and no existing critique is adequately comprehensive.[4]

That is not to say, however, that demonstrating the flaws in existing accounts of culpability without awareness is a worthless endeavour. Seeing the pitfalls and useful starting points in existing accounts of culpable carelessness that are not premised exclusively on awareness of

[1] See, however, the discussion of unreflective choices above at Chapter 6, section on 'The Significance of Choice'.

[2] See Michael S. Moore, *Placing Blame: A Theory of the Criminal Law* (Oxford: Oxford University Press, 1998), ch. 13. Moore also objects to capacity-based theories, such as Hart's (discussed below).

[3] See, e.g. Larry Alexander and Kimberly K. Ferzan with Stephen J. Morse, *Crime and Culpability: A Theory of Criminal Law* (Cambridge: Cambridge University Press, 2009), chs. 2–3.

[4] Cf. the rather cursory treatment of some arguments in ibid., ch. 3.

risk allows for the development of a better alternative. This chapter is thus dedicated to clearing some ground in the existing literature on accounts of culpability for unjustified risk-taking that do not require the defendant to have been aware of the relevant risk at the time of taking it. Some previous treatments of culpability beyond awareness are more similar to the account presented in the next chapter, and will be dealt with there.

This chapter begins by exploring accounts of culpability without awareness that are based (to a large extent) on the defendant's conduct. Accounts of culpability without awareness that rely on 'tracing' – i.e. looking for culpability in previous decisions made by the defendant before she was unaware of the risks attendant upon her conduct (φ-ing) – are then analysed. Next, the chapter discusses theories of culpability premised on counterfactual assessments of what the defendant *would have* chosen had she been aware of the risk she in fact missed (or the clash of values that the risk raises). Finally, attitudinal accounts of culpability without awareness are considered, with Antony Duff's 'practical indifference' – the most developed such account – being critiqued at length and ultimately rejected.

Conduct: Hart's Insight

Attempts to explain the place of inadvertent, unjustified risk-taking in the criminal law sometimes focus on the *extent* of the defendant's unjustified risk-taking (her wrongdoing), rather than her mental state.

There is some doctrinal support for such conduct-centred approaches in some of the Anglo-American systems surveyed in Chapter 2. In certain Australian jurisdictions, for example, negligence is defined in the following terms: 'such a great falling short of the standard of care that a reasonable person would exercise in the circumstances; and . . . such a high risk that the physical element exists or will exist, that the conduct merits criminal punishment for the offence'.[5] Such definitions of culpable unjustified risk-taking do not focus on the defendant's beliefs about risk at all.[6] This allows for a clear line to be drawn between

[5] See, e.g. Criminal Code Act 1983 (NT), sch. 1, s. 43AL; Criminal Code Act 1995 (Cwlth), s. 55. The same constituent definitional elements appear in a slightly different order in the Criminal Code 2002 (ACT), s. 21.

[6] Jeremy Gans, *Modern Criminal Law of Australia* (Cambridge University Press, 2011), p. 111.

recklessness (which, as seen above, is a concept connected to beliefs about risk) and negligence. This clear distinction might be viewed as a virtue.[7]

If *criminal* negligence is conceived of as being conduct-based, it is plain why it is controversial: if the defendant is censured simply for not behaving as another (hypothetical) person would have, then the criminal inquiry seems anti-individualised.[8] Convicting the defendant tells her (and others) little about *her* and the concern that *she* failed to show for others' interests.[9] Without this personalised message of condemnation, the communicative aspect of conviction is absent.[10]

The challenge for proponents of criminal liability for negligence who support the communicative enterprise of criminal law is thus to 'get personal'[11] and demonstrate that punishment for inadvertent, unjustified risk-taking communicates something meaningful not only about the standards of conduct expected of 'reasonable persons', but also about the defendant, her culpability and the community criticism her wrongdoing attracts.

There is, then, a need to move beyond bare conduct alone – many Anglo-American systems have gone wrong in their explanation of negligence. A significant development in the debate over whether inadvertent risk-taking could be the stuff of criminal liability was H.L.A. Hart's essay 'Negligence, *mens rea* and criminal responsibility'.[12] As will be seen, Hart's focus seems at first to be mainly conduct-based, but soon falls into consideration of the defendant's beliefs about risk. The contention in this section is that Hart points the way to a more defensible conception of criminal negligence, but does not flesh out the details sufficiently to make his account acceptable.

7 See, further, Sally Cunningham, 'Recklessness: being reckless and acting recklessly' (2010) 21 *King's College Law Journal* 445.

8 See, similarly, George P. Fletcher, 'The fault of not knowing' (2002) 3 *Theoretical Inquiries in Law* 265 at 277.

9 See Moore, *Placing Blame*, p. 412.

10 On the communicative aspects of conviction, see above pp. 1–2. See, similarly, A.P. Simester, 'Can negligence be culpable?', in Jeremy Horder (ed.), *Oxford Essays in Jurisprudence: Fourth Series* (Oxford: Oxford University Press, 2000), p. 85, at pp. 85–88.

11 John Gardner, 'On the general part of the criminal law', in R.A. Duff (ed.), *Philosophy and the Criminal Law: Principles and Critique* (Cambridge: Cambridge University Press, 1998), p. 205, at p. 236.

12 H.L.A. Hart, *Punishment and Responsibility*, 2nd edn. (Oxford: Oxford University Press, 2008), ch. 6.

Exploring Hart's Account

In common with some of the authors discussed in the previous chapter, (sufficiently free) choices are of central importance to Hart's view of culpability.[13] He nevertheless contends that punishment for *negligence* (or, as he sometimes refers to it, 'gross, unthinking carelessness')[14] might be appropriate in certain circumstances.[15] Hart is not, in short, an Exclusive Theorist.

It is important to note, before proceeding further, the distinction Hart draws between *inadvertence* (the psychological state of the defendant who is not aware of the risks attendant upon her behaviour) and *negligence*, which Hart introduces as being about bare conduct, i.e. 'reasonable care' and 'reasonable precautions against harm'.[16] When first explained by Hart, the core concern in negligence is not the defendant's inadvertence but the failure of the defendant to *behave* sufficiently carefully.[17] Hart might be misread here as endorsing a bare conduct-based account of negligence. This would be unacceptable for the criminal law, for it would fail to draw a clear, personalised link between the defendant and her wrongdoing.

When Hart begins to develop his account of negligence, a surer basis for personalised findings of culpability nevertheless becomes visible. Hart moves to focus on whether the defendant could 'have thought about what he was doing',[18] i.e. done more to form appropriate beliefs about the risk attendant upon φ-ing. The negligent defendant fails to 'exercise a capacity to advert to, and think about ... conduct and its risks'.[19] This role for inadvertence can be read into Hart's famous test for negligence:[20]

> (i) Did the accused fail to take those precautions which any reasonable man with normal capacities would in the circumstances have taken?
> (ii) Could the accused, given his mental and physical capacities, have taken those precautions?

These are referred to as the 'invariant standard of care' and the 'individualised conditions of liability', respectively. The invariant standard of care contains no clue as to the role of the defendant's inadvertence in

[13] Ibid., pp. 120–121. [14] Ibid., p. 136.
[15] Hart is agnostic on the question of whether negligence *should* be punished: ibid., p. 157.
[16] Ibid., pp. 136–137, 147–148. [17] Ibid., pp. 147–148. [18] Ibid., p. 152.
[19] Ibid., p. 157. [20] Ibid., p. 154.

establishing culpability. It avowedly is not concerned with individual features of the defendant (because Hart is worried that, if it were, the standard would ultimately become the defendant's and nobody would ever fall short of it)[21] and draws a distinction between the defendant's *situation* and the defendant's particular attributes.[22] All the first part of Hart's test is doing, then, is identifying wrongdoing, i.e. unjustified risk-taking.

The use of the 'reasonable man' standard ensures that the extent of criminal liability for risk-taking is circumscribed.[23] It is not negligent, on Hart's view, to fail to take precautions against risk unless the defendant could be expected – as a member of the community, which it is assumed the 'reasonable man' stands in for[24] – to have done more. This should stave off concerns about negligence liability requiring defendants to make an effort to avoid risks in *every* circumstance, which would have significant implications for individual freedom.[25] Sometimes, on Hart's view of negligence, risks are not wrongful to take. All of these points cohere with the account of justification sketched in Chapter 1.[26]

Hart's individualised standard of care might be thought of as a guarantee of culpability – a personal connection between defendants and wrongdoing. First, it deals well with cases where the defendant simply could not, because of an absent or undeveloped 'mental or physical capacity', have taken the required steps to cater to the risk attendant upon φ-ing. Cases of physical incapacity are perhaps straightforward, but it is his mentioning of *mental* incapacity that takes Hart away from bare

21 See, further, James B. Brady, 'Punishment for negligence: a reply to Professor Hall' (1972–1973) 22 *Buffalo Law Review* 107 at 115; Glanville Williams, *Textbook on Criminal Law*, 2nd edn. (London: Stevens, 1983), pp. 94–95; Larry Alexander, 'Reconsidering the relationship among voluntary acts, strict liability and negligence in criminal law', in Ellen F. Paul, Fred D. Miller and Jeffrey Paul (eds.), *Crime, Culpability and Remedy* (Oxford: Basil Blackwell, 1990), p. 84, at p. 98.

22 For alternative suggestions regarding which attributes to consider, see Kent Greenawalt, *Law and Objectivity* (New York: Oxford University Press, 1992), p. 104; R.A. Duff, *Criminal Attempts* (Oxford: Oxford University Press, 1996), p. 175.

23 There are various problems with the 'objective' standard, which are less relevant to the present discussion. See, however, Mayo Moran, *Rethinking the Reasonable Person: An Egalitarian Reconstruction of the Objective Standard* (Oxford: Oxford University Press, 2003).

24 Cf. the discussion of justification and risk-taking, above at Chapter 1, section on 'Justifying Risk-taking'.

25 See the discussion of the extent to which negligence liability is compatible with autonomy, below at Chapter 8, section on 'Virtue Ethics and a Liberal Criminal Law'.

26 Section on 'Justifying Risk-taking'.

conduct and towards inadvertence (i.e. the absence of a belief that the relevant risk existed) as an important aspect of negligence. The (in) famous English case of *Elliott* v. *C (A Minor)*[27] is instructive here. The defendant was fourteen years old and of low intelligence. After spending the night wandering the streets, C happened upon a shed, which contained white spirit. She decanted the spirit onto the floor and set fire to it. The shed was destroyed.

Because of her limited intelligence, there were doubts over C's ability to appreciate that her conduct carried with it a risk of property damage. As a result, she was acquitted, and the prosecution appealed. On appeal, the court denied that C's incapacity made a difference to the matter of *recklessness*, as that concept was not dependent on awareness of risk in relation to criminal damage in English law at the time.[28] If the 'ordinary' person would have believed that the relevant risk existed, then the defendant was reckless for taking it, despite her inadvertence.[29]

The decision in *C* is clearly problematic. It meant that the English law of recklessness, at least in some contexts, 'admitted of no exceptions'.[30] This situation was rightly criticised strongly by academics[31] and the Law Commission.[32] It is 'perhaps the nadir of modern English criminal law'.[33] The imposition of criminal liability (for a relatively serious offence) on a child of low intelligence further seemed to communicate little to the individual defendant (other than she was expected to reason and then act better than she apparently *could* have done), the shed's owner, or the public more generally. It thus seemed fruitless,[34] and a

27 [1983] 1 WLR 939 (E&W). 28 At 947.

29 This was not an isolated case. For other cases reaching similar conclusions, see *Stephen* v. *R* (1984) 79 Cr App R 334 (E&W); *R* v. *Coles* [1995] 1 Cr App R 157 (E&W); *R* v. *Bell* [1985] RTR 202 (E&W).

30 Andrew Ashworth and Jeremy Horder, *Principles of Criminal Law*, 7th edn. (Oxford: Oxford University Press, 2013), p. 180. See, further, *R* v. *Stephens*, unreported, Auckland High Court, 8 December 1983 (cited in *R* v. *Harney* [1987] 2 NZLR 576 (NZ), at 579).

31 See P.R. Glazebrook, 'Criminal negligence' (1984) 43 *Cambridge Law Journal* 1; Stewart Field and Mervyn Lynn, 'The capacity for recklessness' (1992) 12 *Legal Studies* 74; Glanville Williams, 'The unresolved problem of recklessness' (1988) 8 *Legal Studies* 74 at 78; John E. Stannard, 'Subjectivism, objectivism and the Draft Criminal Code' (1985) 101 *Law Quarterly Review* 540 at 547; Barry Mitchell, 'Recklessness could still be a state of mind' (1988) 52 *Journal of Criminal Law* 300 at 303.

32 See e.g. *Legislating the Criminal Code: Offences against the Person and General Principles* (Law Com. No. 218, 1993), para. 14.22.

33 Simester, 'Can negligence be culpable?', p. 102 (n. 67).

34 R.A. Duff, *Intention, Agency and Criminal Liability: Philosophy of Action and the Criminal Law* (Oxford: Basil Blackwell, 1990), p. 164.

violation of the principle that criminal liability ought to be reasonably easy to avoid.[35]

Hart's theory can deal with *Elliott* v. *C (A Minor)* in a sensible manner, by taking into account the defendant's individual shortcomings in considering whether she could legitimately be expected to have formed a belief about the relevant risk associated with her behaviour and taken steps to avoid it.[36] This is, indeed, the basis of its strength over simple 'reasonable person' test conceptions of negligence, such as those found in some Anglo-American systems (if those are not then supplemented by certain of the defendant's personal attributes).[37] It is important to note, however, that to deal with *Elliott* v. *C (A Minor)*, Hart cannot be concerned with bare conduct alone. Surely C *could* have taken the relevant steps against the risk of fire (not spilling the white spirit, not lighting it, etc.), but the point is that – if she is viewed as credible – she did not *believe* that such steps were necessary, because she did not *believe* that the relevant risk of inflammation attended her conduct. Her plea is not one concerned with bare conduct, but one concerned with consideration of her beliefs, and her ability to form the belief that the risk of inflammation attached to her conduct, at the time of acting. This moves the focus back where it ought to be: can C legitimately be expected to have better managed her beliefs regarding risk? That is the basis of the account of negligence to be presented in the next chapter, but it moves beyond what Hart explained in his seminal essay.

Indeed, the main difficulty with Hart's theory is that it is so undeveloped. Although Hart's theory can deal with somewhat clear cases such as *C*, there remains a question over *which* of the defendant's attributes are relevant to the question of whether she had the capacity to comply with the invariant standard of care. For example, C was both of subnormal intelligence and extremely tired (having spent the night wandering the streets). Both of these factors could impact upon her mental capacity to appreciate risk. Are both equally relevant to the question of culpability?

Any answer to this question is likely to be difficult and controversial.[38] It might be assumed that a tired person is less alert to risk than a rested

[35] For a defence of this principle, see above at Chapter 6, section on 'Choice and Fair Warning'.

[36] Cf. Oliver W. Holmes, *The Common Law* (Boston: Little, Brown, 1881), p. 108.

[37] See e.g. *RSPCA* v. *C* [2006] EWHC 1069 (Admin) (E&W), where (along with other factors) the defendant's age was used to contextualise the reasonable person test in a case of animal neglect.

[38] *R* v. *G and Another* [2003] UKHL 50, [2004] 1 AC 1034 (E&W), at [37].

one, which might count in favour of considering C's tiredness as relevant to assessing her failure to reach the invariant standard of care. It could be countered, however, that C was free to have slept at home. She was not forced into being tired, or breaking into the shed and setting fire to the white spirit she found inside.

Even taking C's low level of intelligence into account might provoke controversy. If C *believed*, for instance, that she did careless things and took risks with the interests of others without noticing, it might be argued that she was at fault for going out unaccompanied in the first place. C's decisions, in light of her beliefs about her capacities with regard to risk perception, might well have showed a facet of her agency that grounds responsibility and, potentially, culpability.[39]

Having to address meaningfully the difficult question of which attributes should be taken into account is a major drawback of accepting wholeheartedly Hart's theory of culpability without awareness. It might be thought that, in view of the value pluralism that permeates modern societies, it is unlikely that real consensus could be reached on when incapacity should excuse,[40] a difficulty that Hart adverts to (but does little to address).[41] This is not to say that no such clarifications can in theory be made, but simply to note that Hart does not make them.

Even if Hart's account were specified adequately so as to remove the doubts above, it might still fail to detect clearly culpable defendants. On a natural understanding of *could*, most defendants *could* have recognised the risk attendant upon their conduct, but this does not necessarily say anything about their insufficient concern for others, the gist of culpability. Indeed, a more sensible approach than Hart's would be to take all of the defendant's features into account, other than her concern for others, and ask what level of concern with regard to others' interests *a reasonable person with her attributes would have shown.*[42] But that

[39] This type of argument is discussed below in the section on 'tracing' theories.

[40] Nicola Lacey, *State Punishment: Political Principles and Community Values* (Abingdon: Routledge, 1988), p. 65; Samuel H. Pillsbury, 'The meaning of deserved punishment: an essay on choice, character and responsibility' (1991–1992) 67 *Indiana Law Journal* 719 at 748.

[41] Hart thinks only 'gross forms of incapacity' (whatever these are) could be demonstrated in practice: Hart, *Punishment and Responsibility*, p. 155. The difficulty of 'subjectivising' standards is of course prevalent in other areas. See e.g. Eimear Spain, *The Role of Emotions in Criminal Law Defences: Duress, Necessity and Lesser Evils* (Cambridge: Cambridge University Press, 2011), pp. 175–189.

[42] A broadly similar suggestion is made in Peter Weston, 'Individualizing the reasonable person in criminal law' (2008) 2 *Criminal Law and Philosophy* 137.

gets very far away from what Hart said, and closer to the theory espoused in the next chapter.

In summary, the choice and capacity theory espoused by Hart is significant in its acceptance of culpability in the absence of a choice to do wrong. It demonstrates that one can be committed to choice as a marker of culpability and yet endorse alternative grounds of fault. Hart does not excuse automatically persons who fail to live up to standards of carefulness expected by the community. Rather, he opens concern up to the question of whether the defendant *could have* done better in terms of her beliefs and, as a result, her conduct. He certainly indicated a meaningful way forward in the debate over culpable carelessness, but the details are for others to fill in. To an extent, many of the accounts discussed below and in the next chapter can be seen as attempts to follow Hart's lead and shore up his account of culpability without awareness.

The next account to be considered here is, like Hart's, superficially about conduct alone.

Conduct: Horder's Reasons-Based Account

Jeremy Horder argues that failing to meet a set standard of conduct *can* demonstrate something about the actor's personal culpability, even when she did not believe the relevant risks attendant upon φ-ing existed.[43] Horder's focus is on, instead of belief, the relationship between the defendant, the reasons that ought to guide her, and her wrongdoing.

In the light of its intricate nature, it is helpful to have an example to come back to whilst discussing Horder's theory. Hana is a doctor, who is charged with the care of Dan. Hana injects Dan with a drug that he is allergic to, and he dies. A cursory check would have indicated the allergy, but Hana states (truthfully) that she did not believe that Dan might be allergic to the drug. Horder's route to establishing whether Hana is culpable with regard to Dan's death would take the following steps.

First, Horder would note that Hana came to be in charge of Dan's care as a result of voluntarily becoming a doctor.[44] Although she might occasionally face emergency decisions, this does not undermine the fact

[43] Jeremy Horder, 'Gross negligence and criminal culpability' (1997) 47 *University of Toronto Law Journal* 495. Horder also describes a form of negligence which concentrates upon the defendant's attitude of *indifference*. This is discussed later in this chapter.

[44] Hana must have made a *series* of choices to become a doctor (taking the correct exams at school, applying to medical schools, etc.), demonstrating her commitment to that goal.

that Hana was not forced to become a doctor. It can be assumed that, when making this decision, she was aware of the practical and ethical responsibilities attendant upon that role (if not, Hana surely became aware of these as her studies progressed).[45] This means that she had fair warning of the responsibilities she would assume if she ultimately became a doctor (rather than, say, a medical researcher).[46] By electing to become a doctor, Hana has therefore fairly assumed the prospective responsibilities associated with that role[47] and agreed to be governed by a well-known code of conduct and ethics.

The code of conduct and ethics that governs her profession gives rise to certain restrictions on Hana's actions. For instance, if a procedure is not carried out in the accredited way, this might be cause for professional (and perhaps legal)[48] censure. This is the sort of conduct element that some theorists concentrate on in their denials of culpability for inadvertent, unjustified risk-taking. Up until this point, it could even be argued that – if punished for Dan's death – Hana is being held *strictly liable* for the consequences of an omission to follow guidelines:[49] the polity has decided to declare certain conduct – and its consequences – criminal and Hana has (for whatever reason) fallen short of its expectations.[50] Understood this way, the element of *personal* culpability demonstrated by Hana's action is at first unclear. All that has been identified is a failure of conduct, which seems like an element of wrongdoing, as distinct from culpability.

There is, however, another aspect of Hana's assumption of the responsibilities of being a doctor which shows more transparently the root of her culpability for Dan's death. For Horder, this wider aspect of responsibility comes from the voluntary undertaking of a doctor to act in the patient's best interests at all times. This commitment to patients permeates the codes of conduct to which doctors subscribe, and it ought to motivate a doctor's reasoning and make her act in

[45] Cf. the term 'role responsibility' in Hart, *Punishment and Responsibility*, pp. 212–214.

[46] See Horder, 'Gross negligence and criminal culpability', at 516–517.

[47] On prospective responsibilities, see Peter Cane, *Responsibility in Law and Morality* (Oxford: Hart, 2002), pp. 31–35; Victor Tadros, *Criminal Responsibility* (Oxford: Oxford University Press, 2005), pp. 21–22; R.A. Duff, *Answering for Crime: Responsibility and Liability in the Criminal Law* (Oxford: Hart, 2007), pp. 30–36.

[48] Cf. *R* v. *Adomako* [1995] AC 171 (E&W).

[49] Some authors think that negligence folds into strict liability. See e.g. Larry Alexander, 'Reconsidering the relationship among voluntary acts, strict liability, and negligence'.

[50] Strict liability is not considered in this book.

selfless ways which would not be required of other citizens.[51] Although the hospital janitor may leave Dan alone, Hana *must* treat him in line with his best interests. Walking away is not an option for her in virtue of her role – she would have to answer (to her colleagues, to Dan and/or his family, perhaps to the criminal courts)[52] for acting in that manner. Hana's assumption of responsibility for others has thus done more than simply provide her with accredited ways of carrying out medical procedures – it has also provided her with what Raz calls 'exclusionary reasons'.[53]

As their name suggests, exclusionary reasons exclude certain other reasons from consideration.[54] For example, that a person has promised to lend her car to her mother ought to exclude reasons which would point towards selling the car.[55] Even though selling the car would normally be a viable option (it might, on the balance of reasons, be the right thing to do), the exclusionary reason – the promise – changes things. Exclusionary reasons can thus 'tip the scales' against the balance of reasons.[56]

Similarly, Hana's assumption of responsibility over Dan's healthcare alters her situation by excluding certain reasons and closing off options that would otherwise be open to her (walking away, etc.).[57] A prohibition on giving a patient a drug without checking – when the opportunity presented itself – for allergies would exist *because* acting in that way would be detrimental to that patient's best interests. Through taking exactly that course of conduct (even if for the first time),[58] Hana has done more than *merely* act contrary to an 'objective' standard. She has also acted on reasons that ought to be excluded, that should not even

[51] Horder, 'Gross negligence and criminal culpability', at 515. Whether citizens should have legal duties to assist others is a difficult question, which cannot be addressed here. See, however, Andrew Ashworth, 'The scope of criminal liability for omissions' (1989) 105 *Law Quarterly Review* 424; Andrew Ashworth, *Positive Obligations in Criminal Law* (Oxford: Hart, 2013), ch. 2.

[52] On the matter of to *whom* a person is responsible, see Duff, *Answering for Crime*, ch. 2.

[53] See Joseph Raz, *Practical Reason and Norms* (rev. edn.) (Oxford: Oxford University Press, 1990), pp. 37–45.

[54] Ibid., p. 190. [55] Ibid., p. 39.

[56] Ibid., p. 41. Clashes between exclusionary reasons are resolved by weight: Joseph Raz, 'Facing up: a reply' (1988–1989) 62 *Southern California Law Review* 1153 at 1168.

[57] Cf. Raz, *Practical Reason and Norms*, p. 39.

[58] Cf. Michael D. Bayles, 'Character, purpose and criminal responsibility' (1982) 1 *Law and Philosophy* 5 at 10–11; Michael D. Bayles, *Principles of Law: A Normative Analysis* (Dordrecht: Reidel, 1987), p. 299.

have occurred to her.[59] In doing so, Hana 'has betrayed her very role as a doctor',[60] because the thought 'I will give him the drug . . .' *should never have entered her mind* without the caveat '. . . if he is not allergic' and the attendant motivations (to check for allergies, etc.). The fact that it did suggests that Hana was insufficiently motivated, in terms of her reasoning (not necessarily her *beliefs* about the situation), by Dan's legally protected interest in bodily integrity and life.[61] This is so even though Hana was not aware of the risk that Dan had an allergy at the time that she administered the drug.

Not all failures of conduct are thus 'minor moral lapses' that can be dealt with only through strict liability offences or the civil courts.[62] On Horder's reasons-based view, they can be culpable in the sense that criminal law usually requires.

The culpability outlined above surely *is* personal to Hana in that *she* voluntarily accepted a standard of conduct and failed to act in line with the exclusionary reasons that flowed from it. Although these reasons are external (in the sense that they will be dictated by bodies of professional opinion), it is still *Hana's* reasoning and the way she conducted *herself* – not the reasonable doctor's imagined reasoning or conduct – which matters for culpability. Thus Horder has identified a way of linking defendants to their unjustified risk-taking and its consequences in a manner that suggests personalised blame is appropriate but that does not focus on the unjustified absence of a particular belief about risk.

It is submitted that Horder's argument is nevertheless problematic. First, it is important to consider *why* Hana failed to adhere to the standard of reasoning required of her by her role as a doctor. Hana might be able to rebut the inference of culpability for Dan's death by offering an excuse for her failure to check for allergies which explains why, despite appearances, she showed sufficient regard for Dan's interests. Such an excuse will be difficult to make out in Hana's circumstances. There was no emergency, so she had time to stop and consider Dan's best

[59] Bernard Williams, *Ethics and the Limits of Philosophy* (Cambridge, MA: Harvard University Press, 1985), p. 185; Raz, *Practical Reason and Norms*, p. 181; Horder, 'Gross negligence and criminal culpability', at 514–515.

[60] Horder, 'Gross negligence and criminal culpability', at 516.

[61] Cf. Tadros, *Criminal Responsibility*, p. 85.

[62] Kenneth W. Simons, 'Culpability and retributive theory: the problem of criminal negligence' (1994) 5 *Journal of Contemporary Legal Issues* 365 at 386. It is doubtful that *all* offences of strict liability concern 'minor' behaviour, but that is an issue that need not be resolved here.

interests. Even if Hana was distracted with thoughts of other, sicker patients, she would still show herself to be insufficiently motivated by *Dan's* interests in failing to act in line with the exclusionary reasons which bore upon her. Her duty was to Dan *and* her other patients – not *just* her sickest patients. It is submitted that it is Hana's *demonstration of insufficient concern* for Dan's interests, in the formation of her beliefs about the reasons that bore upon her, which matters for criminal culpability, not simply that she had signed up voluntarily for a standard of conduct and failed to be guided by the reasons it supplied.

Further to this point about insufficient concern, Horder's account is necessarily very limited as an explanation of negligence on the Standard Account. To summarise the discussion thus far, Horder's account requires the following: (i) a voluntary decision to undertake an activity, (ii) a well-publicised code of conduct governing that activity, (iii) exclusionary reasons arising from that conduct and (iv) a failure to act in accordance with those exclusionary reasons resulting in substantial, unjustified risk-taking and demonstrating insufficient concern for the interests of others.

Such situations obviously exist in everyday activity. For instance, (legal) drivers voluntarily assume a range of responsibilities, in line with a well-publicised (and examined) code of conduct,[63] which fosters the demonstration of sufficient regard for the interests of other road-users, thus providing drivers with exclusionary reasons which ought, in normal circumstances,[64] to prohibit the contemplation of selfish conduct. Options which would otherwise be open to a person are excluded by virtue of her assumption of the responsibilities of being a driver.[65]

This show of consideration for others is essential to being a proper driver.[66] By not following the legal regulations (or non-legal documents such as the 'Highway Code') surrounding driving, a driver *can* thus

[63] In the UK jurisdictions, the Highway Code and the various pieces of (UK-wide) Road Traffic legislation.

[64] Cf. *McNab* v. *Guild* 1989 JC 72 (Scot), where the accused thought his passenger needed medical attention and so drove at great speed. This motivation might suggest that he *did* show sufficient concern for others in driving as he did, despite initial signs to the contrary.

[65] Even an unlicensed (and/or uninsured) driver could have assumed these responsibilities, implicitly, by driving on public roads. The same argument could be made where the defendant has undertaken a regulated activity without expertise (e.g. 'fixing' a faulty gas fire – see *R* v. *Singh* [1999] *Criminal Law Review* 582 (E&W)).

[66] Horder, 'Gross negligence and criminal culpability', at 517.

demonstrate her attitude towards those regulations and, more importantly, her lack of concern for the values that they promote. This close connection between responsibility, conduct and culpability is perhaps the source of the misconception that negligence is *just* about action.

Although Horder explains well the blameworthiness in failing to drive safely, or follow medical procedure, his account fares less well in other situations[67] – making a voluntary-duty-based approach to negligence seem narrow indeed. This is for a number of reasons.

First, some activities are not regulated sufficiently to satisfy Horder's conditions. Consider walking on the pavement:[68] there is not a system of legal regulation (or, presumably, sufficient social consensus) on whether it is acceptable to, for instance, walk along engrossed in reading a text message to make doing so wrong and a matter of responsibility and culpability, *even if* this conduct puts other people at significant risk of serious injury or worse.[69]

Second, even if a social consensus appears to exist over such mundane things, it might be wondered whether citizens have any meaningful alternatives to entering certain spheres of conduct. Is it possible to avoid using a pavement? If not, then the element of voluntariness (and, consequently, the assumption of responsibility for living up to expected standards) appears to be vitiated. Citizens could legitimately complain if they were unable easily to avoid the threat of the criminal sanction.[70] Similar problems are encountered when citizens have no acceptable option but to enter areas of specialist expertise. Consider laypersons forced, by the circumstances, into giving medical aid:[71] although there are well-publicised expectations concerning how this should be undertaken, which promote values and provide exclusionary reasons, the layperson has not (meaningfully) *volunteered* to enter that sphere of regulation and meet its expectations. Horder's account of negligence presumably does not cater for such situations.[72]

[67] Cf. the discussion of rape in ibid., at 518. See, further, Richard H.S. Tur, 'Rape, reasonableness and time' (1981) 1 *Oxford Journal of Legal Studies* 432 at 437.

[68] Or on the road. Cf. *Evgeniou* v. *R* (1964) 37 ALJR 508 (HCA).

[69] Cf. driving whilst using a mobile phone, which is now criminalised in some jurisdictions – e.g. Road Traffic Act 1988 (UK), s. 41D.

[70] See the discussion of fair warning, above at Chapter 6, section on 'Choice and Fair Warning'.

[71] Cf. *R* v. *Stone and Dobinson* [1977] QB 354 (E&W).

[72] Horder, 'Gross negligence and criminal culpability', at 519.

Horder's conduct-based account of negligence identifies, at best, a *special* case of negligence. It relies upon the voluntary (i.e. avoidable) assumption of responsibilities, a well-publicised code of conduct (and/or ethics) and the provision of exclusionary reasons, rather than simply a *simple* failure to act (or omit to act) as others might have. Given its limited sphere of application, some opponents of criminal liability for negligence might accept Horder's argument as developed here.[73] It seems appropriate that those who voluntarily adopt special roles (which might mean the difference between another person living or dying) are held, on pain of punishment, to a high standard of conduct and to demonstrate sufficient concern for the interests of others in their reasoning.

Criminal negligence is not, however, usually limited to such special contexts in doctrinal criminal law. Horder's view cannot therefore be an adequate descriptive account in itself – indeed, as will be seen later in this chapter, Horder offers an additional account of 'gross' negligence. It is of course open to Horder to complain that his account is not merely descriptive, but rather could lead to revisions of doctrine. Even if that point is accepted (which is reasonable), it is submitted that his account is unnecessarily complicated and limited compared with the alternative account of negligence presented in the next chapter. Furthermore, for the reasons given in Chapter 3, it would be preferable if *one* account of negligence could be given,[74] and it will be contended that the account in Chapter 8 is superior descriptively and theoretically.

This section has rejected (primarily) conduct-based accounts of culpability without awareness. The next section moves to consider arguments that look for the defendant's culpability not at the time of taking the relevant risk or in the presence of a relevant circumstance or consequence, but at an earlier point in time. These can be classed together as 'tracing' accounts of culpable inadvertence.

'Tracing' Accounts

There are three main tracing strategies in the existing literature. As with the accounts discussed thus far, there is some truth in these views, but they also have their limitations. To anticipate the conclusion drawn in

[73] See e.g. J.C. Smith, 'Subjective or objective? Ups and downs of the test of criminal liability in England' (1981–1982) 27 *Villanova Law Review* 1179 at 1204.

[74] For pessimism about unified accounts of negligence, see Michael S. Moore and Heidi Hurd, 'Punishing the awkward, the stupid, the weak, and the selfish: the culpability of negligence' (2011) 5 *Criminal Law and Philosophy* 147 at 191–192.

the sections below, tracing strategies tend to require choices that very few (intuitively) negligent defendants are likely to have made.[75]

An Earlier Disregarding of the Relevant Risk

The first 'tracing' strategy usually makes reference to cases such as the well-known *People* v. *Decina*,[76] from New York. Decina knew that he was susceptible to epileptic seizures. Despite this knowledge, he decided to drive despite not having taken his medication. Predictably, Decina experienced a seizure. Four schoolchildren died as a result of the crash that followed.

The Court of Appeals of New York found that Decina had been *negligent*, insofar as his decision to drive, despite his awareness of his condition and the risks of driving whilst experiencing a seizure, had shown a 'disregard of the consequences which may ensue from the act, and indifference to the rights of others'.[77] The situation would have been different if the defendant did not have awareness of his propensity towards seizures.[78]

Alexander, Ferzan and Morse describe *Decina* as a case of recklessness *if* the defendant consciously disregarded the risk of a collision.[79] When consideration is given to *Decina* itself, however, doubts arise about whether this can be a plausible reading of the facts. Although, as the Court of Appeals of New York noted, the defendant no doubt *could have* thought about the risk of a collision, and the further risk of death, it is unlikely that a belief about these risks was present at the time of decision to expose others to the relevant risk (by getting behind the wheel). That would be a question of evidence, but it is plausible Decina did not believe, at the time of driving, that he was exposing others to *that particular risk*. He might have had beliefs about the risks associated with having a seizure when behind the wheel *in general*, but that is not a belief that he was exposing others to the risk of death at the time of driving. Because of the personalised message that a criminal conviction sends about a defendant and her relationship with a particular instance of risk-taking (and, typically, its consequences), it is crucial that her culpability relates to *that relevant risk*.

[75] Matt King, 'The problem with negligence' (2009) 35 *Social Theory and Practice* 577 at 581.

[76] 2 NY 2d 133, 138 NE 2d 799 (1956, NY).

[77] At 139 (building on *People* v. *Angelo* 246 NY 451 (1927, NY)).

[78] *Decina*, at 140.

[79] Alexander and Ferzan with Morse, *Crime and Culpability*, pp. 80–81.

The similar case of *People* v. *Eckert*[80] (again from New York) makes this point more clearly. There it was held that culpable negligence required:[81]

> knowledge of the highly dangerous nature of his actions *or* knowledge of such facts as under the circumstances would disclose to a reasonable man the dangerous character of his action, and despite this knowledge he so acts. That he does not view his conduct as dangerous is of no consequence; his lack of realization of the danger involved may arise from his abnormally reckless temperament or from unexpectedly favorable results of previous conduct of the same sort. [Emphasis added]

In short, there was no need for the defendant to *believe* that his conduct carried with it the specific risk of death (or indeed a belief in 'danger' in general) in order for him to be negligent with regard to the risk of killing others. That there was such awareness in *Eckert* was *sufficient* for establishing the requisite 'indifference' to others.[82] It was not, however, *necessary* for establishing culpability.

Although there is nothing necessarily *wrong* with the argument that acting in spite of awareness at t_1 of a risk of a specific instance of wrongdoing at t_2 is an example of recklessness, *Decina* and *Eckert* suggest that such cases are going to be extremely rare.[83] It seems unlikely that many defendants will have such precise beliefs about their later potential inadvertence to specific risks. This is the problem, it will be remembered from Chapter 2, with deeming those who become voluntarily intoxicated, to the extent at which they cannot form *mens rea*, to have been 'reckless' as to the commission of an *actus reus*.[84] It is that wrongdoing that is to be traced back to the defendant's agency, and this requires a sense of correspondence between her fault and the specific risk that led to the relevant wrongdoing.[85]

All of this is to say that the concession to prior recklessness in choice-based tracing cases is not a terribly large one. Again, if any attempt at a descriptive *and* normative account is to be offered, it will need to be applicable in wider circumstances.

80 2 N.Y. 2d 126, 138 N.E. 2d 794 (1956, NY).
81 2 N.Y. 2d 126, 138 N.E. 2d 794 (1956, NY), at 130–131. 82 Ibid., at 132.
83 See, similarly, Moore and Hurd, 'Punishing the awkward, the stupid, the weak, and the selfish', at 179.
84 See above at pp. 30–32.
85 See Michael S. Moore, *Act and Crime: The Philosophy of Action and Its Implications for Criminal Law* (Oxford: Clarendon, 1993), p. 35.

Pillsbury's Perception Choices

An alternative, ostensibly wider tracing account would focus not only on the defendant's failure to be moved by a risk of which he is aware (even at an earlier time), but also on his failure to be motivated to notice certain features of his situation from which a belief in risk could have been formed.

It is obvious that human beings cannot perceive every aspect of their situation. This is primarily because of the limitations of the sensory organs.[86] Without technology, for instance, it is impossible to see further than eyesight allows. It would be wrong, Pillsbury contends, to think that these physiological features of perception set the only boundaries on culpability, that all failures to perceive an aspect of a situation are accidents of biology and thus not an instantiation of agency. Instead, he notes that 'the gathering and selecting of relevant information represents an affirmative mental activity. Information processing is something we *do*, not something that is *done* to us.'[87] By this, Pillsbury is appealing to the idea that, even given their limitations, the sensory organs take in far more information than can be appraised consciously. He explains that the filtering of information is thus necessary for our consciousness to avoid becoming overwhelmed and argues that this filtration process is a 'learned activity'.[88] Human beings avoid clouding their minds with sensory information, Pillsbury posits, by making 'decisions about what to hear or see and what to ignore'.[89]

Pillsbury explains that perception choices apparently 'follow our interests';[90] they reflect what the chooser cares about:[91]

> A kind, sensitive person is kind and sensitive because she places a high priority on addressing the needs of others . . . Callous individuals set a low priority on respecting others' needs, explaining why they may consciously disregard the harmful consequences of their actions . . .

By drawing these connections between perception, value and agency, Pillsbury is able to explain a form of 'culpable indifference' that he

[86] Samuel H. Pillsbury, 'Crimes of indifference' (1997) 49 *Rutgers Law Review* 105 at 142.

[87] Ibid., at 143. See, further, John R. Searle, *Mind: A Brief Introduction* (Oxford: Oxford University Press, 2004), p. 179.

[88] Pillsbury, 'Crimes of indifference', at 143. See, similarly, Hyman Gross, *A Theory of Criminal Justice* (Oxford: Oxford University Press, 1979), p. 92.

[89] Pillsbury, 'Crimes of indifference', at 144. See also Daniel C. Dennett, *Consciousness Explained* (Boston: Little, Brown, 1991), p. 308.

[90] Pillsbury, 'Crimes of indifference', at 144.

[91] Ibid., at 151.

thinks Anglo-American criminal justice systems ought to recognise. He contends that blame is appropriate where the defendant's perception choices show indifference towards (or 'not caring enough' about)[92] the interests of others.[93] In such circumstances, the defendant is blamed not for her eventual inadvertence, but for her prior *choices* about what to perceive, and what these choices demonstrate about her concern for the interests of others.[94]

Pillsbury's thesis is objectionable for a number of reasons. First, the oddity of the perception choices that he posits should be considered. It is simply not clear that many people *do* make the posited reflective decisions about what to 'hear or see . . . [or] ignore'.[95] Even if it is granted, for the sake of argument, that *some* such preferences might be expressed deliberately by agents, Pillsbury accepts that not *all* perception preferences are chosen.[96] It might be a person's genetics or environment (rather than her reflective choices) that determine what she pays (and does not pay) attention to, and a defendant might have no *experience* of having had alternative options in crafting those perception preferences.[97] Pillsbury does not appear to view this deterministic slant as a problem for his theory.[98] It nevertheless undermines severely the plausibility of his thesis.[99] It is difficult to see, if choice is not really necessary, how Pillsbury is able to draw a meaningful link between the defendant, as an agent, her perceptive preferences and her eventual risk-taking. That is to say not that linkage between a person's inadvertence and her wrongdoing is unavailable *in principle*, but merely that Pillsbury's account does not offer it convincingly.

It might be thought that focussing only on reflective, conscious, deliberative perception preferences could save Pillsbury's account. Perception preferences that were not adopted in this manner would, on this revised account, not be a basis for culpability. Even on this revised model, issues with Pillsbury's account arise. In his examples of culpable perception choices, Pillsbury tends to concentrate on actors who decide

[92] Ibid., at 107. [93] Ibid., at 151. [94] Ibid., at 151.

[95] See Angela M. Smith, 'Responsibility for attitudes: activity and passivity in mental life' (2005) 115 *Ethics* 236 at 236–242.

[96] Pillsbury, 'Crimes of indifference', at 151.

[97] See Robert Audi, 'Dispositional beliefs and dispositions to believe' (1994) 28 *Noûs* 419 at 428.

[98] Pillsbury, 'Crimes of indifference', at 151.

[99] Kimberly K. Ferzan, 'Opaque recklessness' (2000–2001) 91 *Journal of Criminal Law & Criminology* 597 at 640.

(reflectively) not to perceive certain matters almost immediately before acting.[100] This might be telling: if a choice to not perceive a certain fact is made immediately before the defendant fails to perceive it takes hold, then responsibility for inadvertence, and any attendant finding of culpability, seems relatively straightforward. Indeed, the concessions made by other theorists to accommodate cases such as *Decina* (discussed above) seem to apply in such examples. Pillsbury's account is unnecessarily complicated if all it does accommodate is such cases, but on the basis of unrealistic perception choices.

The situation becomes more complicated when the perception choice was made hours, days or even years before the relevant act of inadvertent, unjustified risk-taking. Pillsbury does not deal convincingly with this problem of linking historical preferences (and attendant attitudes) to future inadvertence. It nevertheless poses significant difficulties for his account. Without showing a meaningful connection between historical perception choices and contemporary unjustified risk-taking, it seems that his 'indifference' theory explains only a small percentage of peculiar cases where a reflective decision in engaged with almost immediately before taking a particular, relevant risk. In other cases, the vital link that culpability is meant to draw between the defendant and her act of wrongdoing is absent.

Another problem concerns the nature of Pillsbury's perception choices themselves, a matter on which he does not say much. What exactly does the actor have to prefer in order to demonstrate her culpable indifference?[101] Does the preference have to be specific (such as the choice to never perceive the signs of non-consent in a sexual partner) or more general (such as the choice to not perceive social signs in others)? Pillsbury does not reach a settled view on this issue. At points, he suggests that culpable indifference must relate to a specific interest, such as the signs of non-consent in sex, rather than simply social signs relevant to the perception of consent/non-consent more generally.[102] If this *is* the case, then Pillsbury's account seems to encounter difficulties. Again, the question is whether many alleged rapists can be said to have *reflectively chosen* not to perceive the signs of non-consent to the extent that these fail to register with them at all at a later time.[103] It is more likely that no

[100] See e.g. Pillsbury, 'Crimes of indifference', at 151–152.

[101] See, further, Ferzan, 'Opaque recklessness', at 639.

[102] Pillsbury, 'Crimes of indifference', at 171–173.

[103] See, similarly, Alexander and Ferzan with Morse, *Crime and Culpability*, p. 57; George Sher, *Who Knew? Responsibility without Awareness* (Oxford: Oxford University Press,

such choice is made and that it is rather the defendant's indifferent *attitude*, or his failure to control himself adequately, divorced from deliberative decisions regarding risk perception, that prevents such signs from registering properly with him.[104]

If Pillsbury's perception choices were more general in their nature, there is a difficulty in explaining why that decision links the defendant meaningfully to later wrongdoing. Ferzan states this objection well: 'When an actor learns [chooses] to be selfish, to what extent does he appreciate that he might cause future harm?'[105] The answer, it is assumed, is rarely.[106] This makes tracing accounts such as Pillsbury's seem weaker still: only exceptional cases of inadvertent risk-taking are going to be caught by his expanded *choice*-based view of culpability. This is not to say that generalised attitudes towards risk are necessarily irrelevant to the question of culpable carelessness, but rather to doubt that Pillsbury's focus on *choice* is helpful.

Finally, from a more practical perspective, it is worth noting the obvious point that *proving* a culpable perception choice is going to be nigh on impossible.

All of these points cast significant doubt on Pillsbury's tracing account, which is why it will not be followed here.

Tracing Character

A third tracing theory looks at the defendant's character formation and asks whether something in it discloses culpability with regard to future ignorance. Some such accounts suffer from similar problems to Pillsbury's. An example from the criminal law literature is Jean Hampton's account of negligence.[107] She contends that, in general,

2009), p. 25; M.J. Zimmerman, 'Moral responsibility and ignorance' (1996–1997) 107 *Ethics* 410 at 421.

104 Zoe Lodrick, a psychotherapist with extensive experience with victims and offenders in sexualised violence cases, has explained to me that many sex offenders do not view themselves as 'sex offenders'. This psychological point supports the thesis that most sexual offenders will not make reflective choices relevant to sexual offending.

105 Ferzan, 'Opaque recklessness', at 640.

106 Cf. Manuel Vargas, 'The trouble with tracing' (2005) 29 *Midwest Studies in Philosophy* 269, with John M. Fischer and Neal A. Tognazzini, 'The truth about tracing' (2009) 43 *Noûs* 531. See, further, Moore and Hurd, 'Punishing the awkward, the stupid, the weak and the selfish', at 178.

107 Jean Hampton, '*Mens rea*', in Ellen F. Paul, Fred D. Miller and Jeffrey Paul (eds.), *Crime, Culpability and Remedy* (Oxford: Basil Blackwell, 1990), p. 1.

culpability consists in choosing to defy the law's commands and that punishment is the means of educating[108] defiant offenders in what society requires of them.[109] This defiance is demonstrated typically in a free choice to engage in conduct, despite knowledge that the law deems it wrongful.[110]

This focus on defying the law's commands does not, however, lead Hampton to the conclusion that inadvertent risk-taking is not a legitimate basis of culpability in the sense required by the criminal law.[111] Hampton argues that negligence can be a ground of culpability if defiance is evidenced 'not at the time of the act [of inadvertent risk-taking], but earlier, during the process of character formation'.[112]

Hampton's theory thus maintains her focus on choice as the mark of culpability but recognises that there might be blameworthiness attendant upon later, inadvertent, unjustified risk-taking. Hampton's theory of character development is, however, peculiar. To see this, it is necessary to return to Aristotle's theory of character formation. It will be remembered from the brief discussion in Chapter 6 that Aristotle admitted of liability for inadvertent risk-taking and harm-doing where it was 'in the power' of the defendant to have developed her character differently and been more careful.[113] If the defendant could have possessed a different character (understood as a set of stable traits concerning conduct and value),[114] then she could be held responsible and liable for the consequences of her inadvertence.

Any resemblance to Hampton's theory is fleeting. On Aristotle's view, virtuous traits (such as acting with appropriate care in the circumstances) were internalised through the performance of careful actions: repeated careful action begets careful character (which, in turn, leads to the consistent performance of careful action). Aristotle did not contend, as Hampton appears to, that a person chooses to act in such a way as to demonstrate cruelty, carefulness, or bravery, and that this decision promptly transforms a person into a cruel, careful or brave person

[108] See also Jean Hampton, 'The moral education theory of punishment' (1984) 13 *Philosophy and Public Affairs* 208.

[109] Hampton, '*Mens rea*', pp. 5, 12. [110] Ibid., p. 14.

[111] This distinguishes her account from Brudner's view, discussed above at Chapter 6, section on 'Choice and Punishment'.

[112] Hampton, '*Mens rea*', p. 27.

[113] See above at Chapter 6, section on 'Ferzan's "Opaque" Recklessness'.

[114] There is not space here to discuss the *best* definition of character. The account presented in the next chapter is character-based, and its nature is more fully explained there.

who will defy the law's commands.[115] Instead, Aristotle required a long commitment to certain types of action, and it is not entirely clear that becoming vicious (e.g. becoming cruel) required a *choice* to do vicious acts. Although it is difficult to become virtuous, it seems possible, in theory, for an actor to become vicious with reflectively choosing that course. Perhaps this happens entirely by chance,[116] where – for instance – the defendant has lived exclusively in a community that simply does not exhibit the relevant virtue.[117]

The problem for Hampton is therefore that her theory 'adopts the eccentric notion that people choose the characters . . . and the dispositions that they want to have, almost as if these were goods in a shop.'[118] It is very unlikely that *this* sort of control over character – and, in particular, *vicious* character traits – exists in many cases.[119] Hampton's account, like the previous two 'tracing' strategies, endorses an explanation of culpable inadvertence that is unrealistic and, ultimately, explains too little. This is not to say that (some understanding of) character is *irrelevant* to the best understanding of culpability without awareness. Indeed, (a particular sense of) character will play a core role in explaining negligence in the next chapter. It is simply that liability for inadvertent, unjustified risk-taking should not be founded on Hampton's choice-based tracing model. Like Hart, Hampton points in a worthwhile direction (that of character, in Hampton's case) but does not explain culpable

[115] See also Rosalind Hursthouse, *On Virtue Ethics* (Oxford: Oxford University Press, 1999), p. 12; Sophia R. Moreau, 'Reasons and character' (2005) 115 *Ethics* 272 at 277.

[116] Edmund L. Pincoffs, 'Legal responsibility and moral character' (1972–1973) 19 *Wayne Law Review* 905 at 919.

[117] Such actors might be 'ethically disabled', as this phenomenon is explained in Jonathan Jacobs, *Choosing Character: Responsibility for Virtue and Vice* (Ithaca, NY: Cornell University Press, 2001). This situation would be almost unimaginable in the modern (Western) world, but it is plausible that certain remote communities might cultivate vice and persons brought up in that environment might simply fall, ignorantly, into following that example. These situations pose special problems for the acceptance view of responsibility (discussed below at Chapter 8, section on 'A Wider View: Reflecting Character').

[118] Jeremy Horder, 'Criminal culpability: the possibility of a general theory' (1993) 12 *Law and Philosophy* 193 at 197. See, similarly, Nomy Arpaly, *Unprincipled Virtue: An Inquiry into Moral Agency* (Oxford: Oxford University Press, 2002), p. 141.

[119] For discussion of this point, see Stephen J. Morse, 'Reasons, results and criminal responsibility' [2004] *University of Illinois Law Review* 363 at 368–369. P.J.T. O'Hearn, 'Criminal negligence: an analysis in depth' (1964–1965) 7 *Criminal Law Quarterly* 27, 407 (published in two parts) at 421; Samuel H. Pillsbury, 'The meaning of deserved punishment: an essay on choice, character and responsibility' (1991–1992) 67 *Indiana Law Journal* 719 at 749; Moreau, 'Reasons and character', at 277.

inadvertence in a suitably compelling manner, because of her commitment to choice as the sole possible explanation of culpability.

Tracing accounts thus explain too little, or at least in an unconvincing manner, because the choices they envisage are bizarre. The next set of theories focuses not on choices that *have* been made, but instead on choices that *could have been made*, and what these counterfactual choices demonstrate about the defendant's attitude towards risk and the interests of others. The next section exposes the pitfalls of such accounts.

Culpability and Counterfactuals

Horder[120] and Simons[121] present the two most developed counterfactual choice accounts.[122] Their theories are similar, yet distinct. This is because of their slightly different *foci*: Horder is concerned to see if the defendant would have recognised a value clash raised by the existence of the relevant risk and chosen differently, whereas Simons is concerned simply with whether the bare fact of awareness of risk would have made the defendant choose differently. Given this distinction, it is worth explaining the accounts separately. Their common difficulties will then be discussed.

Simons's 'Culpable Indifference'

In an important attack on the approach to recklessness and negligence under traditional understandings of *mens rea*, Simons seeks to distinguish amongst 'the different cognitive (belief-related), conative (desire-related), and conduct-related senses of both negligence and recklessness'.[123] He identifies 'culpable indifference'[124] as the conative state that best explains when a defendant is culpable, in spite of the absence of awareness of the risk(s) attendant upon behaviour. This variety of culpability:[125]

> is often described as a form of recklessness (though it could also be categorized as a form of negligence). An actor who is culpably indifferent

120 Horder, 'Gross negligence and criminal culpability'.

121 Simons, 'Culpability and retributive theory'.

122 See also Alan C. Michaels, 'Acceptance: the missing mental state' (1997–1998) 71 *Southern California Law Review* 953.

123 Simons, 'Culpability and retributive theory', at 366.

124 Simons initially distinguished three forms of reckless indifference: Kenneth W. Simons, 'Rethinking mental states' (1992) 72 *Boston University Law Review* 463 at 486–487.

125 Simons, 'Culpability and retributive theory', at 377–378.

> to a harmful result neither desires the result nor desires to avoid it. Rather, she cares much less than she should about bringing it about. This ... attitude could genuinely be described as 'unreasonable' or 'negligent', since it is explicitly linked to the attitudes and desires that a reasonable person would have.

Simons complicates matters by suggesting that indifference can be present in *both* recklessness and negligence. The distinction between these two types of indifference is, apparently, that the former 'is a more aggravated degree of blameworthy indifference'.[126] This view is not particularly edifying when used by some Anglo-American courts to distinguish between 'civil' and 'criminal' negligence (and between different senses of 'negligence' in the criminal law),[127] and it is not much more helpful in discerning Simons's thoughts concerning culpable carelessness.

Simons might reply that the line between negligence and recklessness is unimportant, or at least less important than the Standard Account and much criminal law literature assumes. After all, he argues that traditional *mens rea* categories are misconceived. His account is revisionary, rather than explanatory.

Accepting Simons's revisionary justification for muddying the recklessness/negligence distinction, for now, it becomes clear that Simons believes that 'culpable indifference' is present where the defendant's conduct demonstrates 'that he would not have avoided the risk even if he had appreciated it'.[128] Such defendants are, essentially, counterfactually reckless. The 'callous insensitivity'[129] to the interests of others that such counterfactual recklessness points to is – on Simons's view – a form of culpability that ought to merit criminal punishment, even in the absence of actual awareness of the relevant risk associated with φ-ing.

Before critiquing Simons's approach, it is useful to explain Jeremy Horder's similar view.

Horder's 'Weak' and 'Strong' Indifference

Like his conduct-based view (discussed above), Horder's counterfactual conception of negligence is built on Razian foundations.[130] Raz famously distinguishes between 'agent-relative' and 'agent-neutral' values and their

126 Ibid., at 378.
127 Cf. Kenneth W. Simons, 'Deontology, negligence, tort and crime' (1996) 76 *Boston University Law Review* 273.
128 Simons, 'Culpability and retributive theory', at 381. 129 Ibid.
130 See Raz, *Practical Reason and Norms*, p. 34.

impact upon practical reasoning.[131] Raz explains that everybody has reason to respect agent-neutral values when deciding what to do; they ought *always* to count in practical reasoning.[132] Agent-relative values, by contrast, need be respected only by the person who holds them.[133] This means that agents may permissibly ignore the agent-relative values of others in deciding what to do or may prefer their own agent-relative values over them.

Horder thinks this distinction is important to 'gross' negligence (a concept that is hard to distinguish from recklessness in many doctrinal systems, particularly in the context of manslaughter) because it is possible to use it to identify defendants who display the appropriate *attitude* of indifference towards risk that is morally equivalent to taking a risk of which one is aware. He suggests that this type of indifferent defendant will, contrary to what Raz's account of morality requires, place their agent-relative values ahead of the agent-neutral values of others and will continue to do so *even after* the clash of values has been pointed out to them.

To make Horder's account less abstract, it is useful to consider an example. In the Scottish case of *Transco plc* v. *HM Advocate*,[134] a gas supply company had failed to maintain a gas pipe that supplied a house. Following cold weather, some gas built up under the house and eventually exploded. The explosion killed the house's occupants (the Findlay family). Assume, for the moment, that this maintenance failure occurred because it would have harmed Transco's profits to check the house's gas supply as often as would be ideal. This profiteering would seem an agent-relative value: only Transco (i.e. its management and employees) had reason to promote the making of as much profit as possible. It was not the case that *everybody* had reason to promote Transco's profit-making enterprise when considering what to do.

The interests of the Findlay family in life were, by contrast, agent-neutral values. Everybody has reason to promote the interests of others in life and to place this interest above their own, agent-relative values.[135]

131 Horder, 'Gross negligence and criminal culpability', at 502. Note that Raz calls agent-neutral values 'objective', a term that is useful to avoid, given its overuse (and thus opacity) in criminal theory.

132 Raz, *Practical Reason and Norms*, p. 34.

133 Ibid. Persons other than the agent *may*, of course, promote her agent-relative values (consider family members supporting and furthering one another's interests). But morality does not, on Raz's view, *require* them to do so.

134 2004 JC 29.

135 There are difficult questions concerning how far the agent-neutral value of life should be promoted, as the discourse around alleviating poverty and the debate surrounding assisted dying demonstrate.

Transco's management, in the counterfactual turn of events proposed here, appears to have confused this situation and put an agent-relative value (profit) above the agent-neutral values involved in their activities (the lives of the Findlays and other people whose gas supplies were maintained by Transco).

What matters, for Horder, is what would have happened had this fact been pointed out to Transco's management.[136] The company's board might have been persuaded to change the company's policies, accepting that the business *had* – as a point of morality – to be less profitable. This would reflect a proper recognition of the agent-neutral values at stake and show Transco's management to be, in Horder's terms, 'weakly indifferent'.[137] Had they had the relevant beliefs about the risks they were imposing, and the clash of values that bore upon their business activities, they would have been motivated to act differently from how they in fact did.

Weakly indifferent actors can be contrasted with 'strongly indifferent' ones.[138] Horder explains that:[139]

> [t]he strongly indifferent person is not swayed by agent-neutral values, such as the victim's interests, but is moved only by his own agent-relative values ... like the weakly indifferent person, the strongly indifferent person is usually too obsessed by his agent-relative values to appreciate the existence of the agent-neutral values at stake ... But, even if the strongly indifferent person discovers agent-neutral values giving rise to reasons not to act on his agent-relative values, they make no difference to his practical reasoning.

In short, the strongly indifferent actor would not have been persuaded to act differently if she had possessed the relevant beliefs about the risks

[136] In the event, the prosecution could not prove any awareness of the risk of death on the part of the accused company, and it was acquitted of culpable homicide. This led to the creation of a new offence, based on death resulting from the manner in which a company's being run constituting a 'gross' breach of a duty of care: Corporate Manslaughter and Corporate Homicide Act 2007 (UK), s. 1. It is not yet clear what 'gross' breaches amount to.

[137] Horder, 'Gross negligence and criminal culpability', at 502.

[138] See Dirk Ruimschotel, 'The psychological reality of intentional and negligent criminal acts', in Peter J. van Koppen, Dick J. Hessing and Grat van den Heuvel (eds.), *Lawyers on Psychology and Psychologists on Law* (Lisse: Swets & Zeitlinger, 1988), p. 83. Ruimschotel distinguishes between knowledge deficits (weak indifference) and value deficits (strong indifference). For further use of this distinction, see Barry Mitchell, 'Culpably indifferent murder' (1996) 25 *Anglo-American Law Review* 64 at 72–78; Celia Wells, *Corporations and Criminal Responsibility*, 2nd edn. (Oxford: Oxford University Press, 2001), pp. 116–117.

[139] Horder, 'Gross negligence and criminal culpability', at 503.

attendant upon her conduct, and the value conflict they raised. She was both inadvertent *and* indifferent,[140] a person who – if aware of the interests that she threatened, and their agent-neutral nature – would view them as obstacles to getting what she wanted rather than reasons worthy of respect.[141] In consequence, if Transco's management had been strongly indifferent, they would not have endeavoured to check the gas supply more frequently, even if they had been aware of the significant risk that this posed to the lives of others.

Horder concludes that 'gross' negligence in manslaughter[142] should be understood as 'strong' indifference: to convict the defendant, the finder of fact should be sure that she would have acted in the same way even if she had been aware of the risk of death, i.e. that she would not have been moved by the reasons she had for not acting.[143]

There is one specific worry about Horder's account that it is useful to discuss before moving to consider difficulties common to both his and Simons's counterfactual-based accounts. This is that Horder has identified only *one* way of going seriously wrong in the assessment of values. Just as an inappropriate weighing of agent-relative and agent-neutral values might demonstrate a lack of sufficient concern for others, so might an error in the assessment of agent-neutral values. What if, had he possessed the relevant beliefs about the situation, the defendant would have valued the interest of some rare flowers over the life of a human being?[144] If this point about clashes of agent-neutral values is accepted, then Horder's question really becomes whether, had the defendant had appropriate beliefs about the risks attendant upon φ-ing, she would have valued a less weighty agent-neutral or agent-relative value over a weightier agent-neutral value. This hints at one problem with Horder's account in

[140] It might be objected that, by using a counterfactual test, Horder and Simons fail to tie culpable indifference and the defendant's ignorance concerning risk to her act of wrongdoing. This might give rise to a so-called significance in action problem. On such problems, see below at Chapter 8, section on 'Significance of Action'. Some writers suggest that ignorance must arise *through* indifference for the defendant to be culpable: e.g. R.A. Duff, '*Caldwell* and *Lawrence*: the retreat from subjectivism' (1983) 3 *Oxford Journal of Legal Studies* 77 at 97. Duff's version of this argument is discussed later in this chapter. He avoids the 'significance in action' difficulty by positing a theory based in part on the interpretation of actions.

[141] See, similarly, Jeanette Kennett, *Agency and Responsibility: A Common-Sense Moral Psychology* (Oxford: Oxford University Press, 2001), pp. 179–180.

[142] Horder is concerned only with manslaughter in the relevant part of his article.

[143] Horder, 'Gross negligence and criminal culpability', at 504.

[144] I am grateful to Victor Tadros for suggesting this example.

comparison with the one presented in the next chapter – it seems to bring in a distinction between types of value that ultimately might not be necessary. Again, Horder's theory is ornate and complex, and a simpler account (if available) would, it is submitted, be preferable if it still identifies culpable inadvertence sufficiently well. It will be contended in Chapter 8 that the account of negligence as failure of belief is such a preferable model.

Now that Simons's and Horder's views have been explained, it is time to explore their common difficulties.

Criticisms of Counterfactual Choice

There are three main difficulties with the counterfactual-choice model of culpable inadvertence. First, there is room for significant doubt concerning what the defendant might have done *had she* been aware of the risks involved in her conduct and (on Horder's view) the clash of values they raised.[145] Consider Simons's example of a babysitter who 'departs the children's house for her boyfriend's as soon as the parents have left'.[146] Simons contends that the babysitter's 'willingness to abandon the children entirely may suggest that, had she been present in the house and heard noises calling for further inquiry and action, she would not have inquired further'.[147] The operative word in this sentence is surely 'may' – with these bare facts, there is no reliable basis upon which to infer what the babysitter *would have done* had she been aware of indicators that the children might, for instance, have fallen and injured themselves. Her irresponsible attitude might stem from naïve overconfidence in the maturity of the children left in her care, rather than indifference towards their welfare. There is, therefore, in one of Simons's few concrete examples of culpable indifference, little upon which to hang culpability. The same difficulty impacts on the persuasiveness of Horder's account.

The obvious reply is that culpable mental states are almost always evidenced in epistemologically questionable ways.[148] A jury might

[145] A.J.P. Kenny, *Freewill and Responsibility* (London: Routledge and Kegan Paul, 1978), p. 62; Larry Alexander, 'Inculpatory and exculpatory mistakes and the fact/law distinction: an essay in memory of Myke Bayles' (1993) 12 *Law and Philosophy* 33 at 63; Simester, 'Can negligence be culpable?', p. 89; Kimberly K. Ferzan, 'Don't abandon the Model Penal Code yet! Thinking through Simons's rethinking' (2002–2003) 6 *Buffalo Criminal Law Review* 185 at 212.

[146] Simons, 'Culpability and retributive theory', at 381. [147] Ibid.

[148] See Mitchell, 'Culpably indifferent murder', at 81–82; Cath Crosby, 'Recklessness – the continuing search for a definition' (2008) 72 *Journal of Criminal Law* 313 at 325. Often,

interpret conduct as pointing towards the proper ascription of a belief that there was a risk attendant upon certain behaviour, when features of the situation, of which the jury cannot be certain (perhaps the defendant's own memory of her phenomenal experience at the time of the *actus reus*), point to the opposite conclusion. Unless the jury is told (honestly) of *all* features of a situation – if this is even possible – their verdict is always going to be epistemologically imperfect. The means by which juries reach verdicts, however, are accepted as appropriate in matters of criminal justice. The bare presence of epistemic doubt cannot, therefore, undermine Horder's and Simons's theories, or else it endangers the entire process of establishing key concepts such as awareness of risk.

It is nevertheless clear that there are *greater* epistemological difficulties involved in conducting 'speculative'[149] counterfactual enquiries than there are in interpreting factual behaviour and that Horder and Simons would presumably need to propose changes to the law of evidence for their theory to work properly in practice.[150]

A second difficulty is that it is unclear *why* the criminal courts should be involved in inquiries into what the actor *would* have done had the circumstances been different. Culpability judgments are useful insofar as they bridge the gap between what a defendant has *done* (her wrongdoing) and her agency. There is thus good reason to concentrate on what defendants *have* done (wrong), rather than what they *might have done* had they had different beliefs about risk (on Simons's view) or been alerted to a clash of value (on Horder's).[151] If this approach is not taken, the criminal inquiry risks becoming an unreal journey into fiction, rather than a personalised assessment of responsibility and blameworthiness *in relation to* a factual instance of wrongdoing.

A third, connected, concern is raised by Ferzan: if hypothetical inquiries into what the actor would have done were she aware of risk/value

this objection is couched in terms of inferring 'internal' mental states from 'external' evidence. Cf. the discussion of belief above at Chapter 4.

149 *G and Another*, at [38].

150 See Glanville Williams, 'A reply to Mr Duff' (1982) 41 *Cambridge Law Journal* 286 at 287–288; Diane J. Birch, 'The foresight saga: the biggest mistake of all?' [1988] *Criminal Law Review* 4 at 13. See Horder, 'Gross negligence and criminal culpability', at 504–505. With regard to Horder's thesis, changes to the law on bad character evidence in English law might allow the prosecution to adduce evidence to show that, even if the defendant had been aware of risk, she would have carried on regardless: see, generally, Criminal Justice Act 2003, pt. 11, ch. 1; Crosby, 'Recklessness', at 325.

151 See, similarly, Alan Brudner, *Punishment and Freedom: A Liberal Theory of Penal Justice* (Oxford: Oxford University Press, 2009), p. 96.

clashes are worthwhile, why stop there?[152] Consider the defendant in the tragic New South Wales case of *R* v. *Lavender*,[153] who drove a heavy (but slow) vehicle after children playing at the mine where he worked. Lavender ran over one child (who was, from the vantage point in the vehicle, difficult to see), killing him. Lavender claimed to be unaware of the risk of running over a child, his intention being to scare the children away.[154] On Simons's and Horder's accounts, the relevant question is whether Lavender would have ceased the chase had he believed there was a risk he would kill one of the children, and the value conflict that such conduct raised. Ferzan queries why matters should stop there: why not, if one counterfactual enquiry is permissible, ask what Lavender would have done if it were his sworn enemy, rather than a child, in front of him? Might he have intended to cause death or serious harm?

Ferzan's objection is that once the counterfactual door is open, it is difficult to know when to close it. This worry is, however, overstated. If the criminal law is (and criminal law theorists are) to engage in counterfactuals, it is presumably desirable to stay as close to reality as possible when speculating about what might have been.[155] Although nothing in Horder's or Simons's articles prevents the rampant supposition that Ferzan envisages, presumably the relevant counterfactual situation is where *only* the defendant's beliefs regarding the risks attendant upon her conduct, and the clash of values they present, are altered. The stronger objection is the one made above: the criminal law has no business in asking what persons would have done had their beliefs about the situation been different.

Counterfactual choice models of culpable inadvertence are thus deeply problematic and should not be employed. The final set of theories to be considered in this chapter concern not *choices* regarding risks but *attitudes* towards them.

Attitudinal Accounts

The most common attitude that is linked to culpability without awareness is *indifference*, and it is worth beginning by noting some aspects of

[152] Ferzan, 'Opaque recklessness', at 622–623.

[153] [2005] HCA 37, (2005) 222 CLR 67. See Penny Crofts, *Wickedness and Crime: Laws of Homicide and Malice* (Abingdon: Routledge, 2013), ch. 6.

[154] This situation is reminiscent of the famous English case of *Hyam* v. *DPP* [1975] AC 55.

[155] See Leo Katz, *Bad Acts and Guilty Minds: Conundrums of the Criminal Law* (Chicago, IL: University of Chicago Press, 1987), pp. 232–233.

this term. First, it should be noted that some of the accounts discussed thus far are, in fact, presented as accounts of indifference to risk. They equate that attitude with choices (whether about perception or counterfactual decisions). Not all theoretical accounts of 'indifference' are defended in this manner, however. They focus on the *attitude* of indifference itself, independent of the defendant's awareness of risk. It is those theories that are now under consideration.

Second, although indifference is a concept that occurs often in doctrinal and theoretical debates over culpable carelessness, it is not a particularly apt word to employ. To be indifferent is to have 'no particular interest or sympathy', to be 'unconcerned'.[156] Most indifference theorists (and courts, presumably) do not in fact require that the actor was *utterly* unconcerned with the interests she put at risk.[157] Rather, they tend to focus on actors who do not care *enough* about the interests of others.[158] This is clear from some of the accounts discussed above. Simons, for instance, is concerned with 'whether the actor cared much less than he should about bringing about a harmful result';[159] Pillsbury with the vice of 'not caring enough'.[160] Of the indifference theorists discussed in this chapter, perhaps[161] only Antony Duff talks truly of indifference – of actors who 'cared nothing for' the consequences of their actions.[162]

156 See http://oxforddictionaries.com/view/entry/m_en_gb0407440#m_en_gb0407440.

157 William J. Winslade, 'Recklessness' (1970) 30 *Analysis* 135 at 136; James B. Brady, 'Recklessness' (1996) 15 *Law and Philosophy* 183 at 190–191.

158 Accepting this point allows most indifference theorists to explain cases where the actor took an acknowledged risk, whilst apparently caring *somewhat* about whether harm resulted or not: P.J. Fitzgerald and Glanville Williams, 'Carelessness, indifference and recklessness: two replies' (1962) 25 *Modern Law Review* 49 at 54–55; Nils Jareborg, *Scraps of Penal Theory* (Uppsala: Iustus Förlag AB, 2002), p. 51. Cf. James B. Brady, 'Recklessness, negligence, indifference and awareness' (1980) 43 *Modern Law Review* 381 at 387–388.

159 Simons, 'Culpability and retributive theory', at 390. See also Simons, 'Rethinking mental states', at 487; Kenneth W. Simons, 'Does punishment for "culpable indifference" simply punish for "bad character"? Examining the requisite connection between *mens rea* and *actus reus*' (2002–2003) 6 *Buffalo Criminal Law Review* 219 at 226.

160 Pillsbury, 'Crimes of indifference', at 107.

161 Horder's 'strongly indifferent' actors might be utterly unconcerned with risk, but this is far from clear: as explained above, 'strongly indifferent' actors fail to show *adequate respect* to 'agent-neutral' values. This surely allows an actor to be 'strongly indifferent' through not caring *enough*.

162 Duff, *Intention, Agency and Criminal Liability*, p. 163 (cf. R.A. Duff, 'Recklessness' [1980] *Criminal Law Review* 282 at 284). See, further, Alan R. White, 'Carelessness, indifference and recklessness' (1961) 24 *Modern Law Review* 592.

Most *attitudinal* accounts of indifference (as opposed to those premised on choice or counterfactual choice) are undeveloped. The same is true of the doctrinal accounts found in the Anglo-American jurisdictions surveyed in Chapter 2. Indifference has been used historically and is still employed occasionally by contemporary Anglo-American systems, at least in some contexts, as a synonym for recklessness and/or negligence.[163] Indifference itself is rarely defined, but it appears that at least in some jurisdictions indifference as an attitude can exist independently of awareness of risk. That is a point that will be returned to in due course.

In other court decisions, indifference is presented as though it is an *additional* ingredient of recklessness, as distinct from bare awareness of risk.[164] This is in fact the model adopted in civilian systems that endorse 'conditional intention', or *dolus eventualis.*[165] There is not space to engage here in a detailed discussion of *dolus eventualis*. It is nevertheless useful, before addressing Duff's approach to indifference, to recognise that, at least in South African law (which is a useful comparator to Anglo-American systems), *dolus eventualis* is perhaps less different to recklessness than some Anglo-American lawyers might think.

Dolus Eventualis: *A South African View*

Conditional intention requires two elements. First, the actor must be aware that it was 'a not entirely distant possibility' that a certain risk would materialise.[166] This is analogous to the Standard Account's focus on awareness of risk in cases of recklessness.

The distinctiveness of conditional intention arises from its second element: the defendant must have 'accepted',[167] 'consented to',[168] 'not cared'[169] about or been indifferent to the materialisation of the relevant risk. This requirement is sometimes expressed in terms of

[163] See e.g. the definition of recklessness at work in Scots common law offences: *Quinn* v. *Cunningham* 1956 JC 22, at 24–25.

[164] See e.g. *R* v. *Leary* [1978] 1 SCR 29 (Can), at 34.

[165] See Paul T. Smith, 'Recklessness in *dolus eventualis*' (1979) 96 *South African Law Journal* 81. On the related German concept of *Bedingter Vorsatz*, see Michael Bohlander, *Principles of German Criminal Law* (Oxford: Hart, 2009), pp. 63–65; Greg Taylor, 'Concepts of intention in German criminal law' (2004) 24 *Oxford Journal of Legal Studies* 99; Dan W. Morkel, 'On the distinction between recklessness and conscious negligence' (1982) 30 *American Journal of Comparative Law* 325.

[166] See Taylor, 'Concepts of intention in German criminal law', at 108.

[167] Ibid., at 109.

[168] *State* v. *Ngubane* 1985 (3) SA 677 (ZA), at 685.

[169] *State* v. *De Bruyn* 1968 (4) SA 498 (ZA), at 508.

'recklessness'.[170] This volitional element of *dolus eventualis*, apparently, is vital – a conviction cannot be sustained without proof of it beyond reasonable doubt.

Despite (or perhaps because of) its apparent importance, various competing accounts of the volitional element in conditional intention exist.[171] There is, for example, an expansive South African jurisprudence on the volitional element, but Jonathan Burchell argues that the attitudinal component of *dolus eventualis* very rarely makes a difference in concrete cases.[172] The core question is whether the defendant engaged voluntarily in unjustified risk-taking, *aware* of the risk attendant upon her conduct. If she did, Burchell contends, then she has evidenced *dolus eventualis*. Burchell thus argues that, absent conditions negating a voluntary choice to take the relevant risk (e.g. incapacity or excuse), the defendant will have *dolus eventualis* simply in virtue of her decision to act in spite of her beliefs about the associated risks. This makes *dolus eventualis*, at least in South Africa, similar to recklessness in those jurisdictions that discuss 'disregard' of or 'indifference' towards risk as if it is a synonym for a failure to be moved by a belief in risk, or simply superfluous.[173] In the light of these points, it is submitted that the Standard Account can learn little from *dolus eventualis*, at least as understood in South Africa.

Duff's sense of indifference is distinct from (at least the South African conception of) *dolus eventualis* insofar as, as will be seen, he does not require an indifferent defendant to be aware of the risk attendant upon her behaviour, and the attitude of indifference in his theory definitely thus has genuine independent significance.

Duff's 'Practical Indifference'

Duff's influential account of recklessness as 'practical indifference'[174] and his explanation of how it differs from negligence are ornate. To be appreciated fully, they must be approached patiently.

170 See e.g. *State* v. *Sigwahla* 1967 (4) SA 566 (ZA); *State* v. *Sethoga* 1990 (1) SA 270 (ZA), at 276.

171 See George P. Fletcher, *Rethinking Criminal Law* (Boston: Little, Brown, 1978), pp. 445–446; Jonathan Burchell, *Principles of Criminal Law*, 4th edn. (Claremont: Juta, 2013), pp. 365–370.

172 Cf. *Humphreys* [2013] ZASCA 20, 2013 (2) SACR 1 (ZA), discussed in Burchell, *Principles of Criminal Law*, pp. 368–369.

173 See Smith, 'Recklessness in *Dolus Eventualis*', at 81–84. It also makes it difficult to distinguish between *dolus eventualis* and conscious negligence: Leo Zaibert, *Five Ways Patricia Can Kill Her Husband: A Theory of Intentionality and Blame* (Peru, IL: Open Court, 2005), p. 106.

174 See, most comprehensively, Duff, *Intention, Agency and Criminal Liability*, ch. 7. For earlier versions of Duff's theory, see Duff, 'Recklessness'; R.A. Duff, 'Recklessness and

The first building block in understanding Duff's 'practical indifference' is his position on dualism. Dualism, it will be remembered,[175] is the belief 'that human beings consist of two distinct elements: a physical body, which occupies and moves in space, and a non-physical mind, which thinks and feels'.[176] Dualism holds that the only way for an external observer to ascertain the content of another's intentions or attitudes is to observe her physical actions, in their context, and make inferences *back to* the mental processes that accompanied them. For instance, if Gavin hits Allan, it might be inferred from Gavin's actions that he had the attendant psychological experience of the intention to hit Allan or, alternatively (if the circumstances suggest it), that the 'punch' was an accidental movement or an involuntary spasm, unaccompanied by mental deliberation.[177]

This dualist approach to intentionality and action has clearly influenced the criminal trial around the Anglo-American world: the judge or jury is asked to draw inferences from conduct (*actus reus*) and other 'objective' evidence to ascertain the 'subjective' thoughts (*mens rea*) accompanying the defendant's actions (or the lack thereof).[178] Despite its pervasiveness in the practice of criminal law, Duff thinks that dualism is a 'deeply mistaken doctrine'.[179] This is a problem for those theorists who argue that recklessness must be understood exclusively in terms of an explicit, conscious mental experience (a thought such as 'I might kill someone . . .'), as Duff sees their theories as dualist.[180]

Duff's main difficulty with dualism is that he believes there is more to discovering a person's attitudes and intentions than asking what thoughts happen to go (or not go) through her head at the time of acting. The external observer should thus not understand her role as trying to uncover a 'hidden mental realm to which only the agent has direct access'.[181] Instead, inferences should be drawn 'from the actions, or

rape' (1981) 3 *Liverpool Law Review* 49; R.A. Duff, 'Professor Williams and conditional subjectivism' (1982) 41 *Cambridge Law Journal* 273; R.A. Duff, '*Caldwell* and *Lawrence*: the retreat from subjectivism' (1983) 3 *Oxford Journal of Legal Studies* 77.

175 See the brief discussion of dualism, above at Chapter 4, section on 'Behaviourism'.

176 Duff, *Intention, Agency and Criminal Liability*, p. 116.

177 See Gerald H. Gordon, 'Subjective and objective *mens rea*' (1974–1975) 17 *Criminal Law Quarterly* 355 at 359–361.

178 Alan W. Norrie, *Punishment, Responsibility and Justice: A Relational Critique* (Oxford: Oxford University Press, 2000), p. 133.

179 Duff, *Intention, Agency and Criminal Liability*, p. 119. See, further, Fruchtman, 'Recklessness and the limits of *mens rea*', at 323.

180 Duff, *Intention, Agency and Criminal Liability*, p. 159.

181 Ibid., p. 131.

aspects of action, which we observe, to the broader patterns of meaning of which they are part'.[182] On this view, an actor's intentions are revealed as much through her actions, in their context, as through her occurrent mental states.[183] It does not therefore matter whether, in the example above, Gavin thought 'I intend to hit Allan' when he threw the punch. The context of the action (in a crowded bar, following the spilling of Gavin's drink) might reveal that intention, even if it did not figure in Gavin's conscious deliberations over his conduct, because of the speed with which he reacted.

Until this point, Duff's account is similar to that presented in the discussion of *belief* in Chapter 4. From here, however, Duff's approach and that adopted in this book diverge. Duff is not looking to establish, from conduct, what the defendant *believed* about risk, because – as will be seen – he does not require an indifferent defendant to be aware of the risks attendant upon φ-ing. He is rather looking for a more abstract *attitude towards* risk, which can exist independent of awareness of risk.

Duff contends that the need to extend recklessness beyond the awareness-based paradigm arises because of what a failure to notice risk demonstrates about the 'practically indifferent' defendant's values: 'What I notice or attend to reflects what I care about; and my very failure to notice something can display my utter indifference to it'.[184] In at least *some* situations, if the defendant *cared* adequately, she would have believed that there were dangers inherent in her action.[185] She would then have been in a position to decide whether to take those risks or not. The absence of such awareness of risk is thus an indicator, rather than a defeater, of culpability.

By looking to action, rather than just the defendant's mental state, Duff argues that the law would be able to better reflect a form of moral equation because:[186]

[182] Ibid.

[183] See, similarly, Hans Oberdiek, 'Intention and foresight in criminal law' (1972) 81 *Mind* 389 at 399; Gordon, 'Subjective and objective *mens rea*', at 361.

[184] Duff, *Intention, Agency and Criminal Liability*, p. 163.

[185] The phrase 'inherent in' is used in preference to 'attendant upon' because of the distinction Duff draws between intrinsic and contingent risks.

[186] Duff, *Intention, Agency and Criminal Liability*, p. 162. See, similarly, Gordon, 'Subjective and objective *mens rea*', at 384; George P. Fletcher, *The Grammar of Criminal Law: American, Comparative and International* (Oxford: Oxford University Press, 2007), p. 315. Cf. Alan R. White, *Grounds of Liability: An Introduction to the Philosophy of Law* (Oxford: Clarendon, 1985), p. 109; Alan R. White, *Misleading Cases* (Oxford: Clarendon, 1991), p. 37.

> there is [in some contexts] no significant moral difference between one who does and one who does not notice that his action endangers [others] ... the latter's very failure to notice that risk displays just the kind of practical indifference which is displayed in the former's conscious risk-taking.

For Duff, indifference – therefore – can be a mental state that is associated with awareness of risk[187] *or*, at least *sometimes*, an aspect of conduct.[188] In *some* instances, this will not make a (moral) difference to the question of culpability for unjustified risk-taking. The law, therefore, should not draw a sharp distinction between advertence (recklessness) and inadvertence (negligence). It should instead try to establish the circumstances in which advertence and inadvertence are morally equivalent.

Duff argues that context is the key here. When further context is given to an act of inadvertent, unjustified risk-taking, it might become clear that the actor's failure to believe that a specific risk existed resulted from something other than indifference, such as stupidity or inexperience,[189] or that her indifference was detached from, rather than bound up in, her action. In these circumstances, the defendant's risk-taking does not, for Duff, demonstrate indifference in the right way.[190] What is important, in cases of inadvertence, are the reasons *why* the defendant failed to be aware of the relevant risk, and what attitude was demonstrated *by her actions*.[191]

It is useful to stop the explanation of Duff's theory here temporarily, in order to dispose with some general objections to it. It will then be possible to consider more specific difficulties with particular aspects of Duff's argument about when 'practical indifference' is displayed.

Some General Criticisms

Some authors have argued that Duff's approach is wrong-headed because it is impossible to be *indifferent* to something without first being

[187] It has been doubted that advertent recklessness *always* displays indifference: John Gardner and Heike Jung, 'Making sense of *mens rea*: Antony Duff's account' (1991) 11 *Oxford Journal of Legal Studies* 559, at 577; A.P. Simester, 'A disintegrated theory of culpability', in Dennis J. Baker and Jeremy Horder (eds.), *The Sanctity of Life and the Criminal Law: The Legacy of Glanville Williams* (Cambridge: Cambridge University Press, 2013), p. 178, at p. 187.

[188] Duff, *Intention, Agency and Criminal Liability*, p. 163.

[189] Ibid., pp. 164–165.

[190] See, similarly, Duff, *Criminal Attempts*, p. 179; Tadros, *Criminal Responsibility*, pp. 252–253.

[191] Duff, 'Professor Williams and conditional subjectivism', at 276.

aware of it.[192] White presents the example of fearlessness to demonstrate this point:[193] it would be peculiar to think of an actor as being fearless if she was not aware of the features of her situation which ought to inspire fear. If Alyson walks into a building which is susceptible to collapse to investigate the cry of a child, and rescues the child from imminent death, she can, White suggests, be described as fearless only if she was aware of the danger she was in. Otherwise, what appears to be an act of fearlessness might simply be an act carried out through ignorance – had Alyson been aware of the danger, she might not have entered the building.

The same might be alleged in cases of indifference:[194] without being aware of the features of her situation which make it risky, the defendant could not be described as 'indifferent' to the relevant risk. The person who has no beliefs about the relevant risk attendant upon φ-ing (or wrongly concludes that there is no risk) might be better described as ignorant.

Two responses are available to Duff. First, as noted above, indifference is defined as 'having no particular interest or sympathy; unconcerned'.[195] Nothing in that definition suggests that Duff is wrong about the inadvertent actor being 'indifferent' in the sense of being unconcerned, though at times Duff seems to adopt a higher standard of indifference. It is not clear that he *needs* to do so.

Second, it has already been noted that Duff argues that the *acts* of the defendant, in their context, tell the external observer important information about her attitude towards the risks she is taking. White could be alleged to have concentrated too much on the mental aspects of various traits and ignored their behavioural or attitudinal components. In the example immediately above, Alyson might not notice the features of her situation that call for fear *precisely because* she is fearless – fear simply does not register with her.[196] This is an important distinction between Duff's approach and that adopted in this book. Again, Duff is not looking

[192] See White, *Misleading Cases*, p. 38. See also Brady, 'Recklessness, negligence, indifference and awareness', at 381; Williams, 'The unresolved problem of recklessness', at 83. Cf. Edward W. Hautamaki, 'The element of *mens rea* in recklessness and "criminal negligence"' (1951–1952) 2 *Duke Bar Journal* 55 at 63.

[193] White, *Misleading Cases*, p. 38.

[194] It is assumed that virtues (such as fearlessness) and vices (such as indifference) may be compared with one another.

[195] See http://oxforddictionaries.com/view/entry/m_en_gb0407440#m_en_gb0407440.

[196] Christopher Hookway, 'Epistemic norms and theoretical deliberation' (1999) 12 *Ratio* 380 at 395.

for manifested dispositions in virtue of which an ascription of belief about risk can be made. He is simply looking for what a person's behaviour and cognitive processes tell us about her *attitude* towards risk. Alyson's attitude towards the threat of harm might be clearly visible for Duff, even if it might be difficult to ascribe to her a belief that she is in danger, or perhaps even the ingredients for the formation of that risk (discussed in the next chapter).[197]

A second objection concerns the matter of establishing the defendant's attitude, particularly in the context of a criminal trial.[198] Fruchtman contends that[199]

> Attitudes . . . are inherently personal, the result of the accused's particular background and history. Ironically, indifference can be seen as so radically subjective that ordinary principles of evidence may not provide a satisfactory basis for the requisite inferences.

This may be contrasted with more usual mental states such as belief, which are – it is assumed – more capable of proof in the courtroom.

This argument might cast doubt on some of Duff's examples of 'practical indifference', such as a parent omitting to get medical care for his child: 'if the child's need was sufficiently obvious and lasting, we may discern in the parent's failure to notice that need his indifference to the child's health (he did not notice because he did not care)'.[200] A comparison with the facts of the famous Washington case, *State* v. *Williams*,[201] shows how this type of case is not necessarily clear-cut when it comes to assessing attitudes (accounting, perhaps, for Duff's use of the word 'may'). In that case, which will be analysed again in the next chapter,[202] Native American parents omitted to seek medical care for their baby out of fear, it appears, that the social services would take the child away, alleging abuse. This explanation means that it may have been fear of losing the child, not simple indifference to its welfare, which meant that the Williamses did not seek medical attention for their son. Fruchtman might marshal this

197 For criticism of Duff's 'shaky metaphysical assumptions' on this front, see Ferzan, 'Opaque recklessness', at 611–617.

198 Ibid., at 617–618; Jennifer Temkin, 'The limits of reckless rape' [1983] *Criminal Law Review* 5 at 11.

199 Fruchtman, 'Recklessness and the limits of *mens rea*', at 440. See also Birch, 'The foresight saga', at 9.

200 Duff, *Intention, Agency and Criminal Liability*, p. 166.

201 484 P 2d 1167 (1971).

202 See below at Chapter 8, section on '*State* v. *Williams*'.

case in support of his argument that Duff's theory is impractical and/ or likely to lead to intuitively unjust results.

This objection would, however, be too strong. Just as a judge or jury might misinterpret certain conduct as giving rise to an inference of indifference (when, in fact, the defendant failed to advert to a risk because she is, for example, of low intelligence), they could surely misinterpret some accidental conduct as intentional or carried out in the light of a belief. Again, this element of uncertainty has not prevented the 'objective' proof of mental states from being employed in criminal trials in the Anglo-American world.

Furthermore, it is possible to distinguish the example Duff provides from *Williams*: once the relevant background facts (the parents' level of intelligence, their motivations, etc.) are brought into consideration, these give further context to the act of risk-taking. The Williamses' failure to notice the need for medical attention would then take on a different meaning when placed in its context and perhaps would not demonstrate a 'practical indifference' towards their child's interests. Again, context and meaning are determinative *if* the jury is given the relevant information. This information will surely be available in many cases, meaning that Duff's theory is not too 'subjective' to be useful, even if it requires the jury to ask slightly harder questions than they consider at present.[203] That is, however, an important point: if a surer basis of identifying culpable inadvertence can be defended, then Duff's looks a less secure, and thus less desirable, alternative. It will be contended in the next chapter that the account of negligence as failure of belief is a surer basis for recognising culpability without awareness of risk than Duff's 'practical indifference'.

A third, connected, objection levelled at Duff (and applicable to many indifference theories)[204] concerns the use of 'indifference' in his theory.[205] The concept is not well defined,[206] and it is entirely possible

[203] It should be noted that juries are often asked difficult questions (e.g. What constitutes a 'reasonable' belief in consent?) and seem to cope: Dori Kimel, 'Inadvertent recklessness and the criminal law' (2004) 120 *Law Quarterly Review* 548 at 552–553.

[204] See, similarly, D.J. Galligan, 'Responsibility for recklessness' (1978) 31 *Current Legal Problems* 55 at 72.

[205] See Andrew Ashworth, 'Principles, pragmatism and the Law Commission's recommendations on homicide law reform' [2007] *Criminal Law Review* 333 at 338; Williams, 'The unresolved problem of recklessness', at 83.

[206] 'Duff . . . tells us remarkably little about what he understands by [indifference]': Horder, 'Gross negligence and criminal culpability', at 501.

that a judge or jury could share a completely different view of 'indifference' from the defendant and other members of society.[207] This opens Duff's theory up to the objection that it allows unmitigated jury discretion on the question of culpability. This is problematic because juries do not give public reasons for their decisions and their verdicts are virtually unassailable.

An obvious response to this criticism is that the concept of recklessness is vague in a few Anglo-American jurisdictions, but juries still manage to reach decisions (although it is not clear how consistent these decisions are, which is troubling).[208] A more developed response is to attempt to concretise the concept of indifference through providing examples.[209] Some examples might already be found in the doctrine of certain jurisdictions. In Scotland, for example, the fact that a death followed an assault involving 'lethal' weapons provides strong evidence of 'wicked' recklessness,[210] a concept premised on indifference to life.[211] The inference is that using a 'lethal' weapon against another is almost necessarily to demonstrate indifference towards life.[212] Similarly, in order to avoid the vagueness of indifference in rape cases,[213] English law recognises the absence of a *reasonable* belief in consent as a form of *mens rea*, and also a range of indicators of where a person is presumed not to be consenting, and the defendant is presumed not to believe reasonably in consent.[214] These could be taken as examples of when having sexual intercourse with someone

207 Alan Norrie, *Crime, Reason and History: A Critical Introduction to Criminal Law*, 3rd edn. (Cambridge: Cambridge University Press, 2014), pp. 91–92.

208 A 2011 study of involuntary manslaughter in England and Wales did not consider this issue but did find that 'gross' negligence manslaughter (which employs a vague conception of 'recklessness') is rare in comparison to its unlawful, dangerous act and (advertently) reckless counterparts: Barry Mitchell and R.D. Mackay, 'Investigating involuntary manslaughter: an empirical study of 127 cases' (2011) 31 *Oxford Journal of Legal Studies* 165 at 190. This makes investigating jury decisions regarding 'gross' negligence difficult.

209 See, similarly, G.R. Sullivan, 'Intent, subjective recklessness and culpability' (1992) 12 *Oxford Journal of Legal Studies* 380 at 390–391.

210 *HM Advocate* v. *McGuinness* 1937 JC 37, at 40. See, further, Gerald H. Gordon, *The Criminal Law of Scotland*, 3rd edn., ed. M.G.A. Christie, 2 vols. (Edinburgh: W. Green and Son, 2001), vol. 2, para. 23.23 (n. 20).

211 'Wicked' recklessness is explained above at Chapter 2, section on 'Scotland'.

212 Cf. Alan W. Norrie, 'Between orthodox subjectivism and moral contextualism: intention and the consultation paper' [2006] *Criminal Law Review* 486 at 492.

213 See e.g. *R* v. *Pigg* [1982] 1 WLR 762 (E&W).

214 See Sexual Offences Act 2003, ss. 1, 75–76.

presumptively suggests an indifference to the matter of consent, independent of the defendant's beliefs.

These doctrinal examples illustrate that the concept of indifference can be firmed up. There are, of course, limits on how definite it can become: recklessness is employed in relation to a wide range of offences, and it would be difficult (if not impossible) to provide a list of examples of indifference for each context.[215] Some jury/judicial discretion would therefore have to remain. Such discretion is not, however, avoided by other theorists. For instance, many accounts of culpability rely on normative standards that will admit of flexibility. Consider the idea of *insufficient concern* for the interests of others. This is similarly malleable to Duff's idea of indifference, which is part of its strength in allowing for nuanced judgments regarding culpability.

Duff's general theory of 'practical indifference', therefore, is defensible against popular objections. It will be argued in the next section that the culpability of inadvertence should not be understood, however, in terms of 'practical indifference'. This is because Duff has difficulty distinguishing between different varieties of inadvertence ('practical indifference' /recklessness and negligence) in a compelling manner.[216]

Distinguishing Recklessness and Negligence

It is useful to consider Duff's treatment of (inadvertent) recklessness and negligence as it appears in *Intention, Agency and Criminal Liability*, rather than his earlier (less expansive) work. Duff begins by discriminating between the actor who has no beliefs about the risks that she is taking and the actor who positively believes there is no risk attendant upon her conduct. In relation to the former, the distinction between negligence and recklessness is 'difficult to fathom'.[217] Duff explains that[218]

> What makes a reckless agent more culpable, more fully responsible for the risk she creates, is that she displays a gross indifference to that particular risk or to the *particular interests* which she threatens: negligence, however,

215 As seen below, 'practical indifference' can exist only in *some* cases of inadvertence, and so this point about the widespread use of recklessness should not be taken too far when considering Duff's theory. Other theorists are, however, less restrictive in their use of reckless indifference.

216 See, similarly, Brady, 'Recklessness', at 197; Horder, 'Gross negligence and criminal culpability', at 501.

217 Brudner, *Punishment and Freedom*, p. 95.

218 Duff, *Intention, Agency and Criminal Liability*, p. 165.

> involves a *less specific kind of carelessness* or inattention which does not relate the agent so closely, as an agent, to the risk which she creates. To show that I recklessly endangered someone's life it must be shown that my action manifested a culpable indifference to her life: but negligently endangering her life need involve only a lack of attention to what I am doing – not a specific indifference to that particular risk. [Emphasis added]

This distinction may seem too abstract to apply easily.[219] Things become clearer through Duff's consideration of examples. The risk of death is apparently specific to and 'inseparable' from a serious physical assault.[220] Therefore, 'the assailant's failure to notice [a risk of death] cannot but manifest an utter indifference to his victim's life'.[221] A parent failing to notice obvious signs of illness in her child (see above) *may* display indifference: 'he did not notice because he did not care'.[222] A driver failing to foresee the risks attendant upon driving at high speed in a busy urban street is *sometimes* 'practically indifferent' to the safety of others (and no doubt himself);[223] the threat to their safety is *sometimes* bound up in her careless conduct.[224]

It is clear that these examples work best when the circumstances are extremely grave. The parent who fails to notice obvious signs that her child needs medical attention might fail to notice because she does not care, but – as noted above – also because she fears social services might take the child from her.[225] Her action does not seem to be structured around ignoring or threatening the child's interests. Similarly, the driver who speeds in an urban area does not seem automatically indifferent to the lives of others. Endangering life does not necessarily structure the actor's intentional action. She might be evading pursuit, rather than seeking, through her actions, to threaten the interests of others (and, indeed, herself) in life and bodily integrity.[226] As noted above, Duff holds that context is everything. He is not, then, bound to reject the arguments in this paragraph.

[219] L.H. Leigh, 'Recklessness after *Reid*' (1993) 56 *Modern Law Review* 208 at 216; Brady, 'Recklessness', at 197; C.M.V. Clarkson, 'Aggravated endangerment offences' (2007) 60 *Current Legal Problems* 278 at 279.

[220] Duff, *Intention, Agency and Criminal Liability*, p. 166. [221] Ibid. [222] Ibid.

[223] Cf. the discussion of *dolus eventualis* in *Humphreys* v. *State* [2013] ZASCA 20, 2013 (2) SACR 1 (ZA).

[224] Duff, *Intention, Agency and Criminal Liability*, pp. 166–167.

[225] Cf. *State* v. *Williams*, 484 P 2d 1167 (1971, WA).

[226] Cf. *HM Advocate* v. *Purcell* [2007] HCJ 13, 2008 JC 131 (Scot).

The possibility of neutering or explaining away some of Duff's examples is also present in some of the cases where risks are allegedly not 'specific' in the sense required for inadvertent recklessness. The defendant in the famous English case of *Commissioner of Police for the Metropolis* v. *Caldwell*[227] set fire to his former place of employment (a hotel) to settle a grudge. He was charged with aggravated criminal damage, which includes an allegation of recklessness as to the endangerment of life.[228] Caldwell was convicted, but Duff contends that this was an error. Caldwell 'intended only to damage property, not to cause injury: his intended action was not so closely related to the risk of death which it in fact created; it did not by itself show him to be reckless as to that risk'.[229] It may, however, be alleged that, through adopting the *means* that he did to achieve property damage, Caldwell necessarily (and intentionally) unleashed the risk of death upon the hotel guests.[230] His intentional action was to damage property through setting *fire* to it, and it is not too difficult to draw – from Caldwell's conduct, rather than simply his extant beliefs – the inference that his posing a risk to the interests in bodily integrity and life of those within the hotel was intrinsic to his action (that it structured his act of 'revenge') and that he simply did not care if that risk materialised.[231]

These disagreements about Duff's examples are not nit-picking – they are legitimate doubts about the way that actions are described, interpreted and understood in their context. The fact that alternative readings of Duff's examples are available suggests that the specific/general line he draws between recklessness and negligence lacks structural integrity, especially when contrasted with the Standard Account's comparatively clear line drawn by awareness of risk. As well as lacking the clarity of the Standard Account, it is possible that the benefit of understanding inadvertent 'practical indifference' could be wrought not by warping the idea of recklessness to include defendants who were not aware of the risk, but instead by taking the culpability of negligence more seriously, as argued for in the next chapter.

[227] [1982] AC 341. [228] Criminal Damage Act 1971, s. 1(2).

[229] Duff, *Intention, Agency and Criminal Liability*, p. 166.

[230] The fact that Caldwell was voluntarily intoxicated will be ignored. It was argued in Chapter 2 that rules regarding voluntary intoxication should be entirely divorced from rules concerning recklessness and negligence.

[231] See, further, Norrie, *Crime, Reason and History*, p. 92. The famous case of *Hyam*, where a woman set fire to a love rival's house, intending to scare her but killing two children, can be analysed similarly.

Duff nevertheless perseveres in drawing a distinction between recklessness and negligence. It is useful next to consider Duff's treatment of cases where the defendant believed positively that there was no risk involved in φ-ing, as these are the clearest examples of defendants who are 'practically indifferent' and yet do not believe there is a risk attendant upon φ-ing (whether in terms of their explicit conscious experiences or their behaviour and cognitive processes). In such cases, Duff's approach to separating out recklessness and negligence seems far clearer and more defensible. Duff begins from the premise that '[t]here is sometimes a significant difference between one who does what he realizes will probably cause some harm, and one who does what he realizes might, but probably will not, cause such harm'.[232] This can be the dividing line between recklessness and negligence in Duff's view. A person who throws debris off a roof without checking for passers-by below, for instance, is negligent, not reckless:[233] the risk of harming another person in this situation is *contingent* upon, rather than *intrinsic* to, the activity.[234] Apparently, this risk would be intrinsic if the debris was thrown in order to frighten a neighbour. In such circumstances, a failure to notice a risk of injury could be reckless, rather than simply negligent.

Duff gives other examples of intrinsic circumstances which, when ignored by an agent, can give rise to an inference of 'practical indifference'. For instance, as consent is central to a proper understanding of sexual intercourse,[235] a person who fails to notice obvious signs of non-consent is 'practically indifferent' – and reckless – as to consent, even if he believes positively that consent exists.[236] Consent is not a circumstance which floats in the ether (as the circumstance of a neighbour being below floats alongside the act of throwing debris off a roof to dispose of it): 'his action is structured by a disregard for (an indifference to) *her* integrity, and *her* right to make up and express her own mind about her sexual partners, which does not differ significantly from that displayed by one who persists with intercourse realizing that the woman might not consent'.[237]

[232] Duff, *Intention, Agency and Criminal Liability*, p. 168.

[233] Ibid. See, similarly, Hart, *Punishment and Responsibility*, pp. 147, 149.

[234] Duff, *Intention, Agency and Criminal Liability*, p. 168. See, similarly, George P. Fletcher, *Basic Concepts of Criminal Law* (Oxford: Oxford University Press, 1998), p. 116.

[235] T.M. Scanlon, *What We Owe to Each Other* (Cambridge, MA: Harvard University Press, 1998), p. 175.

[236] Duff, 'Recklessness and rape'; Duff, *Intention, Agency and Criminal Liability*, pp. 168–171.

[237] Duff, *Intention, Agency and Criminal Liability*, p. 170.

These examples lead to the conclusion that the distinction between *attacks* and *endangerments*[238] (a theme Duff has returned to in later work)[239] is central to separating inadvertent recklessness from negligence. A person who aims at causing serious bodily injury (even if she believes that this attack will not kill), for instance, engages in an attack against the interests of the victim in life; she acts for the very reason that the attack puts the victim's life in peril.[240] A person who engages in the same conduct – and fails to be guided by reasons which ought to motivate her[241] – but does not have the same *aim* of causing serious injury merely endangers the victim; her action is not structured by the end of causing serious injury or imperilling life, and she will be happy (even relieved)[242] if those consequences are avoided.[243]

It is thus only the attacker who is, though inadvertent, 'practically indifferent' to the 'intrinsic' risks she is imposing.[244] The endangerer is not connected so closely through her intentional action to those risks, and so does not demonstrate 'practical indifference' through her failure to note them. This means that, for Duff, inadvertent recklessness is quite a slim category, where the risk is bound up in the actor's intentional conduct or flows naturally from it.[245] Endangerments require awareness of risk – i.e. a belief that there is a specific risk attendant upon φ-ing – in order for the defendant to be culpable.[246]

Again, this reasoning sounds compelling,[247] but some of Duff's examples have proved controversial. It was noted above that Duff views

238 Ibid., p. 176.

239 See R.A. Duff, 'Criminalizing endangerment', in R.A. Duff and Stuart P. Green (eds.), *Defining Crimes: Essays on the Special Part of the Criminal Law* (Oxford: Oxford University Press, 2005), p. 43; Duff, *Answering for Crime*, ch. 7; R.A. Duff, 'Whose luck is it anyway?', in C.M.V. Clarkson and Sally Cunningham (eds.), *Criminal Liability for Non-aggressive Death* (Aldershot: Ashgate, 2008), p. 61.

240 Duff, *Intention, Agency and Criminal Liability*, p. 177.

241 See Kennett, *Agency and Responsibility*, p. 177; Clarkson, 'Aggravated endangerment offences', p. 286; Duff, *Answering for Crime*, p. 151.

242 Duff, 'Criminalizing endangerment', p. 68.

243 Duff, *Intention, Agency and Criminal Liability*, p. 61.

244 The fact that this connection exists in limited circumstances has led some theorists to conclude that recklessness is not what Duff is describing. For instance, it has been suggested that his example of assaults and death describes not recklessness but *implied malice* (in fact, that is the title of the section in which his thoughts on murder are expressed (ibid., p. 173)): Gardner and Jung, 'Making sense of *mens rea*', at 578.

245 See, further, Clarkson, 'Aggravated endangerment offences', p. 293.

246 Duff, *Answering for Crime*, p. 157.

247 Cf. Kimberly K. Ferzan, 'The structure of criminal law' (2009) 28 *Criminal Justice Ethics* 223 at 227–230.

'practical indifference' as relevant in cases of rape.[248] Although it is obvious to Duff (and others)[249] that a person who engages in sexual intercourse without adverting to obvious signs of non-consent is misunderstanding what sex *ought* to be about (mutual respect, communication, etc.), Norrie points out that there is no real coherence in social conceptions of what is (and is not) inherent in the practice of ('proper') sex.[250] This suggests that explaining what is, and is not, intrinsic to sex (properly understood) is a difficult enterprise, making Duff's example concerning rape at least debatable.

Even if such social agreement about the 'proper' content of sex existed (and few would deny that proper consideration of the matter of *consent* is crucial), it is clear that the rape and serious physical attack examples used by Duff are not making the same point. Where the defendant does not intend non-consensual intercourse (and despite Duff's best efforts to say otherwise),[251] it is difficult to conceive of his action as an *attack* on interests in the way that a serious physical assault attacks the life of another person.[252] Unless the defendant intended to have non-consensual intercourse, he surely only *endangers* his partner's sexual autonomy; he will not have failed in his action if – consistent with his belief – the complainant was, in fact, consenting. Contrary to what Duff argues, it appears that the matter of consent is – in the relevant sense – contingent, rather than intrinsic, and this leads to the suggestion that the defendant who fails to note obvious signs of non-consent is possibly *negligent* but not reckless.

Perhaps Duff has warped the rape example to fit his model of inadvertent recklessness.[253] This move is, to a degree, understandable: negligence is perceived as being non-serious by most theorists, and it is therefore

248 See the text accompanying nn. 235–237, above.

249 See, e.g. Pamela R. Ferguson, 'Controversial aspects of the law of rape: an Anglo-Scottish comparison', in Robert F. Hunter (ed.), *Justice and Crime: Essays in Honour of the Right Honourable the Lord Emslie* (Edinburgh: T&T Clark, 1993), p. 180, at p. 194.

250 Norrie, 'Subjectivism, objectivism and the limits of criminal recklessness', at 51.

251 See also Duff, *Criminal Attempts*, p. 374.

252 This perhaps accounts for the restatement of the rape example (in a footnote) in Duff's later work: see Duff, 'Criminalizing endangerment', at p. 54 (n. 38). There, Duff suggests that 'the actualisation of the risk' of non-consent turns sexual intercourse 'into an attack'. This explanation is mysterious: why is the structure of the defendant's action determined by a matter (the circumstance of non-consent) beyond his control?

253 There are hints of this argument in Gardner and Jung, 'Making sense of *mens rea*', at 578. They postulate that Duff might have to employ different *mens rea* terms in contexts where recklessness-as-indifference does not 'fit'.

more palatable to extend the concept of recklessness to accommodate cases of seeming culpable inadvertence. If negligence as failure of belief (outlined in the next chapter) were taken seriously in the criminal law, this manoeuvre would be unnecessary. It would be possible to argue that the defendant failed to form a belief in risk where he could legitimately be expected to have done so, and *this* (rather than recklessness understood in terms of 'practical indifference') is why he ought to be convicted of rape.

For now, it is clear that when the rape example (and the other examples criticised above) are examined in detail, Duff's account of 'practical indifference' is even narrower than his views in *Intention, Agency and Criminal Liability* suggest. In the assault example (and others like it), the core points that Duff makes about attacks, endangerments and risks are defensible in theory. But they seem to lack much explanatory value.[254] The argument here is not that Duff's account is unsustainable but that it explains even less than Duff claims it does. It is a tremendously narrow conception of inadvertent fault, and it will be argued in the next chapter that it is possible to explain a wider, and more defensible, sense of culpable inadvertence.

Conclusion

This chapter has critically analysed a number of existing accounts of culpable carelessness that include inadvertent risk-taking. Some of these accounts challenge the veracity of the Exclusive Thesis, insofar as there are no knockdown arguments that render them *utterly unsustainable.* A more muted conclusion is called for, and that is that there are difficulties with the accounts discussed in this chapter. If an account of culpable inadvertence can be crafted that has fewer theoretical, explanatory and practical shortcomings, then it is submitted that it will be preferable to the theories discussed here and represents a stronger challenge to the Exclusive Thesis. The next chapter will outline an account of culpability without awareness that, it will be contended, is more defensible than those discussed thus far.

[254] There is also the perhaps obvious point that it is difficult to imagine a situation where a person embarks on an intentionally serious physical attack against another person without a belief that the attack *could* result in death. See Ferzan, 'Opaque recklessness', at 615 (n. 62). See also David Lanham, 'Murder, recklessness and grievous bodily harm' (1978) 2 *Criminal Law Journal* 255 at 271.

8

Negligence as Failure of Belief

The previous chapter analysed some conceptions of culpable carelessness that are not based on the defendant's failure to be moved by her belief about a particular risk at the time of taking it (in circumstances where doing so was unjustified). It found that although there are sometimes no knockdown arguments against such theories, each suffers from deficiencies, in terms of realism, explanatory value or complexity. This chapter presents an account of culpability without awareness which, it will be argued, is realistic, explains well the role of negligence in the 'Standard Account' of culpable carelessness that the Anglo-American systems surveyed in Chapter 2 are converging around, and fares better against objections relating to complexity. It will be presented as the *best* account of culpability without awareness, and thus the best account of negligence on the Standard Account.

It will be contended that negligence is best understood in terms of the defendant's failure to form a belief that there was a *specific risk* attendant upon her behaviour (φ).[1] In other words, negligence is the failure to be in the epistemic position of the putatively reckless defendant. It will be explained when such failures of belief are culpable, and the kind of circumstances in which that culpable negligence should be recognised as sufficient fault to merit the personalised condemnation communicated by a criminal conviction.[2]

It is sensible to begin by explaining once again the focus on beliefs, rather than behaviour, in the account of negligence defended in this book.

[1] This chapter thus assumes that negligence must relate to a specific risk and not exist 'in the air'. See, further, Michael S. Moore, *Causation and Responsibility: an Essay in Law, Morals and Metaphysics* (Oxford: Oxford University Press, 2009), ch. 7.

[2] On the condemnation of conviction, see above at pp. 1–2.

Beliefs, not Behaviour

It was noted in the previous chapter that some doctrinal accounts of culpability without awareness have focussed on the extent of the defendant's careless *behaviour*, rather than a more personalised basis of fault.[3] It was argued that this is why a bare conduct-based model of negligence is inappropriate for the criminal law, even if it is appropriate for other areas of the law – for instance, tort law/delict. The appropriateness of conduct-based models of negligence in other areas of the law is, however, not a matter on which a settled conclusion need be expressed here.

Not all doctrinal accounts of criminal negligence focus simply on conduct, however. For instance, the American Law Institute's Model Penal Code (MPC) defines negligence in the following terms:[4]

> A person acts negligently with respect to a material element of an offense when he should be aware of a substantial and unjustifiable risk that the material element exists or will result from his conduct. The risk must be of such a nature and degree that the actor's failure to perceive it, considering the nature and purpose of his conduct and the circumstances known to him, involves a gross deviation from the standard of care that a reasonable person would observe in the actor's situation.

At first glance, the MPC's definition of negligence might seem to be concerned with conduct alone: it begins '[a] person *acts* negligently . . .' (emphasis added), and the reasonable person's standard of care, the mark of most Anglo-American doctrinal, conduct-based accounts of negligence, is again mentioned. The MPC's definition of negligence nevertheless proceeds to locate the defendant's fault not in her conduct itself, but instead in her unreasonable failure to be *aware* of the relevant risk(s) associated with φ-ing.[5] It is that absence of awareness of risk that links the defendant, as an agent, to her wrongdoing – her unjustified risk-taking and its consequences. It is that epistemic failure, twinned with an unjustified instance of risk-taking (and, if relevant, the materialisation of that risk), which explains why the defendant can legitimately be condemned as a culpable wrongdoer.

[3] At Chapter 7, section on 'Conduct: Hart's Insight'.

[4] American Law Institute, *Model Penal Code and Commentaries (Official Draft and Revised Comments)*, 3 vols. (Philadelphia: American Law Institute, 1980), vol. 1, s. 2.02(2)(d).

[5] The Model Penal Code's definition of recklessness also begins by explaining that 'A person acts recklessly': ibid., s. 2.02(2)(c). Nobody, to my knowledge, claims that the MPC's definition of recklessness is about conduct, rather than awareness of risk.

The MPC uses the concept of awareness of risk in explaining negligence (with perception apparently being a synonymous term). In the light of the discussion of awareness of risk in Chapters 4 and 5, it is best to view the MPC's variety of negligence as being concerned with the defendant's failure to *believe* that φ-ing carries with it a particular risk or risks.[6] Following the account of belief presented in Chapter 4, the failure to have a belief that there is a particular risk attendant upon φ-ing is synonymous with the failure to have a sufficient number of phenomenal, behavioural and cognitive dispositions relevant to the proper ascription of a belief that there is a risk attendant upon φ-ing.

The switch from conduct to belief described above is natural. The criminal law's other fault terms are all related, to a greater or a lesser extent, to beliefs. A person cannot intend to bring about a certain result unless she believes that she *can* bring that result about (however unlikely she believes that result is).[7] A person cannot intend to run at 50 miles per hour. At least as far as the criminal law is concerned, a person cannot know a certain proposition unless she has a belief about it.[8] Recklessness, as has been argued in this book, is a belief-based concept. In short, beliefs are core to understanding criminal culpability – in linking defendants meaningfully to their wrongdoing.

The problem with negligence is, of course, that it is the very *absence* of the relevant belief about risk that is vital to recklessness. That is what the MPC identifies as the problem in negligence: it is the failure of the defendant to form a belief about the risks attendant upon φ-ing.[9] In the discussion that follows, it is envisaged that such failures can arise in relation to two distinct situations.[10] First, there are cases where the defendant forms a false belief about the extent of a relevant risk or concludes (incorrectly) that the risk does not exist at all (so-called

[6] See, similarly, A.P. Simester, 'Can Negligence Be Culpable?', in Jeremy Horder (ed.), *Oxford Essays in Jurisprudence: Fourth Series* (Oxford: Oxford University Press, 2000), p. 85, at p. 95. See also Michael S. Moore, *Placing Blame: A Theory of the Criminal Law* (Oxford: Oxford University Press, 1997), p. 412.

[7] Cf. Moore, *Placing Blame*, p. 410.

[8] For discussion of knowledge, see above at Chapter 5.

[9] Peter W. Low, 'The Model Penal Code, the common law and mistakes of fact: recklessness, negligence or strict liability?' (1987–1988) 19 *Rutgers Law Journal* 539 at 549.

[10] This distinction is drawn clearly in Leo Zaibert, 'For negligence liability', in Paul H. Robinson, Stephen P. Garvey and Kimberly K. Ferzan (eds.), *Criminal Law Conversations* (Oxford: Oxford University Press, 2009), p. 281, at p. 281.

Caldwell lacuna cases).[11] Second, there are cases where the defendant simply has *no* beliefs about the riskiness of φ-ing.

It is useful to begin the explanation of negligence as failure of belief by looking at the process of belief-formation itself. This discussion will segue into consideration of an obvious concern about the level of *control* that persons have over their beliefs. The focus can then switch to the circumstances in which a failure to form a belief that the relevant risk exists can be a basis for culpability.

A Preliminary Sketch of Belief Formation

It is posited here that the dispositions relevant to the ascription of a belief that a certain proposition is the case are formed through a process of combining information gleaned from perception[12] and the defendant's 'background' beliefs.[13] It was suggested in Chapter 4 that such background beliefs are best analysed in dispositional terms: a person has a background belief that water conducts electricity if she is disposed to act cautiously around water if she has noticed electrical items nearby, has a phenomenal experience of the proposition that water conducts electricity, plans to avoid leaving electrical items near water, and so on. The idea of negligence as failure of belief is that a person with that relevant background belief has failed to form, in the light of her perceptions about the situation she is in, a further belief that attached to φ-ing is a risk to a specific interest (a risk that, in the circumstances, it is unjustified for her to take).

For instance, if a person smells rotting cabbage upon entering a room, and has the relevant background beliefs regarding the proposition that leaking gas makes a smell like rotting cabbage, then the ingredients are there for the formation of the dispositions consistent with a new belief that there is, at this moment, a risk of a gas leak. Assuming additional background dispositions, further fresh dispositions regarding the matter

[11] Such cases were introduced above at Chapter 1, section on 'Why Is Justification Required?'.

[12] It might be contended that perception is a form of belief formation – see e.g. Nomy Arpaly, *Unprincipled Virtue: An Inquiry into Moral Agency* (Oxford: Oxford University Press, 2002), p. 53. It is not obvious that accepting this point would cause any difficulties for the account of negligence as failure of belief presented in this chapter.

[13] On such beliefs, see Victor Tadros, *Criminal Responsibility* (Oxford: Oxford University Press, 2005), p. 250; Stephen P. Garvey, 'What's wrong with involuntary manslaughter?' (2006–2007) 85 *Texas Law Review* 333 at 342.

of whether turning the light on at this time would be unjustifiably risky are, in principle, capable of being formed.[14] If these dispositions *are* formed, then the ascription of a belief about the risk(s) associated with flicking the switch will be merited.

In cases of negligence, the concern should be with the defendant's *failure* to display the dispositions that merit this ascription of a belief that there is a specific risk attendant upon φ-ing.[15] The important matter is whether and – if so – when a person can be responsible for failing to possess and manifest the dispositions that merit the ascription of this new belief that a particular risk exists in the circumstances.

Before proceeding further, it is important to emphasise that the two posited ingredients for belief – perception and background beliefs – are *necessary* (but not sufficient) conditions for negligence as failure of belief.[16] A person who could not be credited with the relevant background belief, on the basis of her dispositions, that gas smells that way or who has a blocked nose would be missing a vital part of the belief formation puzzle involved in the example above.[17] Regarding a person as criminally culpable for her failure to form the dispositions that merit the ascription of the belief about the risks attendant upon flicking the light switch, etc. in these circumstances would be unfair.[18] It is useful to dwell on the nature of this unfairness.

It might be thought that any argument about unfairness is premised on concerns about avoidability. Without the relevant background beliefs or perceptions required to form the relevant belief about risk, the defendant is not in a position easily to avoid her failure to form a belief that there is a risk attendant upon φ-ing. In such circumstances, it would be legitimate for her to complain about any finding of responsibility or culpability for her risk-taking or its consequences. It might be doubted, however, that the defendant could have such a complaint if she is at *fault*

[14] It is accepted that perceptions and background dispositions may exist in degrees of strength. See, further, Samuel H. Pillsbury, 'Crimes of indifference' (1996–1997) 49 *Rutgers Law Review* 105 at 141.

[15] Or, perhaps, the absence of a disposition *to* believe the relevant risk exists. See Robert Audi, 'Dispositional beliefs and dispositions to believe' (1994) 28 *Noûs* 419.

[16] See, similarly, Edwin R. Keedy, 'Ignorance and mistake in the criminal law' (1908–1909) 22 *Harvard Law Review* 75 at 81; P.J.T. O'Hearn, 'Criminal negligence: an analysis in depth' (1964–1965) 7 *Criminal Law Quarterly* 27, 407 (published in two parts) at 419. Cf. Simester, 'Can negligence be culpable?', at pp. 99–100.

[17] Keedy, 'Ignorance and mistake in the criminal law', at 81.

[18] Cf. Kenneth W. Simons, 'When is negligent inadvertence culpable?' (2011) 5 *Criminal Law and Philosophy* 97 at 99.

for lacking a particular background belief or set of background beliefs.[19] If such a fault exists, the argument would run, then the defendant *did* have an adequate opportunity to avoid being unaware of the relevant risk, and that is why she may be adjudged responsible and perhaps even culpable for the absence of the relevant belief about the risk(s) attendant upon φ-ing.

Consider if the reason that the gas smell is not perceived in the example above is that the defendant had not dried her hair before heading out on a cold day, and thus can fairly be said to have been responsible for her having a blocked nose. Would it be permissible, in such circumstances, to hold her responsible for her failure to perceive the risk of explosion, on the basis that she could have avoided having the blocked nose through taking the simple step of drying her hair?

Consider also Tadros's example of a person (call her Fiona) who does not believe that water conducts electricity.[20] In the absence of a belief about water and conductivity, Fiona would presumably not be able to form a belief that she was putting others at risk by leaving a plugged-in radio close to the bath, *because* she lacks the necessary background beliefs that would lead to the formation of that belief about risk.[21] What if Fiona played truant from school when the conductivity of water was covered? Had she not, she might[22] have had the relevant dispositions towards thought and action consistent with the belief about conductivity and been in a position to form a further belief about the specific risk(s) associated with her behaviour. Again, Fiona is in the position where a simple step would have led her to be in a better epistemic position, and so it might be argued that she is adequately responsible for her failure to have the relevant belief about the risks attendant upon her conduct.

The difficulties that arose in the previous chapter in relation to Pillsbury and Hampton's accounts of culpable carelessness[23] are encountered again here. There are significant problems involved in showing adequate

19 Cf. Simester, 'Can negligence be culpable?', p. 96.

20 Tadros, *Criminal Responsibility*, pp. 251–252. See also Jonathan Dancy, *Practical Reality* (Oxford: Oxford University Press, 2002), p. 57.

21 Cf. *R* v. *Whybrow* (1951) 35 Cr App R 141 (E&W), at 144 (it is 'common knowledge' that water conducts electricity).

22 Fiona might well have forgotten the relevant information and lack the dispositions consistent with the relevant belief about conductivity, by the time it becomes relevant to her behaviour. See below.

23 See Chapter 7, section on 'Tracing Accounts'.

freedom, foresight and culpability in an earlier decision not to take steps to gain background beliefs or to ensure certain aspects of the situation are perceived. Did the defendant know what was on the lesson plan the day that she played truant? Were other opportunities for the relevant background belief to be formed, or perception made, missed? How much time has passed since the last available opportunity was passed up? Such questions, and many more politically charged ones (Can the state legitimately expect that citizens develop and retain certain dispositions towards propositions regarding risk, and perceive certain aspects of their situation, on pain of criminal punishment?), cannot easily be resolved in the criminal courtroom.[24] For the sake of feasibility, the focus ought, therefore, to be on the background beliefs and perceptions that the defendant *had* at the time she engaged in unjustified risk-taking, rather than those that she *could or should have had.*

Information that the defendant has forgotten about ought to be considered similarly.[25] The absence of such recallable information is, on the account defended here, the absence of the relevant background dispositions towards thought and behaviour required for the formation of the new specific belief about the risk(s) attendant upon φ-ing. Without such background beliefs, defendants cannot exhibit negligence as failure of belief with regard to the specific risks attendant upon φ-ing.[26]

Now that the posited necessary ingredients of belief formation have been outlined, it is important to consider the role of control and the will in the process of belief formation.

Belief Formation and the Will

It is widely accepted that the *complete* absence of control over a certain thing negates responsibility for that thing.[27] Belief formation, it might be thought, is one of those matters that is beyond a person's control. This is because belief formation often does not seem to require an exercise of

[24] See, similarly, Nicola Lacey, *State Punishment: Political Principles and Community Values* (London: Routledge, 1994), p. 71.

[25] Cf. the treatment of defendant whose capacities to retain information and form justified beliefs in risk have deteriorated, subtly, over time in Robert L. Rabin, 'The fault of not knowing: a comment' (2003) 4 *Theoretical Inquiries in Law* 427 at 431–432.

[26] Cf. Glanville Williams, 'The unresolved problem of recklessness' (1988) 8 *Legal Studies* 74 at 86.

[27] See the discussion of control and criminal responsibility/culpability above at Chapter 6, section on 'Choice and Control'.

will, at least in all instances.[28] On entering a room smelling of rotting cabbage, a person might immediately manifest the dispositions consistent with a belief that there is a risk of a gas leak, and a further belief that turning on the lights would carry with it particular risks. In such circumstances it seems peculiar and misleading to speak of the defendant having to *will* the formation of the dispositions that she in fact manifested and the beliefs that she can therefore be attributed.[29] She just formed and manifested them, and there seems little role for the will in that process.[30] Tadros has described such beliefs as 'cognitive',[31] but a better label would be 'unreflective'.[32]

The existence of unreflective beliefs might be thought to cause difficulties for a theory of criminal negligence premised on the defendant's failure to form a belief about a particular risk.[33] If the defendant had absolutely *no control* over what she believed (or did not believe), then any finding of responsibility and blame premised on the absence of a particular belief seems out of the question.[34] However relaxed the control requirement can be, it cannot be obliterated entirely.

There is good reason to think, however, that defendants do have a relevant sense of control over their beliefs, which opens the door to findings of responsibility and culpability based on the absence of particular beliefs. The most obvious context in which this control is demonstrated is in relation to what Tadros calls 'evaluative' beliefs (though a better term, for both evaluations and deliberative beliefs, might be 'reflective').[35] Tadros gives the example of forming the belief that a garden of roses is beautiful.[36] The formation of this belief requires

[28] Joseph Raz, *Engaging Reason: On the Theory of Value and Action* (Oxford: Oxford University Press, 2002), p. 13; Tadros, *Criminal Responsibility*, pp. 240–241.

[29] See, similarly, Audi, 'Dispositional beliefs and dispositions to believe', at 421. Cf. Bernard Williams, *Problems of the Self: Philosophical Papers 1956–1972* (Cambridge: Cambridge University Press, 1973), p. 143.

[30] Raz, *Engaging Reason*, p. 10.

[31] Tadros, *Criminal Responsibility*, p. 241.

[32] Audi calls the process that leads to such beliefs 'non-voluntarist', which also captures the lack of reflection involved: Audi, 'Dispositional beliefs and dispositions to believe', at 427.

[33] Tadros, *Criminal Responsibility*, p. 239. Cf. Barbara Winters, 'Believing at will' (1979) 76 *Journal of Philosophy* 243.

[34] Duff, *Answering for Crime*, p. 59.

[35] Tadros, *Criminal Responsibility*, p. 240. There are also beliefs that track matters under direct physical control. If I want to believe that my cat is inside, then I can pick her up and put her inside. This kind of control is not particularly relevant to the criminal law's treatment of culpable risk-taking. See, however, Richard Feldman, 'The ethics of belief' (2000) 60 *Philosophy and Phenomenological Research* 667 at 671–672.

[36] Tadros, *Criminal Responsibility*, p. 241.

consideration of the actor's perceptions – the sensory information available to her – and her other extant beliefs about value (about what constitutes beauty, for instance).[37]

A person is clearly exercising her will in the process of belief formation when she considers – or is asked to consider – whether the garden of roses is beautiful (contrast this with the formation of the belief that the roses in the garden are red or white). She engages her capacity for reason based on the (perceptive and background) evidence available to her, meaning that reflective beliefs need not simply 'happen upon' a person.[38] A person thus *can* make decisions with regard to the formation of a new *reflective* belief, in the sense that she can engage in consideration of evidence that she has, search for new evidence and so on. When fresh beliefs are formed after such reflection and investigation, they seem inappositely described as 'involuntary'.[39] This point about reflective beliefs makes any general claim that the formation of a belief is *utterly* beyond the control of a person – and therefore not a matter of responsibility, never mind criminal responsibility and culpability – too strong.[40] There is still, then, a plausible basis for a theory of culpable negligence that is premised on the defendant's beliefs (or lack thereof).

Given the analysis above, it might be argued that it is the formation of reflective beliefs that the defendant has any sense of control over. This might lead to the conclusion that it is only where a defendant has deliberated over a certain matter that she can be negligent in the formation of her beliefs. It will, by now, nevertheless be apparent that the distinction between reflective and unreflective beliefs is not as important as it might have at first seemed. First, surely some of the beliefs that Tadros terms 'evaluative' are formed immediately, without any obvious deliberation. A person can be struck by injustice or beauty immediately without extended deliberation. The theoretical distinction between reflective and unreflective beliefs (as presented above) is thus difficult to maintain.

[37] Cf. Cohen's views on belief 'acceptance', as distinct from belief formation: L. Jonathan Cohen, *An Essay on Belief and Acceptance* (Oxford: Oxford University Press, 1992), ch. 1.

[38] See Raz, *Engaging Reason*, pp. 9–10. See also Pamela Hieronymi, 'Responsibility for believing' (2008) 161 *Synthese* 357; Pamela Hieronymi, 'Controlling attitudes' (2006) 87 *Pacific Philosophical Quarterly* 45 at 49–50.

[39] Hieronymi, 'Controlling attitudes', at 46; Duff, *Answering for Crime*, p. 61; Matthias Steup, 'Doxastic voluntarism and epistemic deontology' (2000) 15 *Acta Analytica* 25 at 51.

[40] Tadros, *Criminal Responsibility*, p. 241.

Second, if what makes an agent responsible for her reflective beliefs is that she is indirectly in control of their formation (through her ability to look for evidence, to weigh it, etc.), then there is reason to think that a person can be responsible also for her unreflective beliefs, insofar as she could exercise similar indirect control over them. A person can seek evidence to challenge the beliefs formed immediately upon perception, and thus she can be responsible for those beliefs as well.[41] A general claim that beliefs are utterly impervious to control, and thus beyond the scope of responsibility, is thus much too strong.

If these points about belief and control are right, then a defendant can be responsible for both the reflective and unreflective beliefs that she holds, on the basis that she could have searched for more evidence, weighed that evidence more carefully, etc. – matters under her control. Once again, if the objection is that this control is not of the right sort to ground criminal responsibility, a more developed argument to that effect needs to be presented. No convincing account has been developed in the existing literature on culpable carelessness, but the matter of what can reasonably be expected of defendants in terms of their belief formation will be returned to later in this chapter.

It is important not to overstate the claim made in this section. It is not being suggested that persons can control the *content* of their beliefs, of how they are, in fact, disposed to think and behave with regard to a particular matter.[42] A person who believes (after reflection) that the garden of roses is not beautiful is not in control of *that* feature of her belief.[43] Similarly, a person who concludes after adequate investigation that there is no risk attendant upon φ-ing is not responsible for the content of that belief. What agents *can* control is the *process* of encouraging the formation of appropriate beliefs – of looking for evidence and weighing it, etc. – rather than the *outcome* of that process. That is an important feature of negligence as failure of belief that will be returned to in due course. It will be contended that such failures are not *culpable* if the defendant has, through her efforts in terms of belief formation, demonstrated sufficient concern for the interests of others.

[41] Thomas Kelly, 'The rationality of belief and some other propositional attitudes' (2002) 100 *Philosophical Studies* 163 at 170.

[42] L. Jonathan Cohen, 'Belief and acceptance' (1989) 98 *Mind* 367 at 370. Cf. Tadros, *Criminal Responsibility*, p. 240.

[43] Tadros, *Criminal Responsibility*, p. 241. See, further, Williams, *Problems of the Self*, pp. 149–151; Hieronymi, 'Responsibility for believing'; Robert Audi, 'The ethics of belief: doxastic self-control and intellectual virtue' (2008) 161 *Synthese* 403.

As mentioned above, negligence as failure of belief envisages two distinct situations. The first of these is where the defendant *has* a belief about the risks attendant upon φ-ing, but it is – on some basis – not an appropriate one. The next section unpacks this idea of the beliefs that it is appropriate to hold.

Incorrect Beliefs about Risk

If (as contended in the previous section) a person can exercise a relevant degree of control over the formation processes of her beliefs to ground responsibility for her beliefs, then it is possible to sketch an argument that she might be held responsible, and potentially found culpable and liable, for the beliefs that she has (and those that she does not have), which relate to her wrongdoing. This could then be used to connect the defendant meaningfully to her wrongdoing, in the manner required for the condemnation of conviction to be applied legitimately.

One difficulty is how to decide if a defendant who has particular beliefs about risk (as opposed to a defendant who has *no* beliefs about the risks attendant upon φ-ing) is subject to criticism for not having *correct* beliefs about risk. Consider, for instance, the '*Caldwell* lacuna' cases thought up by English commentators, where the defendant concludes (incorrectly) that there is *no* risk attendant upon φ-ing.[44]

Beliefs can be evaluated in a number of ways.[45] First, on the assumption that beliefs aim at truth,[46] it might be asked whether a belief is true or false.[47] A belief that the UK Supreme Court sits in Liverpool is false, and this might lead to a negative evaluation of those who hold it. They might *want* the Supreme Court to sit in Liverpool (viewing state power in the United Kingdom as unduly centred on London), but this does not make their belief beyond criticism. In cases such as this, it seems legitimate that the agent be expected to try to make her beliefs – her dispositions towards thought and behaviour – fit the world as it *is*, not how she would

[44] Such cases are introduced above at Chapter 1, section on 'Why Is Justification Required?'.

[45] See Conor McHugh and Daniel Whiting, 'The normativity of belief' (2014) 74 *Analysis* 698.

[46] For discussion, see David J. Owens, 'Does belief have an aim?' (2003) 115 *Philosophical Studies* 283; Lucy O'Brien, 'Imagination and the motivational view of belief' (2005) 65 *Analysis* 55; J. David Velleman, *The Possibility of Practical Reason* (Oxford: Oxford University Press, 2000), pp. 247–253.

[47] See, further, Williams, *Problems of the Self*, pp. 136–137.

like it to be.[48] In the light of this expectation, a number of questions follow logically when asking if the belief-holder deserves censure. Why did the agent come to hold the dispositions relevant to the ascription of her belief?[49] Did she demonstrate some form of epistemic or investigatory failings in doing so?[50]

Already, the discussion has moved away from talk of truth or fallacy of the believed proposition alone.[51] Reconsider Tadros's garden example: beauty is not a fact, like the Supreme Court's location. It is an evaluative judgment. Although in ordinary discourse[52] it is sometimes assumed that evaluative opinions and judgments simply are 'true' or 'false', 'right' or 'wrong', this language might be misleading.[53] It is preferable to talk of whether a belief in the beauty of a garden is *justified* or *unjustified*.[54] The question again then becomes *how* the belief came about, and what grounds can be advanced for its retention, not whether that belief was empirically true or false.[55]

Truth and justification can, therefore, come apart.[56] A person can have a belief that is true, but nonetheless unjustified (she guessed some vital piece of information relevant to the belief);[57] or vice versa (she is – through no investigatory or epistemic fault of her own – ignorant of information which would have led her to a different conclusion).[58] It is submitted that the criminal law ought to be concerned only with the justification (rather than the truth) of a belief

48 Martha C. Nussbaum, *Upheavals of Thought: The Intelligence of Emotions* (Cambridge: Cambridge University Press, 2001), p. 48; Philip Pettit, *The Common Mind: An Essay on Psychology, Society and Politics* (Oxford: Oxford University Press, 1993), p. 18.

49 See Hieronymi, 'Responsibility for believing', at 371.

50 This question brings in consideration of the intellectual virtues and vices, which are beyond the scope of this book. See, however, Linda T. Zagzebski, *Virtues of the Mind: An Inquiry into the Nature of Virtue and the Ethical Foundations of Knowledge* (Cambridge: Cambridge University Press, 1996).

51 Cf. Stephen Shute, 'Knowledge and belief in the criminal law', in Stephen Shute and A.P. Simester (eds.), *Criminal Law: Doctrines of the General Part* (Oxford: Oxford University Press, 2002), p. 171, at pp. 183–184.

52 See Philip Pettit and Michael Smith, 'Freedom in belief and desire' (1996) 93 *Journal of Philosophy* 429 at 430. See, further, Ronald Dworkin, *Justice for Hedgehogs* (Cambridge, MA: Belknap, 2011), ch. 2.

53 Carl Elliot, 'Beliefs and responsibility' (1991) 25 *Journal of Value Inquiry* 233 at 240.

54 Tadros, *Criminal Responsibility*, p. 244; Duff, *Answering for Crime*, p. 267.

55 See, similarly, Hieronymi, 'Responsibility for believing', at 359.

56 Martha C. Nussbaum, *Hiding from Humanity: Disgust, Shame and the Law* (Princeton, NJ: Princeton University Press, 2004), p. 25; Tadros, *Criminal Responsibility*, p. 244.

57 Cf. Simester, 'Can negligence be culpable?', p. 105.

58 T.M. Scanlon, *What We Owe to Each Other* (Cambridge, MA: Belknap, 1998), p. 26.

in risk or safety[59] when assessing culpability. This is because the matter of justification reflects clearly the defendant's agency, and her belief-formation efforts, in a way that the truth of a proposition does not. That a belief is true or false does not, immediately, tell us anything useful about a person who holds it or the care she took in cultivating the relevant dispositions towards thought and behaviour.

To see the importance of justification, it is useful to consider the Scottish case of *Jamieson* v. *HM Advocate*[60] (though similar cases exist in other Anglo-American jurisdictions).[61] The accused apparently believed the complainer was consenting to sex and (it can be inferred) that there was no risk of non-consent. He was wrong, but this should not, in itself, make him culpable for rape.[62] The resolution of that question depends on whether Jamieson was *justified* in forming his belief in consent or whether he demonstrated some failure in terms of his seeking and consideration of the evidence, based on his background beliefs and perceptions. However convinced or deluded the accused was in his belief,[63] the question should be whether it was based on adequate grounds to show that he was sufficiently motivated by the interests of the complainer in the management of his beliefs about her consent, and the risk that she might not be consenting.

The question of sufficiency of evidence and investigation is, accordingly, central to justification. Ultimately, the issue is resolved by asking what it means to be a responsible citizen in forming the dispositions consistent with the ascription of beliefs, in the light of extant background beliefs and perceptions.[64] In most contexts, and certainly those with which the criminal law is concerned, it is submitted that there should – at least – be *some* evidential basis for a belief, which would justify holding it.[65] The quality of the evidence required will change with the

59 Simester, 'Can negligence be culpable?', p. 106. The matter of whether the beliefs that led to the formation of the ultimate belief are *themselves* justified is left to the side here. See, however, Jonathan Dancy, *An Introduction to Contemporary Epistemology* (Oxford: Blackwell, 1985), pp. 55–57, 127–130.

60 1994 JC 88.

61 See e.g. *DPP* v. *Morgan* [1976] AC 182 (E&W); *Pappajohn* v. *R* [1980] 2 SCR 120 (Can).

62 See, similarly, Tadros, *Criminal Responsibility*, p. 245.

63 Cf. *Rusk* v. *State*, 43 Md App 476, 406 A 2d 624 (1979, MD), where the defendant's (incorrect) belief in consent was so strong that he asked whether he could see a woman again after having (non-consensual) sex with her. See Pillsbury, 'Crimes of indifference', at 163–165.

64 See, similarly, Simester, 'Can negligence be culpable?'.

65 Tadros, *Criminal Responsibility*, p. 245.

circumstances and the gravity of the consequences of any failure to form a justified belief.[66] For instance, more can be expected of those assessing whether there is consent to sex than those who are investigating whether they might damage a non-valuable piece of property.[67] Connectedly, as the importance of forming a justified belief increases, the inferences that the defendant draws from the available evidence should demonstrate a greater regard for the interests of others.[68]

Jamieson's argument at trial could be understood as follows: the complainer's[69] removing her boots and tights, and apologising for biting him, was sufficient evidence upon which to premise his belief in consent, and no further investigation was required.[70] This evidence might be sufficient in certain contexts (a relationship where such conduct is a normal prelude to consensual sex), but no such circumstances seem to have existed in his case. Indeed, there were outward signs of non-consent: the complainer – a stranger to Jamieson – said repeatedly that she did not want 'that' (i.e. sex) and had screamed at and bitten him.[71] In the light of this conflicting evidence, it is submitted that more could legitimately be expected of Jamieson.

This is not to endorse a wholly 'objective' approach to liability (whatever that is understood to mean) but to mix adequately the 'subjective' with the 'objective' in assessing whether Jamieson merits the personal condemnation attendant upon a conviction for rape. Assuming he had background dispositions consistent with a belief that women do not *always* consent to sex[72] and perceived the complainer's signs of unwillingness, he seems to have had the 'subjective' tools to attempt to 'put two and two together' and form the dispositions consistent with a fresh belief that there was a risk of non-consent *in these circumstances*, and could have been expected to carry out further investigation.[73] That he did not make this effort makes Jamieson's belief in consent unjustified and the conduct that he carried out in the light of it open to potential criticism, including the specialist criticism at issue in a criminal trial. The

66 See Audi, 'The ethics of belief', at 405.
67 Simester, 'Can negligence be culpable?', p. 105.
68 Tadros, *Criminal Responsibility*, p. 248.
69 This is the terminology adopted in Scotland (cf. 'complainant' in other systems).
70 *Jamieson*, at 89. 71 Ibid.
72 As noted above, if Jamieson lacked this background belief, he could not have been culpably negligent in his failure to form a belief in non-consent.
73 If he had formed this belief, the question would be whether Jamieson was *reckless* regarding the risk of non-consent. See above at Chapter 6.

resolution of that matter depends, ultimately, on *why* Jamieson failed to form the relevant belief about the risk of non-consent,[74] and that subject is returned to again below.

Negligence as failure of belief can be categorised, thus far, as the demonstration of an 'intellectually irresponsible attitude' with regard to the formation of beliefs about the risks attendant upon φ-ing.[75] It is present in familiar cases of mistake in defences[76] – for instance in self-defence[77] – and is generally (though not always)[78] captured in a legal requirement of *reasonableness*. Reasonableness calls for justification, which in turn calls for sufficient grounds for holding the dispositions consistent with the ascription of a particular belief, and an adequate display of concern for the interests of others.[79]

The difference between the accused in *Jamieson* and a person faced with an immediate decision over whether to kill an aggressor is that nothing prevented the former from taking time to consider his beliefs more carefully, to exercise the type of indirect control spoken to above.[80] The law can afford to be more forgiving to the self-defender, as the situation forces her to act with less reflection.[81] It would be unreasonable to require defendants to exercise as much control over their beliefs in such circumstances. Ultimately, negligence as failure of belief – and the relevant level of sufficient concern for others – will have to be sensitive to the circumstances in which the defendant acted.

[74] Cf. P.J. Fitzgerald and Glanville Williams, 'Carelessness, indifference and recklessness: two replies' (1962) 25 *Modern Law Review* 49 at 51.

[75] See James A. Montmarquet, 'Culpable ignorance and excuses' (1995) 80 *Philosophical Studies* 41 at 43.

[76] See Stephen Sverdlik, 'Pure negligence' (1993) 30 *American Philosophical Quarterly* 137 at 139–142; Victor Tadros, *The Ends of Harm: The Moral Foundations of Criminal Law* (Oxford: Oxford University Press, 2011), p. 225.

[77] For an overview, see Fiona Leverick, *Killing in Self-Defence* (Oxford: Oxford University Press, 2006), ch. 9.

[78] For instance, English law allows a defendant to rely on self-defence if he honestly (even if unreasonably) believed that force was necessary: *R* v. *Williams* [1978] 3 All ER 411; Criminal Justice and Immigration Act 2008, s. 76(4).

[79] David Archard, 'The *mens rea* of rape: reasonableness and culpable mistakes', in Keith Burgess-Jackson (ed.), *A Most Detestable Crime: New Philosophical Essays on Rape* (Aldershot: Dartmouth Pub., 1999), p. 213, at p. 219; John Gardner, 'The mysterious case of the reasonable person' (2001) 51 *University of Toronto Law Journal* 273 at 273.

[80] E.M. Curley, 'Excusing rape' (1976) 5 *Philosophy and Public Affairs* 325 at 346.

[81] See, similarly, Celia Wells, 'Swatting the subjectivist bug' [1982] *Criminal Law Review* 209 at 214; Jeremy Horder, 'Cognition, emotion and criminal culpability' (1990) 106 *Law Quarterly Review* 469 at 477–478; Simester, 'Can negligence be culpable?', at p. 99.

It is useful to stop the consideration of defendants who have inappropriate beliefs about the risks attendant upon φ-ing here, to consider briefly those who hold *no* beliefs about such risks.

No Beliefs about Risk

To a large extent, the defendant who does not form *any* belief about the risks attendant upon φ-ing is to be assessed in the manner explained in the section above. It is to be asked whether, in the light of her background beliefs and perceptions, the defendant could legitimately be expected to do more in terms of forming appropriate beliefs about the risks attendant upon φ-ing.

One point that it is worth considering here is so-called wilful blindness. On some accounts, the wilfully blind actor is *positively* motivated to avoid the confirmation of her *suspicions*;[82] she will choose to neglect to investigate the risks attendant upon φ-ing where a properly motivated person would, for fear that she will acquire a belief that she would rather not have.[83] Such defendants, it will be argued here, are exhibiting a kind of negligence, if the reason that they fail to carry out further investigations, in spite of their background beliefs and perceptions, demonstrated insufficient concern for others.[84] This element of 'cheating'[85] to avoid beliefs that a defendant would rather not have is not present in cases of recklessness.[86] This explains one way in which wilful blindness can be conceptually distinguished from recklessness.[87]

This point about wilful blindness and recklessness does not answer the question of whether they ought to be treated as equivalents, as some writers

[82] See e.g. *Redgate* v. *Haynes* (1875–1876) LR 1 QBD 89 (E&W); *Ross* v. *Moss* [1965] 2 QB 396 (E&W); *Westminster City Council* v. *Croyalgrange Ltd and Another* [1986] 1 WLR 674 (E&W), at 684.

[83] *The Zamora No 2* [1921] 1 AC 801 (E&W), at 812; Rollin M. Perkins, '"Knowledge" as a *mens rea* requirement' (1977–1978) 29 *Hastings Law Journal* 953 at 962–963; Douglas N. Husak and Craig A. Callender, 'Wilful ignorance, knowledge, and the "equal culpability" thesis: a study of the deeper significance of the principle of legality' [1994] *Wisconsin Law Review* 29 at 54.

[84] Cf. Deborah Hellman, 'Wilfully blind for good reason' (2009) 3 *Criminal Law and Philosophy* 301.

[85] David Lanham, 'Wilful blindness and the criminal law' (1985) 9 *Criminal Law Journal* 261 at 267.

[86] Cf. Alexander and Ferzan with Morse, *Crime and Culpability*, pp. 33–35.

[87] See Robin Charlow, 'Wilful ignorance and criminal culpability' (1991–1992) 70 *Texas Law Review* 1351 at 1429. See, further, Husak and Callender, 'Wilful ignorance', at 42; D. Luban, 'Contrived ignorance' (1998–1999) 87 *Georgia Law Journal* 957 at 969.

have suggested.[88] Such equivalences are, it will be suggested, based on psychologically odd cases where the defendant positively *chooses* to remain without a particular belief. It is submitted that such cases are rare, and – when more realism is applied to the kind of wilful blindness that arises in cases of risk-taking – it becomes clearer how wilful blindness is more similar to negligence. This allows for space to be opened up between recklessness and wilful blindness. As will be explained at the close of this chapter, recklessness reflects more meaningfully the defendant's insufficient concern for the interests of others and should not be equated with negligence (where the reflection of the defendant's culpability is present but less secure).

Consider the famous English case *R* v. *Parker*.[89] The defendant, in a state of extreme anger, smashed the receiver of a public payphone against its cradle. Both parts of the phone were made out of plastic, and broke. Parker was charged with criminal damage, but argued that he had, because of his emotional state, failed to apply his mind at all to the risk that he might break the phone. He thus argued that he was not aware of the relevant risk of damage, and thus was not reckless with regard to it. Clearly wanting to avoid the situation where a state of ignorance brought about by the defendant's excited emotional state could exculpate him (and not, due to the relevant statute, having negligence to fall back on as a fault element), the Court of Appeal explained that Parker should be considered as 'reckless' because[90]

> [a] man is reckless in the sense required [by the Criminal Damage Act 1971] when he carried out a deliberate act knowing *or closing his mind to the obvious* fact that there is some risk of damage resulting from that act but nevertheless continuing in the performance of that act.

The idea of closing one's mind to risk, a form of wilful blindness, is mysterious. First, it might mean (as in the view discussed above) that the defendant *deliberately chose* not to ascertain the risks attendant on smashing down the phone receiver, as he did not want to form the belief that the relevant risk of damage existed.[91] Choices, it will be remembered, are limited by beliefs. On this view, then, Parker *did* believe that there was a

[88] Michael S. Moore and Heidi M. Hurd, 'The culpability of negligence', in Rowan Cruft, Matthew H. Kramer and Mark R. Reiff (eds.), *Crime, Punishment and Responsibility: The Jurisprudence of Antony Duff* (Oxford: Oxford University Press, 2011), p. 311, at p. 319.

[89] [1977] 1 WLR 600 (E&W). See also *R* v. *Booth* [2006] EWHC 192 (Admin) (E&W).

[90] *Parker*, at 604.

[91] See, further, *Roper* v. *Taylor's Central Garages (Exeter) Limited* [1951] 2 TLR 284 (E&W), at 289; *Westminster City Council* v. *Croyalgrange Ltd and Another*, at 684.

risk of damaging the phone but put it out of his mind. This, as many authors noted, would make him reckless on the normal understanding of that term.[92] No *equivalence* with recklessness would be required.

The first view of the Court of Appeal's statement in *Parker* is, nevertheless, peculiar. It seems implausible that, in raising up the phone receiver before smashing it down, Parker *decided* to put a belief out of his contemplation. What is more convincing is the idea that Parker was prevented by his anger from forming that particular belief about the risks associated with his proposed conduct. The core question, on this view of Parker's situation, is whether the defendant could legitimately be expected to have done more, given his background beliefs (about the fragility of the plastic phone, etc.) and his perceptions, to form an appropriate belief about the risks attendant upon his conduct. On this account, *Parker* is not a case of wilful blindness or its equivalence with recklessness. The case is, rather, a good example of negligence.[93]

This chapter has, thus far, sketched an outline of negligence as failure of belief and indicated two situations in which it can be the basis of a finding of culpability: where the defendant formed an incorrect belief about the presence or extent of the risks attendant upon φ-ing and where no belief about the relevant risk was formed at all. In both cases, the defendant has similarly failed to put 'two and two together', when he could legitimately be expected to have at least *tried* to do so, in the light of his background beliefs and his perceptions.

The next section builds on this outline by considering whether *all* such failures to form appropriate beliefs about the risk(s) attendant upon φ-ing can draw a meaningful bridge between defendants and their wrongdoing. It will be suggested that the answer to this question is 'No'.

The Reason for the Failure of Belief

It is implausible that *all* failures to form appropriate beliefs about the risks attendant upon φ-ing could ground culpability. Some such failures

92 See D.J. Galligan, 'Responsibility for recklessness' (1978) 31 *Current Legal Problems* 55 at 68; *Caldwell*, at 358; *R* v. *Crabbe* (1985) 156 CLR 464 (HCA), at [12]; Earl Fruchtman, 'Recklessness and the limits of *mens rea*: beyond orthodox subjectivism' (1986–1987) 29 *Criminal Law Quarterly* 315, 421 (published in two parts) at 328–329; Diane J. Birch, 'The foresight saga: the biggest mistake of all?' [1988] *Criminal Law Review* 4 at 7.

93 See, further, William Wilson, *Criminal Law: Doctrine and Theory*, 5th edn. (Harlow: Pearson, 2014), p. 140; David J. Ibbetson, 'Recklessness restored' (2004) 63 *Cambridge Law Journal* 13 at 15.

will arise from matters that reflect no aspect of the defendant's agency, and thus fail to draw a meaningful connection between her, as an agent, and her unjustified risk-taking (and, if relevant, the materialisation of those risks and the associated harm). For instance, if the defendant fails to form the relevant belief because of her absence of intelligence, this should not ground culpability. The defendant's intelligence does not reflect anything meaningful about her, as an agent, in the same way that her short-sightedness, and her not being taller than she is, would not.[94]

Other reasons for the defendant's failure to form an appropriate belief about the risks attendant upon φ-ing, however, are going to be more clearly reflective of agency. In the most developed such account in the existing literature,[95] Garvey attempts to isolate the reflection of agency by focussing on the defendant's *desires* and their interaction with the formation of beliefs. Garvey argues that failures to form justified beliefs about risk typically result from the defendant's failure to control a desire that then interferes with the actor's belief formation process.[96] On Garvey's account, the defendant is prevented, by such a desire, from putting the pieces together in the way that she, given her perceptions and background dispositions, *could* otherwise have done.[97] It will be contended that Garvey's account points towards an appropriate account of negligence as failure of belief, but needs modification and expansion.

Garvey summarises his argument (which is developed in the context of manslaughter, hence the references to causing death) as follows:[98]

> An actor who creates a risk of causing death but who was unaware of that risk is fairly subject to retributive punishment if he was *nonwillfully ignorant* or *self-deceived* with respect to the existence of the risk, and if such ignorance or self-deception was due to the influence of a desire he should have controlled. The culpability of such an actor does not consist in any choice to do wrong, but rather in the culpable failure to exereise [sic] *doxastic self-control*, i.e. control over desires that influence the formation and awareness of one's beliefs . . . the actor could and should

[94] Cf. Peter Westen, 'Individualizing the reasonable person in criminal law' (2008) 2 *Criminal Law and Philosophy* 137 at 144; Angela M. Smith, 'Control, responsibility and moral assessment' (2008) 138 *Philosophical Studies* 367 at 381.

[95] Cf. the broadly similar, but far less developed, account in Williams, 'The unresolved problem of recklessness'.

[96] Garvey, 'What's wrong with involuntary manslaughter?'.

[97] See, similarly, Sher, *Who Knew?*, p. 21.

[98] Garvey, 'What's wrong with involuntary manslaughter?', at 337–338 (emphasis in original). Cf. Ishtiyaque Haji, 'An epistemic dimension of blameworthiness' (1997) 57 *Journal of Philosophy & Phenomenological Research* 523 at 537.

> have controlled his wayward desire, thereby allowing the relevant belief to form and surface into awareness.

For example, Jamieson's desire to have sex may have led him to give insufficient weight to obvious prompts that the complainer was not consenting, and to fail to form, or become (consciously) aware of, the belief that there was a risk of non-consent.[99]

It is submitted that there are three respects in which Garvey's stated position on negligence would benefit from development. The first development would emphasise the role of *culpability* to a greater extent. The matter of *when* a failure to exercise self-control over desires is culpable is not addressed convincingly. At one stage, Garvey argues that a failure to maintain control over desires is itself the basis of culpability.[100] This does not seem right: consider a person on a diet who fails to prevent her desire to eat cake from stopping her from forming the belief that eating cake would be inconsistent with her losing weight. Such a person is surely not culpable in the sense required for the criminal law (her 'fault' does not even appear to implicate the interests of others), but she has failed to exercise doxastic control in the manner that Garvey describes. She has failed to turn her attention away from her desire and towards features of her situation which would encourage her to abstain.[101]

This difficulty is easy to address. Garvey could point to the need to show that the defendant took an unjustified risk of the death of another person before the question of criminal culpability even arises. He is simply presenting an account of manslaughter, and so the other-regarding nature of doxastic failures is clear.

Even if this point is accepted, it is submitted that it would be a good idea to add at least one further condition to Garvey's account. This is that, to be culpable in the sense required for a criminal conviction, a negligent agent must manifest – through her failure to control her desires – *insufficient concern for the interests of others.*[102] When modified in this manner, Garvey's account switches focus from just the beliefs about risk that a person *has* (and their justification) towards the management of her desires and her attitude towards the interests of others,

[99] See, similarly, Horder, 'Cognition, emotion and criminal culpability', at 476–477.

[100] Garvey, 'What's wrong with involuntary manslaughter?', at 360.

[101] See Jeanette Kennett, *Agency and Responsibility: A Common-Sense Moral Psychology* (Oxford: Oxford University Press, 2001), p. 163.

[102] Garvey might accept this condition – see Garvey, 'What's wrong with involuntary manslaughter?', at 365.

providing a wider basis for establishing the type of connection between the defendant's wrongdoing and her agency that a criminal conviction should require.

Second, the circumstances in which self-control could be expected of a defendant should be expanded beyond Garvey's stated position on negligence. Alexander and Ferzan worry that Garvey's original account of culpable negligence is 'fatally circular'.[103] This is because, if the defendant did not have a mental experience of the proposition that the relevant risk *might* exist at the time of acting, there was no internal, psychological prompt to urge her to engage in control over the management of her desires and the formation of her beliefs.[104] For instance, Jamieson was apparently unaware of the risk of non-consent – he had no doubt that the complainer was consenting – and Alexander and Ferzan worry that, in such circumstances, there was nothing to put him 'on notice' that he needed to control his desires and carry out further investigations into the matter of consent.

Garvey's answer to this point is to admit that a defendant can be fairly expected to exercise doxastic self-control only where 'he suspects that [the risk] exists or is dimly aware of its existence'.[105] In making this move, it is submitted that Garvey largely endorses what Ferzan calls 'opaque' recklessness (a concept critiqued in Chapter 6)[106] – a mentally experienced decision to disregard a nagging, psychological sense of danger or risk (where a moment's conscious reflection would have revealed the defendant's 'preconscious' awareness of the precise danger or risk). In short, Garvey's account becomes very narrow indeed (and susceptible to the criticisms of 'opaque' recklessness made in Chapter 6).[107]

It is submitted that Garvey has given up too much ground in responding to Alexander and Ferzan's critique. Assuming he was not in a state of automatism, Jamieson was presumably aware that he was engaged in

[103] Larry Alexander and Kimberly K. Ferzan with Stephen J. Morse, *Crime and Culpability: A Theory of Criminal Law* (Cambridge: Cambridge University Press, 2009), p. 77.

[104] Ibid.

[105] Stephen P. Garvey, 'Fatally circular? Not!', in Paul H. Robinson, Stephen P. Garvey and Kimberly K. Ferzan (eds.), *Criminal Law Conversations* (Oxford: Oxford University Press, 2009) p. 286, at p. 287.

[106] Section on 'Ferzan's "Opaque" Recklessness'.

[107] See, similarly, Larry Alexander and Kimberly K. Ferzan, 'Reply', in Paul H. Robinson, Stephen P. Garvey and Kimberly K. Ferzan (eds.), *Criminal Law Conversations* (Oxford: Oxford University Press, 2009) p. 291, at pp. 292–293.

sexual intercourse. Consent is a core component in sexual relations.[108] Furthermore, the consequences of non-consensual intercourse are grave; it is an inherently risky activity.[109] It is submitted that *these* features of Jamieson's situation (which it is assumed he was aware of, in the sense of having the relevant beliefs about them) put him sufficiently 'on notice' that he ought to consider the possibility that his desire to have sex might prevent him from forming a justified belief about whether there was a risk of non-consent.[110] Although Jamieson's desire may have dominated his (conscious) mind to the extent that he did not have a nagging sense of riskiness,[111] the point of negligence as failure of belief is that he could still be legitimately expected to have done more in terms of forming appropriate beliefs about the risks attendant upon his conduct.

The third concern regarding Garvey's account also relates to narrowness. It is not clear why it is *only* the role of desire that is emphasised on Garvey's account. For instance, laziness or a general trait of 'carelessness' might explain the defendant's failure to form adequate beliefs about risk.[112] Such traits are reflective of agency, in a way that makes a potential finding of responsibility and culpability possible, but are not *desires*. Rather than focussing on desires, it should be asked whether *any* feature of the defendant's character that is *reflective of agency* prevented the formation of the relevant belief regarding risk-taking. In short, the argument is that Garvey's account focuses on too few facets of agency. The next section develops a wider, character-based account of when negligence as failure of belief is made out.

A Wider View: Reflecting Character

The question of when features of a person – her dispositions towards thought and behaviour – are truly representative of *her*, as an agent, is a difficult one. As seen in the previous chapter, one answer to this quandary looks to choice and asks whether the agent chose to, for example, be lazy or be the kind of person who is not disposed to see the signs of

[108] R.A. Duff, *Intention, Agency and Criminal Liability: Philosophy of Action and the Criminal Law* (Oxford: Basil Blackwell, 1990), pp. 168–169; Scanlon, *What We Owe to Each Other*, p. 175.

[109] Cf. Tadros, *Criminal Responsibility*, p. 257.

[110] See, further, Sverdlik, 'Pure negligence', at 142; Alfred R. Mele, *Autonomous Agents: From Self-Control to Autonomy* (Oxford: Oxford University Press, 2001), p. 98.

[111] Cf. Garvey, 'Involuntary manslaughter', at 369 (n. 117).

[112] Kennett, *Agency and Responsibility*, p. 255.

non-consent in a sexual partner. Such accounts were rejected in the previous chapter,[113] on the basis that this is not how persons tend to develop their dispositions. Although a person *can* make choices about how she is disposed to act and react in certain circumstances, character development is more often unreflective, and the connection between any such choices and results is far looser than writers such as Hampton might be read to suggest.[114] It seems more plausible that the grounds for responsibility for character are far wider than a choice-based account would capture.

Rather than asking whether a particular disposition was positively *chosen*, it is submitted that it would be preferable to ask whether the feature of the defendant's motivational set-up that prevented her from forming the relevant belief about risk *is* in fact reflective of her as an agent, that it is not 'alien' to her, in the sense that it springs from somewhere outside the framework of dispositions towards thought and behaviour that makes *her* – the person who will be punished – who she is.[115]

More will be said about this conception of the self in due course, but it is sensible to address the question of why the law should inquire into whether the reason that the defendant failed to notice a risk is properly reflective of *her*, as an agent. Why not just ask, as Simester does, whether a character trait (as opposed to something impervious to agency, such as blindness or intelligence) accounted for the failure to form the relevant belief?[116]

There is a sense in which 'alienation' is indeed difficult to fathom. Absent external intervention (such as hypnosis), 'alien' desires must spring from *somewhere* within the agent;[117] they may surely properly be described as part of her 'character' in a *general* sense.[118] The point remains, however, that there is a tension between the relevant feature of

[113] Chapter 7, section on 'Tracing Character'.

[114] See the discussion of Hampton's theory, above at ibid.

[115] This is how 'out of character' acts should be understood in this book. See also Fields, 'Moral beliefs and blameworthiness', at 411.

[116] A.P. Simester, 'A disintegrated theory of culpability', in Dennis J. Baker and Jeremy Horder (eds.), *The Sanctity of Life and the Criminal Law: The Legacy of Glanville Williams* (Cambridge: Cambridge University Press, 2013) p. 178, at pp. 193–194.

[117] Gary Watson, 'Reasons and Responsibility' (2001) 111 *Ethics* 374 at 389. Perhaps from her subconscious: see Andrew E. Taslitz, 'Forgetting Freud: the courts' fear of the subconscious in date rape (and other) cases' (2006–2007) 16 *Boston University Public Interest Law Journal* 145 at 179.

[118] Sher, *Who Knew?*, p. 135.

the person and who she *really* is.[119] This point leads to an alternative, more compelling, strategy, which is to deny that 'alien' features of a person's dispositional set-up are part of her *true* character and – given the personal nature of criminal condemnation – to affirm that it is a person's true character that ought to matter when assessing her culpability in relation to φ-ing.[120]

It is submitted that there are two reasons why the criminal law ought to inquire further into whether the character trait that accounts for the defendant's inadvertence is 'alien' to her. First, in order to ensure that the fault that connects the defendant to her wrongdoing does so in a sufficiently personal way to merit the condemnation of conviction, it is essential to ensure that the feature of her character that made her fail to form a belief that there is a risk attendant upon φ-ing is 'truly representative' of her character,[121] that it belongs to her 'in the deepest sense'.[122] It is important to remember, in this regard, that the criminal law does not punish isolated character traits.[123] Rather, it is *the defendant* who is punished. Aspersions will be cast on *her wider character* and *she* will bear the criminal record.[124] To ensure that such messages are not shallow,[125] it should be asked whether the relevant character trait was reflective of the defendant's wider personality in this manner.

There is a second possible reason to consider the coherence of the feature of the defendant's identity that prevented the formation of an appropriate belief about the risks attendant upon φ-ing: control.[126]

119 This might lead to a distinction between being blameworthy (which might not take alienation into account) and *being blamed* (which would). See e.g. Arpaly, *Unprincipled Virtue*, p. 144.

120 Cf. Harry G. Frankfurt, *The Importance of What We Care About: Philosophical Essays* (Cambridge: Cambridge University Press, 1988), ch. 2. Frankfurt's account of identification is discussed briefly above at Chapter 6, section on 'The Significance of Choice'.

121 Joel Feinberg, *Doing and Deserving: Essays in the Theory of Responsibility* (Princeton, NJ: Princeton University Press, 1970), p. 36. Cf. Ekow N. Yankah, 'Good guys and bad guys: punishing character, equality and the irrelevance of moral character to criminal punishment' (2003–2004) 25 *Cardozo Law Review* 1019 at 1060.

122 Sophia R. Moreau, 'Reasons and character' (2005) 115 *Ethics* 272 at 275.

123 Kimberly K. Ferzan, 'Act, agency and indifference: the foundations of *Criminal Responsibility*' (2007) 10 *New Criminal Law Review* 441 at 444.

124 Gardner, 'On the general part of the criminal law', at p. 236. See, further, Lloyd Fields, 'Moral beliefs and blameworthiness' (1994) 69 *Philosophy* 397 at 408; Haji, 'An epistemic dimension of blameworthiness', at 529.

125 Arenella, 'Character, choice and moral agency', p. 83.

126 For scepticism on this point, see Stephen J. Morse, 'Culpability and control' (1994) 142 *University of Pennsylvania Law Review* 1587 at 1629.

Consider the phenomenon of 'alien' desires – i.e. desires to act in a certain way that are inconsistent with a defendant's general motivational set-up.[127] It has been suggested that 'alien' desires are not susceptible to control in the way that – at least in *enkratic* (self-controlled) actors – other desires are, because they are not woven into the agent's more general motivational system.[128] The thought is that it would be illegitimate to draw an inference regarding the defendant's general character from her failure to control an 'alien' desire. The necessary link between the defendant and the instance of wrongdoing that culpability is meant to draw would not be made out.

A similar problem could be raised in relation to other 'alien' features of a person's identity. If a disposition possessed by a person is inconsistent with the rest of her character, she might struggle to control it in a way that meaningfully casts doubt on blame for a failure to do so.

This point about control is, to a degree, mysterious (it is seldom explained in great detail why control is not possible), and it is submitted that the concern should instead be whether the defendant has meaningfully taken *responsibility* for that feature of character. If such responsibility has been taken, it is irrelevant whether or not it could have been controlled at the time where the defendant failed to form a belief that the relevant risk(s) existed.[129]

It is submitted that the feature of the defendant's character that prevents the formation of a belief that there is a risk attendant upon φ-ing should give rise to a finding of culpability only if it has been *accepted* as being representative of, and in line with, the defendant's wider motivational framework.[130] Such accepted character traits reflect the defendant's agency in the appropriate manner to secure a finding of criminal responsibility and culpability for her failure to form the relevant belief about risk. If, however, a disposition possessed by the defendant is inconsistent with her wider identity and is rejected by her, then it will be contended that it cannot be the genesis of culpability.

[127] See Frankfurt, *The Importance of What We Care About*, pp. 20–22; Laura W. Ekstrom, 'Alienation, autonomy and the self' (2005) 29 *Midwest Studies in Philosophy* 45.

[128] George Sher, *Desert* (Princeton, NJ: Princeton University Press, 1987), pp. 172–173. Cf. Raz, *Engaging Reason*, p. 20.

[129] Cf. the discussion of taking ownership in John M. Fischer and Mark Ravizza, *Responsibility and Control: A Theory of Moral Responsibility* (Cambridge: Cambridge University Press, 1998), ch. 7.

[130] See, similarly, Arenella, 'Character, choice and moral agency', p. 76. Cf. the idea of 'preferences', explained in Ekstrom, 'Alienation, autonomy and the self'.

It is important to clarify that what is described here as an 'alien' feature is one that is *radically* outside the defendant's normal personhood.[131] This point should not be misunderstood, so that any of a person's character traits with which she is dissatisfied might be disowned by her. 'Alien' features of a person's character are, it is submitted, best viewed as being initially outside the framework of true character, of representations of who the defendant really is. When a person is presented with an 'alien' feature of herself, however, it seems appropriate that she engage in self-reflection about how she is motivated towards it.[132] If the agent recognises the desire as inconsistent with her values – those interests she views as important to promote – then she might try and remove the desire (or prevent it from habitually occurring to her),[133] to show her commitment to those values.[134] She might fail no matter how hard she tries, but such a failure is not acceptance. It is submission, and this should not be enough to render the failure to form a justified belief concerning risk to be an adequate bridge between the defendant, as an agent, and her wrongdoing. Such submission would be shown where apparently sincere steps to combat a feature of the defendant's character have been taken.

Acceptance, nevertheless, may take a number of forms. For example, the agent might realise that a desire is inconsistent with her values, and yet not attempt to remove it.[135] This is surely acceptance through

[131] Cf. Simester, 'A disintegrated theory of culpability', at p. 199. Simester contends that Patty Hearst was responsible for her actions when she became – at the hands of her captors – her alter ego 'Tania', who participated in armed robberies. Simester is correct that *after some time being 'Tania'*, Hearst could be held criminally responsible for her actions: see, further, Scanlon, *What We Owe to Each Other*, p. 284. It is submitted, however, that such a radical character change (from heiress to armed robber) at least temporarily destabilised the connection between Hearst's body's actions, and *her*, as an agent, raising problems in relation to blaming her *for those initial actions*. Cf. Stephen J. Morse, 'Rationality and responsibility' (2000) 74 *Southern California Law Review* 251 at 257.

[132] See, similarly, Gary Watson, 'Free agency', in Gary Watson (ed.), *Free Will*, 2nd edn. (Oxford: Oxford University Press, 2003), p. 337.

[133] Joel J. Kupperman, *Character* (Oxford: Oxford University Press, 1991), p. 53.

[134] For further discussion, see Richard B. Brandt, 'Traits of character: a conceptual analysis' (1970) 7 *American Philosophical Quarterly* 23 at 27; Fields, 'Moral beliefs and blameworthiness', at 413–414; Nomy Arpaly and Timothy Schroeder, 'Praise, blame and the whole self' (1999) 93 *Philosophical Studies* 161 at 184; Harry G. Frankfurt, *The Reasons of Love* (Princeton, NJ: Princeton University Press, 2004), p. 19. Cf. Aristotle, *Nicomachean Ethics*, trans. Roger Crisp (Cambridge: Cambridge University Press, 2000), III.5.1114a.

[135] Kupperman, *Character*, p. 50; Jonathan Jacobs, *Choosing Character: Responsibility for Virtue and Vice* (Ithaca, NY: Cornell University Press, 2001), p. 32; Tadros, *Criminal Responsibility*, p. 37.

acquiescence.[136] Alternatively, the agent might realise that she is simply deceiving herself and that her *true* character is revealed by the 'alien' trait. This is surely a comprehensive form of acceptance, which might lead the agent to change *other* aspects of her character to accommodate the previously 'alien' feature.

The method of acceptance does not matter, and in many cases it will be subtle. The issue of concern is whether the feature of the defendant that prevented the formation of a belief about risk (the reason why, for instance, further investigations were not carried out) *has* been accepted into the agent's wider character prior to the act of risk-taking.[137] In such circumstances, it is submitted that the offending feature of the person's character will be sufficiently her responsibility to be the proper basis for a finding of culpability for her failure to form adequate beliefs about the risks associated with φ-ing.[138] To fail to form such beliefs because of an accepted character trait, where this failure indicates an insufficient regard for the interests of others, is to demonstrate negligence as failure of belief.[139]

With these points made about the role of character in negligence, the account of negligence as failure of belief now has far more flesh on its bones. It is useful to consider some objections to the argument presented thus far, in order to clarify certain aspects of negligence as failure of belief. Some examples of the application of negligence as failure of belief will then be presented, in the hope of clarifying matters further.

Objections and Clarifications

Thus far, the concentration has been on factors internal to the defendant: her beliefs, her desires, her character traits, etc. It is necessary to now consider the physical element of negligence as failure of belief.

[136] Cf. Fischer and Ravizza, *Freedom and Responsibility*, p. 235 (n. 29).

[137] See, similarly, Arpaly and Schroeder, 'Praise, blame and the whole self', at 173.

[138] Note that if a desire is not accepted, then the beliefs that spring from it will also not be accepted. There is thus cause for holding that the actor is not responsible for them. See Elliot, 'Beliefs and responsibility'. Cf. Raz, *Engaging Reason*, p. 16.

[139] Cf. Holly M. Smith, 'Non-tracing cases of culpable ignorance' (2011) 5 *Criminal Law and Philosophy* 115 at 143, who argues that negligence must be traceable to 'a full enough set of her evaluative attitudes at the time that they adequately represent her moral personality'. This is similar to the view in Sher, *Who Knew?*, but – it is submitted – is too vague a standard to employ.

'Significance in Action'

The first matter of concern is what is referred to by some writers as the 'significance in action' problem.[140] Those who raise this difficulty suggest that, in theories such as Garvey's, there is a gap between the defendant's act of wrongdoing (the taking of an unjustified risk in offences of endangerment, or its materialisation in complete offences) and her culpability (on Garvey's account, her failure to exercise doxastic self-control and form a belief that the relevant risk existed). This apparently makes it illegitimate to hold an actor responsible and liable for the *actions* she performs in light of her beliefs (and their consequences).[141]

The significance in action problem is also associated with accounts of culpable carelessness that deal with attitudes. For instance, as explained in the previous chapter, Simons concentrates on the attitude of 'indifference',[142] as demonstrated through counterfactual questions about what the defendant would have done had she been aware of a particular risk.[143] As Alexander, Ferzan and Morse explain,[144] an attitude of indifference plays no part in a defendant's practical reasoning, and so is disconnected from action. Indifference is not a reason for acting, they argue; it is a mood contemporaneous with action. It can thus only explain *behaviour*, and not why that behaviour was culpable.[145] Allegedly, character-based approaches to negligence (such as that outlined above) suffer from the same 'significance in action' problem.[146]

At the most basic level, as Dempsey points out, there is nevertheless a necessary connection between actions and (on the view defended in this chapter, *accepted*) character traits: 'An actor is not properly criminalised for being a jerk: but he might properly be subject

[140] See Kenneth W. Simons, 'Culpability and retributive theory: the problem of criminal negligence' (1994) 5 *Journal of Contemporary Legal Issues* 365 at 391–393; Kenneth W. Simons, 'Does punishment for "culpable indifference" simply punish for "bad character"? Examining the requisite connection between *mens rea* and *actus reus*' (2002–2003) 6 *Buffalo Criminal Law Review* 219; Alexander and Ferzan with Morse, *Crime and Culpability*, pp. 72–73.

[141] See Alexander and Ferzan with Morse, *Crime and Culpability*, pp. 72–73; Simester, 'Can negligence be culpable?', p. 88.

[142] Or, rather, 'whether the actor cared much less than he should about bringing about a harmful result': Simons, 'Culpability and retributive theory', at 390.

[143] See above at Chapter 7, section on 'Simons's "Culpable Indifference"'.

[144] Alexander and Ferzan with Morse, *Crime and Culpability*, p. 72.

[145] See Michael S. Moore, 'Responsibility and the unconscious' (1980) 53 *Southern California Law Review* 1563 at 1631.

[146] Alexander and Ferzan with Morse, *Crime and Culpability*, pp. 74–75.

to criminal liability because, *in virtue of being such a jerk*, he ended up killing someone'.[147] The same connection may be drawn between an actor who is negligent in the formation of her beliefs and the wrongful actions which she performs as a result. Jamieson would not properly be blamed for the unjustified belief in consent accompanying his action. He is, instead, blamed for the fact that – *as a result* of his failure to form adequate beliefs about the risks of non-consent due, presumably, to his strong desire to have sex (which, it is assumed, was not 'alien' to his general motivational set-up) – he had non-consensual sex with another person.[148] On this account, there is no problem connecting Jamieson's culpability with the act of wrongdoing. The connection between the two is more than simply explanatory. It is – if anything – causal.

Drawing this connection between character and action endorses properly the expectations that bore upon Jamieson with regard to his belief formation and emphasises his culpable failure to meet them (which resulted in an inadvertent act of grave wrongdoing).

If this point is accepted, a further objection presents itself. It was noted above that even 'alien' desires can ground findings of responsibility if the relatively low bar of acceptance is overcome. This means, Ferzan suggests, that punishing failures to form beliefs attendant upon wrongdoing is simply punishing for omitting to resist aspects of one's character that are inconsistent with the agent's wider character.[149] This omission is again apparently divorced from action.

This restatement of the 'significance in action' objection is not compelling. Arguably, it misses the point, which concerns what could legitimately be expected of the defendant in terms of the formation of beliefs about risk. The contention is that only features of the defendant's personality which have been accepted – in some sense – by the defendant are acceptable bases for judgments of responsibility and fault. Agents are faulted not simply for failing to remove a trait, but rather for, once that trait has been accepted, failing as a result to form the relevant belief about risk and – as a result – inadvertently engaging in wrongdoing. Ferzan's objection conflates these two issues.

147 Michelle M. Dempsey, 'The object of criminal responsibility', in Paul H. Robinson, Stephen P. Garvey and Kimberly K. Ferzan (eds.), *Criminal Law Conversations* (Oxford: Oxford University Press, 2009) p. 283, at p. 284. See, similarly, Kupperman, *Character*, p. 60.

148 See, similarly, Sher, *Who Knew?*, p. 87.

149 Ferzan, 'Act, agency and indifference', at 452.

The 'significance in action' problem can now be left behind. A separate concern arises from confusion over the significance *of* action in character formation.

Significance of Action

Actions might be seen as *evidence* of existing character traits.[150] On this view, a character trait can exist even if it has never been manifest in action[151] – a person is *first* a callous character (she has the relevant dispositions towards callous thoughts and behaviour) and then, when given the opportunity, performs callous acts (manifests those dispositions).

The difficulty, it might be suggested, is that it is not clear from *one* callous action that a person has a callous character. Acts might give rise to ambiguous estimations of character, making them of dubious evidential worth. As a result, it might be argued, talk of character and its interaction with belief should be abandoned, and *chosen* wrongdoing concentrated upon when considering isolated acts of wrongdoing.[152]

This conclusion is too rash. To begin with, actions provide more than just evidence of an existing character trait: they are partially *constitutive* of character.[153] Duff gives the example of a person performing a dishonest act.[154] Before the act is performed, the defendant has dispositions to act in a certain way but is not *yet* a dishonest person. It is only through performing a dishonest action that, as well as *evidencing* a trait, the actor *confirms* that trait as part of her character. In short, a person cannot be dishonest without acting dishonestly.[155]

Michael Moore thinks this claim is both 'false' and 'irrelevant'.[156] On the falseness front, Moore argues that it is difficult to see how anybody, on Duff's account, can demonstrate a character trait for the first time. But surely a person can carry out such a demonstration, on the basis that her

150 Glanville Williams, 'A reply to Mr Duff' (1982) 41 *Cambridge Law Journal* 286 at 288.

151 Holly Smith, 'Culpable ignorance' (1983) 92 *Philosophical Review* 543 at 555; Pettit, *The Common Mind*, p. 30.

152 Yankah, 'Good guys and bad guys', at 1052.

153 Sometimes the distinction between the two views contrasted here is far from clear: see Joseph Raz, *From Normativity to Responsibility* (Oxford: Oxford University Press, 2011), p. 239.

154 R.A. Duff, *Criminal Attempts* (Oxford: Oxford University Press, 1996), p. 188.

155 The reverse is not true: to steal is not to be a dishonest person, as this action might not stem from a dishonest character trait.

156 See Moore, *Placing Blame*, pp. 586–588.

action *reveals* the underlying trait. That inference from action to disposition and character might well sometimes be questionable, epistemically,[157] but it is not utterly implausible. Moore's argument is strongest in relation to the view that character must be demonstrated by a string of consistent actions. This is not assumed here (although the inferences to be drawn from conduct to character will be stronger in cases where the defendant has acted in a similar fashion on multiple occasions).

Moore's second argument is that Duff's view is irrelevant:[158]

> Suppose [the defendant] has committed a rape and a murder in the past, so that now his aggressive, hostile, uncaring character has been manifested. Suppose also that [he] has been punished for such past wrongs, which punishment in no way diminished [his] dispositions to do more rapes and murders in the future. Now: is not the character theorist committed to punishment being deserved by [the defendant] for his bad character, despite that character not yet having resulted in more acts of violence?

Moore hits upon a real worry, but only *if* proportionate punishment is meted out *for* simply having a particular character trait, rather than for *acting upon it*.[159] If punishment is restricted to those instances where, through her wronging of another citizen, the defendant has made her character 'public' – i.e. the concern of the polity – then this concern need not arise.[160] It would be illiberal to require the defendant to change in the sense of losing the relevant character trait. Thus the state's demand, through conviction and punishment, should be to communicate that *acting* on the relevant trait again in the future will incur hard treatment.[161] (Incidentally, this response goes to answering more general critiques of character theories of culpability that are premised on concerns about the defendant's privacy.)

157 Matt King, 'The problem with negligence' (2009) 35 *Social Theory and Practice* 577 at 584; Smith, 'Non-tracing cases of culpable ignorance', at 119–120.

158 Moore, *Placing Blame*, p. 587.

159 Cf. Douglas Husak's view that a crime of having a particular trait could be created: 'Preventive detention as punishment? Some potential obstacles', in Andrew Ashworth, Lucia Zedner and Patrick Tomlin (eds.), *Prevention and the Limits of the Criminal Law* (Oxford: Oxford University Press, 2013), p. 178. See Findlay Stark, 'Review of Ashworth, Zedner and Tomlin (eds.), *Prevention and the Limits of the Criminal Law*' (2016) 10 *Criminal Law and Philosophy* 389 at 391–392.

160 See the hints of a similar argument in Tadros, *The Ends of Harm*, pp. 97–98, and Duff, *Answering for Crime*, p. 116.

161 R.A. Duff, *Punishment, Communication and Community* (Oxford: Oxford University Press, 2001), pp. 121–125

It is submitted that Moore's challenges to Duff's account fail. Actions are not simply evidence of character traits but play an important part in confirming that the defendant is insufficiently motivated by the interests of others in the management of her character and behaviour.[162] Acts can secure culpability, strengthening the connection between the defendant's wider personality and her wrongdoing.[163] Although they can give rise to dubious estimations of the defendant's motivational structure, it is submitted that epistemic uncertainty around the inferences drawn from action is not fatal to character theories of culpable carelessness. Furthermore, if those objections were fatal, then 'objective' means of proving 'subjective' mental states also seem problematic.[164]

Two prominent objections concerning the role of character in action have thus been dispensed with. The next criticism to be considered at this stage concerns the role of 'objectivity' in negligence as failure of belief.

The Role of 'Objectivity'

In the previous chapter, it was contended that asking whether the defendant's conduct fell short of the reasonable person's conduct is insufficient to ground criminal blame.[165] Such accounts of negligence lack the personal linkage between defendant and wrongdoing that ought to be required for conviction. From this, it might be taken that 'objective' standards are anathema to the context of culpable carelessness.

This is not, however, the case. 'Objective' standards will have a role to play in assessing culpability as well as justification under the theory of negligence as failure of belief presented here. The court will have to establish whether the defendant demonstrated, in her failure to form the relevant belief(s) about risk(s), *insufficient* concern for the interests of others. This assumes a standard of sufficiency of motivation, which will presumably be set by 'objective', impersonal standards, for largely the same reasons – discussed briefly in Chapter 1 – that justification must be

162 Cf. Michael S. Moore and Heidi M. Hurd, 'Punishing the awkward, the stupid, the weak and the selfish: the culpability of negligence' (2011) 5 *Criminal Law and Philosophy* 147 at 176.

163 Cf. Duff, *Criminal Attempts*, p. 191.

164 Susan Bandes, 'Is it immoral to punish the heedless and clueless? A comment on Alexander, Ferzan and Morse: *Crime and Culpability*' (2010) 29 *Law and Philosophy* 433 at 447.

165 At Chapter 7, section on 'Conduct: Hart's Insight'.

'objectively' assessed.[166] Recall that allowing the defendant to set the standard of justification would be to withhold blame in cases that merit it. The same would be true of allowing the defendant to set the level of sufficient concern for the interests of others. That standard must be set 'objectively'. It might, therefore, be objected that the theory of negligence as failure of belief presented here is not in fact as 'personalised' as it claims to be.

Although this point is sometimes missed by theorists,[167] relying on concepts such as insufficient concern or 'indifference' veils the 'objective' elements of culpable carelessness but cannot eradicate them. Even if *choice* is the mark of culpability, writers such as Alexander, Ferzan and Morse admit of culpability only where insufficient concern was demonstrated, necessitating an 'objective' estimation of sufficient concern for others.[168] A measure of 'objectivity' is inescapable, even if negligence is denied as a basis for criminal fault.[169]

This is not a cause for concern, however. The 'objective' aspects of negligence as failure of belief are not unduly troubling. Absent a strong attachment to 'subjectivity' – which would require independent justification of the sort that the Exclusive Thesis needs[170] – the presence of some 'objectivity' is not fatal to a defensible theory of culpable carelessness. 'Objectivity' comes in degrees, and the argument here is that negligence as failure of belief is 'subjective' *enough* to suffice for criminal conviction, in a way that a conduct-based view of negligence is not. Where there is disagreement over the proper social expectations concerning risk-taking and belief formation, important moral and political questions are, of course, raised.[171] But it is not the aim of this book to remove them from the attribution of criminal responsibility and liability. If anything, 'objective'

166 See Chapter 1, section on 'Justifying Risk-taking'. Cf. Simester's person of ideal character: 'A disintegrated theory of culpability', p. 202.

167 This is perhaps a pitfall of the decision to move from a standard of reasonableness to one of 'practical indifference' (a concept discussed in Chapter 7) in Mayo Moran, *Rethinking the Reasonable Person: An Egalitarian Reconstruction of the Objective Standard* (Oxford: Oxford University Press, 2003), ch. 8.

168 See Alexander and Ferzan with Morse, *Crime and Culpability*, ch. 2.

169 George P. Fletcher, *Basic Concepts of Criminal Law* (Oxford: Oxford University Press, 1998), p. 119. This might lead to a lack of precision, to which some authors object: Kenneth Simons, 'When is negligent inadvertence culpable?' (2011) 5 *Criminal Law and Philosophy* 97 at 113.

170 See above at Chapter 6.

171 Alan W. Norrie, *Crime, Reason and History: A Critical Introduction to Criminal Law*, 3rd edn. (Cambridge: Cambridge University Press), pp. 99–100.

considerations are simply made more transparent by the theory of negligence as failure of belief. This might be a good reason to limit the use of negligence as failure of belief, but that is a point not about *culpability* but about *criminalisation*. This point will be returned to later in this chapter.

For now, it is useful to consider another objection to the account presented above – that 'character' (in the sense explained above) is an illusion.

The Illusion of Character

The account of negligence as failure of belief is reliant on the idea of character. Aside from the concerns about the role of character in the criminal law that have been discussed thus far, a more general worry comes from the insights of psychology. Doris, for instance, argues that character – understood as a set of stable dispositional traits concerning conduct and value – does not exist and that philosophy (and, presumably, the law) should look to other concepts when discussing responsibility.[172] Doris's argument is premised on empirical evidence, which suggests that *circumstances*, rather than character, determine conduct. Asking whether a person has a certain character, and whether a feature of her dispositional set-up fits in a wider nexus of desires and values, is thus unwise.

This conclusion is too strong. First, it is not required that *every* opportunity to perform an in-character act is taken by agents. Someone with the trait of dishonesty does not have to lie at every given opportunity. This means that, even if a focus on character is maintained, circumstances can play an important explanatory role in demonstrating why a person disposed to perform action *x* performed action *y*.[173] Second, the studies relied upon by Doris surely show only that *few* (as opposed to *no*) people have a virtuous character which will defy authority when told, for instance, to electrocute another person or animal. Some test subjects did, after all, defy authority in Milgram's infamous experiments.[174] It cannot,

[172] John M. Doris, *Lack of Character: Personality and Moral Behaviour* (Cambridge: Cambridge University Press, 2002). See, further, Gilbert Harman, 'Moral philosophy meets social psychology: virtue ethics and the fundamental attribution error' (1999) 99 *Proceedings of the Aristotelian Society* 315. Cf. John Sabini and Maury Silver, 'Lack of character? Situationism critiqued' (2005) 115 *Ethics* 535; Mark Alfano, *Character as Moral Fiction* (Cambridge: Cambridge University Press, 2013).

[173] Kupperman, *Character*, p. 59.

[174] Many people will no doubt be familiar with these experiments, but for the uninitiated, Milgram sought volunteers who were ordered to give increasingly powerful electric

therefore, be objected that the theory of negligence presented in this chapter relies on an illusionary notion. The fact that it is sometimes *difficult* to form beliefs concerning risks does not detract from the fact that failing to try to do so because of an accepted facet of character *sometimes* shows insufficient regard for others.

This conclusion segues into the next foreseen complaint: that the approach defended above aims to punish those who do not display *virtue*, rather than those who display *vice*.

Virtue Ethics and a Liberal Criminal Law

Negligence as failure of belief might be alleged to enforce virtue ethics through the criminal law, which is controversial.[175] This objection, however, is misguided, because culpability is *legally* relevant only where an agent shows insufficient concern for the *legally protected* interests of others in failing to form a belief in risk. There are, therefore, two limitations on negligence as failure of belief. First, *insufficient concern* should be imagined as quite a high standard to meet, given the serious consequences attendant upon a criminal conviction. This will ensure that punishment is for obvious displays of viciousness, rather than mere failures to attain virtue.[176] A useful comparator to the insufficient concern test, as envisaged here, is again glimpsed in the MPC. There, negligence requires 'a gross deviation from the standard of care that a reasonable person would observe in the actor's situation'.[177] The idea of something like a 'gross deviation' from what can reasonably be expected of citizens in the formation of beliefs about risk is what is envisaged here.

Second, the ambit of negligence as failure of belief can be circumscribed by limiting the range of legally protected interests to which

shocks to a subject who was not visible but could be heard. Many volunteers applied 'lethal' shocks. The experiments are meant to demonstrate that, when ordered by someone in a position of apparent authority to act in a particular way, a surprising number of people will bend to authority. See Stanley Milgram, *Obedience to Authority: An Experimental View* (London: Tavistock, 1974); Doris, *Lack of Character*, pp. 39–53.

175 Cf. Kyron Huigens, 'Virtue and inculpation' (1994–1995) 108 *Harvard Law Review* 1423 with R.A. Duff, 'Virtue, vice and criminal liability: do we want an Aristotelian criminal law?' (2002–2003) 6 *Buffalo Criminal Law Review* 147.

176 See, similarly, Tadros, *Criminal Responsibility*, p. 89.

177 American Law Institute, *Model Penal Code and Commentaries*, 3 vols. *(Official Draft and Revised Comments)* (Philadelphia: American Law Institute, 1980), vol. 1, s. 2.02(2)(d).

criminal negligence can attach. More needs to be said about this second response.

Although it *is* found in Anglo-American law, and forms part of the Standard Account, it should be borne in mind that negligence liability is relatively rare, especially in serious offences. This makes a *wide-ranging* argument for negligence liability in the criminal law seem suspicious.[178]

Some of those writers who accept that negligence is a legitimate basis for culpability nevertheless doubt that it would be good *policy* to include negligence in the criminal law's arsenal of fault concepts.[179] First, expanding the reach of the criminal law to cover the inadvertent, unjustified taking of risks with a wide range of interests would result – throughout most of the Anglo-American world – in a greater number of trials, leading to higher costs for the criminal justice system.[180] This practical argument means that limiting the ambit of negligence liability to *severe* instances of inadvertent risk-taking should be taken seriously, an idea returned to below.

Second, there might be concern over using negligence liability too liberally, as it relies on the court's estimation of what *sufficient concern* is, which might allow excessive jury/judicial discretion.[181] If this is a real concern, then surely it cuts deeper than negligence liability. As noted earlier in this chapter, recklessness also relies on estimations about the concern that citizens should show to others in considering the risks attendant upon their conduct. If this gives the jury undue discretion, then recklessness liability is also problematic in the criminal context, and nobody (at least as far as I am aware) makes this argument.

Many of the arguments that might be raised against the theory in this chapter are thus weak. Of more concern is a final, more principled point: that punishing negligence too zealously would result in an overly intrusive criminal law, which requires citizens to investigate aspects of their conduct at all times to ensure that there are no attendant, unjustifiable risks about which (because of an accepted facet of their characters) they are failing to form beliefs. This seems to be the logical conclusion of

[178] Fletcher, *Basic Concepts of Criminal Law*, p. 117. Cf. Jeremy Horder, 'Criminal culpability: the possibility of a general theory' (1993) 12 *Law and Philosophy* 193 at 196.

[179] Bandes, 'Is it immoral to punish the heedless and clueless?', at 434, 447; Andrew D. Leipold, 'A case for criminal negligence' (2010) 29 *Law and Philosophy* 455 at 462.

[180] J.C. Smith, 'Subjective or objective? Ups and downs of the test of criminal liability in England' (1981–1982) 27 *Villanova Law Review* 1179 at 1204; Glanville Williams, 'Intention and recklessness again' (1982) 2 *Legal Studies* 189 at 189–190; Glanville Williams, *Textbook of Criminal Law*, 2nd edn. (London: Stevens, 1983), p. 97.

[181] Simons, 'Culpability and retributive theory', at 377.

Simon Gardner's view that – as a 'concomitant of their partaking in the life of the planet' – citizens should investigate all possible dangers attendant upon their activities.[182]

There is no doubt a sense in which 'people ought to believe the fairly obvious consequences of what they believe'[183] and carry out investigations relevant to matters on which they are not sure. Gardner's proposal is, however, fraught with difficulties.[184] Primarily, it is incompatible with any meaningful conception of individual autonomy,[185] of citizens leading their own lives.[186] In fact, it would surely stymie (to quite a large extent) personal development. How many citizens would have time for hobbies, leisure activities and other aspects of a 'good life' if their lives were spent incessantly testing their beliefs about the riskiness of their conduct?[187] Careful thought should be given to keeping the criminal law's interference with citizens' life plans to an absolute minimum, consistent with adequate respect for the interests of others.[188] There is also a sense in which fair warning – a crucial aspect of the Rule of Law – requires a clear indication of *which* risks must be looked out for.[189]

Furthermore, there are instances where investigating a risk will be impractical. Consider Tadros's example of a substance which might be poison, but the only way to be sure is to conduct 'an expensive ten-year study'.[190] Surely a citizen is not duty-bound (in virtue of her citizenship

[182] Simon Gardner, 'Recklessness refined' (1993) 109 *Law Quarterly Review* 21 at 27. See, similarly, Stephen Shute, 'Second Law Commission consultation paper on consent: (1) something old, something new, something borrowed: three aspects of the project' [1996] *Criminal Law Review* 684 at 686–688; Richard J. Hall and Charles R. Johnson, 'The epistemic duty to seek more evidence' (1998) 35 *American Philosophical Quarterly* 129; Kumaralingam Amirthalingam, '*Caldwell* recklessness is dead, long live *mens rea*'s fecklessness' (2004) 67 *Modern Law Review* 491 at 500.

[183] Frank Jackson, 'Non-cognitivism, normativity, belief' (1999) 12 *Ratio* 420 at 421. See, further, Richard Feldman, 'The ethics of belief' (2000) 60 *Philosophy and Phenomenological Research* 667 at 676–689.

[184] See Tadros, *Criminal Responsibility*, pp. 246–247.

[185] Cf. Pillsbury, 'Crimes of indifference', at 127.

[186] This point has been considered in the context of omissions liability. See A.P. Simester, 'Why omissions are special' (1995) 1 *Legal Theory* 311 at 333–335.

[187] Toni Pickard, 'Culpable mistakes and rape: relating *mens rea* to the crime' (1980) 30 *University of Toronto Law Journal* 75 at 88; Glanville Williams, 'Recklessness redefined' (1981) 40 *Cambridge Law Journal* 252 at 272; Zagzebski, *Virtues of the Mind*, p. 154; Christopher Hookway, 'Epistemic norms and theoretical deliberation' (1999) 12 *Ratio* 380 at 386; Tadros, *Criminal Responsibility*, p. 248.

[188] Cf. Alexander and Ferzan with Morse, *Crime and Culpability*, p. 84.

[189] See, similarly, Ashworth, *Positive Obligations*, pp. 66–68.

[190] Tadros, *Criminal Responsibility*, p. 247.

or participation 'in the life of the planet') to carry out this study, assuming she had the tools available to do so.

Connectedly, it is possible that being overcautious when carrying out some activities might increase their riskiness.[191] Driving at 10 miles per hour might be a display of commendable caution on a blind bend,[192] but adopting the same strategy on a motorway – for fear of preventing the formation of justified beliefs about risk – is likely only to *increase* the risk of harm to others.

These objections are all good ones, but the most critical reason for not adopting a duty to investigate all potentially unjustifiable risks at all times is that it would result in many people being convicted and punished.[193] It would be difficult for citizens – however well meaning – to avoid being culpably negligent. This would dilute substantially the message of the criminal sanction and cause undue, widespread hardship through punishment.[194]

For all of these reasons,[195] negligence as failure of belief should be used sparingly in the criminal law. All kinds of behaviour demonstrate insufficient concern for the interests of others but are not criminal (consider barging in front of others in a queue).[196] The only limit on outright legal moralism (understood as the prosecution and punishment

191 See, similarly, Hookway, 'Epistemic norms and theoretical deliberation', at 385.

192 Cf. H.A. Prichard, *Moral Writings*, ed. Jim MacAdam (Oxford: Clarendon, 2002), p. 93.

193 Alexander and Ferzan with Morse, *Crime and Culpability*, p. 71.

194 Alan W. Mewett, 'The shifting basis of criminal law' (1963) 9 *McGill Law Journal* 124 at 135; Douglas N. Husak, *Overcriminalization: The Limits of the Criminal Law* (Oxford: Oxford University Press, 2008), p. 12.

195 Tadros further argues that autonomous agents have the *right* not to know about some risks (Tadros, *Criminal Responsibility*, p. 247). He is, however, let down by his example: somebody who has the results of an HIV test in an envelope which he does not open. This person might be exercising autonomy at this stage, but surely if he continues to engage in (unprotected) intercourse with others, it is legitimate to expect him to be appraised of his HIV status if he has gone to the extent of having a test. There is a clash of autonomy here, and it seems to over-privilege one party to hold – on the grounds of *his* individual autonomy – that he should not investigate his HIV status when it is easy for him to do so and the consequences for his sexual partners (and *their* autonomy) might be severe. Such ignorance might demonstrate insufficient concern for the interests of others.

196 This, it is submitted, accounts for Tadros's unwillingness to define clearly the 'moral vices' (vices which demonstrate insufficient concern for others). See Tadros, *Criminal Responsibility*, pp. 86–89, 252–254. For this reason, the book prefers to rely simply on the notion of insufficient concern itself. This standard has rarely been developed in criminal law theory, but for a sketch of its possible meanings, see Kenneth W. Simons, 'Retributivism refined – or run amok?' (2010) 77 *University of Chicago Law Review* 551 at 556–558.

of all culpable actors)[197] is to require that the defendant demonstrated a *serious* lack of concern for the interests of others, and to classify the specific interests which the polity declares[198] it would be criminal or potentially criminal to put at inadvertent, unjustified risk.[199] The key to limiting negligence as failure of belief is to consider the interests being (inadvertently) put at risk.[200] For instance, citizens could be put under a legal duty to do enough to form (on the basis of their background beliefs and perceptions) justified beliefs about whether their conduct endangers interests *x*, *y* or *z*, rather than interests in general. They would be answerable only for those specific failures, and even then culpability is not assured. It might be that sufficient concern for others was nevertheless demonstrated, or there might be an 'alien' explanation for the failure to form the relevant belief.

Identifying interests *x*, *y* and *z* will, naturally, be difficult for any polity. In effect, it must decide which interests are important enough that risks to them must be paid attention to by all citizens at all times. *Some* common ground is, surely, imaginable. For instance, life, bodily integrity and sexual autonomy are sacrosanct in Anglo-American criminal law. It would therefore appear sensible to start with these interests, covering negligence with regard to the taking of an unjustified risk with the life,[201] bodily integrity[202] or sexual autonomy of another person. It is instructive that some Anglo-American jurisdictions possess some of these offences already,[203] and some Continental systems contain similarly wide-ranging offences of negligence.[204] Rather than Brudner's

[197] Admittedly, this is a caricature of legal moralism. See, however, R.A. Duff, 'Towards a modest legal moralism' (2014) 8 *Criminal Law and Philosophy* 217; James R. Edwards, 'An instrumental legal moralism' 3 *Oxford Studies in Philosophy of Law*, forthcoming.

[198] There is a debate over whether the criminal law *prohibits* or *declares*. See, further, Duff, *Answering for Crime*, pp. 85–87.

[199] See above at Chapter 1.

[200] See Heidi M. Hurd, 'What in the world is wrong?' (1994) 5 *Journal of Contemporary Legal Issues* 157 at 198–199.

[201] See, similarly, Andrew Ashworth, 'Manslaughter: general or nominate offence?', in C.M.V. Clarkson and Sally Cunningham (eds.), *Criminal Liability for Non-aggressive Death* (Aldershot: Ashgate, 2008), p. 235, at p. 236.

[202] See, similarly, Paul H. Robinson, *Structure and Function in Criminal Law* (Oxford: Oxford University Press, 1997), p. 225.

[203] Cf. Sexual Offences Act 2003 (E&W), s. 1; Sexual Offences (Scotland) Act 2009 (Scot), ss. 1, 16.

[204] See the discussion of French law's approach to negligently caused death and personal injury in J.R. Spencer and Marie-Aimée Brajeux, 'Criminal liability for negligence – a lesson from across the Channel?' (2010) 59 *International and Comparative Law Quarterly* 1.

'mistakes',[205] these offences are examples of the recognition of the fact that negligence in relation to particularly important interests is what the criminal law should be concerned with.

Beyond these cases, the situation seems less clear. Consider property – another important interest in the criminal law. Should it be incumbent on citizens to take adequate steps to ensure that they do not inadvertently put property at unjustifiable risk of damage or destruction? Intuitively, the answer might appear to be 'Yes', but there is reason for deeper inquiry.[206] Are risks to *all* property serious enough to be investigated by citizens when engaging in *any* activity? The answer will surely depend on the property: consider the negligent burning of a copy of a magazine as opposed to the negligent burning of the Mona Lisa.

The question thus becomes, which factors are relevant to discovering whether a piece of property is important enough to be protected from negligently caused damage? A number of factors might be imagined: cost, purpose, uniqueness, sentimental attachment, etc. However easy it is to imagine these criteria, it is clear that they would be impractical. Consider cost: a crime might involve the fault element of inadvertently (and without justification) putting property of a value above £1000 at risk. It might be difficult for a non-expert citizen to assess whether she should stop and engage in further investigation about the riskiness of her actions. She would have to do an investigation into monetary value *prior to* her risk investigation, which sounds even *more* burdensome and potentially illiberal. Furthermore, given the difficulty of predicting accurately the financial worth of an item of property (Is *that* television worth over £1000?), it is possible that the relevant background beliefs would often be absent, or virtually all mistakes would be reasonable (i.e. demonstrate sufficient concern for others), and this would presumably negate any finding of culpability.

For these reasons, it is submitted that *criminal* negligence liability would be inappropriate in cases of property damage or destruction. It is thus to be applauded that the House of Lords removed inadvertent risk-taking from the ambit of English offence of criminal damage in 2003, after a twenty-year experiment[207] and that the criminal laws of

205 Brudner, *Punishment and Freedom*, p. 79.

206 Cf. Leo Katz, 'Harm and justification in negligence' (2003) 4 *Theoretical Inquiries in Law* 397 at 407.

207 *Commissioner of Police for the Metropolis* v. *Caldwell* [1982] AC 341; *R* v. *G and Another* [2003] UKHL 50, [2004] 1 AC 1034.

many other Anglo-American systems do not criminalise the inadvertent taking of risks with property. It is similarly to be regretted that systems such as Scotland's *might* criminalise inadvertent property damage or destruction.[208] If a legal remedy for such damage is to be available, it should be extracted via the civil courts or insurance, not the criminal law.

It is possible, through debates such as these, to limit the impact of negligence as failure of belief on the criminal law.[209] This is, however, a question of criminalisation, rather than of culpability. This demonstrates that issues of culpability and criminalisation cannot be considered in isolation. Not every case that *could* be identified as negligence ought to potentially be the stuff of criminal liability, and the debate sketched immediately above shows the process by which the polity should decide where to draw the line. It is noteworthy, from the perspective of explaining and justifying the Standard Account's conception of culpable carelessness, that it already draws such lines. As already noted, in relation to serious criminal offences (as opposed to regulatory offences), negligence is a rare form of culpability.

The account of negligence as failure of belief has now been given and defended against counter-arguments. The next section considers two examples of negligence as failure of belief, to demonstrate its application.

Two Examples

From the discussion thus far, negligence as failure of belief has three necessary components beyond the taking of a substantial, unjustified risk (i.e. wrongdoing):

(i) Background beliefs relevant to the risk involved in the defendant's planned behaviour.
(ii) Perception of features of the situation relevant to the risk involved in the defendant's planned behaviour.
(iii) An accepted facet of character that prevents the formation of a belief that the relevant, specific risk exists in circumstances demonstrating the defendant's insufficient concern for the interests of others.

[208] Property offences would presumably involve the *Quinn* v. *Cunningham* 1956 JC 22 definition of recklessness (which is unclear on the question of awareness of risk), discussed above at Chapter 2, section on 'Scotland'.

[209] A further limit would be to refuse to criminalise negligent *endangerment*, but this point is not considered here because of constraints of space.

To see these elements in action (and how difficult decisions about negligence can be), it is useful to consider the oft-discussed Washington case, *State* v. *Williams.*[210]

State *v.* Williams

The defendants' child became seriously ill. Despite obvious indicators of this fact (e.g. the child's cheek turned blue), of which the Williamses were aware, they decided that their son had toothache and did not take him to a doctor. He died and his parents were charged with manslaughter which, under Washington law at the time, required 'ordinary' civil negligence.[211] The case was thus approached on the basis of whether the defendants had failed to *act* as reasonable parents would have in the circumstances. For the reasons explored at the start of Chapter 7, such a bare, conduct-based approach is objectionable.[212]

With just these facts, it remains unclear whether culpability was present in *Williams.* Assuming an unjustified risk was taken with the child's life, the first important matter is whether the defendants had the relevant background beliefs and perceptions to form a specific belief that there was a risk of death associated with their omission to seek medical attention. With regard to background beliefs, the defendants had received only a basic education.[213] Although they had perceived that the child was sick, there is thus a possibility that the Williamses lacked the relevant background beliefs that could lead to a belief concerning *how* sick their child was and that his life was in danger.[214] This makes it questionable whether they had the ingredients required to form the further dispositions consistent with the belief that their child might die if *medical attention* were not sought. If they did not possess the relevant

[210] 4 Wash App 908, 484 P 2d 1167 (1971, WA). For previous discussions, see Sanford H. Kadish, *Blame and Punishment: Essays in the Criminal Law* (New York: Collier Macmillan, 1987), pp. 95–98; Pillsbury, 'Crimes of indifference', at 193–198; Garvey, 'What's wrong with involuntary manslaughter', at 333–339; Peter Westen, 'Individualizing the reasonable person in criminal law' (2008) 2 *Criminal Law and Philosophy* 137 at 152–155.

[211] *Williams*, at 1171. The penal code now requires 'criminal negligence' for manslaughter in the second degree: West's RCWA 9A.32.070. The definition of 'criminal negligence' largely resembles the MPC's definition of negligence : West's RCWA 9A.08.010(1)(d).

[212] See section on 'Conduct: Hart's Insight'.

[213] *Williams*, at 1169–1170.

[214] Cf. the evidence of the defendant in *R* v. *Stone and Dobinson* [1977] QB 354 (E&W), at 362, to the effect that he was not aware of how gravely ill his sister was, when he had taken in and then failed to care adequately for her.

background dispositions, then negligence as failure of belief cannot be made out with regard to risking the child's life, for the reasons explained above.

If it is assumed that the Williamses *did* have the relevant background beliefs and perceptions to form a belief that seeking medical attention was warranted, consideration turns to the reason(s) why a belief to that effect was not formed. Why, for example, did the Williamses not take steps to check with a medical professional about *how* ill their child was? The Williamses were Native Americans and feared that their child would be taken by social services if they took him to a doctor.[215] This fear was apparently well founded.[216] The primary feature of their characters that prevented the Williamses from seeking medical attention was, thus, the desire to ensure that they remained connected to their son. The question is, then, whether this desire was truly representative of the defendants' characters, whether it was reflective of what made them *them*. It is assumed that it was.[217]

The matter of culpability can then be addressed: did the Williamses – in their failure to form a belief in the relevant risk to their son's life – show insufficient concern for the interests of their child? This is a complicated question, but it seems that the Williamses were deeply concerned with their child's welfare. Although this (perversely) led to the child's death,[218] it is submitted that the Williamses showed sufficient regard for his interests in the formation of beliefs *in the dire circumstances in which they were placed*.[219] More could not legitimately be expected of them in those severe circumstances. They ought not, therefore, to have been adjudged culpably negligent and declared manslaughterers.

215 *Williams*, at 1170.

216 Garvey, 'What's wrong with involuntary manslaughter?', at 334–335.

217 It is envisaged that desires will, in practice, be assumed to be part of the agent's accepted character and that she will bear the burden of adducing evidence to the contrary. See below at Chapter 9, section on 'Evidential Concerns'.

218 This may give rise to the suspicion that the Williamses showed a greater regard for *their* enjoyment of the child than *the child's* welfare: Pillsbury, 'Crimes of indifference', at 197.

219 Moran, *Rethinking the Reasonable Person*, p. 313. More difficult cases are imaginable – e.g. *Walker* v. *Superior Court* 47 Cal 3d 112, 763 P 2d 852 (1988, CA), where a mother refused to take her child to the doctor because she believed – wrongly, yet consistently with her religious beliefs – that prayer would lead to the child's recovery. A conviction in such circumstances is described as 'scandalous' in Glanville Williams, 'Criminal omissions: the conventional view' (1991) 107 *Law Quarterly Review* 86 at 91.

Williams is no doubt a powerful example because of its emotive facts.[220] It is thus prudent to consider a less highly charged case from Scotland, *Cameron* v. *Maguire*.[221]

Cameron *v.* Maguire

Cameron fired his rifle at a low wall in his back garden. The wall backed onto a wood, which was popular with walkers, and a public road. Assuming, again, that Cameron had the relevant background beliefs regarding the risks of firing his rifle, that someone might be in the woods around his home, etc., and that he perceived that he was firing a gun in the direction of the woods, the question becomes whether the feature of his character that led him to fire his rifle in such circumstances was accepted as part of his character. Again, it is assumed that it was.

If Cameron had accepted his desire to fire the rifle, then the question is whether his failure to form a belief in risk demonstrated insufficient concern for the interests of others. It is unclear why, other than wanting to check the accuracy of his rifle, Cameron was shooting in his back garden. As a result, it does not seem that his failure to perform any checks about the wall showed *any* regard for the lives of others. In such circumstances, it is submitted that he ought to have been convicted of a crime. As he believed it was *safe* for him to be shooting in his back garden,[222] however, it is again difficult to conceive of his crime as one involving 'recklessness' (as the court did), rather than negligence.

The two examples provided above explain how, in principle, negligence as failure of belief establishes culpability for unjustified risk-taking. In practice, some assumptions might need to be made, in order to facilitate the proof of culpability, and Chapter 9 explains briefly how these might look.

It is useful, in concluding this chapter, to explain its relationship with Tadros's superficially similar account of *recklessness*.

Tadros's Account of Recklessness (and/or Negligence)

Those readers familiar with Tadros's account of recklessness[223] will note the similarities between it and negligence as failure of belief. Tadros

[220] Cf. Pillsbury, 'Crimes of indifference', at 111. [221] 1999 JC 63.

[222] *Cameron* v. *Maguire*, at 66.

[223] See Victor Tadros, 'Recklessness and the duty to take care', in Stephen Shute and A.P. Simester (eds.), *Criminal Law Theory: Doctrines of the General Part* (Oxford: Oxford University Press, 2002), p. 227; Tadros, *Criminal Responsibility*, ch. 9.

thinks that recklessness is made out where a defendant fails to investigate further her *belief* that her action is *risky in general* for a reason that is generally reflective of agency. All he requires is that – 'passively' – the defendant believed that the activity was of the type with which risks are associated – for instance, driving.[224] This sounds like the mere presence of background beliefs about risks in general which the defendant *could* but has *failed to* actualise in her belief formation processes, as a result of some accepted feature of her personality.[225] This is a more specific form of negligence as failure of belief, because the defendant must have a background belief that his conduct is *risky in general.*[226] It is, nevertheless, broadly similar to the account above.

The reason Tadros's account is problematic is that he conflates recklessness and negligence. It is not particularly clear whether he is talking consistently about recklessness or whether negligence is introduced at points.[227] Tadros does not consistently put a name to the form of culpability that he is describing, but there are frequent references to 'objective' recklessness in the earlier version of his argument concerning recklessness.[228] Beyond this, Tadros describes the type of fault he is discussing as 'carelessness', which could apply to either reckless or negligent wrongdoing.[229] Ultimately, it is not clear what Tadros thinks negligence is, or, indeed, whether a distinction between recklessness and negligence is worth having.[230]

The distinction between recklessness and negligence is nevertheless worth having, which is why Tadros's account should not be followed wholeheartedly. The Standard Account gets that much right. On the account presented in this book, the reckless actor fails to be moved as a properly motivated agent would be by the beliefs that she has about the specific risk(s) attendant upon φ-ing;[231] the negligent defendant fails,

224 Ibid. 225 For Tadros's view of acceptance, see Tadros, *Criminal Responsibility*, ch. 1.

226 Ferzan also thinks that Tadros is considering negligence, not recklessness: Ferzan, 'Act, agency and indifference', at 450–454. See also Garvey, 'Involuntary manslaughter', at 359 (n. 87).

227 Cf. Tadros, 'Recklessness and the duty to take care', p. 227.

228 See, particularly, ibid., pp. 237–239. 229 Ibid., p. 255.

230 Talk of negligence is largely absent from Tadros, *Criminal Responsibility*, ch. 9. It is mentioned only briefly: ibid., p. 245. There is only one reference to negligence in *Criminal Responsibility*'s index, which directs the reader to a page where Tadros equates it with 'objective' recklessness: ibid., p. 30.

231 See, further, R. Jay Wallace, *Responsibility and the Moral Sentiments* (Cambridge, MA: Harvard University Press, 1994), p. 138; Michael Smith, 'Rational capacities, or how to distinguish recklessness, weakness and compulsion', in Sarah Stroud and Christine

because of an accepted facet of her character, to form those beliefs about risk(s). It is submitted that, on this account, the reckless defendant more immediately and clearly shows her insufficient concern for the interests of others than the negligent defendant.[232] There is a clear link between the harm to an interest of another person, the risk of that outcome taken by the defendant, and the defendant's beliefs. Those theorists who are concerned with choice get that much right (though, as seen in Chapter 6, their accounts of why choice is the *only* basis of culpability are unconvincing).

That is not to say that there is *no* adequate personalised link between the defendant and her wrongdoing in cases of negligence. The account of negligence as failure of belief ensures that such a personalised link exists, but it is necessarily a *weaker* link than exists in recklessness. The defendant's lack of concern for the interests put at risk is less clear when she does not *believe* that a specific risk attends φ-ing. As explained in Chapter 7, it is difficult to know what a person would have done had her beliefs been different.[233] Thus a defendant who is negligent in the management of her belief-formation processes should not be equated with a reckless one, as Tadros would have it. That is another grain of truth in choice theories of recklessness, but the falsehood is that the Exclusive Thesis is right and choice is the be-all and end-all of culpability.

Thus, although Tadros's account of recklessness offers insights that pave the way towards negligence as failure of belief, it collapses an important distinction between recklessness and negligence. This distinction should be recognised, and this chapter and the ones that preceded it have explained the best way to understand it, with reference to the Standard Account of culpable carelessness in Anglo-American systems.

Conclusion

This chapter has presented an account of when negligence ought to be recognised as culpable on the Standard Account. This is, broadly, when a defendant was possessed of the background beliefs and perceptions that

Tappolet (eds.), *Weakness of Will and Practical Irrationality* (Oxford: Clarendon, 2003), p. 17.

232 See, similarly, Nils Jareborg, *Scraps of Penal Theory* (Uppsala: Iustus Förlag AB, 2002), p. 52. This might explain why the community will be more concerned with reckless than negligent harm-doing: Mark R. Reiff, *Punishment, Compensation and Law: A Theory of Enforceability* (Cambridge: Cambridge University Press, 2005), p. 128.

233 See section on 'Criticisms of Counterfactual Choice'.

could have led to the belief that a risk was present, but failed to form that belief – in circumstances demonstrating insufficient concern for others – because of an accepted facet of her character. A variety of potential objections to this view have been parried. The chapter also sketched an answer to the question of when a display of negligence should be used as a fault element, concluding that life, bodily integrity and sexual autonomy are the only interests that should be protected through negligence-based offences. The option was nevertheless left open for a polity to discuss wider deployment of negligence in the criminal law, a discussion that relates to criminalisation, rather than culpability.

The next chapter considers some practical implications arising from the theory of culpable carelessness defended in this book.

9

Some Practicalities

This concluding chapter considers how the theoretical defence of the 'Standard Account' developed in the previous chapters could inform reform of the approach to culpable carelessness adopted in the Anglo-American jurisdictions surveyed in Chapter 2. It also contemplates some practical challenges that will require theoretical compromises. The first section explores possible changes to the substantive criminal law. The second section then addresses certain evidential matters.

The Substantive Law

It is useful first to consider the changes to the substantive law that flow from the theory defended the preceding chapters, before considering whether the understandings of negligence and recklessness developed in this book could be translated into statute and jury directions.

Culpable Carelessness: Statutory Formulations

Criminal law theorists rarely present statutory formulations of *mens rea* terms. In jurisdictions such as England and Wales, and Scotland – where there is no criminal code to speak of – this is perhaps understandable. Codification of the criminal law is, it is accepted, an unattainable aim there,[1] despite its still being an original aim of the Law Commissions (bodies charged with reviewing the law and proposing reforms).[2]

[1] See Tom Bingham, *The Business of Judging: Selected Essays and Speeches* (Oxford: Oxford University Press, 2000), pp. 295–297; Ian Dennis, 'RIP: the criminal code (1968–2008)' [2009] *Criminal Law Review* 1; Eric Clive, 'Codification of the criminal law', in James Chalmers, Fiona Leverick and Lindsay Farmer (eds.), *Essays in Criminal Law in Honour of Sir Gerald Gordon* (Edinburgh: Edinburgh University Press, 2010), p. 54.

[2] Law Commissions Act 1965, s. 3. The (English and Welsh) Law Commission's tenth programme of law reform nevertheless abandoned the aim of codifying the criminal law – see Dennis, 'RIP: the criminal code'.

A similar trend would be understandable in other un-codified jurisdictions (or jurisdictions that do not, at least, codify their *mens rea* terms).[3]

The assumption here is, however, that *mens rea* terms ought to be capable of being codified, or else there are genuine concerns about their being understood by ordinary citizens. Such understanding is central to the communicative enterprise of the criminal law, as explained in Chapter 3 of this book. Furthermore, many jurisdictions with more modern codes (such as those in parts of Australia and the United States) *do* define their *mens rea* terms in statutory form. It is thus important that the understandings of negligence and recklessness provided in this book could, potentially, be put into statutory form. Otherwise, they might be deemed inferior to existing definitions, even if they contain theoretical flaws.

Of course, no translation from theory to practice is ever going to be perfect: judges and jurors are not philosophers or criminal law theorists.[4] There are also complicated matters concerning proof that pose practical problems for basic and ornate theories alike. Given these concerns, it is necessary to try and explain *mens rea* concepts in 'everyday' language where possible and to allow the judge or jury to use inferences where features of the crime (the defendant's beliefs, desires, etc., at the time of acting) cannot easily be demonstrated.[5]

The argument in the following sections is not, therefore, that the theory in this book could be implemented *directly*. Rather, the contention is that the positive criminal law in the main Anglo-American jurisdictions can be *improved upon* in line with that theory but that certain pragmatic compromises must be made. The theory defended in this book, however, will help to explain and justify the law's approach in individual cases and help to stymie the divergences in approach detected in Chapter 2.

Attention will now turn to the statutory definitions of the concepts described in the previous chapters. It is sensible, for reasons which will

[3] For instance, Canada, which defines 'criminal negligence' in relation to some offences (see the discussion above at Chapter 2, section on 'Canada'), but not in relation to *all* offences. Similarly, recklessness is not defined in the code. See, further, Don Stuart, 'A case for a General Part: lessons from Canada's experience with Stephen's Code since 1892 and entrenched Charter standards since 1982' (2009) 20 *Criminal Law Forum* 113.

[4] Gerald H. Gordon, 'Subjective and objective *mens rea*' (1974–1975) 17 *Criminal Law Quarterly* 355 at 375.

[5] Even if the defendant gives evidence, there are still issues of credibility that might make her representation of her beliefs, desires, etc., untrustworthy. Inferences, therefore, will still be necessary.

become clear, to start by considering the concept of justification, even though the discussion of it in Chapter 1 was necessarily truncated.

Justification

Justification of risk-taking: The defendant can be reckless or negligent with regard to a substantial risk that a particular piece of conduct will be engaged in, consequence will materialise or circumstance will exist (the relevant risk) only when it was unjustifiable for him[6] to take the relevant risk. A lack of justification is established where, given social expectations concerning risk-taking, the dangers posed by the defendant's behaviour went beyond acceptable limits. The defendant's views concerning justification are relevant but not determinative. It is possible for the defendant to be convicted of an offence involving negligence or recklessness even if he honestly and mistakenly believed – at the time of acting – that he was justified in taking the relevant risk.

This section sets out the view of justification outlined in Chapter 1. As lack of justification and the taking of a substantial risk permeate both forms of culpable carelessness recognised by the Standard Account, they should be set out in their own section, rather than inserted into the definition of each form of culpable carelessness, as they are in instruments such as the American Law Institute's Model Penal Code (MPC).[7] This approach shortens and simplifies the wording of the sections concerning recklessness and negligence and gives courts more specific guidance on the issue of justification. Additionally, it has the benefit of ensuring that wrongdoing and culpability are kept conceptually distinct.

As noted in Chapter 1,[8] the court may – in determining the matter of justification – have regard to the views of the 'reasonable person' (or, as the MPC has it, in relation to recklessness, 'law-abiding person')[9] on risk-taking. It is not, however, necessary to set this standard out in statutory form.[10] It is a heuristic device, rather than a formal legal

[6] Statutory language has historically employed 'he', not 'she', in the United Kingdom and elsewhere.

[7] See American Law Institute, *Model Penal Code and Commentaries (Official Draft and Revised Comments)*, 3 vols. (Philadelphia: American Law Institute, 1980), vol. 1, ss. 2.02(2)(c)–2.02(2)(d).

[8] Section on 'Justifying Risk-taking'.

[9] American Law Institute, *Model Penal Code*, s. 2.02(2)(c).

[10] Cf. ibid., s. 2.02(2)(d) (explaining the reasonable person standard in relation to negligence).

requirement. The 'reasonable person', however, could be referred to in jury directions (on which, see below). In order to avoid doubt on this point, it is desirable that the statute explicitly sets out the view defended in Chapter 1 concerning *mistakes* as to justification. It will be remembered that it was argued that a defendant's views on justification are *not* determinative: the question is whether her risk-taking was *in fact* justified by reference to social expectations.

The next definition concerns recklessness.

Recklessness

The challenge with regard to recklessness is defining in it in an accessible manner. Chapter 4 introduced the various mental states that have been alleged to be relevant to recklessness and argued that these distinct states were actually identifying distinct types of *disposition* upon which an ascription of a belief about the risks attendant upon her behaviour (φ) might be based. It was concluded that, for recklessness, there is no need for a defendant to have a conscious, phenomenal experience of risk (a thought such as 'This might catch on fire . . .'); that is simply a manifestation of *one* disposition relevant to the ascription of a belief that there is a risk attendant upon φ-ing. It is possible that *other* dispositions towards thought and behaviour could also merit the ascription of the relevant belief, even if the defendant's conscious mind is focussed elsewhere. For the avoidance of doubt, this point should be mentioned in a statutory definition of recklessness.

There has been at least one previous attempt to explain similarly complex ideas in a statutory definition. Consider Ferzan's revised version of the MPC definition of recklessness:[11]

> Where the evidence does not establish that the actor consciously disregarded the risk, but the actor (1) consciously recognized that her conduct was dangerous; (2) at some level appreciated that the reasons why her conduct was dangerous was because it presented a substantial and unjustifiable risk that a material element existed or would result from her conduct; and (3) she nevertheless chose to engage in the conduct, the actor is reckless. The actor is not reckless where she (1) did not realize her action was dangerous but should have; (2) realized it was dangerous, but thought the risk of harm was not substantial or unjustifiable; or (3) realized it was dangerous but defined dangerous in a way that did not include harm that occurred.

[11] Kimberly K. Ferzan, 'Opaque recklessness' (2000–2001) 91 *Journal of Criminal Law & Criminology* 597 at 644.

There are two main difficulties with this definition. First, it is not clear that this definition captures accurately Ferzan's understanding of 'opaque' recklessness, a concept discussed in Chapter 6.[12] The language of 'at some level' appreciating a risk is ambiguous. A person might appreciate, in theory, the risks attendant upon her conduct at a level that she cannot hope to access consciously.[13] This appreciation of risk cannot suffice for 'opaque' recklessness[14] (and might well make it unsafe to ascribe a belief about risk to the defendant).

It is submitted that it would be far simpler, rather than engaging in discussions of consciousness, to explain awareness of risk in terms of the defendant's beliefs regarding risk, and his failure to be moved by them in circumstances demonstrating his insufficient concern for the interests of others.

Recklessness: A person is reckless with regard to a risk that a particular piece of conduct will be engaged in, consequence will occur or circumstance will exist (the relevant risk) where he: (i) believed that the relevant risk was connected with his behaviour and (ii) failed to alter his behaviour, in circumstances where this demonstrated insufficient concern for the interests of others. The belief that the relevant risk existed need not be at the forefront of the defendant's mind at the time of acting.

It is submitted that cases of 'alienation', introduced at the end of Chapter 6, need not be dealt with explicitly in the definition of recklessness; they could fall under the concept of insufficient concern for others. To choose to take a risk on the basis of an 'alien' feature of the defendant's character is not, the argument would run, to demonstrate insufficient concern for the interests of others.

A second problem with Ferzan's definition of recklessness is that it explains what recklessness *is and* what recklessness *is not*. This causes difficulties because, primarily, definitions should be positive: the court should not have to work out what culpability *is* through excluding what it is *not*.[15] Additionally, if negligence is defined as a culpability term in its own right (something Ferzan would not support,[16] but the account

[12] Section on 'Ferzan's "Opaque" Recklessness'.

[13] John R. Searle, *Mind: A Brief Introduction* (Oxford: Oxford University Press, 2004), pp. 167–168.

[14] Ferzan, 'Opaque recklessness', at 636–638.

[15] Glanville Williams, *The Mental Element in Crime* (Jerusalem: Magnes Press, 1965), p. 16.

[16] See Larry Alexander, Kimberly K. Ferzan and Stephen J. Morse, *Crime and Culpability: A Theory of Criminal Law* (Cambridge: Cambridge University Press, 2009), ch. 3.

presented in this book does), then discussing it in relation to recklessness becomes unnecessary and, once again, liable to confuse. It is thus submitted that the definition of negligence should appear in a separate section.

Negligence

Chapter 8 set out the most defensible account of negligence available. This could be explained, in statutory form, in the following terms.

Negligence: A person is negligent with regard to a risk that a particular piece of conduct will be engaged in, consequence will occur or circumstance will exist (the relevant risk) where he: (i) possessed the beliefs and perceptions relevant to the formation of an additional belief that the relevant risk was involved in his behaviour and (ii) through his failure to form the belief that the relevant risk existed, showed insufficient concern for the interests of others.

Questions about whether the defendant lacked the relevant background beliefs (e.g. that water conducts electricity) or perceptive information required to form a belief about the specific risks attendant upon φ-ing could be raised in relation to the first part of the definition. If it cannot be proved beyond reasonable doubt that the defendant had the relevant background beliefs or perceptions, negligence cannot be established. Of course the jury will need to rely on inferences concerning the defendant's background beliefs, but they must be *sure* that she had them, and resolve any doubts in her favour.

An additional concern is whether the defendant was prevented from forming the relevant belief about the risk attendant upon φ-ing because of an 'alien' facet of her character – a concept explained in Chapter 8.[17] It is once again submitted that such arguments could be considered under the heading of insufficient concern for the interests of others. If there was a case of 'alienation', then the defendant could contend that there is no proof beyond reasonable doubt of *her* insufficient concern for the interests of others. It is thus unnecessary to advert explicitly to cases of 'alienation' in the definition of negligence. The idea of 'alienation', however, will be returned to below, when consideration turns to the rules of evidence.

[17] Section on 'A Wider View: Reflecting Character'.

Statutory Formulations: Summary

The subsections above have demonstrated that statutory definitions of culpable carelessness are possible. It is clear, however, that the explanations of recklessness and negligence in earlier chapters require explanation in slightly different and inevitably less precise/detailed language for them to be useful in criminal trials. As mentioned above, this is mainly because lay jurors might become confused by complex legal and/or philosophical concepts. Assuming juries are to be maintained, then the statutory provisions imagined above would have to become even more basic. This matter is taken up in the next section.

The Jury

There is not space to consider the form or merits and demerits of the jury system as it exists in the various Anglo-American systems surveyed in Chapter 2. It will therefore be assumed that juries will continue to grapple with *mens rea* concepts, including recklessness and negligence, even if those concepts were reconceptualised in the manner proposed in this book.

Given this concession, it might be thought that – as a matter of pure pragmatism – the current, unanalysed dichotomy between awareness and unawareness of risk, or a dichotomy between awareness of risk and bare careless conduct, is easy to explain to the jury and is therefore superior to the more nuanced approach to these terms defended in the previous chapters of this book. Indeed, in *R* v. *G and Another*,[18] the House of Lords shied away from a definition of recklessness in terms other than simple (unanalysed) awareness of risk on the basis that juries might become confused, particularly if they must ask counterfactual questions.

If the argument is that a developed theory of culpable carelessness is necessarily so complex as to be worthless and that – as a matter of pure pragmatism – an unanalysed awareness/unawareness dichotomy is the least worst option available, then two responses might be offered. First, that dichotomy is not an accurate description of the positive law in many jurisdictions, which – as has been seen – warp recklessness to fit cases where unawareness appears to be culpable, e.g. voluntary intoxication. Second, this anti-theoretical standpoint is precisely what has resulted in the doctrinal mess that many Anglo-American jurisdictions have experienced (and some are still experiencing) in the development of their approach towards

[18] [2003] UKHL 50, [2004] 1 AC 1034 (E&W), at [38].

culpable carelessness. It is not sufficient to take comfort in the fact that the current approach 'works' if it is reliant on judges and juries, through gut feeling, to determine whether the defendant was reckless or negligent.

Consider, for instance, the direction on recklessness to be given in cases of 'culpable and reckless conduct' from the Scottish Judicial Studies Committee's *Jury Manual*: 'The accused must have acted with an utter disregard of the consequences of his conduct on the public, with total indifference to their safety.'[19] No more contextualisation is given in the model direction (although of course it *could* be open to a trial judge to provide it). The jury is thus given wide definitional power. Other systems hardly fare better if they do not do anything to 'unpack' awareness of risk. More must be done.

Not many criminal law theorists have gone into detail about how they would translate their accounts in jury directions. Two notable exceptions are the draft jury directions given by Alexander, Ferzan and Morse, and Pillsbury.[20]

Alexander, Ferzan and Morse suggest an 'initial instruction' which provides, as far as relevant, that[21]

> It is criminal for an actor to take an unjustified risk of causing harm to a legally protected interest or to take an unjustified risk that his conduct constitutes prohibited behaviour . . . For behaviour to be justified, the reasons that the actor has for engaging in his behaviour should be weighed against the risk that the actor perceives that his conduct will cause a prohibited result or results . . . The actor's reasons for action include not only the reason or reasons that motivate his conduct but also any other reason that might justify his conduct of which he is aware. These reasons should be accorded weight by (1) their positive or negative force and (2) the actor's perception of the likelihood that the facts underlying the reasons do or will obtain.

This direction on recklessness (which the authors think explains *the whole* of criminal culpability)[22] requires the members of the jury to ask themselves some difficult questions. Justification must be assessed on the basis of the actor's (presumably inferred, unless he gives evidence) reasons (themselves to be weighed in terms of their force and the actor's belief regarding their existence)[23] against the actor's perception (again,

[19] Judicial Studies Committee, *Jury Manual: Some Notes for the Guidance of the Judiciary* (2012), p. 37.2. The manual is available at http://www.scotland-judiciary.org.uk/24/720/Jury-Manual-Published.

[20] See also Peter Westen, 'Individualizing the reasonable person in criminal law' (2008) 2 *Criminal Law and Philosophy* 137 at 154–155.

[21] Alexander and Ferzan with Morse, *Crime and Culpability*, pp. 327–329.

[22] See ibid., ch. 2.

[23] See above at Chapter 1, section on 'Justifying Risk-taking'.

presumably inferred from 'objective' evidence) of the risks his conduct involves. It is likely that a jury will simply be confused by this direction – especially its current wording – and go with 'gut feeling'.

Pillsbury's direction is much longer (too long to warrant quoting in full), because its content regarding risk-taking is far more contextualised.[24] What Pillsbury's direction demonstrates is that juries will need detailed guidance concerning the various elements of culpable carelessness, preferably with examples and indications of the type of heuristic devices (such as the 'reasonable person') that they may employ in reaching a decision.[25] He also shows that the jury can be informed of matters which need not figure in the statutory definition of *mens rea* terms.

In the following jury instructions (which could be given in written form), Pillsbury's detailed approach will be preferred. It will be assumed that no question over exactly *what* the relevant risk was has arisen, as this would presumably be a question that would require expert evidence (in order to establish the relevant reference classes, etc.).[26] It should further be noted that questions of evidence and procedure are ignored in the directions given below. Their concern is primarily with the *mens rea* component of the offence charged.

Possible Direction on Recklessness

Count[27] *[count number]* is of *[name of offence]*.

[Set out parts of the actus reus *which do not concern justification of risk-taking or* mens rea*]*.

There is a fault element to this crime *[set out* mens rea*]*.[28]

To be reckless, the defendant must take a substantial and unjustified risk that *[set out relevant risk]*. It is for you to decide what a substantial risk is. You must be satisfied that, taking the substantial risk that *[set out relevant risk]* went beyond the bounds of socially accepted risk-creation.

24 See Samuel H. Pillsbury, 'Crimes of indifference' (1996) 49 *Rutgers Law Review* 105 at 209–212.

25 Pillsbury actually refers (ibid., at 209) to 'one in the defendant's position', which is ambiguous.

26 See the discussion of risk assessment above at Chapter 1, section on 'Why Is Justification Required?'.

27 The English term 'count' is used here, but of course other systems will use different terminology.

28 Some offences will have more than one form of *mens rea* (e.g. recklessness and intention).

You – as representatives of the community – must ask whether it was socially acceptable for the defendant to put others at risk in the manner that she did, and it might be helpful to consider what you imagine the 'reasonable citizen' would think of the defendant's risk-taking. If you are sure that the defendant's risk-taking went beyond socially acceptable levels, and was therefore unjustified, you may proceed to consider the other matters I will direct you towards. If you are not sure that the defendant's risk-taking went beyond socially acceptable levels, and was therefore unjustified, you must acquit on this count.

If the defendant gives evidence as to justification:

In reaching a conclusion concerning the justification of the defendant's risk-taking, you must consider the defendant's evidence. This is important, but should not be determinative: it can be unjustifiable to take a risk even if the defendant believes that she is justified in doing so. The question is always whether the defendant's risk-taking *actually* went beyond socially acceptable levels, not whether the defendant *believed* that to be the case.

If you decide that the defendant's risk-taking was substantial and unjustifiable, you must ask whether she was reckless as to the risk that *[set out relevant risk]*. Recklessness is an everyday word, but it has a specific legal meaning, which you must apply. To be reckless, the defendant must have believed that *[set out relevant risk]* and must have, in spite of this belief, continued with her behaviour.

To establish whether the defendant has a particular belief about *[set out relevant risk]*, you should ask whether she acted, thought and planned in the way that you would expect someone with the relevant belief about *[set out relevant risk]* to have acted, thought and planned. You may look at all of the evidence in the case, including the defendant's reaction to the materialisation of the risk. If she was surprised by its materialisation, is it fair to attribute a belief in the risk to her at the time of acting? Or is surprise really simply regret that a risk that the defendant believed to exist has in fact materialised? That is a decision that you have to make. You must be sure that the defendant had the relevant belief that *[set out relevant risk] at the time* that she took that risk.[29]

[29] This excludes cases such as *People* v. *Decina* 2 N.Y 2d 133, 138 N.E. 2d 799 (1956, NY), discussed above at Chapter 7, section on 'An Earlier Disregarding of the Relevant Risk'. If a *Decina*-type case is argued on grounds of recklessness, this part of the direction could be amended suitably.

I should explain that belief in law does not require the defendant to have been thinking consciously (in her 'mind's eye') about the risk attendant upon her behaviour. We all know what it is like to be distracted and yet still manage to successfully navigate obstacles and take account of risks in our actions. *[Thereafter give an example.]*[30] So long as you find it proved that, in the light of the evidence of the defendant's conduct and planning, such a belief was in fact formed, you may proceed further.

'Caldwell *Lacuna'-type cases:*

If you are not sure that the defendant believed that *[set out relevant risk]*, then you must acquit. If, as contended by the defence, the defendant investigated the risk that *[set out relevant risk]* and came to the conclusion that the risk had been completely removed, the defendant cannot be reckless in law. *[If relevant, give direction on negligence – see below.]*

Finally, if you find that the defendant had a belief – in the sense I have described to you – that *[set out relevant risk]*, the final question is whether her failure to alter her behaviour to avoid taking that risk demonstrated insufficient concern for the interests of others. You, as representatives of the community, must decide on the level of concern that might legitimately be expected of the defendant in the circumstances in which she found herself. You must pay attention to any explanation for the taking of the risk that is offered by the defendant. You might find it useful to consider what the 'reasonable citizen', possessed with exactly the same beliefs as the defendant, might have done in the circumstances.

[END]

Possible Direction on Negligence

[Set out elements of recklessness (but replace that term with 'negligence' until after the matter of whether the defendant gives evidence as to justification.]

If you are satisfied that the defendant's risk-taking was substantial and unjustifiable, you can approach the question of whether she was negligent with regard to *[set out relevant risk]*. The ingredients of negligence are as follows. First, the defendant must have had the relevant beliefs, and perceived the relevant features of her situation, required to form the belief that *[set out relevant risk]*. *[Give examples of the type of beliefs and perceptions pertaining to the relevant risk.]*

[30] For instance, the example of driving, given above at Chapter 4, section on 'Tacit Knowledge'.

Second, if you are sure the defendant had the beliefs and perceptions necessary to form the further belief that there was a risk of *[set out relevant risk]*, the question becomes *why* she failed to form that further belief that there was a risk of *[set out relevant risk]*. Why did she not conduct further checks or apply her beliefs to her perceptions? If you find this failure resulted from a factor which shows the defendant to be insufficiently motivated by the interests of others, then she was culpably negligent and you may convict her, assuming the other elements of the offence are made out.

If you are not convinced beyond reasonable doubt that the defendant's failure to believe that the risks attendant upon her conduct demonstrated insufficient concern for the interests of others, then you must acquit her. Again, you – as representatives of the community – must decide on the level of sufficient concern for others which was appropriate in the circumstances. Once again, you might find it useful to consider what level of concern a 'reasonable citizen', with all of the defendants beliefs and perceptions (but no *other* beliefs and perceptions), could be expected to do in terms of forming beliefs about the risks attached to her behaviour.

If the defendant gives evidence as to background beliefs or perceptions:

You have heard evidence from the defendant that, because she did not believe or perceive that *[relevant proposition]*, she was unable to form the belief that there was a risk of *[set out relevant risk]*. You must consider this evidence – and decide on its weight – in reaching your decision concerning guilt. Again, you must be sure that the defendant had the relevant beliefs and perceptions necessary to form the further belief that there was a risk of *[set out relevant risk]*.

[END]

It is submitted that the directions suggested above would be comprehensible to lay jurors, and make clear that recklessness and negligence – although 'everyday' terms – have specific legal meanings.

The questions of whether the defendant can raise evidence of character and the idea of 'alienation' (introduced in Chapters 6 and 8) have been left to the side in the directions. This is because the question of what the jury should be told about such arguments depends on a matter of proof, which is discussed in the next section.

Evidential Concerns

In Chapters 6 and 8, it was contended that if an 'alien' feature of a defendant's personality (i.e. one not accepted as part of the defendant's character) explains why she failed to be motivated appropriately in the light of her beliefs about risk (recklessness) or to form an appropriate belief about the risks associated with φ-ing (negligence), a finding of culpability would be too fragile to support the kind of personalised condemnation that is core to a criminal conviction.[31]

A concern with character and 'alienation' raises difficulties in the trial environment, which is perhaps why so few criminal theorists take these matters into account beyond situations such as duress and necessity. How, for example, is the prosecution to prove that the feature of the defendant that explains her failure to form appropriate beliefs was truly reflective of her, as an agent?[32] Such proof would be a hard task for the prosecution to undertake in the majority of cases and might result in unmerited acquittals.

One answer to this problem is to bite the bullet and claim that *any* explanation for the failure to form the relevant belief about risk can be traced to the defendant, excepting features such as height, intelligence, etc. which are not reflective of agency.[33]

An alternative response, and the one defended here, is to propose a rebuttable *presumption* that all traits, desires, etc. possessed by a person are accepted and are a meaningful reflection on the defendant's character. This proposal is not meant as an empirical claim that agents *are* usually accepting of the entirety of their character. Rather, it is a normative claim. A useful comparison can be drawn with the law on insanity/mental disorder: the law in Anglo-American jurisdictions assumes that the defendant was sane, and this is – at least in part – a normative stance which respects properly the defendant as a citizen. By default, to conduct an enquiry into whether the defendant is an appropriate participant in the criminal trial would be disrespectful to the defendant's agency in the vast majority of cases (i.e. cases where it is not immediately apparent that the defendant might be incapacitated). It is submitted that it is important to respect the defendant – to take her seriously as a full, rather than potential, moral agent – even if this means that the defendant (and in some systems the prosecution)[34] must

[31] See above at Chapter 8, section on 'A Wider View: Reflecting Character'.

[32] See, similarly, Joshua Dressler, 'Reflections on excusing wrongdoers: moral theory, new excuses and the Model Penal Code' (1987–1988) 19 *Rutgers Law Journal* 671 at 696–697.

[33] See Simester, 'A disintegrated theory of culpability', at 201.

[34] Systems of law vary on the question of whether the prosecution can raise the matter of insanity (with or without leave) and whether the standard of proof is beyond reasonable doubt or the balance of probabilities/preponderance of evidence. For concerns of space, these differences are glossed over here.

overcome a presumption of sanity by satisfying a (frequently persuasive) burden of proof.[35]

Taking this analogy further, it might be presumed that the defendant is responsible for character traits insofar as she has accepted them.[36] To overcome this presumption, she would have to bring evidence (presumably character witnesses) concerning her ability to typically form appropriate beliefs about the relevant type of risk or the steps she has taken to attempt to rid herself of traits with which she does not identify.

This proposal raises worries over reverse burdens of proof. It might be imagined that the defendant would have to satisfy the jury on the balance of probabilities (or equivalent standard) that the features of her motivational set-up that, for instance, led her to fail to form the relevant belief about risk were 'alien' and that she should not, in consequence, be held liable for her unjustified risk-taking and its results. This is the approach taken towards insanity in many Anglo-American systems. It must be asked, however, whether imposing a persuasive burden on the defendant would be compatible with her rights. There is not space here to consider this matter in relation to each of the distinct Anglo-American jurisdictions discussed in Chapter 2. The next section considers this question specifically in the context of the European Convention on Human Rights

[35] See *R* v. *M'Naghten* (1843) 10 Cl & F 200 (E&W), at 210 (see also *Woolmington* v. *DPP* [1935] AC 462 (E&W)); Criminal Code Act 1924 (Tas), s. 15; Criminal Code Act 1899 (Qld), s. 26; Crimes (Mental Impairment and Unfitness to Be Tried) Act 1997 (NSW), ss. 21(1)–21(2); Criminal Code Act (NT), s. 43D; Criminal Code Act 1995 (Cwlth), s. 7.3(3); Criminal Law Consolidation Act 1935 (SA), ss. 269D, 269F(A)(3), 269G(B)(3); Criminal Code Act 2002 (ACT), ss. 28(4)–28(5); Criminal Code Compilation Act 1913 (WAus), s. 26; Criminal Code, RSC 1985, c. C-46 (Can), s. 16(2); Crimes Act 1961 (NZ), s. 23(1); Criminal Procedure (Scotland) Act 1995 (Scot), s. 51A(4). There is not space here for a detailed survey of the various US approaches to the insanity defence, but the presumption is found in various state codes, e.g. Alabama (Ala Code 1975, s. 13A-3-1(c)), Connecticut (CGSA, ss. 53a-12, 53a-13 (CON)) and New York (NY Stat., ss. 25.00(2), 40.15). For theoretical discussion of the defensibility of imposing this reverse legal burden in insanity cases, see David Hamer, 'The presumption of innocence and reverse burdens: a balancing act' (2007) 66 *Cambridge Law Journal* 143 at 162–163.

[36] See, similarly, Edmund L. Pincoffs, 'Legal responsibility and moral character' (1972–1973) 19 *Wayne Law Review* 905 at 922. Note that the prosecution would still have to prove the other substantive elements of *mens rea*, as at present. It might be objected that, in removing part of the prosecution's responsibility to prove moral fault, this book endorses an illegitimate reverse burden. See Ian Dennis, 'Reverse onuses and the presumption of innocence: in search of principle' [2005] *Criminal Law Review* 901 at 919–920. Dennis does not consider a character-based theory of criminal responsibility/liability. His thinking might be different if one were adopted.

(ECHR), in order to demonstrate the type of debate relevant to determining whether a reverse burden would be appropriate in theory.

Reverse Burdens and the Right to a Fair Trial: An Argument in the Context of the European Convention on Human Rights

In the case of UK jurisdictions, the question of whether a reverse burden concerning character could be imposed would be governed by the ECHR. Whether a reverse persuasive burden would be compatible with Article 6 of the ECHR's guarantee of a fair trial[37] is determined by the vague test in *Salabiaku* v. *France*.[38] There, the European Court of Human Rights decided that reverse burdens of proof were compatible with the defendant's Article 6 right *provided that* they are confined 'within reasonable limits which take into account the importance of what is at stake and maintain the rights of the defence'.[39] It should be noted from the outset that this decision was made in the context of a reverse burden forming part of a particular criminal offence. In the paragraphs below, the focus is on a reverse burden which concerns the defendant's *responsibility* for her character, which – although important in explaining culpability in the circumstances of an offence – is not tied to a specific criminal offence.[40] The character presumption is again akin to insanity, in this regard.

It is submitted that a reverse burden concerning the acceptance of character traits would satisfy the 'reasonable limits' spoken of in *Salabiaku*, particularly given the normative justification underlying the presumption of responsibility for character.[41] This is not simply a case of a difficult prosecution task being eased by placing a burden of proof upon the defence;[42] it is a matter of respect for citizens who are called to account for their alleged wrongdoing. It is thus envisaged that there is a difference between asking the defendant to defeat an inference of *mens rea*, or the lack of a defence (something that, usually, the defendant

[37] On which, see Victor Tadros and Stephen Tierney, 'The presumption of innocence and the Human Rights Act' (2004) 67 *Modern Law Review* 402 at 416–420.

[38] (1991) 13 EHRR 379. [39] At [28].

[40] This means that the seriousness of the offence under consideration ceases to be crucial in deciding whether a reverse burden is acceptable. For discussion, see Hamer, 'The presumption of innocence', at 149–151; Tadros and Tierney, 'The presumption of innocence', at 430–432.

[41] It would be for the state to justify the reverse burden: *R* v. *Lambert* [2001] UKHL 37, [2002] 2 AC 545 (E&W), at [37].

[42] See, further, Hamer, 'The presumption of innocence', at 159.

knows about but the prosecution may prove by reference to the circumstances of the offence),[43] and asking her to show that her choice to take a risk (recklessness) or failure to form a relevant belief (negligence) was 'out of character', i.e. not a true reflection of her accepted motivational set-up and general concern for others (something that the defendant knows about, but the prosecution will presumably have great difficulty in showing, even by external evidence relating to the specific behaviour under consideration at trial).[44] This approach shows adequate respect to both the public's interest in having factually guilty offenders convicted *and* the defendant's interest in self-respect.

Tadros and Tierney demonstrate the dangers of taking the difficulty of proof argument too far: rape is difficult to prove, so should elements of that offence be presumed to be present, and the defendant bear a reverse burden?[45] No: the prosecution should prove the elements of the offence. The argument here is that proving acceptance of character traits is beyond the competence of the prosecution in most cases. This would lead to (unmerited) acquittals, which would be contrary to the public's interest in the conviction of the factually guilty.

An important consideration in the context of the ECHR is, however, whether this burden upon the defendant would be a *persuasive* one (requiring the defendant to meet the balance of probabilities (or similar) standard) or an *evidential* one (requiring the defendant to present evidence to make an issue 'live' in proceedings). Answering this question requires asking whether the defendant can realistically bring evidence to meet the standard required by a persuasive burden.[46] If not, the practice in jurisdictions applying the ECHR has been to 'reduce' the burden from persuasive to evidential.[47]

It should be practicable to bring character witnesses to attest to the defendant's normal tendency towards, for instance, care concerning

[43] 'Usually' because some *mens rea* terms (e.g. negligence) do not relate to matters of which, at the time of the offence, the defendant was aware: Tadros and Tierney, 'The presumption of innocence', at 427 (n. 66).

[44] See Hamer, 'The presumption of innocence', at 161.

[45] See Tadros and Tierney, 'The presumption of innocence', at 427.

[46] This factor was emphasised in *DPP* v. *Sheldrake; Attorney-General's Reference (No 4 of 2002)* [2004] UKHL 43, [2005] 1 AC 264 (E&W). See also *R* v. *Hunt* [1987] AC 352 (E&W), at 374. This is a negative proposition: a burden will be illegitimate if it is difficult for the defendant to satisfy it. See, further, Paul Roberts, 'The presumption of innocence brought home: *Kebilene* deconstructed' (2002) 118 *Law Quarterly Review* 41 at 65–66.

[47] See e.g. *Sheldrake; Attorney-General's Reference (No 4 of 2002)*; Human Rights Act 1998 (UK), s. 3.

certain risks.[48] It might be more difficult for the Crown to discover these witnesses, making the case for a reverse burden of proof seem compelling. This does not, however, distract too much from the difficulties that the defendant might encounter in trying to meet the standard of a persuasive burden (i.e. proof on the balance of probabilities). These practicalities might lead to imbalance in the trial proceedings, rendering them unfair to the defendant.[49] Just because the defendant has peculiar knowledge of her general belief-formation processes, for instance, does not mean that it is easy for her to establish this in court.[50] It therefore appears that an evidential burden – i.e. the presentation of *some* credible evidence that, for instance, the defendant's failure to believe a certain risk existed was the result of an 'alien' feature of her personality – is all that can be imposed.[51] It is submitted that, given the relatively low bar of acceptance set out in Chapter 8,[52] it will be difficult for a defendant to *falsely* and *credibly* raise such evidence, and not have the prosecution prove beyond reasonable doubt that the relevant trait was in keeping with the defendant's wider motivational framework, and thus an adequate reflection on *her*, as an agent.

A connected consideration is whether the prosecution should be able to counter the defendant's evidence of good character by relying on her past misdeeds, including any relevant convictions. Without going into a long discussion of the doctrinal approaches towards what is often called 'bad character' evidence around the Anglo-American world, it is submitted that such evidence should be admissible where the defendant has chosen to make her character a live issue in proceedings.[53] Such an approach prevents a culpable defendant from escaping liability by presenting questionable evidence of the good parts of her character, whilst withholding more negative facets of her past conduct. Importantly, however, the defendant must *first* raise the issue of character for any negative evidence of past misconduct to be brought forward. This, it is submitted, respects the reluctance of some Anglo-American systems to allow the indiscriminate admission of bad character evidence and its

[48] This appears to have been acceptable in early cases of culpable homicide under Scots law, e.g. *HM Advocate* v. *McHaffie* (1827) Syme 33.

[49] For discussion of when, in principle, a reverse burden is justified on the basis of ease of proof, see Hamer, 'The presumption of innocence', at 158.

[50] Tadros and Tierney, 'The presumption of innocence', at 427.

[51] See, similarly, Hamer, 'The presumption of innocence', at 159.

[52] Section on 'A Wider View: Reflecting Character'.

[53] See e.g. *Lowery* v. *R* [1974] AC 85 (PC); Criminal Justice Act 2003 (E&W), s. 101(1)(f).

commitment to protecting the privacy of the defendant.[54] If the defendant does not mention her character, on this model, the prosecution cannot do so, either. This seems appropriate, in allowing the defence the decision over whether the issue of character is litigated.

Ultimately, then, a presumption that the defendant had accepted the character traits relevant to her unjustified risk-taking, which can be displaced by the meeting of an *evidential* burden, is envisaged. To explain these matters to the jury, this supplementary direction could be given in cases of alleged 'alienation'.

> You have heard evidence from the defence which suggests that the defendant failed to be moved by a belief in risk/form a belief in risk *[delete as appropriate]* because of *[set out feature of character]*. The law assumes that the defendant's character traits are accepted by her, and thus her responsibility, but it might be that the defendant's evidence has raised reasonable doubt on this matter. If you have reasonable doubt over the representativeness of *[set out feature of character]* that caused the defendant's failure to be moved by her beliefs about risk/to appreciate the riskiness of her conduct *[delete as appropriate]*, then you should acquit the defendant. I should point out that the defendant does not need to *prove* anything; the question for you is simply whether – taking all evidence into consideration – you are satisfied beyond reasonable doubt that the defendant's unjustified risk-taking reflected on *her*, as a person.

The above discussion has demonstrated in outline that sort of evidential discussion that would need to be had to accommodate the understandings of culpable carelessness developed in this book. It has also shown that the practicalities of the criminal trial will require a balance between competing interests, and this will sometimes require compromises. The theory of culpability developed in this book, if left unaltered, would allow the prosecution to prove guilt in a frustratingly small number of cases if no evidential presumptions were put in place. This would be contrary to the public's interest in the conviction of the factually guilty.[55]

[54] Art. 8 of the ECHR protects 'the right to respect for his private and family life, his home and his correspondence'.

[55] The presence of presumptions concerning character and knowledge no doubt opens the door to unmerited convictions, but this risk is inherent in all systems of criminal law. It is not, therefore, fatal to the argument in this book.

Conclusion

This chapter has presented two main arguments. First, those jurisdictions that do not possess clear and consistent definitions of their *mens rea* terms in, for instance, a code, should enact statutory definitions of justification, recklessness and negligence. Those systems that have codified their definitions of *mens rea* terms, including recklessness and negligence, should reform their definitions in line with the theory presented in this book. However clear the law becomes, it is nevertheless plain that – if laypersons are to be involved in trials – *mens rea* terms concerning culpable risk-taking must be translated into accessible jury directions. It was shown that such directions could be crafted, based on the account of culpable carelessness defended in the preceding chapters.

Second, it was argued – by drawing an analogy with a common approach to insanity – that the rules of evidence, in principle, could accommodate a greater reliance on character evidence in relation to recklessness and negligence and that a reverse (evidential) burden of proof upon the defendant in these circumstances would be consistent with due regard for the defendant's rights.

The account of culpable carelessness in this book is now complete. The result, it is submitted, is a practical, yet theoretically defensible, account of the Standard Account of culpable carelessness in Anglo-American criminal law.

BIBLIOGRAPHY

Adams, Robert M., 'Involuntary sins' (1985) 94 *The Philosophical Review* 3.

Adler, Matthew D., 'Risk, death and harm: the normative foundations of risk regulation' (2003) 87 *Minnesota Law Review* 1293.

'Against "individual risk": a sympathetic critique of risk assessment' (2005) 153 *University of Pennsylvania Law Review* 1121.

Alexander, Larry, 'Reconsidering the relationship among voluntary acts, strict liability and negligence in criminal law', in Ellen F. Paul, Fred D. Miller and Jeffrey Paul (eds.), *Crime, Culpability and Remedy* (Oxford: Basil Blackwell, 1990), p. 84.

'Inculpatory and exculpatory mistakes and the fact/law distinction: an essay in memory of Myke Bayles' (1993) 12 *Law and Philosophy* 33.

'Deontology at the threshold' (2000) 37 *San Diego Law Review* 893.

Alexander, Larry, and Ferzan, Kimberly K., 'Culpable acts of risk creation' (2007–2008) 5 *Ohio State Journal of Criminal Law* 375.

'Reply', in Paul H. Robinson, Stephen P. Garvey and Kimberly K. Ferzan (eds.), *Criminal Law Conversations* (Oxford: Oxford University Press, 2009), p. 291.

Alexander, Larry, and Ferzan, Kimberly K., with Morse, Stephen J., *Crime and Culpability: A Theory of Criminal Law* (Cambridge: Cambridge University Press, 2009).

Alfano, Mark, *Character as Moral Fiction* (Cambridge: Cambridge University Press, 2013).

Alldridge, Peter, 'Rules for courts and rules for citizens' (1990) 10 *Oxford Journal of Legal Studies* 487.

'Making criminal law known', in Stephen Shute and A.P. Simester (eds.), *Criminal Law Theory: Doctrines of the General Part* (Oxford: Oxford University Press, 2002), p. 103.

Allmark, Peter, 'An Aristotelian account of autonomy' (2008) 42 *Journal of Value Enquiry* 41.

American Law Institute, *Model Penal Code and Commentaries (Official Draft and Revised Comments)*, 3 vols. (Philadelphia: American Law Institute, 1980), vol. 1.

Amirthalingam, Kumaralingam, '*Caldwell* recklessness is dead, long live *mens rea*'s fecklessness' (2004) 67 *Modern Law Review* 491.

Anon, 'Negligence and the general problem of criminal responsibility' (1971–1972) 81 *Yale Law Journal* 949.

Archard, David, 'The *mens rea* of rape: reasonableness and culpable mistakes', in Keith Burgess-Jackson (ed.), *A Most Detestable Crime: New Philosophical Essays on Rape* (Aldershot: Dartmouth, 1999), p. 213.

Arenella, Peter, 'Character, choice and moral agency: the relevance of character to our moral culpability judgments', in Ellen F. Paul, Fred D. Miller and Jeffrey Paul (eds.), *Crime, Culpability and Remedy* (Oxford: Basil Blackwell, 1990), p. 59.

Aristotle, *Nicomachean Ethics*, trans. Roger Crisp (Cambridge: Cambridge University Press, 2000).

Armstrong, D.M., *Belief, Truth and Knowledge* (Cambridge: Cambridge University Press, 1973).

'Perception and belief', in Jonathan Dancy (ed.), *Perceptual Knowledge* (Oxford: Oxford University Press, 1988), p. 127.

Arpaly, Nomy, *Unprincipled Virtue: An Inquiry into Moral Agency* (Oxford: Oxford University Press, 2002).

Arpaly, Nomy, and Schroeder, Timothy, 'Praise, blame and the whole self' (1999) 93 *Philosophical Studies* 161.

Ashworth, Andrew, 'Belief, intent and criminal liability', in John Eekelaar and John Bell (eds.), *Oxford Essays in Jurisprudence: Third Series* (Oxford: Oxford University Press, 1989), p. 30.

'The scope of criminal liability for omissions' (1989) 105 *Law Quarterly Review* 424.

'Interpreting criminal statutes: a crisis of legality?' (1991) 107 *Law Quarterly Review* 419.

'Principles, pragmatism and the Law Commission's recommendations on homicide law reform' [2007] *Criminal Law Review* 333.

'Manslaughter: general or nominate offence?', in C.M.V. Clarkson and Sally Cunningham (eds.), *Criminal Liability for Non-aggressive Death* (Aldershot: Ashgate, 2008), p. 235.

Positive Obligations in Criminal Law (Oxford: Hart, 2013).

Sentencing and Criminal Justice, 6th edn. (Cambridge: Cambridge University Press, 2015).

Ashworth, Andrew, and Horder, Jeremy, *Principles of Criminal Law*, 7th edn. (Oxford: Oxford University Press, 2013).

Audi, Robert, 'Dispositional beliefs and dispositions to believe' (1994) 28 *Noûs* 419.

'The ethics of belief: doxastic self-control and intellectual virtue' (2008) 161 *Synthese* 403.

Epistemology: A Contemporary Introduction to the Theory of Knowledge (New York: Routledge, 2011).

Baker, Brenda M., '*Mens rea*, negligence and criminal law reform' (1987–1988) 6 *Law and Philosophy* 53.

'Theorizing about responsibility and criminal liability' (1992) 11 *Law and Philosophy* 403.

Baldwin, Thomas, 'Foresight and responsibility' (1979) 54 *Philosophy* 347.

Bandes, Susan, 'Is it immoral to punish the heedless and clueless? A comment on Alexander, Ferzan and Morse: *Crime and Culpability*' (2010) 29 *Law and Philosophy* 433.

Barton, Joshua, 'Recklessness in Scots criminal law: subjective or objective?' 2011 *Juridical Review* 143.

Bayles, Michael D., 'Character, purpose and criminal responsibility' (1982) 1 *Law and Philosophy* 5.

Principles of Law: A Normative Analysis (Dordrecht: Reidel, 1987).

Bingham, Tom, *The Business of Judging: Selected Essays and Speeches* (Oxford: Oxford University Press, 2000).

Birch, Diane J., 'The foresight saga: the biggest mistake of all?' [1988] *Criminal Law Review* 4.

Bohlander, Michael, *Principles of German Criminal Law* (Oxford: Hart, 2009).

Bok, Hilary, 'Freedom and practical reasoning', in Gary Watson (ed), *Free Will*, 2nd edn. (Oxford: Oxford University Press, 2003), p. 162.

Boonin, David, *The Problem of Punishment: A Critical Introduction* (Cambridge: Cambridge University Press, 2008).

Botterell, Andrew, 'Understanding the voluntary act principle', in Francois Tanguay-Renaud and James Stribopoulos (eds.), *Rethinking Criminal Law Theory: New Canadian Perspectives in the Philosophy of Domestic, Transnational and International Criminal Law* (Oxford: Hart, 2012), p. 117.

Brady, James B., 'Punishment for negligence: a reply to Professor Hall' (1972–1973) 22 *Buffalo Law Review* 107.

'Recklessness, negligence, indifference and awareness' (1980) 43 *Modern Law Review* 381.

'Recklessness' (1996) 15 *Law and Philosophy* 183.

Braithwaite, R.B., 'The nature of believing' (1932–1933) 33 *Proceedings of the Aristotelian Society* 129.

Brandt, Richard B., 'Traits of character: a conceptual analysis' (1970) 7 *American Philosophical Quarterly* 23.

Bratman, Michael E., *Intention, Plans and Practical Reason* (Cambridge, MA: Harvard University Press, 1987).

Briggs, Adrian, 'Judges, juries and the meaning of words' (1985) 5 *Legal Studies* 314.

Bronitt, Simon, and McSherry, Bernadette, *Principles of Criminal Law*, 3rd edn. (Sydney: Thomson Reuters, 2010).

Brudner, Alan, 'Is negligence blameless?', in Paul H. Robinson, Stephen P. Garvey and Kimberly K. Ferzan (eds), *Criminal Law Conversations* (Oxford: Oxford University Press, 2009), p. 285.

Punishment and Freedom: A Liberal Theory of Penal Justice (Oxford: Oxford University Press, 2009).

'A reply to critics of *Punishment and Freedom*' (2011) 14 *New Criminal Law Review* 495.

Burchell, Jonathan, *Principles of Criminal Law*, 4th edn. (Claremont: Juta, 2013).

Campbell, Kenneth, and Ashworth, Andrew, 'Recklessness in assault – and in general?' (1991) 107 *Law Quarterly Review* 187.

Cane, Peter, *The Anatomy of Tort Law* (Oxford: Hart, 1997).

'Fleeting mental states' (2002) 59 *Cambridge Law Journal* 273.

Responsibility in Law and Morality (Oxford: Hart, 2002).

Carroll, Lewis, *Through the Looking Glass and What Alice Found There* (London: Dent, 1929).

Carruthers, Peter, *Consciousness: Essays from a Higher-Order Perspective* (Oxford: Oxford University Press, 2005).

Chalmers, David J., *The Conscious Mind: In Search of a Fundamental Theory* (Oxford: Oxford University Press, 1996).

Chalmers, James, 'Lieser and misconceptions' 2008 *Scottish Criminal Law* 1115.

Chalmers, James, and Leverick, Fiona, *Criminal Defences and Pleas in Bar of Trial* (Edinburgh: SULI/W. Green, 2006).

'Fair labelling in criminal law' (2008) 71 *Modern Law Review* 217.

Chan, Winnie, and Simester, A.P., 'Four functions of *mens rea*' (2011) 70 *Cambridge Law Journal* 381.

Charlow, Robin, 'Wilful ignorance and criminal culpability' (1991–1992) 70 *Texas Law Review* 1351.

Chisholm, Roderick, *Theory of Knowledge*, 3rd edn. (Englewood Cliffs, NJ: Prentice-Hall International, 1989).

Clarkson, C.M.V., 'Aggravated endangerment offences' (2007) 60 *Current Legal Problems* 278.

Clive, Eric, 'Codification of the criminal law', in James Chalmers, Fiona Leverick and Lindsay Farmer (eds.), *Essays in Criminal Law in Honour of Sir Gerald Gordon* (Edinburgh: Edinburgh University Press, 2010), p. 54.

Clive, Eric, Ferguson, Pamela, Gane, Christopher, and McCall Smith, Alexander, *A Draft Criminal Code for Scotland with Commentary* (Edinburgh: TSO, 2003).

Coffee, John C., 'Paradigms lost: the blurring of the criminal and civil law models – and what can be done about it' (1991–1992) 101 *Yale Law Journal* 1875.

Cohen, Daniel I.A., 'The jurisprudence of unconscious intent' (1996) 24 *Journal of Psychiatry and Law* 511.

Cohen, L. Jonathan, 'Belief and acceptance' (1989) 98 *Mind* 367.

An Essay on Belief and Acceptance (Oxford: Oxford University Press, 1992).

Coke, Edward, *Third Part of the Institutes of the Laws of England* (London: E&R Brook, 1648).

Coleman, Jules L., *The Practice of Principle: In Defence of a Pragmatist Approach to Legal Theory* (Oxford: Oxford University Press, 2001).

Colvin, Eric, 'Recklessness and criminal negligence' (1982) 32 *University of Toronto Law Journal* 345.

Colvin, Eric, and McKechnie, John, *Criminal Law in Queensland and Western Australia: Cases and Commentary*, 5th edn. (Chatswood, NSW: LexisNexis/ Butterworths, 2008).

Conklin, William E., *Hegel's Laws: The Legitimacy of a Modern Legal Order* (Stanford, CA: Stanford University Press, 2008).

Cowan, Sharon, '"Freedom and the capacity to make a choice": a feminist analysis of consent in the criminal law of rape', in Vanessa E. Munro and Carl Stychin (eds.), *Sexuality and the Law: Feminist Engagements* (Abingdon: Routledge-Cavendish, 2007), p. 51.

Cranor, Carl F., 'Towards a non-consequentialist approach to acceptable risks', in Tim Lewens (ed.), *Risk: Philosophical Perspectives* (London: Routledge, 2007), p. 45.

Crofts, Penny, *Wickedness and Crime: Laws of Homicide and Malice* (London: Routledge, 2013).

Crosby, Cath, 'Recklessness – the continuing search for a definition' (2008) 72 *Journal of Criminal Law* 313.

Cross, Rupert, 'The mental element in crime' (1967) 83 *Law Quarterly Review* 215.

Cross, Troy, 'Recent work on dispositions' (2012) 72 *Analysis* 115.

Cunningham, Sally, 'Recklessness: being reckless and acting recklessly' (2010) 21 *King's College Law Journal* 445.

Curley, E.M., 'Excusing rape' (1976) 5 *Philosophy and Public Affairs* 325.

Dan-Cohen, Meir, 'Decision rules and conduct rules: on acoustic separation in criminal law' (1983–1984) 97 *Harvard Law Review* 625.

Dancy, Jonathan, *An Introduction to Contemporary Epistemology* (Oxford: Blackwell, 1985).

Practical Reality (Oxford: Oxford University Press, 2002).

Dehaene, Stanislas, Changeux, Jean-Pierre, Naccache, Lionel, Sackur, Jérôme, and Sergent, Claire, 'Conscious, preconscious, and subliminal processing: a testable taxonomy' (2006) 10 *Trends in Cognitive Sciences* 204.

Deigh, John, 'Responsibility', in John Deigh and David Dolinko (eds.), *The Oxford Handbook of Philosophy of Criminal Law* (Oxford: Oxford University Press, 2011), p. 194.

Dempsey, Michele M., 'The object of criminal responsibility', in Paul H. Robinson, Stephen P. Garvey and Kimberly K. Ferzan (eds.), *Criminal Law Conversations* (Oxford: Oxford University Press, 2009), p. 283.

Dennett, Daniel C., *Content and Consciousness* (Abingdon: Routledge, 1969).

Elbow Room: The Varieties of Free Will Worth Wanting (Cambridge, MA: MIT Press, 1984).

The Intentional Stance (Cambridge, MA: MIT Press, 1987).

Consciousness Explained (Boston: Little, Brown, 1991).

Dennis, Ian, 'Reverse onuses and the presumption of innocence: in search of principle' [2005] *Criminal Law Review* 901.

'RIP: the criminal code (1968–2008)' [2009] *Criminal Law Review* 1.

Denno, Deborah W., 'Crime and consciousness: science and involuntary acts' (2002–2003) 97 *Minnesota Law Review* 269.

'Criminal law in a post-Freudian world' [2005] *University of Illinois Law Review* 601.

Dillof, Anthony M., 'Transferred intent: an inquiry into the nature of criminal culpability' (1997–1998) 1 *Buffalo Criminal Law Review* 501.

Dilman, Ilman, *Freud and the Mind* (Oxford: Basil Blackwell, 1984).

Dimock, Susan, 'What are intoxicated offenders responsible for? The "intoxication defense" revisited' (2011) 5 *Criminal Law and Philosophy* 1.

Doris, John, *Lack of Character: Personality and Moral Behaviour* (Cambridge: Cambridge University Press, 2002).

Dressler, Joshua, 'Reflections on excusing wrongdoers: moral theory, new excuses and the Model Penal Code' (1987–1988) 19 *Rutgers Law Journal* 671.

'Does one *mens rea* fit all? Thoughts on Alexander's unified conception of criminal culpability' (2000) 88 *California Law Review* 955.

du Bois-Pedain, Antje, 'The wrongfulness constraint in criminalization' (2014) 8 *Criminal Law and Philosophy* 149.

Duff, R.A., 'Recklessness' [1980] *Criminal Law Review* 282.

'Recklessness and rape' (1981) 3 *Liverpool Law Review* 49.

'Professor Williams and conditional subjectivism' (1982) 41 *Cambridge Law Journal* 273.

'*Caldwell* and *Lawrence*: the retreat from subjectivism' (1983) 3 *Oxford Journal of Legal Studies* 77.

Intention, Agency and Criminal Liability: Philosophy of Action and the Criminal Law (Oxford: Basil Blackwell, 1990).

'Choice, character and criminal liability' (1993) 12 *Law and Philosophy* 345.

Criminal Attempts (Oxford: Oxford University Press, 1996).

'Subjectivism, objectivism and criminal attempts', in A.P. Simester and A.T.H. Smith (eds.), *Harm and Culpability* (Oxford: Clarendon, 1996), p. 19.

'Law, language and community: some preconditions of criminal liability' (1998) 18 *Oxford Journal of Legal Studies* 189.

Punishment, Communication and Community (Oxford: Oxford University Press, 2001).

'Rule-violations and wrongdoing', in Stephen Shute and A.P. Simester (eds.), *Criminal Law Theory: Doctrines of the General Part* (Oxford: Oxford University Press, 2002), p. 47.

'Virtue, vice and criminal liability: do we want an Aristotelian criminal law?' (2002–2003) 6 *Buffalo Criminal Law Review* 147.

'Criminalizing endangerment', in R.A. Duff and Stuart Green (eds.), *Defining Crimes: Essays on the Special Part of the Criminal Law* (Oxford: Oxford University Press, 2005), p. 43.

'Theorizing criminal law: a 25th anniversary essay' (2005) 25 *Oxford Journal of Legal Studies* 353.

Answering for Crime: Responsibility and Liability in the Criminal Law (Oxford: Hart, 2007).

'Whose luck is it anyway?', in C.M.V. Clarkson and Sally Cunningham (eds.), *Criminal Liability for Non-aggressive Death* (Aldershot: Ashgate, 2008), p. 61.

'Towards a modest legal moralism' (2014) 8 *Criminal Law and Philosophy* 217.

Dworkin, Gerald, *The Theory and Practice of Autonomy* (Cambridge: Cambridge University Press, 1988).

Dworkin, Ronald, *Taking Rights Seriously* (Cambridge, MA: Harvard University Press, 1977).

Law's Empire (London: Fontana, 1986).

Justice for Hedgehogs (Cambridge, MA: Belknap, 2011).

Edwards, James R., 'Coming clean about the criminal law' (2011) 5 *Criminal Law and Philosophy* 315.

'An instrumental legal moralism' 3 *Oxford Studies in Philosophy of Law*, forthcoming.

Edwards, James R., and Simester, A.P., 'Wrongfulness and prohibitions' (2014) 8 *Criminal Law and Philosophy* 171.

Ekstrom, Laura W., 'Alienation, autonomy and the self' (2005) 29 *Midwest Studies in Philosophy* 45.

Elliot, Carl, 'Beliefs and responsibility' (1991) 25 *Journal of Value Inquiry* 233.

Enoch, David, Spectre, Levi, and Fisher, Talia, 'Statistical evidence, sensitivity and legal knowledge' (2012) 40 *Philosophy & Public Affairs* 197.

Eshleman, Andrew, 'Responsibility for character' (2004) 32 *Philosophical Topics* 65.

Feinberg, Joel, *Doing and Deserving: Essays in the Theory of Responsibility* (Princeton, NJ: Princeton University Press, 1970).

Feldman, Richard, 'The ethics of belief' (2000) 60 *Philosophy and Phenomenological Research* 667.

Ferguson, Pamela R., 'Controversial aspects of the law of rape: an Anglo-Scottish comparison', in Robert F. Hunter (ed.), *Justice and Crime: Essays in Honour of the Right Honourable the Lord Emslie* (Edinburgh: T&T Clark, 1993), p. 180.

Ferguson, Pamela R., and McDiarmid, Claire, *Scots Criminal Law: A Critical Analysis*, 2nd edn. (Edinburgh: Edinburgh University Press, 2014).

Ferzan, Kimberly K., 'Opaque recklessness' (2000–2001) 91 *Journal of Criminal Law & Criminology* 597.

'Don't abandon the Model Penal Code yet! Thinking through Simons's rethinking' (2002–2003) 6 *Buffalo Criminal Law Review* 185.

'Holistic culpability' (2006–2007) 28 *Cardozo Law Review* 2523.

'Act, agency and indifference: the foundations of *Criminal Responsibility*' (2007) 10 *New Criminal Law Review* 441.

'The structure of criminal law' (2009) 28 *Criminal Justice Ethics* 223.

Festinger, Leon, *A Theory of Cognitive Dissonance* (Stanford, CA: Stanford University Press, 1957).

Field, Stewart, and Lynn, Mervyn, 'The capacity for recklessness' (1992) 12 *Legal Studies* 74.

Fields, Lloyd, 'Moral beliefs and blameworthiness' (1994) 69 *Philosophy* 397.

Findlay, Mark, Odgers, Stephen and Yeo, Stanley, *Australian Criminal Justice*, 5th edn. (Oxford: Oxford University Press, 2014).

Fine, Robert P., and Cohen, Gary M., 'Is negligence a defensible basis for penal liability?' (1966–1967) 16 *Buffalo Law Review* 749.

Finkelstein, Claire, 'The inefficiency of *mens rea*' (2000) 88 *California Law Review* 895.

'Is risk a harm?' (2002–2003) 151 *University of Pennsylvania Law Review* 963.

'Responsibility for unintended consequences' (2005) 2 *Ohio State Journal of Criminal Law* 579.

Finnis, John, *Natural Law and Natural Rights*, 2nd edn. (Oxford: Oxford University Press, 2011).

Fischer, John M., 'The importance of Frankfurt-style argument' (2007) 57 *The Philosophical Quarterly* 464.

Fischer, John M., and Ravizza, Mark, *Responsibility and Control: A Theory of Moral Responsibility* (Cambridge: Cambridge University Press, 1998).

Fischer, John M., and Tognazzini, Neal A., 'The truth about tracing' (2009) 43 *Noûs* 531.

Fitzgerald, P.J., and Williams, Glanville, 'Carelessness, indifference and recklessness: two replies' (1962) 25 *Modern Law Review* 49.

Fletcher, George P., 'The theory of criminal negligence: a comparative analysis' (1970–1971) 119 *University of Pennsylvania Law Review* 401.

'Fairness and utility in tort theory' (1971–1972) 85 *Harvard Law Review* 537.

Rethinking Criminal Law (Boston: Little, Brown, 1978).

'What is punishment imposed for?' (1994) 5 *Journal of Contemporary Legal Issues* 101.

Basic Concepts of Criminal Law (Oxford: Oxford University Press, 1998).

'The fault of not knowing' (2002) 3 *Theoretical Inquiries in Law* 265.

The Grammar of Criminal Law: American, Comparative and International (Oxford: Oxford University Press, 2007).

'Remembrance of essays past', in Russell L. Christopher (ed.), *Fletcher's Essays on Criminal Law* (Oxford: Oxford University Press, 2013), p. 269.

France, Simon, 'A reckless approach to liability' (1988) 18 *Victoria University of Wellington Law Review* 141.

'The mental element' (1990) 20 *Victoria University of Wellington Law Review Monograph* 43.

'Reforming criminal law – New Zealand's 1989 code' [1990] *Criminal Law Review* 827.

Frankfurt, Harry G., *The Importance of What We Care About* (Cambridge: Cambridge University Press, 1988).

The Reasons of Love (Princeton, NJ: Princeton University Press, 2004).

Freud, Sigmund, *The Standard Edition of the Complete Psychological Works of Sigmund Freud*, ed. J. Strachey, 24 vols. (London: Vintage, 2001), vol. 19.

Fruchtman, Earl, 'Recklessness and the limits of *mens rea*: beyond orthodox subjectivism' (1986–1987) 29 *Criminal Law Quarterly* 315, 421 (published in two parts).

Galligan, D.J., 'Responsibility for recklessness' (1978) 31 *Current Legal Problems* 55.

Gans, Jeremy, *Modern Criminal Law of Australia* (Cambridge: Cambridge University Press, 2011).

Gardner, John, 'Criminal law and the uses of theory: a reply to Laing' (1994) 14 *Oxford Journal of Legal Studies* 217.

'On the general part of the criminal law', in R.A. Duff (ed.), *Philosophy and the Criminal Law: Principle and Critique* (Cambridge: Cambridge University Press, 1998), p. 205.

'The mysterious case of the reasonable person' (2001) 51 *University of Toronto Law Journal* 273.

'Wrongs and faults', in A.P. Simester (ed.), *Appraising Strict Liability* (Oxford: Oxford University Press, 2005), p. 51.

Offences and Defences: Selected Essays in the Philosophy of Criminal Law (Oxford: Oxford University Press, 2007).

'Ashworth on principles', in Lucia Zedner and Julian V. Roberts (eds.), *Principles and Values in Criminal Law and Criminal Justice: Essays in Honour of Andrew Ashworth* (Oxford: Oxford University Press, 2012), p. 3.

Gardner, John, and Jung, Heike, 'Making sense of *mens rea*: Antony Duff's account' (1991) 11 *Oxford Journal of Legal Studies* 559.

Gardner, Simon, 'Recklessness refined' (1993) 109 *Law Quarterly Review* 21.

Garvey, Stephen P., 'Passion's puzzle' (2004–2005) 90 *Iowa Law Review* 1677.

'What's wrong with involuntary manslaughter?' (2006–2007) 85 *Texas Law Review* 333.

'Fatally circular? Not!', in Paul H. Robinson, Stephen P. Garvey and Kimberly K. Ferzan (eds.), *Criminal Law Conversations* (Oxford: Oxford University Press, 2009), p. 286.

Gendler, Tamar S., 'Alief and belief' (2008) 105 *Journal of Philosophy* 634.

'Alief in action (and reaction)' (2008) 23 *Mind and Language* 552.

Intuition, Imagination and Philosophical Methodology (Oxford: Oxford University Press, 2010).

Gettier, Edmund L., 'Is justified true belief knowledge?' (1963) 23 *Analysis* 181.

Ginet, Carl, 'The epistemic requirements for moral responsibility' (2000) 34 *Noûs* 267.

Glazebrook, P.R. 'Criminal negligence' (1984) 43 *Cambridge Law Journal* 1.

Gordon, Gerald H., *The Criminal Law of Scotland* (Edinburgh: SULI/W. Green & Sons, 1968).

'Subjective and objective *mens rea*' (1974–1975) 17 *Criminal Law Quarterly* 355.

The Criminal Law of Scotland, 3rd edn., ed. M.G.A. Christie, 2 vols. (Edinburgh: SULI/W. Green, 2000–2001).

Gough, Stephen, 'Surviving without *Majewski*?' [2002] *Criminal Law Review* 719.

Grant, Isabel, 'Second chances: bill C-72 and the Charter' (1995) 33 *Osgoode Hall Law Journal* 379.

Greenawalt, Kent, *Law and Objectivity* (New York: Oxford University Press, 1992).

Griew, Edward, 'Consistency, communication and codification – reflections on two *mens rea* words', in P.R. Glazebrook (ed.), *Reshaping the Criminal Law: Essays in Honour of Glanville Williams* (London: Stevens, 1978), p. 57.

'Reckless damage and reckless driving: living with *Caldwell* and *Lawrence*' [1981] *Criminal Law Review* 743.

Gross, Hyman, *A Theory of Criminal Justice* (New York: Oxford University Press, 1979).

Crime and Punishment: A Concise Moral Critique (Oxford: Oxford University Press, 2012).

Haji, Ishtiyaque, 'An epistemic dimension of blameworthiness' (1997) 57 *Journal of Philosophy & Phenomenological Research* 523.

Hall, Jerome, *General Principles of Criminal Law*, 2nd edn. (Indianapolis, IN: Bobbs-Merrill, 1960).

'Negligent behavior should be excluded from criminal liability' (1963) 63 *Columbia Law Review* 532.

Hall, Richard J., and Johnson, Charles R., 'The epistemic duty to seek more evidence' (1998) 35 *American Philosophical Quarterly* 129.

Halpin, Andrew W., *Definition in the Criminal Law* (Oxford: Hart, 2004).

Hamer, David, 'The presumption of innocence and reverse burdens: a balancing act' (2007) 66 *Cambridge Law Journal* 143.

Hampton, Jean, 'The moral education theory of punishment' (1984) 13 *Philosophy and Public Affairs* 208.

'*Mens rea*', in Ellen F. Paul, Fred D. Miller and Jeffrey Paul (eds.), *Crime, Culpability and Remedy* (Oxford: Basil Blackwell, 1990), p. 1.

Harman, Gilbert, 'Moral philosophy meets social psychology: virtue ethics and the fundamental attribution error' (1999) 99 *Proceedings of the Aristotelian Society* 315.

Hart, H.L.A., *Punishment and Responsibility: Essays in the Philosophy of Law*, 2nd edn. (Oxford: Oxford University Press, 2008).

Hautamaki, Edward W., 'The element of *mens rea* in recklessness and "criminal negligence"' (1951–1952) 2 *Duke Bar Journal* 55.

Hegel, Georg W.F., *Philosophy of Right*, trans. S.W. Dyde (Mineola, NY: Dover Publications, 2005 [original: 1896]).

Hellman, Deborah, 'Wilfully blind for good reason' (2009) 3 *Criminal Law and Philosophy* 301.

Hemming, Andrew, 'Reasserting the place of objective tests in criminal responsibility: ending the supremacy of subjective tests' (2011) 13 *University of Notre Dame Australia Law Review* 69.

Hetherington, Stephen, 'The Gettier problem', in Sven Bernecker and Duncan Pritchard (eds.), *The Routledge Companion to Epistemology* (London: Routledge, 2011), p. 119.

Hieronymi, Pamela, 'Controlling attitudes' (2006) 87 *Pacific Philosophical Quarterly* 45.

'Responsibility for believing' (2008) 161 *Synthese* 357.

Holmes, Oliver W., *The Common Law* (Boston: Little, Brown, 1881).

Hookway, Christopher, 'Epistemic norms and theoretical deliberation' (1999) 12 *Ratio* 380.

Horder, Jeremy, 'Cognition, emotion and criminal culpability' (1990) 106 *Law Quarterly Review* 469.

'Criminal culpability: the possibility of a general theory' (1993) 12 *Law and Philosophy* 193.

'A critique of the correspondence principle in criminal law' [1995] *Criminal Law Review* 759.

'Gross negligence and criminal culpability' (1997) 47 *University of Toronto Law Journal* 495.

'Two histories and four hidden principles of *mens rea*' (1997) 113 *Law Quarterly Review* 95.

'Questioning the correspondence principle: a reply' [1999] *Criminal Law Review* 206.

Homicide and the Politics of Law Reform (Oxford: Oxford University Press, 2012).

Hossack, Keith, *The Metaphysics of Knowledge* (Oxford: Oxford University Press, 2007).

Huigens, Kyron, 'Virtue and inculpation' (1994–1995) 108 *Harvard Law Review* 1423.

'Virtue and criminal negligence' (1997–1998) 1 *Buffalo Criminal Law Review* 431.

Hume, David, *A Treatise of Human Nature*, 2 vols., ed. David F. Norton and Mary J. Norton (Oxford: Oxford University Press, 2007), vol. 1.

Hunter, J.F.M., 'Believing' (1980) 5 *Midwest Studies in Philosophy* 239.

Hurd, Heidi M., 'What in the world is wrong?' (1994) 5 *Journal of Contemporary Legal Issues* 157.

'The deontology of negligence' (1996) 76 *Boston University Law Review* 249.

'Introduction: symposium on *Crime and Culpability*' (2010) 29 *Law and Philosophy* 371.

Hursthouse, Rosalind, *On Virtue Ethics* (Oxford: Oxford University Press, 1999).

Husak, Douglas N., *Philosophy of Criminal Law* (Totowa, NJ: Rowman & Littlefield, 1987).

'Ignorance of law and the duties of citizenship' (1994) 14 *Legal Studies* 105.

'Reasonable risk creation and overinclusive legislation' (1997–1998) 1 *Buffalo Criminal Law Review* 599.

'Does criminal liability require an act?', in R.A. Duff (ed.), *Philosophy and the Criminal Law: Principle and Critique* (Cambridge: Cambridge University Press, 1998), p. 60.

'Retribution in criminal law theory' (2000) 37 *San Diego Law Review* 959.

'Strict liability, justice and proportionality', in A.P. Simester (ed.), *Appraising Strict Liability* (Oxford: Oxford University Press, 2005), p. 81.

Overcriminalization: The Limits of the Criminal Law (Oxford: Oxford University Press, 2007).

'Answering Duff: R.A. Duff's *Answering for Crime*' (2010) 29 *Law and Philosophy* 101.

Philosophy of Criminal Law: Selected Essays (Oxford: Oxford University Press, 2010).

'The alleged act requirement in criminal law', in John Deigh and David Dolinko (eds.), *The Oxford Handbook of Philosophy of Criminal Law* (Oxford: Oxford University Press, 2011), p. 119.

'Negligence, belief, blame and criminal liability: the special case of forgetting' (2011) 5 *Criminal Law and Philosophy* 199.

'"Broad" culpability and the retributive dream' (2011–2012) 9 *Ohio State Journal of Criminal Law* 449.

'Distraction and negligence', in Lucia Zedner and Julian V. Roberts (eds.), *Principles and Values in Criminal Law and Criminal Justice* (Oxford: Oxford University Press, 2012), p. 81.

'Preventive detention as punishment? Some potential obstacles', in Andrew Ashworth, Lucia Zedner and Patrick Tomlin (eds.), *Prevention and the Limits of the Criminal Law* (Oxford: Oxford University Press, 2013), p. 178.

Husak, Douglas N., and Callender, Craig A., 'Wilful ignorance, knowledge, and the "equal culpability" thesis: a study of the deeper significance of the principle of legality' [1994] *Wisconsin Law Review* 29.

Husak, Douglas N., and McLaughlin, Brian P., 'Time-frames, voluntary acts, and strict liability' (1993) 12 *Law and Philosophy* 95.

Ibbetson, David J., 'Recklessness restored' (2004) 63 *Cambridge Law Journal* 13.

Ichikawa, Jonathan J., and Steup, Matthias, 'The analysis of knowledge', in Edward N. Zalta (ed.), *The Stanford Encyclopaedia of Philosophy* (Fall 2013 Edition), available at http://plato.stanford.edu/entries/knowledge-analysis/.

Jackson, Frank, 'Non-cognitivism, normativity, belief' (1999) 12 *Ratio* 420.

Jacobs, Jonathan, *Choosing Character: Responsibility for Virtue and Vice* (Ithaca, NY: Cornell University Press, 2001).

Jareborg, Nils, *Scraps of Penal Theory* (Uppsala: Iustus Förlag AB, 2002).

Johnson, Eric A., 'Is the idea of objective probability incoherent?' (2010) 29 *Law and Philosophy* 419.

'Knowledge, risk and wrongdoing: the Model Penal Code's forgotten answer to the riddle of objective probability' (2011) 59 *Buffalo Law Review* 507.

Johnson, Oliver A., 'The standard definition' (1980) 5 *Midwest Studies in Philosophy* 113.

Jones, Timothy H. 'The Scottish law of murder' (1989) 105 *Law Quarterly Review* 516.

Judicial Studies Committee, *Jury Manual: Some Notes for the Guidance of the Judiciary* (2012), available at http://www.scotland-judiciary.org.uk/24/720/Jury-Manual-Published.

Kadish, Sandford H., *Blame and Punishment: Essays in the Criminal Law* (New York: Collier Macmillan, 1987).

Kane, Robert, 'Responsibility, luck and chance: reflections on free will and indeterminism', in Gary Watson (ed.), *Free Will*, 2nd edn. (Oxford: Oxford University Press, 2003), p. 299.

Katz, Leo, *Bad Acts and Guilty Minds: Conundrums of the Criminal Law* (Chicago, IL: University of Chicago Press, 1987).

'Harm and justification in negligence' (2003) 4 *Theoretical Inquiries in Law* 397.

Kaveny, Cathleen M., 'Inferring intention from foresight' (2004) 120 *Law Quarterly Review* 81.

Keedy, Edwin R., 'Ignorance and mistake in the criminal law' (1908–1909) 22 *Harvard Law Review* 75.

Keiter, Mitchell, 'Just say no excuse: the rise and fall of the intoxication defense' (1997) 87 *Journal of Criminal Law & Criminology* 482.

Kelly, Thomas, 'The rationality of belief and some other propositional attitudes' (2002) 100 *Philosophical Studies* 163.

Kennett, Jeanette, *Agency and Responsibility: A Common-Sense Moral Psychology* (Oxford: Oxford University Press, 2001).

Kenny, A.J.P., *Freewill and Responsibility* (London: Routledge, 1978).

Kenny, C.S., *Outlines of Criminal Law*, 15th edn., ed. C.G. Phillips (Cambridge University Press, 1947).

Outlines of Criminal Law, 16th edn., ed. J.W.C. Turner (Cambridge: Cambridge University Press, 1952).

Kimel, Dori, 'Inadvertent recklessness and the criminal law' (2004) 120 *Law Quarterly Review* 548.

King, Matt, 'The problem with negligence' (2009) 35 *Social Theory and Practice* 577.

Kitcher, Philip, 'The naturalists return' (1992) 101 *Philosophical Review* 53.

Korsgaard, Christine M., *The Sources of Normativity* (Cambridge: Cambridge University Press, 1996).

Kumar, Rahul, 'Who can be wronged?' (2003) 31 *Philosophy & Public Affairs* 99.

Kupperman, Joel J., *Character* (Oxford: Oxford University Press, 1991).

Kvanvig, Jonathan L., 'Subjective justification' (1984) 93 *Mind* 71.

Lacey, Nicola, *State Punishment: Political Principles and Community Values* (London: Routledge, 1994).

'Contingency, coherence and conceptualism: reflections on the encounter between "critique" and "the philosophy of the criminal law"', in R.A. Duff (ed.), *Philosophy and the Criminal Law: Principle and Critique* (Cambridge: Cambridge University Press, 1998), p. 9.

LaFave, Wayne R., *Criminal Law*, 5th edn. (St. Paul, MN: West, 2010).

Lanham, David, 'Murder, recklessness and grievous bodily harm' (1978) 2 *Criminal Law Journal* 255.

'Wilful blindness and the criminal law' (1985) 9 *Criminal Law Journal* 261.

Law Commission, *A Criminal Code for England and Wales*, 2 vols. (Law Com. No. 177, 1989), vol. 1.

Legislating the Criminal Code: Offences against the Person and General Principles (Law Com. No. 218, 1993).

Lee, Cynthia, *Murder and the Reasonable Man: Passion and Fear in the Criminal Courtroom* (New York: New York University Press, 2003).

Leigh, L.H., 'Recklessness after *Reid*' (1993) 56 *Modern Law Review* 208.

Leipold, Andrew D., 'A case for criminal negligence' (2010) 29 *Law and Philosophy* 455.

Leverick, Fiona, *Killing in Self-Defence* (Oxford: Oxford University Press, 2006).

Levy, Neil, 'Restoring control: comments on George Sher' (2008) 36 *Philosophia* 213.

Consciousness and Moral Responsibility (Oxford: Oxford University Press, 2014).

Locke, John, *An Essay Concerning Human Understanding* (Oxford: Oxford University Press, 1975 [original: 1690]).

Low, Peter W., 'The Model Penal Code, the common law and mistakes of fact: recklessness, negligence or strict liability?' (1987–1988) 19 *Rutgers Law Journal* 539.

Luban, David, 'Contrived ignorance' (1998–1999) 87 *Georgia Law Journal* 957.

MacCormick, Neil, *Rhetoric and the Rule of Law* (Oxford: Oxford University Press, 2005).

MacMillan-Brown, Heather, 'No longer *Leary* about intoxication: in the aftermath of *R* v. *Daviault*' (1995) 59 *Saskatchewan Law Review* 311.

Marcus, Ruth B., 'Some revisionary proposals about belief and believing' (1990) 50 *Philosophy and Phenomenological Research* 133.

Matthiesson, Sophie, 'Should the law deal with reckless HIV infection as a criminal offence or as a matter of public health?' (2010) 21 *King's Law Journal* 123.

Mayers-Shulz, Blake, and Schwitzgebel, Eric, 'Knowing that *p* without believing that *p*' (2013) 47 *Noûs* 371.

McAuley, Finbarr, and McCutcheon, J. Paul, *Criminal Liability: A Grammar* (Dublin: Round Hall Sweet & Maxwell, 2000).

McBride, Mark, 'Reply to Pardo: unsafe legal knowledge?' (2011) 17 *Legal Theory* 67.

McCarthy, David, 'Rights, explanation and risks' (1997) 107 *Ethics* 205.

McCrone, John, *Going Inside: A Tour Round a Single Moment of Consciousness* (London: Faber, 1999).

McDiarmid, Claire, '"Something wicked this way comes": the *mens rea* of murder in Scots law' 2012 *Juridical Review* 283.

McHugh, Conor, and Whiting, Daniel, 'The normativity of belief' (2014) 74 *Analysis* 698.

Mele, Alred R., *Autonomous Agents: From Self-Control to Autonomy* (Oxford: Oxford University Press, 2001).

Mewett, Alan W., 'The shifting basis of criminal law' (1963) 9 *McGill Law Journal* 124.

Michaels, Alan C., 'Acceptance: the missing mental state' (1997–1998) 71 *Southern California Law Review* 953.

Milgram, Stanley, *Obedience to Authority: An Experimental View* (London: Tavistock, 1974).

Mitchell, Barry, 'Culpably indifferent murder' (1996) 25 *Anglo-American Law Review* 64.

'Recklessness could still be a state of mind' (1988) 52 *Journal of Criminal Law* 300.

Mitchell, Barry, and Mackay, R.D., 'Investigating involuntary manslaughter: an empirical study of 127 cases' (2011) 31 *Oxford Journal of Legal Studies* 165.

Mole, Christopher, 'Attention and consciousness' (2008) 15 *Journal of Consciousness Studies* 86.

Montmarquet, James A., 'Culpable ignorance and excuses' (1995) 80 *Philosophical Studies* 41.

Moore, Michael S., 'Responsibility and the unconscious' (1979–1980) 53 *Southern California Law Review* 1563.

Law and Psychiatry: Rethinking the Relationship (Cambridge: Cambridge University Press, 1984).

Act and Crime: The Philosophy of Action and Its Implications for Criminal Law (Oxford: Oxford University Press, 1993).

Placing Blame: A Theory of the Criminal Law (Oxford: Oxford University Press, 1997).

Causation and Responsibility: An Essay in Law, Morals and Metaphysics (Oxford: Oxford University Press, 2009).

'Intention as a marker of moral culpability and legal punishability', in R.A. Duff and Stuart Green (eds.), *Philosophical Foundations of Criminal Law* (Oxford: Oxford University Press, 2011), p. 179.

Moore, Michael S., and Hurd, Heidi M., 'The culpability of negligence', in Rowan Cruft, Matthew H. Kramer and Mark R. Reiff (eds.), *Crime, Punishment and Responsibility: The Jurisprudence of Antony Duff* (Oxford: Oxford University Press, 2011), p. 311.

'Punishing the awkward, the stupid, the weak, and the selfish: the culpability of negligence' (2011) 5 *Criminal Law and Philosophy* 147.

Moran, Mayo, *Rethinking the Reasonable Person: An Egalitarian Reconstruction of the Objective Standard* (Oxford: Oxford University Press, 2003).

Moreau, Sophia R., 'Reasons and character' (2005) 115 *Ethics* 272.

Morkel, Dan W., 'On the distinction between recklessness and conscious negligence' (1982) 30 *American Journal of Comparative Law* 325.

Morris, J.M., 'The structure of criminal law and deterrence' [1986] *Criminal Law Review* 524.

Morse, Stephen J., 'Culpability and control' (1994) 142 *University of Pennsylvania Law Review* 1587.

'Rationality and responsibility' (2000–2001) 74 *Southern California Law Review* 251.

'Reasons, results and criminal responsibility' [2004] *University of Illinois Law Review* 363.

Nino, C.S., 'A consensual theory of punishment' (1983) 12 *Philosophy and Public Affairs* 289.

Norrie, Alan W., *Law, Ideology and Punishment: Retrieval and Critique of the Liberal Idea of Criminal Justice* (Dordrecht: Kluwer, 1991).

'Subjectivism, objectivism and the limits of criminal recklessness' (1992) 12 *Oxford Journal of Legal Studies* 45.

Law and the Beautiful Soul (London: Glasshouse, 2005).

'Between orthodox subjectivism and moral contextualism: intention and the consultation paper' [2006] *Criminal Law Review* 486.

'Alan Brudner and the dialectics of criminal law' (2011) 14 *New Criminal Law Review* 449.

Crime, Reason and History: A Critical Introduction to Criminal Law, 3rd edn. (Cambridge: Cambridge University Press, 2014).

Nourse, V.F. 'Hearts and minds: understanding the new culpability' (2002–2003) 6 *Buffalo Criminal Law Review* 361.

Nozick, Robert, *Anarchy, State and Utopia* (Oxford: Basil Blackwell, 1974).

Philosophical Explanations (Cambridge, MA: Belknap, 1981).

Nussbaum, Martha C., *Upheavals of Thought: The Intelligence of Emotions* (Cambridge: Cambridge University Press, 2001).

Hiding from Humanity: Disgust, Shame and the Law (Princeton, NJ: Princeton University Press, 2004).

Oberdiek, Hans, 'Intention and foresight in criminal law' (1972) 81 *Mind* 389.

Oberdiek, John, 'Towards a right against risking' (2009) 28 *Law and Philosophy* 367.

'The moral significance of risking' (2012) 18 *Legal Theory* 339.

O'Brien, Lucy, 'Imagination and the motivational view of belief' (2005) 65 *Analysis* 55.

O'Hearn, P.J.T. 'Criminal negligence: an analysis in depth' (1964–1965) 7 *Criminal Law Quarterly* 27, 407 (published in two parts).

Ormerod, David, and Laird, Karl, *Smith and Hogan: Criminal Law*, 14th edn. (Oxford: Oxford University Press, 2015).

Owens, David J. 'Does belief have an aim?' (2003) 115 *Philosophical Studies* 283.

Pardo, Michael S., 'The Gettier problem and legal proof' (2010) 16 *Legal Theory* 37.

'More on the Gettier problem and legal proof: unsafe nonknowledge does not mean knowledge must be safe' (2011) 17 *Legal Theory* 75.

Pardo, Michael S., and Patterson, Dennis, *Minds, Brains and Law: The Conceptual Foundations of Law and Neuroscience* (Oxford: Oxford University Press, 2013).

Perkins, Rollin M., '"Knowledge" as a *mens rea* requirement' (1977–1978) 29 *Hastings Law Journal* 953.

Perry, Stephen, 'Risk, harm and responsibility', in David G. Owen (ed.), *The Philosophical Foundations of Tort Law* (Oxford: Oxford University Press, 1997), p. 321.

'Harm, history and counterfactuals' (2003) 40 *San Diego Law Review* 1283.

'Risk, harm, interests and rights', in Tim Lewens (ed.), *Risk: Philosophical Perspectives* (London: Routledge, 2007), p. 190.

Pettit, Philip, *The Common Mind: An Essay on Psychology, Society and Politics* (Oxford: Oxford University Press, 1993).

Pettit, Philip, and Smith, Michael, 'Freedom in belief and desire' (1996) 93 *Journal of Philosophy* 429.

Pickard, Toni, 'Culpable mistakes and rape: relating *mens rea* to the crime' (1980) 30 *University of Toronto Law Journal* 75.

Pillsbury, Samuel H., 'The meaning of deserved punishment: an essay on choice, character and responsibility' (1991–1992) 67 *Indiana Law Journal* 719.

'Crimes of indifference' (1997) 49 *Rutgers Law Review* 105.

Pincoffs, Edmund L., 'Legal responsibility and moral character' (1972–1973) 19 *Wayne Law Review* 905.

Plantinga, Alvin, *Warrant: The Current Debate* (Oxford: Oxford University Press, 1993).

Posner, Richard, 'The jurisprudence of skepticism' (1987–1988) 86 *Michigan Law Review* 827.

Price, H.H., *Belief* (London: George Allen & Unwin, 1969).

Pritchard, Duncan, *Epistemic Luck* (Oxford: Oxford University Press, 2005).

Pritchard, H.A., 'Knowing and believing', in A.P. Griffiths (ed.), *Knowledge and Belief* (Oxford: Oxford University Press, 1967), p. 60.

Moral Writings, ed. Jim MacAdam (Oxford: Clarendon, 2002).

Quigley, Tim, 'Specific and general nonsense?' (1987–1988) 11 *Dalhousie Law Journal* 75.

Rabin, Robert L., 'The fault of not knowing: a comment' (2003) 4 *Theoretical Inquiries in Law* 427.

Rawls, John, *Political Liberalism* (New York: Columbia University Press, 1993).

A Theory of Justice: Revised Edition (Cambridge, MA: Harvard University Press, 1999).

Raz, Joseph, 'Autonomy, freedom and the harm principle', in Ruth Gavison (ed.), *Issues in Contemporary Legal Philosophy: The Influence of H.L.A. Hart* (Oxford: Clarendon, 1987), p. 313.

The Morality of Freedom (Oxford: Clarendon, 1988).

'Facing up: a reply' (1988–1989) 62 *Southern California Law Review* 1153.

Practical Reason and Norms, rev. edn. (Oxford: Oxford University Press, 1999).

Engaging Reason: On the Theory of Value and Action (Oxford: Oxford University Press, 2002).

The Authority of Law: Essays on Law and Morality, 2nd edn. (Oxford: Oxford University Press, 2009).

'Responsibility and the negligence standard' (2010) 30 *Oxford Journal of Legal Studies* 1.

From Normativity to Responsibility (Oxford: Oxford University Press, 2011).

Reiff, Mark R., *Punishment, Compensation and Law: A Theory of Enforceability* (Cambridge: Cambridge University Press, 2005).

Renzo, Massimo, 'Responsibility and answerability in the criminal law', in R.A. Duff et al. (eds.), *The Constitution of the Criminal Law* (Oxford: Oxford University Press, 2013), p. 209.

Ristroph, Alice, 'When freedom isn't free' (2011) 14 *New Criminal Law Review* 468.

Roach, Kent, 'Dialogue or defiance: legislative reversals of Supreme Court decisions in Canada and the United States' (2006) 4 *International Journal of Constitutional Law* 347.

Roberts, Paul, 'The presumption of innocence brought home: *Kebilene* deconstructed' (2002) 118 *Law Quarterly Review* 41.

Robinson, Paul H., 'A functional analysis of the criminal law' (1994) 88 *Northwestern University Law Review* 857.

'Legality and discretion in the distribution of criminal sanctions' (1988) 25 *Harvard Journal on Legislation* 393.

'Rules of conduct and principles of adjudication' (1990) 57 *University of Chicago Law Review* 729.

Structure and Function in Criminal Law (Oxford: Oxford University Press, 1997).

'Structuring criminal codes to fulfill their function' (2000–2001) 4 *Buffalo Criminal Law Review* 1.

'Fair notice and fair adjudication: two kinds of legality' (2005–2006) 154 *University of Pennsylvania Law Review* 335.

Distributive Principles of Criminal Law: Who Should Be Punished, How Much? (Oxford: Oxford University Press, 2008).

Ruimschotel, Dirk, 'The psychological reality of intentional and negligent criminal acts', in Peter J. van Koppen, Dick J. Hessing and Grat van den Heuvel (eds.), *Lawyers on Psychology and Psychologists on Law* (Lisse: Swets & Zeitlinger, 1988), p. 83.

Ryan, Sharon, 'Doxastic compatibilism and the ethics of belief' (2003) 114 *Philosophical Studies* 47.

Ryle, Gilbert, 'Ordinary language' (1953) 62 *Philosophical Review* 167.

The Concept of Mind (London: Penguin Books, 1999).

Sabini, John, and Silver, Maury, 'Lack of character? Situationism critiqued' (2005) 115 *Ethics* 535.

Sartwell, Crispin, 'Knowledge is merely true belief' (1991) 28 *American Philosophical Quarterly* 157.

Scanlon, T.M., 'The significance of choice', in Sterling M. McMurrin (ed.), *The Tanner Lectures on Human Values, VIII* (Cambridge: Cambridge University Press, 1988), p. 149.

What We Owe to Each Other (Cambridge, MA: Belknap, 1998).

The Difficulty of Tolerance (Cambridge: Cambridge University Press, 2003).

Schloenhardt, Andreas, *Queensland Criminal Law*, 4th edn. (Oxford: Oxford University Press, 2015).

Schulhoffer, Stephen J., 'Harm and punishment: a critique of emphasis on the results of conduct in the criminal law' (1973–1974) 122 *University of Pennsylvania Law Review* 1497.

Schwitzgebel, Eric, 'In-between believing' (2001) 51 *Philosophical Quarterly* 76.

'A phenomenal, dispositional account of belief' (2002) 36 *Noûs* 249.

'Knowing your own beliefs' (2009) 39(1) *Canadian Journal of Philosophy* 41.

'Acting contrary to our professed beliefs or the gulf between occurrent judgment and dispositional belief' (2010) 91 *Pacific Philosophical Quarterly* 531.

Searle, John R., *Intentionality: An Essay in the Philosophy of Mind* (Cambridge: Cambridge University Press, 1983).

The Mystery of Consciousness (New York: New York Review of Books, 1997).

Mind: A Brief Introduction (Oxford: Oxford University Press, 2004).

Shanahan, Michael J., Smith, Paul E., and Ryan, Soraya, *Carter's Criminal Law of Queensland*, 16th edn. (Chatswood, NSW: LexisNexis Butterworths, 2006).

Sheehy, Elizabeth, 'The intoxication defence in Canada: why women should care' (1996) 23 *Contemporary Drug Problems* 595.

Sher, George, *Desert* (Princeton, NJ: Princeton University Press, 1987).

Who Knew? Responsibility without Awareness (Oxford: Oxford University Press, 2009).

Shiner, Roger A., 'Intoxication and responsibility' (1990) 13 *International Journal of Law and Psychiatry* 9.

Shute, Stephen, 'Second Law Commission consultation paper on consent: (1) something old, something new, something borrowed: three aspects of the project' [1996] *Criminal Law Review* 684.

'Knowledge and belief in the criminal law', in Stephen Shute and A.P. Simester (eds.), *Criminal Law Theory: Doctrines of the General Part* (Oxford: Oxford University Press, 2001), p. 171.

Simester, A.P., 'Why omissions are special' (1995) 1 *Legal Theory* 311.

'On the so-called requirement for voluntary action' (1997–1998) 2 *Buffalo Criminal Law Review* 403.

'Can negligence be culpable?', in Jeremy Horder (ed.), *Oxford Essays in Jurisprudence: Fourth Series* (Oxford: Oxford University Press, 2000), p. 85.

Appraising Strict Liability (Oxford: Oxford University Press, 2005).

'Responsibility for inadvertent acts' (2005) 2 *Ohio State Journal of Criminal Law* 601.

'Intoxication is never a defence' [2009] *Criminal Law Review* 3.

'A disintegrated theory of culpability', in Dennis J. Baker and Jeremy Horder (eds.), *The Sanctity of Life and the Criminal Law: The Legacy of Glanville Williams* (Cambridge: Cambridge University Press, 2013), p. 178.

Simester, A.P., and Brookbanks, Warren J., *Principles of Criminal Law*, 4th edn. (Wellington: Thomson Reuters, 2012).

Simester, A.P., Spencer, J.R., Sullivan, G.R., and Virgo, V.J., *Simester and Sullivan's Criminal Law: Theory and Doctrine*, 5th edn. (Oxford: Hart, 2013).

Simons, Kenneth W., 'Rethinking mental states' (1992) 72 *Boston University Law Review* 463.

'Culpability and retributive theory: the problem of criminal negligence' (1994) 5 *Journal of Contemporary Legal Issues* 365.

'Deontology, negligence, tort and crime' (1996) 76 *Boston University Law Review* 273.

'Dimensions of negligence in criminal and tort law' (2002) 3 *Theoretical Inquiries in Law* 283.

'Does punishment for "culpable indifference" simply punish for "bad character"? Examining the requisite connection between *mens rea* and *actus reus*' (2002–2003) *Buffalo Criminal Law Review* 219.

'Should the Model Penal Code's *mens rea* provisions be amended?' (2003) 1 *Ohio State Journal of Criminal Law* 179.

'Retributivism refined – or run amok?' (2010) 77 *University of Chicago Law Review* 551.

'When is negligent inadvertence culpable?' (2011) 5 *Criminal Law and Philosophy* 97.

Singer, Richard, 'On classicism and dissonance in the criminal law: a reply to Professor Meir Dan-Cohen' (1986) 77 *Journal of Criminal Law and Criminology* 69.

Sistare, C.T., 'Models of responsibility in criminal theory: comment on Baker' (1988–1989) 7 *Law and Philosophy* 295.

Skinner, B.F., *Science and Human Behavior* (New York: Macmillan, 1953).

Smith, A.T.H., 'Error and mistake of law in Anglo-American criminal law' (1985) 14 *Anglo-American Law Review* 3.

Smith, Angela M., 'Responsibility for attitudes: activity and passivity in mental life' (2005) 115 *Ethics* 236.

'Control, responsibility and moral assessment' (2008) 138 *Philosophical Studies* 367.

Smith, Holly, 'Culpable ignorance' (1983) 92 *The Philosophical Review* 543.

'Non-tracing cases of culpable ignorance' (2011) 5 *Criminal Law and Philosophy* 115.

Smith, J.C., 'The guilty mind in the criminal law' (1960) 76 *Law Quarterly Review* 78.

'Subjective or objective? Ups and downs of the test of criminal liability in England' (1981–1982) 27 *Villanova Law Review* 1179.

Justification and Excuse in the Criminal Law (London: Stevens, 1989).

Smith, James W., 'Impossibility and morals' (1961) 70 *Mind* 362.

Smith, K.J.M. *Lawyers, Legislators and Theorists: Developments in English Criminal Jurisprudence* (Oxford: Clarendon, 1998).

Smith, Michael, 'Rational capacities, or how to distinguish recklessness, weakness and compulsion', in Sarah Stroud and Christine Tappolet (eds.), *Weakness of Will and Practical Irrationality* (Oxford: Clarendon, 2003), p. 17.

Smith, Paul T., 'Recklessness in *dolus eventualis*' (1979) 96 *South African Law Journal* 81.

Smyth, Thomas W., 'Unconscious desires and the meaning of desire' (1972) 56 *The Monist* 413.

Spain, Eimear, *The Role of Emotions in Criminal Law Defences: Duress, Necessity and Lesser Evils* (Cambridge: Cambridge University Press, 2011).

Spencer, J.R., and Brajeux, Marie-Aimeé, 'Criminal liability for negligence – a lesson from across the Channel?' (2010) 59 *International and Comparative Law Quarterly* 1.

Stanley, Jason, and Williamson, Timothy, 'Knowing how' (2001) 98 *Journal of Philosophy* 411.

Stannard, John E., 'Subjectivism, objectivism and the Draft Criminal Code' (1985) 101 *Law Quarterly Review* 540.

Stark, Findlay, 'Breaking down *Brennan*' 2009 *Juridical Review* 155.

'Culpable carelessness: recklessness and negligence in Scots and English criminal law', PhD thesis, University of Edinburgh (2011).

'Rethinking recklessness' 2011 *Juridical Review* 163.

'Necessity and *Nicklinson*' [2013] *Criminal Law Review* 949.

'Prior fault' (2014) 73 *Cambridge Law Journal* 8.

'Review of Ashworth, Zedner and Tomlin (eds.), *Prevention and the Limits of the Criminal Law*' (2016) 10 *Criminal Law and Philosophy* 389.

Steele, Jenny, *Risks and Legal Theory* (Oxford: Hart, 2004).

Steup, Matthias, 'Doxastic voluntarism and epistemic deontology' (2000) 15 *Acta Analytica* 25.

Strawson, Galen, 'The impossibility of moral responsibility' (1994) 75 *Philosophical Studies* 5.

Freedom and Belief, rev. edn. (Oxford: Oxford University Press, 2010).

Stuart, Don, '*Mens rea*, negligence and attempts' [1968] *Criminal Law Review* 647.

'A case for a General Part: lessons from Canada's experience with Stephen's Code since 1892 and entrenched Charter standards since 1982' (2009) 20 *Criminal Law Forum* 113.

Canadian Criminal Law: A Treatise, 6th edn. (Toronto, Carswell, 2011).

Canadian Criminal Law: A Treatise, 7th edn. (Toronto: Carswell, 2014).

Sullivan, G.R., 'Intent, subjective recklessness and culpability' (1992) 12 *Oxford Journal of Legal Studies* 380.

'Knowledge, belief and culpability', in Stephen Shute and A.P. Simester (eds.), *Criminal Law Theory: Doctrines of the General Part* (Oxford: Oxford University Press, 2002), p. 207.

Sverdlik, Stephen, 'Pure negligence' (1993) 30 *American Philosophical Quarterly* 137.

Tadros, Victor, 'Recklessness and the duty to take care', in Stephen Shute and A.P. Simester (eds.), *Criminal Law Theory: Doctrines of the General Part* (Oxford: Oxford University Press, 2002), p. 227.

'The system of the criminal law' (2002) 22 *Legal Studies* 448.

Criminal Responsibility (Oxford: Oxford University Press, 2005).

'The Scots law of murder', in Jeremy Horder (ed.), *Homicide Law in Comparative Perspective* (Oxford: Hart, 2007), p. 187.

The Ends of Harm: The Moral Foundations of Criminal Law (Oxford: Oxford University Press, 2011).

'Fair labelling and social solidarity', in Lucia Zedner and Julian V. Roberts (eds.), *Principles and Values in Criminal Law and Criminal Justice: Essays in Honour of Andrew Ashworth* (Oxford: Oxford University Press, 2012), p. 67.

Tadros, Victor, and Tierney, Stephen, 'The presumption of innocence and the Human Rights Act' (2004) 67 *Modern Law Review* 402.

Taslitz, Andrew E., 'Forgetting Freud: the courts' fear of the subconscious in date rape (and other) cases' (2006–2007) 16 *Boston University Public Interest Law Journal* 145.

Taylor, Greg, 'Concepts of intention in German criminal law' (2004) 24 *Oxford Journal of Legal Studies* 99.

Temkin, Jennifer, 'The limits of reckless rape' [1983] *Criminal Law Review* 5.

Treiman, David M., 'Recklessness and the Model Penal Code' (1981) 9 *American Journal of Criminal Law* 281.

Tuomela, Raimo, 'Belief versus acceptance' (2000) 2 *Philosophical Explorations* 122.

Tur, Richard H.S., 'Rape, reasonableness and time' (1981) 1 *Oxford Journal of Legal Studies* 432.

Turner, J.W.C. 'The mental element in crimes at common law' (1938) 6 *Cambridge Law Journal* 31.

Turri, John, 'Is knowledge justified true belief?' (2012) 184 *Synthese* 247.

Uleman, Jennifer K., *An Introduction to Kant's Moral Philosophy* (Cambridge: Cambridge University Press, 2010).

Vargas, Manuel, 'The trouble with tracing' (2005) 29 *Midwest Studies in Philosophy* 269.

Velleman, David J., *The Possibility of Practical Reason* (Oxford: Oxford University Press, 2000).

Wallace, R. Jay, *Responsibility and the Moral Sentiments* (Cambridge, MA: Harvard University Press, 1994).

Wasik, M., and Thompson, M.P., '"Turning a blind eye" as constituting *mens rea*' (1981) 32 *Northern Ireland Legal Quarterly* 328.

Watson, Gary, 'Reasons and responsibility' (2001) 111 *Ethics* 374.

'Free agency', in Gary Watson (ed.), *Free Will*, 2nd edn. (Oxford: Oxford University Press, 2003), p. 337.

Wechsler, Herbert, 'On culpability and crime: the treatment of *mens rea* in the Model Penal Code' (1962) 339 *Annals of the American Academy of Political and Social Science* 24.

Wells, Celia, 'Swatting the subjectivist bug' [1982] *Criminal Law Review* 209.

Corporations and Criminal Responsibility, 2nd edn. (Oxford: Oxford University Press, 2001).

Westen, Peter, 'Individualizing the reasonable person in criminal law' (2008) 2 *Criminal Law and Philosophy* 137.

White, Alan R., 'Carelessness, indifference and recklessness' (1961) 24 *Modern Law Review* 592.

Grounds of Liability: An Introduction to the Philosophy of Law (Oxford: Clarendon, 1985).

Misleading Cases (Oxford: Clarendon, 1991).

Williams, Bernard, *Problems of the Self: Philosophical Papers 1956–1972* (Cambridge: Cambridge University Press, 1973).

Ethics and the Limits of Philosophy (Cambridge, MA: Harvard University Press, 1985).

Williams, Glanville, *Criminal Law: The General Part*, 2nd edn. (London: Stevens, 1961).

The Mental Element in Crime (Jerusalem: Magnes Press, 1965).

'Recklessness redefined' (1981) 40 *Cambridge Law Journal* 252.

'A reply to Mr Duff' (1982) 41 *Cambridge Law Journal* 286.

'Divergent interpretations of recklessness III' (1982) 132 *New Law Journal* 313.

'Intention and recklessness again' (1982) 2 *Legal Studies* 189.

Textbook of Criminal Law, 2nd edn. (London: Stephens, 1983).

'The unresolved problem of recklessness' (1988) 8 *Legal Studies* 74.

'Criminal omissions: the conventional view' (1991) 107 *Law Quarterly Review* 86.

Williams, Rebecca, 'Voluntary intoxication – a lost cause?' (2013) 129 *Law Quarterly Review* 264.

Wilson, William, *Central Issues in Criminal Law Theory* (Oxford: Hart, 2002).

Criminal Law: Doctrine and Theory, 5th edn. (Harlow: Pearson, 2014).

Winslade, William J., 'Recklessness' (1970) 30 *Analysis* 135.

Winters, Barbara, 'Believing at will' (1979) 76 *Journal of Philosophy* 243.

Woozley, A.D. 'Negligence and ignorance' (1978) 53 *Philosophy* 293.

Yankah, Ekow N., 'Good guys and bad guys: punishing character, equality and the irrelevance of moral character to criminal punishment' (2003–2004) 25 *Cardozo Law Review* 1019.

Zagzebski, Linda T., 'The inescapability of Gettier problems' (1994) 44 *The Philosophical Quarterly* 65.

Virtues of the Mind: An Inquiry into the Nature of Virtue and the Ethical Foundations of Knowledge (Cambridge: Cambridge University Press, 1996).

Zaibert, Leo, *Five Ways Patricia Can Kill Her Husband: A Theory of Intentionality and Blame* (Peru, IL: Open Court, 2005).

'For negligence liability', in Paul H. Robinson, Stephen P. Garvey and Kimberly K. Ferzan (eds.), *Criminal Law Conversations* (Oxford: Oxford University Press, 2009), p. 281.

Zimmerman, Aaron Z., 'The nature of belief' (2007) 14(11) *Journal of Consciousness Studies* 61.

Zimmerman, M.J. 'Negligence and moral responsibility' (1986) 20 *Noûs* 199.

'Moral responsibility and ignorance' (1996–1997) 107 *Ethics* 410.

INDEX

Lightning Source UK Ltd.
Milton Keynes UK
UKHW021438280921
391322UK00008B/1602

9 781108 465120